The INTERNET UNIVERSITY

College Courses by Computer

Cape Software

Welcome.

Here is the map to your new book: >>>

👉 **Intro** - discusses the burgeoning field of online education and how you can participate *today*; this will give you a <u>vital</u> <u>overview</u>.

👉 **Part I-*Access*** - describes what getting connected will mean to you as an online student; use the Internet for <u>total</u> <u>access</u>.

👉 **Part II-*Sources*** - lists universities that you can attend starting <u>today</u>; presents online students with a cornucopia of academic opportunity.

👉 **Part III-*Study*** - outlines a remarkable 'toolbox' of research resources available to the online student; most are available via simple email.

👉 **Part IV-*Horizons*** - reveals many of the special Internet connections available for CLEP, CEU, high school and personal enrichment.

👉 **Guest Articles** - contributions by foremost online educators, these will give you a strong background in the 'art/science' of this new world.

👉 **Course Catalog** - more than thirty providers and 700 courses profiled, with contact information, course content, prerequisites, fees.

👉 **Lists** - extensive collections of mailing lists, electronic journals, ftp, Telnet and Web sites; most are available for FREE academic access.

👉 **Glossary** - contains many of the most frequently used bits of jargon and buzzwords to help get your feet planted on the *'infobahn'*.

👉 **Index** - alphabetical list of selected keywords with page locations.

Edition 96/01

The INTERNET UNIVERSITY

College Courses by Computer

by

Dan Corrigan

Cape Software

This book is for Amy.

Copyright © 1996 by Cape Software Press

Printed in the United States of America

OVERVIEW

Introduction

☞ An outline of the EXCITING NEW WORLD of ONLINE ACADEMICS

Part I - *Access* - Choose & Connect

☞ Hardware requirements for ONLINE ACADEMICS

☞ Internet tools for the ONLINE STUDENT to use

☞ SERVICE PROVIDERS and choosing the right one

Part II - *Sources* - Providers & Catalog

☞ ACCREDITED Colleges and Universities with ONLINE courses

☞ COURSE DESCRIPTIONS and SUBJECT INDEX

Part III - *Study* - Research & Exploration

☞ Academic use of INTERNET TOOLS outlined

☞ Lists and lists of FREE ACADEMIC RESOURCES

Part IV - *Horizons* - Special Connections

☞ CLEP and CEU sources outlined

☞ Online HIGH SCHOOL sources detailed

☞ PERSONAL ENRICHMENT and other non-credit courses

☞ Online SCHOLARSHIP and FINANCIAL AID sources

See the *COURSE CATALOG* (700+ courses) - Page 187

CONTENTS

Teaching on the Infobahn

Wandered Onto the Information Superhighway

A Diversity of Participants

Not About Technology

Have a Look for Yourself

Personal Internet Access Using SLIP/PPP
How You Use It, How It Works

Me, My Computer, and the Internet

How It All Works

Making Your Mac or PC Internet-Capable

Connecting to the Internet

Using Core Internet Services

Accessing Other Internet Services

From Invisible College to Cyberspace College
Computer Conferencing and Transformation of Informal Scholarly Communication Networks
by John L. Gresham, Jr., Ph.D.
Director of Library Services, Sterling College, Sterling KS

Background to the Invisible College

Computer Conferencing
Introduction to, History of, and Academic Computer Conferencing

From Invisible Colleges to Cyberspace Colleges

Trends and Future Developments

Accessing the Internet by Email
Doctor Bob's Guide to Offline Internet Access

How to Access Internet Services by Email
FTP by Email; Archie by Email; Gopher by Email; Veronica by
Email; A Gophermail Shortcut; Usenet by Email; WAIS Searches
by Email; World-Wide Web by Email; WWW Search by Email

Mailing Lists
Finding a Mailing List; Subscribe to the HELP-NET

Other Services by Email
Finger by Email; 'Directory Assistance' by Email; Address/Name
Server Info by Email

A Few Net-Goodies
Webster by Email; The Usenet Oracle; Almanac, Weather & The
Swedish Chef; Sending a Fax by Email; The Electronic Newstand;
US Congress and the White House; US Government Information;
Patent News Service; The Internet Mall; Finding Email
Addresses; Family Internet MailCall; Usenet Search; Movie Info;
Stock Market; The Contrarian Advisor; Anonymous Email; Net
Journals Listing; Musi-Cal; Ask Dr. Math; Scout Report

Augmenting a Group Discussion Course with CMC
in a Small College Setting

Advantages of CMC
Asynchronicity, Convenience, More Interaction, Increased
Control, Communication in Writing

Efficient Information Access
Online Course Materials, Automatic "Paper Trail", Access to the
Internet, Increased Social Distance

Table 1 - Student Attitudes on Advantages of CMC

Table 2 - Hesitation to Contact Instructor via CMC

Table 3 - Attitudes CMC Advantages Group Communication

Table 4 - Attitudes, Computer Users v. Non-computer Users

The INTERNET UNIVERSITY

Course Descriptions by Provider 211

Lists...391

Glossary...469

Index..481

PLEASE READ THIS DISCLAIMER

This book attempts the impossible - cataloging the educational opportunities on the Internet. Because of the tremendous development and growth of the Internet no catalog or listing of resources available through the Internet can ever be complete. The inherent limitations of print also conspire to prevent anything you read here or anywhere from being truly 'up to date'. In light of this reality, the author and publishers make these statements of limitation.

The title of this book, **The Internet University**, is a metaphor. Please note that there is no educational institution known by the author or publisher as The Internet University. Also, please note that inclusion in this book of any course or provider does not represent an endorsement by the author or publisher.

The information in this book is presented as a service to the reader only. The purpose of this manual is to educate and entertain. While every reasonable effort has been made for factual accuracy herein, no responsibility is assumed for editorial, clerical, or printing error, or error occasioned by honest mistake.

While course descriptions contained in this book are current as of press time, all courses are subject to revision or cancellation. Cape Software suggests that you refer to the providing institutions for information and current status of course offerings. While every effort was made to gather a complete list of courses and providers, we have undoubtedly missed some. Also, Cape Software makes no implied or other statement about the qualifications of any providing institution. In the event of dissatisfaction with any course or provider, Cape Software shall be held harmless and will not offer to provide any mediation or accept any liability for any shortcoming, whether perceived or real.

This book is sold with the understanding that the publisher and author are not engaged in providing any legal or other professional service. If you require legal or other professional expertise, services of a competent professional should be sought. This text should be used only as a general guide and not as an ultimate source.

If you do not wish to be bound by the above, you may return this book to the publisher for a full refund.

Acknowlegements

One problem with including an acknowledgement is the danger of forgetting to mention someone. If I fail to mention your contribution please forgive me. Many of the positive attributes of this book are the result of the help I have received. The errors are mine alone.

This book began in a conversation I had with Matt. Thanks, Matt. Amy was a constant source of encouragement. Thank you, Amy. Tom and Adie gave valuable advice on layout, as well as overview and analysis. Many thanks. Earl helped with early encouragement. Thanks, Earl. Mike, Kevin, Paul and William offered comments on the draft, all of which led to a real improvement of the product. Thank you all. Bill gave vital support at an important time. Thanks alot, Bill. Margaret gave good feedback on the cover and graphic placement. Thanks, Maggie. David provided encouragement, editing and indexing expertise. Thanks, David. Sophie and Ruby encouraged me at every turn. Thanks, kids. Luther provided technical support, with promises of even more to come. Thanks, Luther. Emily followed the whole process with interest. Thanks, Emily. Melissa cheered me on throughout the project. Thanks, Melissa. Jennifer gave insights from the online educator's perspective. Thanks, Jenn. Greg opened my eyes to the way things are going for online ed. Thanks, Greg. Anissa pointed out some embarrassing typos and suggested content additions. Thanks, Anissa. Kim, Marty and Tony and the other professionals at Data Reproductions, Corp., our printers, have been very helpful and, as you can tell from the high quality of the product in your hands, very good at their jobs. Thanks, folks.

I remember discussions with many people who's names I fail to recall now that I am writing this file. I should have kept better notes. Thanks to those who helped with observations and reflections. Please remind me of your contribution so I can update this page for later editions.

The authors of the Guest Articles have contributed mightily to the content of this book, and to its usefulness for the online student. All who gain from this book should thank them.

As this page is being hastily written under the pressure of the printer's deadline, I'm sure I have forgotten somebody, to my embarrassment. My apologies if you are one of these people. And thanks for the help.

- Dan Corrigan

Intro

The Internet University

College Courses by Computer

Introduction

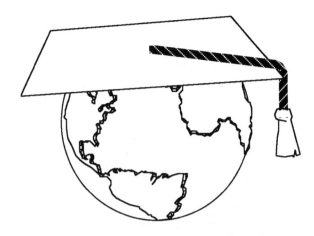

The Internet University: Your Medium of Distance Online Education

In the industrial age, we went to school; in the information age, school can come to us. This is the message implicit in the distance education phenomena of the Internet University.

The Internet University is a <u>virtual organization</u>. There are no campuses, faculty, or classes in this invention of the modern age. The 'virtual reality' of the Internet University exists solely in its connections. Yet, thousands of students already attend this new 'University', and many more are signing on every day. These new and returning students are participating in this *virtual* academic community .

The tools of the electronic age are becoming more well known and available. Thousands of parents, career people and retirees are 'going back to school' - electronically - without dropping the rest of their life activities. Distance education has been under development for decades, but the powerful new tools of the Internet bring this discipline into a new realm through the Internet University process. This book will give you the connections you need to begin.

The Parts of this book have been carefully designed to give you the information you need to 1) 'log on' to the Internet, 2) choose the courses most relevant to you, 3) conduct research and study needed for those courses, and 4) participate in personal enrichment or academic equivalency courses.

You are invited to visit this book's companion website: http://www.caso.com/

A Bit of History: Academics Until Now

From the earliest days of formalized education, the academic process has meant travel and lodging. The first libraries were simple collections of rare books, and only selected people were allowed access. The early universities were armed and barricaded to give carefully selected students relative freedom from want and worry while they carried out their studies.

Even in the days after WWII, when the country's colleges were opened by the GI Bill, accessibility was limited to those who could relocate and totally reorganize their lives - not an option for many young families. This world has changed forever.

The electronic age has revolutionized the delivery of educational services. For the first time people can continue their education from sources they never visit 'in the flesh'. Doctors, lawyers, domestic technicians - all are now able to reach across town, state, country and planet to the world's academic resources. Colleges and universities across the country and the world are rushing to participate in this exploding phenomenon.

The education process is being altered forever, since people are now able to earn their degrees at home according to their own timetables. Populations previously denied equal access due to social or economic factors are now included. This book describes the sources and connections needed in this exciting new world of distance education. With computer and modem anyone can navigate this new world of learning.

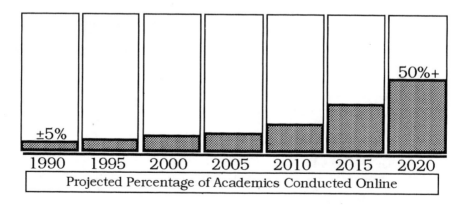

±5% 50%+

| 1990 | 1995 | 2000 | 2005 | 2010 | 2015 | 2020 |

Projected Percentage of Academics Conducted Online

No book on Internet resourses can ever be complete.
If you know of something we've missed please email: tellus@caso.com

Needed to Attend The Internet University:

All that the electronic student needs to participate in this once-elite process is a <u>computer</u>, <u>online access</u>, <u>academic prerequisites</u> and for courses that are not free, the <u>tuition</u>. People with young children, a career, living in remote locations, physical disability, etc. are now able to move freely in the world of college education. Specialty educational activities such as GED preparation and CEU are also available. The essentials:

COMPUTER - An IBM-compatible or Macintosh computer is recommended, and just about any of these will work. There are stories of people who have attended class on a Commodore 64, but this book assumes use of a relatively current model of personal computer, and the basic skills necessary to turn the thing on and get to work with it (primarily word processing).

ONLINE ACCESS - Modem connection to a service provider is another prime ingredient - commercial online services, dialup lines or links to connected local networks are the main sources. An alternative route to the Internet is a corporate, local library or other institutional network. This book gives you the information that you need to select the right service provider for your academic needs.

ACADEMIC PREREQUISITES - Standards parallel those in traditional schools; this book assists in determining these prerequisites during the process of selecting a college, university or other institution.

TUITION - Credit courses are roughly comparable to fees paid at a campus, from $100 to $300 per credit or more. These are fee levels that will undoubtedly drop as economies of scale take effect. If the course is related to skill development for work requirements, these costs may be tax deductible. Many noncredit courses are free, and 'freelance' educational opportunities (unstructured personal development courses) abound on the Internet..

Getting Up To Speed:

New college buildings are still going up, but over the next couple of decades a complete transformation of education will occur. The phenomena described in this book will grow into new institutions. These changes are already occurring. For some the visit to the campus is relegated to a ceremonial role. Others receive their diplomas by 'FedEx' !

Revolutionary changes are occurring on campuses across the country and the globe. Since the beginning the educational community has been a major player in the growth and development of the Internet, but now these services are reaching the individual student on campus as well. As

5

the San Jose Mercury News reported in early 1995, one example of this on-campus revolution is seen at Stanford University.

Stanford was one of the universities that pioneered in the use and development of the Internet, and is now still "at the forefront of the ever-changing technology for collegiate use." For instance, one of the University's engineering classes now provides all of its instructional materials by WWW. Every office on campus has a direct Internet connection, and it is projected that within two years every dormitory room will also have an Internet connection.

The concept of 'place' no longer determines whether you can go to college - as the saying goes, anywhere is everywhere on the Internet. This book is designed to give you immediate access to these new world-wide educational opportunities.

A summary of the sections in this book:

PART I - *ACCESS* - CHOOSE & CONNECT: Part I will help you better understand the world of the virtual Internet University. This section describes academic uses of the various tools and features of the Internet, as well as a listing of service providers. Whether you choose a commercial service such as America Online or Compuserve, or a local Internet connection, you will begin using these tools to improve your learning and earning position.

PART II - *SOURCES* - PROVIDERS & CATALOG: Presents a comprehensive listing of schools and colleges offering online educational opportunities. While current as of publishing date, new providers are continually emerging. Course descriptions, prerequisites and expenses are outlined. This catalog will help you develop an academic strategy that is right for you.

PART III - *STUDY* - RESEARCH & EXPLORATION: Introduces the world's greatest library. The ordinary PC can command access to information and knowledge once only dreamed of by kings, robber barons or high-powered executives. This is access to libraries, mailing lists, Usenet groups and World-Wide Web sites - most of these vast information resources are available to you FREE.

PART IV - *HORIZONS* - SPECIAL CONNECTIONS: Covers the tremendous variety of informational, instructional and equivalency sources 'out there' on the net. These include specialty education resources, equivalency degrees, personal enrichment, electronic high schools, non-credit courses and SCHOLARSHIP connections that can be made through your computer and modem.

The Nature of the Virtual Classroom

A *virtual* experience differs from a *real* experience in that it occurs in the minds of the participants. When we participate in a telephone conversation it can be said that we are involved in a *synchronous* virtual event - that is, we are not actually with the other person, but we are nonetheless involved in a genuine *real-time* conversation. We experience the familiarity of the other person's voice, their interaction with our voice; and in our minds we mutually create a communications event. By using the telephone infrastructure, and despite the physical distance, we are *virtually* face-to-face (or 'mouth-to-ear'). Distance is a state of mind.

Correspondence by mail, with interactions separated by days, can be said to be *asynchronous* virtual conversation. Again, as in the example of the phone conversation, we are exchanging information with our correspondent from different locations, though not at the same time. We substitute the 'mental' senses of our imagination for our real-world senses during the course of this virtual conversation. If our correspondent writes something funny, we laugh as if they are telling it to us in 'real-time'; if the conversation turns sour, we experience it directly.

Creating the Virtual Classroom: With every instance of communication, those *in* communication create a mutually-imagined virtual 'place', whether this communication involves two or twenty persons. From within this 'place' a transfer of knowledge, technique and perspective can occur. With paper mail, a more primitive technology, it naturally takes longer for this 'place' to be established, and effective group interaction is quite limited. Internet access lends an immediacy, creating a powerful educational environment.

In the virtual classroom, the effect of closeness and participation between participants can be as real and engaging as with traditional class structures. Some participants even report an <u>improved</u> performance because the *asynchronous* nature of the discussion allows for a more studied and reflective analysis of the course materials.

Whether by email or paper mail, the students of the *virtual classroom* enter a cooperative conceptual event - they create a 'classroom' that is all their own. With email and a class mailing list, students 'attend' by logging on, downloading the day's correspondence and uploading responses they have written in response to *yesterday's* mail. This interplay of statements, moderated by the instructor, creates a rich academic experience.

Adding to Traditional Approaches: In many ways the experience of the virtual classroom parallels that of the traditional classroom. Students establish personal relationships with each other, and study groups are arranged. This academic discourse reaches a high level due in part to the effect of the correspondence being text-based. This format induces participants to compose their interactions, a process which those who have experienced this report leads to careful consideration and rewriting of submissions.

Unlike with direct perception, reading conveys information to the mind through common understanding of symbols and graphics. Words must be 'decoded' in order for the individual to gather meaning from them. However, once we are literate, information from print tends to be absorbed almost immediately into memories, creating knowledge which is often indistinguishable from that gathered directly from reality.

Paper mail can carry 'words' quite well. Thus, the original paper basis of distance education worked quite well. Imagine though, the early days when mail was long delayed, and arrived irregularly. Even under those conditions distance learning worked, and with the tools of the Internet the process is enhanced. The immediacy and incredible variety of online communications and data sources of the Internet bring people wanting to return to school many unanticipated benefits.

The new world of the Internet University, with email, ftp, Telnet and the Web, provide us with an accelerated and much broadened educational experience. As more people become 'connected', as more educational institutions understand the benefits to providers of distance electronic education, and as required new academic strategies and techniques evolve, the use of Internet University will become commonplace.

Be sure and use The Internet University's companion website:

http://www.caso.com/

This site contains up-to-date listings and current news about online ed.

Four Types of Online Academics

The student of the Internet University will have access to a range of access techniques, ranging from the simplest, low-bandwidth connection (email only) to the most exciting and recently-breaking activities on the Web. Old methods and procedures developed during the era of paper mail are now being coupled with techniques made possible only with the advent of the Internet. These 'types' are inclusive as the user's involvement increases - Web access will include email access, etc.

Online Coursework - by Type

1. Essential Links
- Similar to traditional distance education
- Mailing Lists and Usenet groups, other resources
- Regular mail also used, as are cassettes

2. Mediated Classwork
- Instructor conducts asynchronous classes
- Frequent contributions _from_ all students _to_ all students
- Assignments and drafts posting optional

3. Web Access
- Graphical and hypertext interface
- Maps, charts, drawings, video; audio
- 'Zoom' words and 'buttons'

4. MUD/MOO
- Interactive, real-time discussions
- Classroom environment reproduced electronically

Each increment demands a more robust Internet connection.

Online Academics Described

Many colleges and course-granting institutions identify themselves as being 'online course providers', but in order to understand what this means, some definition of terms is required. If the student can email the instructor, and receive an email response it could be said that the course is being given 'online', but this is only the most rudimentary of Internet-facilitated education. It is the most easily attained, since a simple, low-volume email connection will suffice.

Other, more comprehensive, techniques are available for use by online scholars. These tools are generally employed in an *additive* fashion, that is use of Internet resources expands the further into the medium the providing institution has evolved. Although for the purposes of this book we are describing these 'types' as if they are clearcut categories, in fact there will be considerable blurring between them.

Type 1 - <u>Essential Links</u>: This stage of online academics uses Internet services in an upgrading of traditional distance education methods. Audio and video tapes may be included, as well as 'paper mail'. Some uses of the Internet fit in with this type: receiving and submitting assignments by email; subscribing to mailing lists by email; following Usenet newsgroups.

Type 2 - <u>Mediated Classwork</u>: With this stage of online education we see the creation of the *virtual* classroom, managed and directed by the course instructor. This mediation involves arranging assignments and frequent email correspondence into an effective whole. The benefits of this stage, coupled with the gains from continued Type 1 activities, create a vibrant educational environment.

Type 3 - <u>Web Access</u>: Point-and-click navigation brings your computer to those of the nation's and world's universities and libraries, including the Library of Congress. The new frontier of the Internet, where new approaches are developed, bringing new dimensions to online education.

Type 4 - <u>MUD/MOO</u>: for Multi-User Domain and MUD (Object Oriented), these are terms for 'live' interaction via a host site, where participants are logged on simultaneously (*synchronous* communications). This format allows for immediacy and spontaneous interchange and presents the instructor with a challenging interface to manage. As bandwidth becomes more available, and as student familiarity with Internet use increases, this method of class work is expected to increase in popularity.

Be Sure And Visit The Internet University's Companion Website:
http://www.caso.com/

How to Use this Book

The initial four Parts of this book can be read in sequence for those who are not already online, starting with **Part I - *Access***. This approach will give you the information needed to 1) get online, 2) choose a course provider, 3) conduct successful online study, and 4) continue your education through equivalency and personal enrichment courses. For additional information beyond the overview presented in this Part, be sure to read the Guest Articles, five contributions from online educators who are active in this emerging field.

If you have existing Internet access and an operational familiarity of the net and its workings, you will wish to go directly to **Part II - *Sources***. This Part links directly with the Course Catalog. Scan the listing of courses and course providers. Contact these institutions directly and remember that course offerings change, as do prerequisites and enrollment procedures. The course listings and degree specifications will give you a picture of what the institution will offer you, and you can take it from there through discussions with their counselors.

Those already enrolled in online or traditional courses but wanting assistance in online study will go directly to **Part III - *Study***. Making use of the world-wide information resources that the Internet provides will give you educational opportunities that should benefit you greatly. Remember that the vast majority of these information sources are available to you free of any charges except for your Internet connect fees.

Students interested in the miscellaneous topics covered in **Part IV - *Horizons*** (covering personal enrichment, GED, CLEP, etc.) will benefit by turning directly to that section. These resources are generally lower in cost than the accredited courses described in Part II, and will often be more innovative and exciting in their approach.

```
This 'telephone' has too many shortcomings to be
seriously considered as a means of communication.
The device is inherently of no value to us.
```
-- Western Union memo, 1877

Shortcuts For Using of This Book

What you hope to gain from this book:

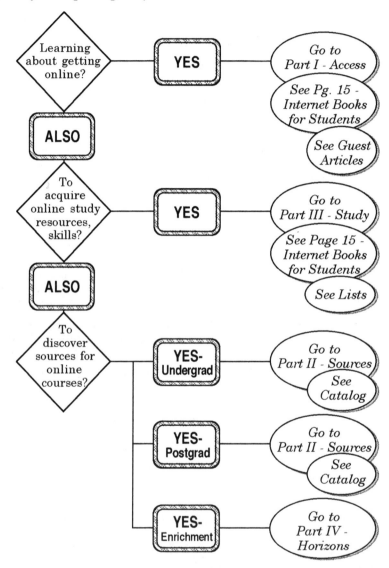

Getting Connected to the Internet

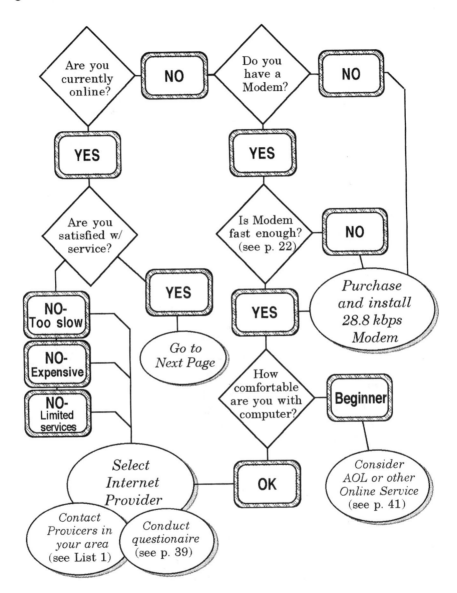

Finding the Right Course

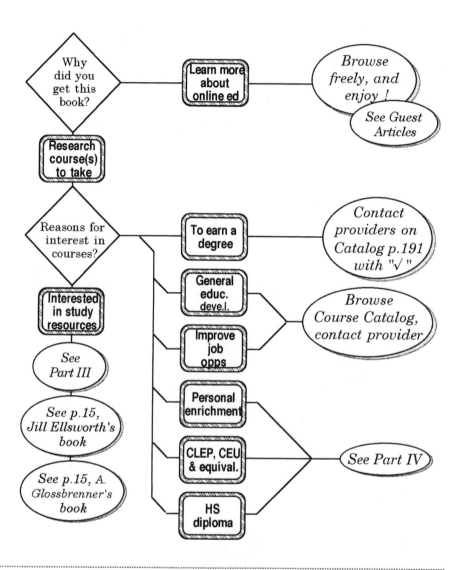

Other books to read

The materials presented in this book are structured in a manner to meet the needs of the widest range of persons interested in online academics. It is anticipated that some readers will want more information than is provided here. We have compiled a short list of books which provide helpful information on the Internet, and education, and advice on navigating the new digital world. Explore freely and make use of these exciting tools.

① Your Internet Consultant - The FAQs of Life Online
By Kevin Savetz - Sams (1994); 800-428-5331 - 550 pages - $25
Provides simple, enlightening answers to hundreds of frequently asked questions about the Internet; arranged in Q&A format.

② Education on the Internet
by Jill Ellsworth - Sams (1994); 800-428-5331 - 591 pages - $25
Curriculum and teaching ideas, college and grad resources, scholarship info, research and distance learning resouces, primer on Internet use.

③ The Whole Internet: User's Guide & Catalog
by Ed Krol - O'Reilly & Assoc. (1994); Sebastopol CA - 544 pages, $25
Lists resource sites on the Internet by category. Succinct descriptions of Internet tools and procedures.

④ The Instant Internet Guide
by Brent Heslop & David Angell - Addison-Wesley - 209 pages, $14.95
Basic introduction to Internet, with reference sections on email, Usenet, gopher, telnet, ftp, basic UNIX, etc. Oriented toward dialup terminal user.

⑤ The Internet by Email
by Clay Shirky - Ziff-Davis Press (1994) - 256 pages, $19.95
For those who have "only Email" access to the Internet or who want to gain more benefit from this fundamental link.

⑥ Internet: The Complete Reference
by H. Hahn & R. Stout - Osborne McGraw-Hill (1994) - 818 pgs., $29.95
A complete guide to the Internet leading the beginner from the fundamentals through the Internet's most important tools.

⑦ Internet 101 - a College Student's Guide
by Alfred Glossbrenner - McGraw Hill (1995) - 350 pages, $19.95
Aimed at college-resident students, this book tells them how to use the Net for all academic and personal needs, emphasises study resources.

⑧ netchat
by Kelly Maloni - Random House (1994) - 281 pages, $19.00
Instructions for maximizing use of newsgroups, mailing lists, IRC chat groups, forums and support groups. Covers many 'alternative' sources.

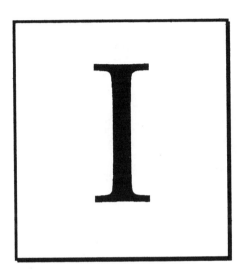

Access

Choose & Connect

Part I - Choose & Connect

Access

Goals for Part I:

☐ **Identify Hardware Requirements**

☐ **Identify Online Needs**

☐ **Select an Internet Provider**

Part I - *Access* - Choose and Connect will assist you in identifying your hardware and online needs, and in making choices best suited to meet those needs. Factors influencing your choices will include your educational online requirements, budget, and proximity to service providers.

An Internet connection will give you the connections you need for online education, allowing you to experience the expanse of information that is available today. Online education will never completely replace the need for traditional campus programs. There are things you can do on paper that are difficult to accomplish by computer, and some courses lend themselves more appropriately to face-to-face meetings. For subjects where the online approach will work, however, expect dramatic numbers of schools to offer online courses.

With these tools and connections, you will be in position to capitalize on the exciting new world of the Internet University.

Hardware Needs: We will be addressing hardware requirements with particular attention to the choice of modems. Naturally, in order to have access to the digital world of the Internet, it is necessary to have a computer and the 'bridge' to the network - the modem. Most popular computers will suffice for this activity, bringing access to most families and individuals in the industrialized world.

In some cases, when a computer is purchased a modem is included ('bundled') along in purchase price. This may not be a bargain, as the enclosed section on modems will demonstrate. A 'free' slow modem may be the 'gift that keeps on taking' and may actually be an impediment to your use of the Internet for academic activities.

Online Needs: We will conduct a review of the basic Internet services to ascertain which you will use. While some terms may now be unfamiliar, and it may take effort to get used to them, it will be worthwhile. In the months and years to come the tools of the Internet will become like old friends and companions. Familiarity with email, comfort using ftp and Telnet, nd excitement toward using the World-Wide Web will soon typify your use of these tools.

It is often not necessary for the online student to have full Internet access - simple email capability may suffice. Research is the academic activity most limited by lack of ftp, Telnet or WWW access, and if your profile demonstrates that external research is not required, access to the more rudimentary (lower cost) services may be all that you need.

Selecting Your Provider: New Internet service providers are coming online every day. These range in size from national to small regional efforts. In some ways the market is reminiscent of the days of the 'Wild West', and selecting from this variety is a challenging task. We provide you with an assessment questionnaire which will assist you in determining the best service to meet your needs, based on projections of what your use of services will be. Compare your local providers for features that are important to you!

Bon Voyage!: If you have never 'surfed' on the Internet, you are about to discover an exciting though occasionally frustrating world. The electronic highway is a reality for millions of people across the world, and you are joining this community. Congratulations! Best wishes for your academic accomplishments, and have a good journey!

If you discover inaccuracies or outdated information in this book please TELL US via email to: `tellus@caso.com`. Your recommendations and corrections will appear in subsequent editions.

✔ Identify Hardware Requirements

The computer world is becoming increasingly 'platform transparent'. Presumably anyone interested in taking college courses online either has a computer or is considering purchasing one. The main point to consider in this section is not which machine to purchase, bytes of RAM, hard disk, etc. Rather, for this book the assumption is made at the outset that your computer is either a Macintosh (Mac Plus or later) or IBM-compatible (IBM/AT, 286 or later). In keeping with the platform-transparent trend of the 'nineties, that's as far as we go on this topic.

Where some important considerations are required is your choice of MODEM, for it is this vital piece of equipment that is the 'bridge' between your computer and the 'electronic highway'. Modems are devices that attach to the computer, either internally or externally, and work to change the digital language of the computer into sound (and *visa versa*) so that 'computerese' can be sent and received over conventional telephone lines.

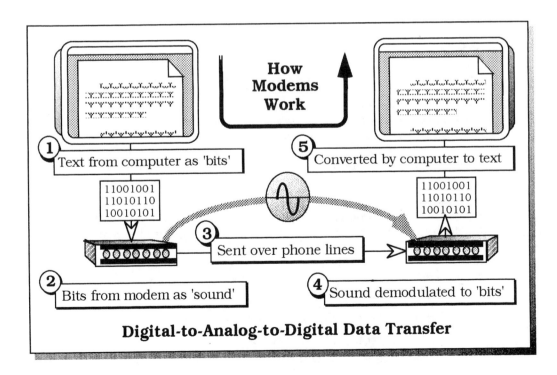

How Modems Work

1. Text from computer as 'bits'
2. Bits from modem as 'sound'
3. Sent over phone lines
4. Sound demodulated to 'bits'
5. Converted by computer to text

11001001
11010110
10010101

Digital-to-Analog-to-Digital Data Transfer

The Modem

This most vital piece of equipment (the modem) is required to take courses online. The modem allows one computer to talk to all others on the network. *Without* a modem your computer is an isolated component of the electronic age - the only way to introduce outside data without a modem is by floppy disk or CD-ROM. Having a good, working modem is a prerequisite in order to enroll in most of the distance education courses outlined in this book.

About *bps* (bits-per-second): Modems work by converting *computer data* (the famous 'bits' and 'bytes') into *sound* which the phone lines can handle. This step is called <u>mo</u>*dulation*. At the other end of the connection, another modem converts the *sound* back into *computer data*. This step is called <u>dem</u>*odulation*. Thus the term *mo-dem*.

Since all computers of the world operate on basic principles, an 'a' on this side of the world is recognized as an 'a' on the other. With a basic 'lingua franca' established as a working protocol, the *information* on all these computers also becomes transferable. Now, twenty-five years into the Internet era, systems and protocols have become established that gives the (modem-equipped) computer owner access to the world's educational opportunities.

A Case of 'Faster is Better': When modems were first invented, as with all these technologies, operational speeds were very slow compared to today's state of the art. Modems work at various speeds, a function of how much was spent on them, and when they were purchased. A 1200 bps (bits per second) modem cost $800 new in 1984; now, modems which transmit data at 24 times that rate, 28.8 kbps (thousand bits per second) are available for under $200. This faster transmission rate means that data is exchanged at up to twenty-four times faster with the faster modem, slashing phone company and/or service provider connect charges while making your online experience far more satisfying.

Until a few years ago, 2400 bps was considered speedy, but the standard has shifted: 9600 bps modems arrived, then 14.4 kbps modems and now 28.8 kbps modems are becoming the norm. Using these new interconnects relieves the Internet user from tedious download sessions by bring while reducing connect charges. Other, more expensive technologies, or those which have not quite arrived' (ISDN, cable-provider connections, etc.) promise even faster access.

Be sure and use the Internet University's companion website:

http://www.caso.com/

This site contains up-to-date listings and current news about online ed.

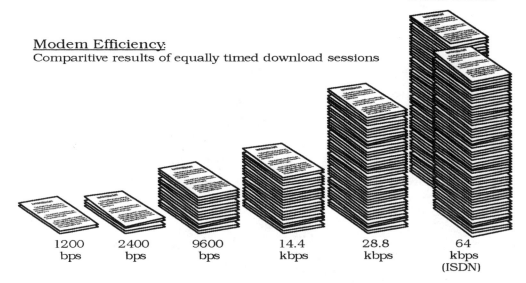

Modem Efficiency:
Comparitive results of equally timed download sessions

| 1200 bps | 2400 bps | 9600 bps | 14.4 kbps | 28.8 kbps | 64 kbps (ISDN) |

Considering the speedy rate of obsolescence in digital technologies, it follows that it might be cost-effective to invest in the fastest model currently available (28.8 kbps) - for another $100 over the cost of a slower modem. Theoretically, the faster modem will transfer data at twice the speed of a 14.4 kbps modem, assuming optimal conditions (i. e.; with another 28.8 kbps modem at the other end, low phone line noise). In the usual case, investment in a fast modem will yield the most academic return, with a very short payback time (3-6 months), even if you currently have a 2400bps or 9600bps device.

Although the purchase price of a slower modem is lower, its slowness will cost you time and money for as long as you have the modem. Internet providers generally base service charges on connect time. The longer processing information takes, as in searching for or downloading files, the higher the service fees will be. Online students from remote areas also have the additional problem of having to pay phone toll calls, which makes the 'slow modem' problem even worse.

Graphics Use Lots of Bits: The slowness of a modem will be more apparent where graphics are used extensively. Any modem slower than 14.4 kbps is an exercise in frustration for a World-Wide-Web connection - 28.8 is recommended. Having a graphical environment allows for 'point-and-shoot' navigation, opening the Internet to non-computer 'techies' and 'nerds'. These factors and others generally point to the truism with modems: purchase the fastest that your budget will allow.

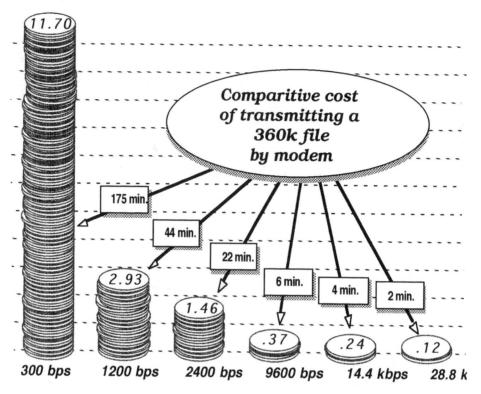

Comparitive cost
of transmitting a
360k file
by modem

11.70

175 min.

44 min.

22 min.

6 min.

4 min.

2 min.

2.93

1.46

.37

.24

.12

| 300 bps | 1200 bps | 2400 bps | 9600 bps | 14.4 kbps | 28.8 k |

Communications Software: A modem is generally hardware (an electronic component that can be held in the hand), and it only works with <u>communications</u> software. Those researching communications software for use with distance learning will discover that there are many of these packages available, ranging in price from free to $150.

Some software is 'free' in that no cash needs to be paid for them. However, such 'free' programs are often quirky or erratic in behavior and possibly not worth the 'savings' for someone wanting to work with these programs strictly for the ability to take college courses, and not to study obscure communications software. There are many contrary examples, the NCSA Mosaic and Netscape web browsers being among the most prominent. Ask for advice and support from your provider; they will also be there to assist you through the connect procedures.

The major online services will provide software for logging on to their systems (AOL wins the contest for best interface 'hands down'), and most local Internet providers will offer at least a rudimentary package. Windows has a module (Terminal) which provides the basic features, as do integrated programs such as Microsoft Works and Claris Works, but these will be totally unsatisfactory. They can handle basic communications functions - including the ability to download binary files - but many users will soon find them too limiting.

Naturally, low-end modems are frequently bundled with only the most basic software (like Bitcom or ProComm), which may require additional fees to use the more powerful features. Replacing the bundled package with a more full-featured program such as ProComm Plus or Crosstalk may be appropriate. Higher end modems generally come with more fully-featured software, with labor-saving capabilities such as automatic email transfer, schedulers, etc.

Consider purchasing one of these off-the-shelf programs, particularly if you have used a free or bundled package and found it lacking in features or ease of use. Remember - calculating the time online needed to figure out how the program works must also be included in figuring the total cost of the package - hard-to-learn 'free' programs may not represent any savings at all.

Data Standards: Any modem purchased to connect the student should fit the international standard v32bis and the matching standard for data compression, v42bis. It is not necessary to know what these standards mean except that they relate to transfer assumptions between machines, and without these capabilities slower operation may result.

Could Less be More? In some cases, a slow modem may be acceptable. If your computer is in a home with local dialup to the service provider (no phone company toll calls) and presuming no extensive online search or download requirements (research completed off-line) a case can certainly be made for staying with a 1200, 2400 or 9600 baud modem. The slower speeds almost certainly infer an 'email-only' or 'email-predominant' use pattern; with ftp, downloading files and research documents could literally take hours *each*; with Telnet the interaction would be more acceptable but still quite time-consuming. This could work if you have no phone tolls and time to kill.

Internal vs. External Modems: An external modem is a separate module that attaches to the computer externally via a serial cable to a plug in the back, typically with its own adapter power cord. An internal modem is on a board which is mounted in one of the 'expansion slots' inside the computer. In both installations a phone 'patchcord' goes from a socket in the modem to a phone wall socket or other 'dial tone' source.

Though a little more expensive, external modems have some advantages over their internal counterparts. They are easier to install and troubleshoot. They are easier to switch between computers. Macs and PCs often can use the same external modems; only the cable connecting them to the computer is different. External modems are about $25 more than the internal version. Before purchasing an internal modem ensure that it is compatible with the computer's expansion slots, or that it will be accepted for return by the vendor. For internally installed modems, it may be best to have a technician install it, though in fact it is generally easy to do.

For true peace and quiet, try a phoneless cord.

Phone Line choices

The least expensive phone connection is a regular telephone line - a so-called 'dedicated line' is not necessary. Of course, since a standard phone line can carry only one signal at a time, when you are online it will not be possible to talk to someone else. Anybody calling your house will get a busy signal; it is essential that you disable 'call waiting' or an interruption may result.

Dedicated Line: Homes with extreme competition for phone access (those with teenagers, a home-operated business, etc.) may not be environments conducive for extended online sessions. For this reason it is reasonable in many cases to install a separate phone line for telecommunications. When factored against the costs saved by online education to traditional methods, with transportation charges, etc., a dedicated phone line may be cost-effective. Factors to consider are:

- Availability of additional lines from local phone company
- Can your budget absorb additional monthly phone charges
- Family use of existing phone lines, particularly during study time

Parallel phone lines: An additional benefit of having a second phone line in the house is that if you are at an impasse while navigating the Internet, it is possible to be online with a knowledgeable advisor using *voice* on one line, while being online through the modem on the other line. In this way, it is possible for your helper to 'talk you through' the problem. For the installation charge, plus the monthly fee, for a second line (prices vary according to local phone company charges) you can give telecommunications a whole new face.

The Future of the Internet? ISDN is the best of dedicated telephone company service available to the house. ISDN is available to some areas for a price comparable to regular phone service, around $25 per month. ISDN provides the user with a 64 kbps connection, which greatly speeds interactions of all sorts. If your education profile indicates extensive online use, this is an option to consider - the first question being if the local phone company provides this service. With the ISDN connection being *digital* rather than *analog* (like a regular phone line) your current modem will not work. An ISDN modem will cost some hundreds more, since no economies of scale are in play yet for manufacturers. This use will be increasing, however, due to the obvious advantages of ISDN, and with compression capabilities, personal ISDN will be even more powerful.

Cable companies are now experimenting with providing Internet access to subscribers over the same line that now carries television programming. It will be necessary for the user to have a 'black box' connected to the incoming cable which will act as the modem. This type of connection will exceed audio-based transfers in speed since it operates on a *digital* to *digital* basis.

Summary of Hardware Considerations: A system of computer, modem and phone line - the basic hardware of the Internet University - could be considered the 'automobile' of the electronic highway. Knowing how to use them is comparable to having your driver's license. Getting introduced to the jargon and technicals of the Internet is challenging, with new terminology and procedures to learn; consider it comparable to knowing about traffic circles, right on red, and how to merge traffic. There is nothing better than experience to help you learn these things - experience that will grow as you continue in your online academic career.

Identify Online Needs

In order to determine your telecommunications requirements and usage patterns it will be necessary to consider what uses you require of the basic Internet services which are available. This next section will briefly describe the basic services and the potential academic uses that you'd have. With an accurate assessment you will be able to then operate a sort system against the multitude of service providers in the market.

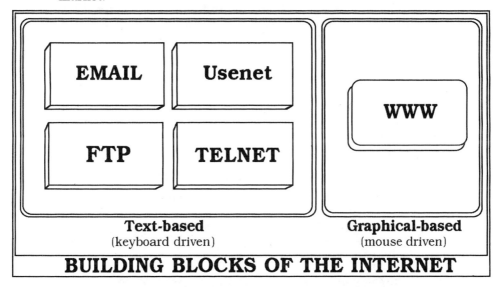

EMAIL	Usenet	
FTP	TELNET	WWW
Text-based (keyboard driven)		**Graphical-based** (mouse driven)

BUILDING BLOCKS OF THE INTERNET

Summary of Internet Services: The basic building blocks of the Internet have been developed over the years to meet the changing needs of users.

They are:
- **email:** *electronic mail*
- **Usenet:** *global bulletin board*
- **ftp:** *file transfer protocol*
- **Telnet:** *remote logon*
- **WWW:** *World-Wide Web*

Each of these features has enough history to entertain and interest the trivia buffs among us for hours (or hundreds of pages). For this book, however, it is sufficient to know what these features are and what they can do for us in our academic pursuits.

What the Basic Internet Services Give the Student:

Under development for one-quarter century, the functions of the Internet will help you overcome distance and time boundaries and secure the future that only education can give. <u>Email</u> and <u>Usenet</u> will change the way you communicate, <u>ftp</u> and <u>Telnet</u> will alter forever your research and study techniques, and the <u>Web</u> gives a powerful scholastic experience.

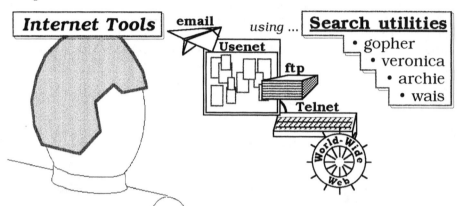

Agents of Research & Communication for the Online Student

Email - everybody's first use of the Internet, in extended uses gives access to mailing lists and journals. Also, email can substitute for other features through 'work-around' techniques.

Usenet - discussion forums and bulletin boards covering more than 8,000 topics where participants can post information that can be read by subscribers anywhere in the world.

FTP - downloads a remotely-stored file to your computer assuming you know the file name and location - works with search utilities like Gopher. Student uses include file retrieval for research purposes.

Telnet - logging onto remote computers, such as a library server, to peruse their contents and use their programs - also works with Gopher.

WWW - the fastest-growing part of the Internet, bringing point-and-click ease of use to the casual user. Hundreds of Universities have established a Web presence, with more coming online daily.

The Student's Use of Email

For the online student, the use of email is essential. This is the medium by which you will be corresponding with your instructor and fellow students, submitting papers and position statements, and inquiring of multiple sources for information needed in the completion of your course work. Happily, any service provider will be giving email access as a bare minimum.

Distance education has traditionally been carried out through correspondence via surface post (paper mail). In using email for this, new possibilities are added. One way email shines is in its speed of 'turnaround'. Papers can be submitted and returned in a schedule similar to or improved over that experienced by on-campus students.

As well, since all correspondence is held in the 'live' medium of online text, inquiries and research will be more easily introduced into compositions. Formulating your thoughts for email transmission will prove to be an aid in organizing course work requirements. The student's use of email is the fundamental building block for your online academics.

Mailing Lists and Journals: Email is also the medium in which mailing lists and journals are operated. In preparing the materials for this book, I subscribed to numerous mailing lists and received their daily downloads. While many of these postings were of no use to me, frequently someone would ask a question or provide information about a resource that I would have otherwise have missed. As well, I was able to post queries to the list, where they were automatically viewed by all subscribers, thus having access to an entire list of people interested in the topic of the mailing list.

Email Workarounds: Email access is a prerequisite for any online student. Even the most rudimentary of Internet access must include email service. In fact, it is possible to participate in a wide variety of courses using nothing more than email, which may be the least expensive alternative for you. Bear in mind, however, that your research efforts will be hampered without some of the more advanced features of full-service Internet providers. Email workarounds for access to expanded features are often slow and unreliable. For more on the student's use of email, including workarounds, see **Part III - *Study***.

When contacting any organization mentioned in this book please tell them that you learned about their services in Cape Software's book:

THE INTERNET UNIVERSITY - COLLEGE COURSES BY COMPUTER

The Student's Use of Usenet

Imagine a bulletin board at a university. Now imagine that all of the powers of the bulletin board format (ease of posting, ease of browsing) have been electronically retained, while the drawbacks (unauthorized removal of postings, stale-dated postings) have been electronically solved. Now further imagine that this bulletin board is electronically sorted into thousands of categories and that it is magically made available world-wide. What you have imagined is the Usenet.

Usenet newsgroups cover the gamut from discussing automobiles and pictures of them to scientific subjects. There are presently many thousands of Usenet newsgroups available to the general public, free of charge. For a selected list of these, see **Part III - *Study***. You will use your provider's newsreader for subscribing to these lists, which are archives of postings by members. These archives are purged according to how long a posting has been online, and most newsreaders are designed to display only those postings that you have <u>not</u> read.

All postings you make automatically have your email address included in them, so that if someone reads a posting of yours and they wish to reply it is very convenient to do so. Responses can either be directed to be posted to the newsgroup as a whole, or to be read individually by the original posting party. Usenet newsgroups provide the user with a convenient meeting place where you can approach someone for further correspondence if you find a posting that intrigues you.

Access to Usenet is essential for the student, and if a prospective Internet service provider does not provide this, for your own satisfaction and interest, seek a connection elsewhere. Also, the provider should give access to a wide range of Usenet domains. Some of these are commercial (ClariNet, for instance) and give useful information to the student. Most providers in these days of competition for customers give access to the full range of Usenet newsgroups, but it is good to check.

If your provider does not give access to a newsgroup that you have discovered you want to employ, request that they provide it. In many cases it is a simple matter for them to add it to their roster, and they will likely be glad to do so. As you become familiar with following the groups you will learn of some of the more obscure ones, and the ability to readily subscribe to them is important. The Usenet will develop into one of your most valuable educational resources.

The Student's Use of FTP

Beyond email, ftp (File Transfer Protocol) - the electronic transfer of files - is perhaps the most useful feature of the Internet. There are thousands of ftp sites around the world that will provide the student with access to a wealth of files for downloading. Transferring files from one Internet-connected computer to another is accomplished by the function known as FILE TRANSFER PROTOCOL. With ftp you will connect your computer to another Internet computer, and locate and download desired files that are stored at the remote site.

Files that can be transferred via FTP include every type of computer file: text files, programs or applications, graphic images, sounds, files formatted for particular software programs (e.g., files with word processing formatting instructions), multimedia files, etc.

For example, in writing this book one of the files that I required was the course catalog for Athena University, among many others. A synopsis of this document had been sent to me via email as a result of an earlier email inquiry, but I wanted the complete record, so I inquired of its location on a distant computer, again by email. I was informed within minutes that the file I wanted was available via the ftp address: `ftp.symnet.net`. It was a simple matter then, using ftp, to go to this site, and following instructions in the earlier email message, search the directory: /users/VOU/incoming; there the files were displayed like this:

```
244224 Feb 24 15:31 catalog.doc   (MS Word for Windows 6)
231424 Feb 24 15:35 catalog.mcw   (MS Word for Mac 5.1)
329718 Feb 24 16:16 catalog.wp    (Word Perfect 5.0)
184806 Feb 24 15:33 catalog.txt   (text only)
```

I selected the 'text only' version of the file and started the download. Since the computer I was using was equipped with an older 2400 bps modem it required about twenty minutes to download. After that process was completed, I was able to open this file in my word processor and view the results, which in this case was text.

Various administrators of computer networks throughout the Internet have dedicated portions of their systems to public access, offering files stored therein for anyone on the Internet to retrieve. These sites support "anonymous" logins; through this technique anyone without a password can have access to these 'anonymous FTP sites.'

The Student's Use of Telnet

Telnet is a service which allows the user to log on to a remote computer. This enables a user in one location on the Internet to act as a terminal on a distant computer. Once logged on, the user can use the remote system as if his computer were part of that network. Telnet is used to allow remote access to everything from library catalogs to databases, computer bulletin boards and interactive role-playing games. With Telnet the student has access to any and all services that the remote computer provides to its local terminals.

Another term for Telnet is 'remote login'. Telnet is initiated by specifying the target computer; from the time of connection everything that is typed on your keyboard is sent to the other computer. In effect, your computer is transformed into a remote terminal of the distant computer - every character you type is sent directly over the Internet connection. Typically, with Telnet, the remote computer will ask you to log in and query you for a password, as if you had just logged in from a terminal on that site. This is the 'catch' with Telnet - you must have the password and logon procedures (a list of various university library logon procedures) is included in **Part III - Study**. Then, when you log off of the remote computer, Telnet exits and you are back in a stand-alone mode with your own computer.

Typical Telnet destinations include library catalogs and bibliographic databases, campus-wide information systems (CWISs), full-text databases and collections of journals and scholarly papers, data files such as census data, scientific compilations and statistical information, and other online services. Many Telnet sites are available for any Internet user free of charge, though access may be limited to certain hours of the day and/or numbers of visitors at any one time.

For an understanding of what happens in a Telnet session, consider that there are two cooperating pieces of software: a *client* which resides on the *requesting* computer; and the *server* which resides on the remote computer. A server is capable of handling a variety of clients, whether operating a Macintosh or PC, whatever happens to seek access. In order for this to occur, an *application protocol* is utilized. By this method your Macintosh or IBM (or compatible) is perfectly suited to use Telnet to work on the incredible network of machines, ranging from IBM mainframes to UNIX servers, that populate the Internet.

No list of Internet resources can ever be complete. If you know of an educational connection or opportunity we've missed, please email to:

tellus@caso.com

The Student's Use of World-Wide Web

The Web (also known as WWW, or World-Wide Web) is the fastest growing part of the Internet - for every user eighteen months ago there are more than 100 users today! This tremendous growth in user base is directly attributable to the development of *browsers* which enable those with no expertise in UNIX to 'surf' (cruise freely) the world's Web sites.

On the Web, users get documents or information in a variety of formats including text, graphics, sound and video. The information is linked through *hypertext* format, which means that the information in one document can be dynamically connected to a different document. For example, while you are reading a document on Frank Zappa, it may be possible to click the mouse on a 'button' (sensitized region) on the screen and within moments you will be able to hear a clip of his work, or click on Zappa's **birth date** to open a new document with his biography.

The Capstone of the Internet: The Web allows even a casual user of the Internet to be amply rewarded for invested time and energy. Information and entertainment for any interest is available entirely by mouse clicks. The point-and-shoot *graphical* interface ties together the text-based building blocks of the Internet, also, bringing an exciting new dimension! Here are a few examples of providers maintaining sites on the Web:

- Museums, including the Smithsonian and the Louvre, which present displays and examples of their holdings;
- Corporations, where product information and service connections are available;
- Government, access information, administrative reports, legislative proceedings, scientific information, census data, etc.;
- Magazines and a range of online publishers ('zines);
- Business sites, with research information about financial markets, investments, etc.;
- Hobby and recreational sites, enabling interaction with other enthusiasts and participants;
- Individuals, who have discovered a new way to meet people.

Academic Resources: Of particular interest to the online student is the extensive list of universities and colleges contained in **Lists**. It is impossible for any printed list to be complete since new additions are being made daily, but here you will find an list of hundreds of sites.

Some colleges are establishing their classrooms on the Web, since the interface is so conducive to interaction. New educational models are evolving to use this remarkable new medium to its fullest. It is not enough to take text-based traditional classroom models and move these over to the Web. These are pioneering days and some innovative projects are ongoing for student participation.

35

The invention of graphical Web browsers gives a boost to the beginner user analogous to the introduction of Macintosh's *graphical user interface* in the mid '80s. Everyday people are suddenly capable of working in a domain only recently populated exclusively by computer 'savvy' people, or those who had supported access through university or corporation. Point-and-shoot interfaces are an important component of the ready use of the globe's computer network by millions of non-computer majors.

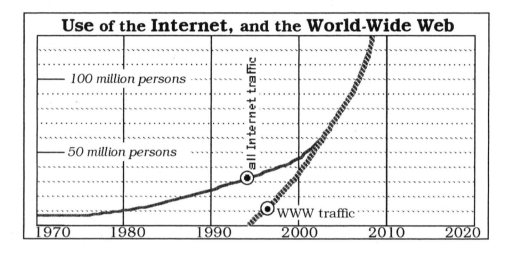

Speed Demons: Remember, in order to access the Web it will be necessary to have a fast modem (14.4 kbps is the <u>bare</u> minimum - with a 28.8 being the practical choice). The medium of the Web is *graphical*, and these documents require more 'bandwidth' and 'throughput' than mere text requires. For access to this brave new world of Internet connections, consider signing on with a provider which gives high-speed access, though most do these days. For truly serious use of the Web, and if ISDN is available within your area and budget, by all means go for it! Once you have experienced the immediacy of the Web on ISDN, the delays for downloads over a modem (even a 28.8kbps model) will seem interminable.

The trouble with our times is that the future is not what it used to be.
- Paul Valery

SLIP and PPP Connections

SLIP (Serial Link Internetworking Protocol) or PPP (Point-to-Point Protocol) represent the new face of the Internet for modem-based connections. SLIP and PPP are protocols that allow for speedy HTTP (Hyper Text Transfer Protocol), making the World-Wide Web a possibility. Hypertext is where **certain words** in a document appearing on the screen are *linked* to another document. Thus by *clicking* on the **highlighted words** the current document disappears and a new one appears which may be located on the same server or across the globe.

SLIP and PPP connections are protocols that make your computer not just connected to the Internet, but actually a part of it. The SLIP/PPP connections can't use standard communications software, but rather require a specialized interface (Netscape being the most popular).

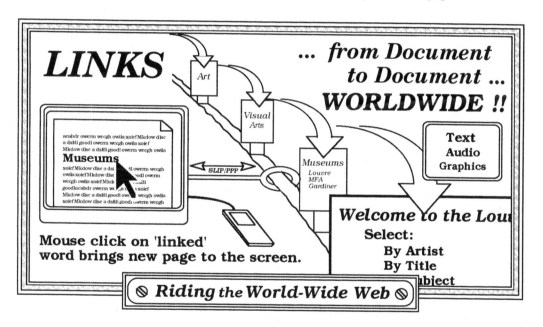

These browsers also allow 'multitasking' (more than one function going on at a time). In one window on your screen you can be reading mail; in another you can be downloading a file via ftp, etc. - limited only by the computer's processing power. FTP is speeded with SLIP/PPP connection - instead of transferring the remote file to your provider's machine and then to your PC, it is copied directly to your home computer.

Selecting an Internet Provider

List1 provides voice phone numbers of Internet service providers according to area code. Note that this list is not complete, as no list of Internet providers ever can be since startups are coming online every day. This is a compilation of providers as reported by multiple sources.

One of these, the Internet Network Information Center (InterNIC) lists some hundreds of commercial access providers around the US (email: `info@internic.net`). Another is Peter Kaminski's PDIAL (<u>email</u>: `info-deli-server@netcom.com`; message: `send pdial`). Of course, these addresses won't help you if you aren't already online, so when searching for a provider, other good sources to consider are local computer magazines, computer stores, of user groups. These latter sources will also be able to provide comparative analysis (otherwise known as 'rumors' and 'reputation') of the local providers.

Questions for Service Provider: Once you have your list of local providers, make a research call to each. Follow this interview format, which records the information needed to make your decision. Remember, this is not a life-and-death choice - you can readily change providers if you discover a better deal in your area. Needs will change, as will technologies and services offered.

Once you have signed on remember to make ample use of the provider's support services. In the given market for Internet service the support people are often overworked though good-natured, and they may require gentle persistence on your part in order to consider your problem higher on their priority list. It is in their best interests to assist you. As it happens, before too many months have passed people will be asking *you* how to use the educational tools that the Internet places in your hands !

Questions for Prospective Internet Providers

Questions:	Average response	Provider's response
Is there a signup fee or one-time connect charge?	Up to $25 one-time charge	
Is there an annual fee in addition to the monthly or usage charge?	No annual fees	
What is the monthly rate? Including how many connect hours? Rate for additional hours?	$25/mo. for 25 hrs, additional $1/hr.	
Are there surcharges for peak hours? If so, what are these and for which hours?	Flat rate	
Do they offer discounts for off-peak hours? If so, what discount, and for what hours?	Flat rate	
Do they offer toll-free access to your area?	Toll free area access offered	
Do they charge for email? Received, or sent? By message? How much?	Unlimited email no extra charges	
Do they charge extra for high speed access (14.4kbps, or 28.8kbps)?	No surcharges for enhanced access speeds	
Is there a charge for any interface software?	Interface or shell provided free of charge	
What are their rates for SLIP/PPP?	No additional charge for SLIP/PPP	

Questions for Prospective Internet Providers (cont'd.):

Which Internet tools do they offer: email? a newsreader? ftp? Gopher, Archie, Veronica? Web browser?	All offered for no additional charges. (Ask about Netscape)	
For a SLIP/PPP account, do they offer documentation, configuration details?	Yes (important)	
Do they offer tech support? What hours of the day is it available?	Good support, convenient time	
Do they support 14.4 kbps, 28.8 kbps, ISDN connections?	(Go 28.8!)	
What are the peak usage hours?	Business hours, evening	
How often are busy signals encountered during peak, evening, and weekend hours?	Best = 'none'; max. 5 min.	
How many subscribers do they have?	Varies	
What is their subscriber/modem ratio?	1 modem /10 subscribers	
Are there times when it is impossible to get through?	Never	
What is their connection to the Internet?	T-1; local or T-3 regional	

Popular Online Services

You may determine that subscribing to a full-fledged Internet provider is not the course for you to take for educational access. The popular online services (AOL, Compuserve, Delphi, etc.) all provide email service to the Internet, though full access is spotty at best, particularly to Telnet, the Web and other advanced services. However, there are factors which recommend their use, nonetheless - these being ease of use, and having access to the numerous services that they provide. While some of the information you find on the Internet is unique, you won't find it on the online services. Similarly, each online service contains a selection of information that you won't find on the Internet.

All the services have forums and services that are available only to subscribers, and thus paying for a membership is the only way to have access to them. Full Internet access will connect you with sources for study that might make you a better student, or make your educational process more effective. On the other hand, it does not make sense to pay for services that remain unused.

Assessment of Educational Support: If you are presently not online in any form (don't feel alone - it is estimated that under 10% of all computer-owners are 'connected'), and are somewhat intimidated by the prospects, using one of these online services may represent an effective 'bridge' for you to get introduced. Also, some of the information you find on the online services is unique; you won't find it anywhere on the Internet. With this in mind, we have assessed the effectiveness for the student of the main six popular online services according to these criteria:

- **ease of interface use**
- **user support services**
- **ease of system navigation**
- **educational services**
- **variety of forums**
- **Internet connections**
- **comprehensiveness**
- **pricing**

America Online ranks highest in most of these categories, and is our recommendation for the student who wants to return to school but is not able or ready to sign on with an Internet provider. The cost of this option will be comparable to regular Internet providers, ease-of-use is improved, comprehensiveness of services is strong, and new services are arriving all the time.

Providing Educational Support: Our study shows that America Online (AOL) is the best choice for online education, not only due to AOL's strong points for interface and variety of information resources, but also due to their arrangement with the Electronic University Network (the EUN is profiled in **Part II - Courses**). All the profiled services have their strong points and they all have weaknesses, but AOL has become the strong service that it is, with its growing popularity, for three main reasons: ease-of-use (graphical interface), relatively low cost, and great variety of online offerings. Only Compuserve exceeds AOL in strength of content; none exceed it in ease of use.

Popular Services Contact Information

AOL
America Online
8619 Westwood Center Drive
Vienna VA 22182-2285
(800) 827-6364

CompuServe, Inc.
5000 Arlington Centre Boulevard
P. O. Box 20212
Columbus OH 43220
(800) 848-8199

Delphi Internet Services Corp.
1030 Massachusetts Avenue
Cambridge MA 02138
(800) 695-4005

eWorld
Apple Computer, Inc.
20525 Mariani Avenue
Cupertino CA 95014
(800) 775-4556

GEnie
General Electric Information Svs
401 N. Washington Street
Rockville MD 20849-6403
(800) 638-9636

Prodigy Services Company
445 Hamilton Avenue
White Plains NY 10601
(800) 776-3449

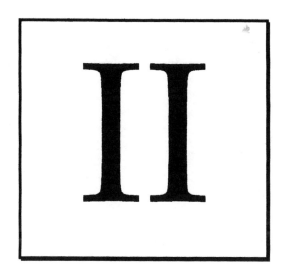

Sources

Providers & Catalog

Part II - Providers & Catalog

Sources

Goals for Part II:

Review Available Courses

Other Sources of Information

Part II - *Sources* - Providers & Catalog will assist you in identifying the course provider which best meets your needs. Some institutions grant degrees and have programs designed to give you enough credits for this, while others will offer only individual courses.

The course providers described in this Part are fully accredited according to the agencies appointed by the US Department of Education. (NOTE: For courses that are non-credit or that are provided by non-accredited institutions, refer to **Part IV - *Horizons*.**) In the Part you are now reading we describe 28 institutions, their degree programs, and their course offerings. Contact information is given for further correspondence and up-to-date course details.

The Internet University student can access these courses through a variety of techniques, ranging from the essential link of email to the exciting World-Wide Web. Traditional methods of distance education are now being coupled with the tools of the Internet. Many institutions identify themselves as being 'online course providers' - in order to understand this, some definition of terms is required. Contact your prospective provider to ensure that the means of transmission is compatible with your needs.

Other, more comprehensive, uses of the Internet are available to online scholars. Internet tools are used in an *additive* fashion; each resource *expands* the use of the network. For this book we are describing these 'types' as if they are clearcut categories, in fact there is often considerable blurring between them.

① **Essential Links**: This stage of online academics uses Internet services in an upgrading of traditional distance education methods. Audio and video tapes may be included, as well as 'paper mail'. Some uses of the Internet with this type: receiving and submitting assignments by email; subscribing to mailing lists, also by email; and following Usenet newsgroups.

② **Mediated Classwork**: With this stage of we see the creation of the *virtual* classroom, managed and directed by the course instructor. This mediation involves arranging assignments and frequent email correspondence into an effective whole. The benefits of this stage, coupled with the gains from continued Type 1 activities, create a vibrant educational environment.

③ **Web Access**: Point-and-shoot navigation from your computer to those of the nation's and world's universities (over 460 university and college Web addresses given) and libraries, including the Library of Congress. The new frontier of the Internet, where new approaches are being developed which is bringing a new dimension to online education.

④ **MUD/MOO**: (Multi-User Domain and MUD-Object-Oriented), these formats provide 'live' interaction via a host site, where participants are logged on simultaneously (*synchronous* communications). This allows for immediacy and spontaneous interchange, and presents the instructor with a challenging interface to manage. As bandwidth becomes more available, and as student familiarity with Internet use increases, this method of class work is expected to increase in popularity.

Contact these institutions directly and remember that course offerings change, as do prerequisites and enrollment procedures. The course listings and degree specifications will give you a picture for what the institution will offer you, and you can take it from there through discussions with their counselors.

Be sure and visit The Internet University's companion website:
http://www.caso.com/
This site contains up-to-date listings and current news about online ed.

About the Course Catalog

These course providing colleges and universities are offering the 650+ courses that are outlined in the Course Catalog included in the rear of this book. Note that the 'code name' is included in each course number so that you can tell at a glance which institution is the provider. The page number refers to the provider's location in the Catalog section of the book.

Institution	Code	Page
Antioch University	AOCH	213
Brevard Community College	BREV	216
California Institute of Integral Studies	CIIS	219
City University	CITY	221
University of California-Dominguez Hills	DOMI	225
Edgewood College	EDGE	227
Embry-Riddle Aeronautical University	ERAU	230
University of Florida	FLOR	235
Front Range Community College	FRCC	243
Heriot-Watt University	HERI	247
Western Illinois University	ILLW	253
University of Iowa	IOWA	258
Internat'l School of Information Mgt.	ISIM	261
Int'l Society for Technology in Ed.	ISTE	268
University of Massachusetts - Dartmouth	MASD	273
New School for Social Research	NEWS	278
Norwich University	NORW	293
Nova Southeastern University	NOVA	295
New York Institute of Technology	NYIT	307
Pennsylvania State University	PASU	324
University of Phoenix	PHOE	327
Rochester Institute of Technology	ROCH	336
Rogers State College	ROGE	348
Salve Regina University	SALV	356
Thomas Edison State College	THOM	360
University of Washington	WASH	364
Webster University	WEBS	374
University of Wisconsin - Madison	WISM	375
University of Wisconsin - Stout	WISS	384

Categories in Catalog Index

The Course Index starts on page Course-2 and it arranges the 650+ courses into the following 24 categories. These distinctions are naturally somewhat arbitrary, since some courses might logically fit in two or more categories (i. e., Management and Computers), so it is recommended that the student scan the entire list for subjects of choice.

Arts	Humanities
Aviation	International
Business	Languages
Communications - Interpersonal	Legal
Communications - Online	Literature
Composition	Management
Computers	Mathematics
Economics	Miscellaneous
Education	Municipal
Government	Psychology
Health Sciences	Science
History	Sociology

To make the most of this book, select the courses of interest and then contact the providing institution for further information on enrollment procedures. Contact information is provided within each of the profiles in the Catalog for the colleges and universities. The information contained herein is current as of the date of press, but if it is no longer up-to-date the college's administrative personnel will inform you of the proper contact person.

The publishers of **The Internet University - College Courses by Computer** have endeavored to maintain an as up-to-date database of courses and providers as is possible, but the field of online education is undergoing a dramatic expansion and it is likely that this listing will not contain every course opportunity. In the event that you discover that a listed course has been discontinued, or any other required revision, we request that you inform us via email at:

tellus@caso.com.

This will enable us to maintain the information as current as possible.

About Accreditation

All of the course providers described in **Part II - *Sources*** are fully accredited according to the agencies appointed by the US Department of Education. (NOTE: For courses that are non-credit or that are provided by non-accredited institutions, see **Part IV - *Horizons*.**) One factor in deciding which college to take courses from is determining whether other universities or your employer will accept the credits you have earned. This is particularly relevant for 'non-traditional' and distance education courses such as those catalogued in this book.

First, for a basic definition of the term, *accreditation* is a process that establishes public recognition that an educational institution meets certain basic criteria, and that it is not a mere 'degree mill'. Accreditation is verification by an outside qualified agency that the college or university you have chosen to attend will provide a high degree of educational quality, and that students attending will have the opportunity to learn proper skills and new perspectives well enough to use them in the 'real world'.

By granting accreditation to a college or university, the accrediting body certifies that the institution meets these basic criteria:

○ Operates on a sound financial basis (will not 'go broke' just after you pay your tuition)
○ Has an approved program of study (course offerings are comprehensive for the degrees offered)
○ Has qualified instructors (generally, a 'top-down' certification, i.e.; instructors attained a higher degree level than they teach)
○ Provides adequate facilities and equipment needed to support the courses that are offered
○ Recruitment and admissions policies are non-discriminatory and are properly operated (all relevant federal and state laws apply)

In order to fully understand accreditation it is necessary to consider the laws of the jurisdiction in which the college or university is located. Some state laws are weak, and it is then possible for 'fly-by-night' abuses to occur. Other states may have laws which on paper are sufficient to protect the consumer, but in which proper enforcement is hindered by budget axes. Another abuse to beware is where institutions hide behind religious exemptions.

All courses listed in the **Catalog** and sources outlined in **Part II - Sources** are offered by institutions which have been accredited by an agency approved by the School Accreditation section of the US Department of Education, which certifies this list:

US Accrediting Agencies

New England Association of Schools and Colleges, Winchester MA
North Central Association of Colleges and Schools, Tempe AZ
Western Association of Schools and Colleges, Burlingame CA
Southern Association of Colleges and Schools, Decatur GA
World Education Services, New York NY
Association of Colleges and Schools, Chicago IL
National Home Study Council, Washington DC
Council on Post Secondary Accreditation, Washington DC
Association of Bible Colleges, Fayetteville AK

The accreditation process is voluntary, and the decision to participate is made by the individual college or university. This process is open to educational institutions that have been operational for a minimum of two years. Success in the process is important; it affects the transferability of the course credits between institutions, and thus the college is encouraged to establish qualification so that prospective students will be interested in applying. The accreditation process is repeated every five years.

Established schools, such as Harvard or Yale, sail through the process, due to their strong reputations and the strength of their organizations. Smaller and less well-endowed institutions, however, often go through a protracted struggle to earn the distinction. Earning and maintaining accreditation becomes a focus for these schools, who must consider implications in all planning and budget discussions. It is not necessary for the applying school to be powerful and wealthy, but it must meet the criteria and demonstrate this through the rigors of the institutional examination.

The American Council on Education, Washington DC publishes an annual directory of accredited schools, colleges and universities. If an institution lacks accreditation, its courses and degrees will not be recognized by virtually any other accredited school. As well, employers and potential employers may take accreditation into consideration when making hiring or promotion decisions. Employee motivation to consider continued academic growth is an important consideration for many employers: a 1994 report by the Distance Education and Training Council, Washington, DC found the unanimous opinion among responding supervisors that distance education graduates were equally well-informed and better performers when compared to other graduates.

If you discover inaccuracies or outdated information in this book please inform us via email at: tellus@caso.com. Your recommendations and corrections will appear in subsequent editions.

✔ Other Sources of Course Information

The data compiled in this book was obtained by contacting the course-providing institutions directly, but there are sources of course info that are available for the student that offer centralized databases. Also, there are sources of information for the online distance ed student which may shorten the time and effort required to obtain that degree or certification that is your academic objective. This section of **Part II - Courses** gives a summary of some of these resources:

National Distance Learning Center

Your Learning Connection: The National Distance Learning Center is a centralized electronic information source for distance learning programs and resources. If you are a user of distance learning services, the NDLC will assist you in distributing and accessing available courseware. The NDLC contains listings of K-12, Higher Education and Continuing Education courses as well as Teleconferences.

Benefits to Users: The NDLC provides you with detailed listings of available courses. You search the database by entering the course subject or audience which interests you. After accepting your input, the NDLC system goes to work and quickly reports with a list of applicable courses and related information. You will find a course's subject, intended audience, distribution format, and most importantly, the exact time and date each course is available. You may print each listing at your personal computer for future reference.

It's Free and Easy: The NDLC does not impose a charge for connection time, a membership fee, or any charge for individual listings. Using the NDLC system is as easy as dialing the telephone and typing on your computer keyboard. You can use almost any communications software to connect to the NDLC. If you need help, NDLC staff are available by voice, phone or fax to assist. Call the NDLC office at (502) 686-4556 and ask the staff for more information

To Log On to NDLC: 1. By modem: 2400 bps - (502) 686-4555
14.4 kbps - (502) 686-4557
2. By Internet Telnet: ndlc.occ.uky.edu

The DistanceLearn Database

This is a searchable database of college credit opportunities available at a distance, which is available for $100 from Regents College. You may consider asking your local library or educational institution to purchase it, or perhaps they have already subscribed. Another alternative is to ask Regents College (the DistanceLearn database publisher) for the name of one of their subscribers who may be local to you, who may let you browse the database. The **DistanceLearn** database runs on any IBM-compatible computer with a hard disk and MS-DOS, and it requires no special computer knowledge to install or operate. It uses a simple window environment with on-screen help.

What does DistanceLearn do?
- Locates credit courses by subject, level, delivery format, cost, etc.
- Greatly increases advising accuracy through frequent updates.
- Significantly reduces time spent on complex searches.
- Operates as a self-directed tool which students can use on their own.

Features of the DistanceLearn database
- Over 8,000 courses using video, audio, computer, or print-only.
- All nationally recognized college credit-by-examination.
- External graduate degree information.
- Search capacity by subject, delivery system, course level, key word.
- Print capacity for all exhibits.
- Mouse support.

Further information about the DistanceLearn database is available from:

Regents College
7 Columbia Circle
Albany, NY 12203-5159
Phone: 518-464-8778
FAX: 518-464-8777
518-464-8500

Attn.: David Brigham

The Princeton Review's Excellent Gopher
Gopher to: `bloggs.review.com`

The Princeton Review assists students in preparing for standardized tests through courses, books, software, audio tapes, and videos. They also maintain rankings of colleges and universities - including candid comments by students. Much of this information is available free of charge on The Princeton's Review's Gopher.

The Princeton Review Gopher Menu:

Business School
    Cracking The GMAT (Graduate Management Admission Test)
    Recent GMATs, What's New On The GMAT
    Financing Business School
    Rankings Of Selected Business Schools
    How The Admissions Criteria Are Weighted
Career Issues
    An Introduction
    Are Internships Worth It?
    What "They" Want, What "You" Want
Graduate School
    What Is The Graduate Record Examination (GRE)
    Information About Graduate Admissions
    Financing Graduate School
Important Testing Phone Numbers
Law School
    Guide To Law Schools
    Law School Information, Admissions
    Financing Law School
    LSAT Info, Registration And Logistics Information
    Professional Recommendations
Medical School
    General Admission Information
    MED School Information
    Financing MED School
Undergraduate Admissions
    College Admissions
    How The Aid Process Works
    Preparing For The SAT
    Student Access Guide To The Best 286 Colleges
    The Secret To Getting Admitted

EUN (Electronic University Network)

The EUN has been providing online student access since 1983. EUN operates through a cooperative arrangement with America Online and participation in their program requires a membership with AOL. EUN provides undergraduate and graduate credit courses and degree programs, and has arrangements with various academic institutions to bring degree programs to students all over the world.

EUN undergraduate credits are accepted by more than 2,500 colleges in the U.S., and the EUN is participating with these institutions:

Brevard Community College	*Associates degrees*
California Institute of Integral Studies	*Ph.D. Integral Studies*
City University	*Undergraduate*
Edgewood College	*Mgt / Leadership Certificate*
Heriot-Watt University	*MBA Program*
Michigan State University	*Associates degrees*
Rogers State College	*Associates degrees*
Salve Regina University	*MA / International Relations*
University of Wisconsin-Stout	*CEUs and Undergraduate*

For credit courses and degrees the participating colleges provide the actual instructions, give the grades and award credits. These courses lead to the same degrees and certificates as are earned by on-campus students, and any credits may be transferred to other colleges to fulfill degree requirements.

The EUN also offers examination programs for credit, which are sponsored by The College Board (with 2,500 member colleges), Thomas Edison State College; DANTES; and the American College Testing service. Credits earned with these exams are accepted by member colleges and many other institutions.

Course schedules: Some courses are open-entry, open-exit; these can be started or completed according to a schedule convenient for the student. Others courses operate on a semester schedule, but within the semester there are no set times to be at your computer, though all work must be completed by a certain date. Naturally, visits to any campus are unnecessary.

Connecting via AOL: The student logs on to the network through a local phone number in most areas, or via access to Tymenet. The amount of online time is determined by upload and download requirements for course work, and any required for online research. There are no online lectures, and so online requirements are not excessive. The student prepares communications to the instructor, reads instructor's messages and prepares all assignments while offline, thus conserving connect time. It is expected that the typical course will easily be communicated well within the five hours allowed monthly in the AOL terms of service.

EUN Counseling Services: This operates as a message board which connects with counselors, and where specific questions can be posed. The topics are organized by degree interests and contain answers to frequently asked questions. As well, for an additional fee of $250, a six-month course of individual counseling can be arranged to develop a degree study plan or other assistance. This counseling does not draw only on EUN courses, but instead will consider all available distance learning resources.

Course Materials and Costs: Costs range from $120 to $182 per semester credit for undergraduate courses; $171 to 285 per credit for graduate courses. For most courses this fee includes a set of course-specific video tapes. For courses which require software, this is available at substantial educational discounts.

Additional Information: Costs and admissions requirements vary according to each school's policies. America Online members can research EUN offerings by going to keyword EUN; for others detailed information is available from:

Electronic University Network
1977 Colestin Road
Hornbrook CA 96044

Phones: (800) 225-3276
(503) 482-5871

When contacting any organization mentioned in this book please tell them that you learned about their services in Cape Software's book:

THE INTERNET UNIVERSITY - COLLEGE COURSES BY COMPUTER

Regents College: The 'No-Campus College':

Regents College has no campus and offers no courses. Instead it is an evaluating and assessing institution. It is flexible, portable, and self-paced. Thousands of students around the world have fulfilled their dreams and earned associate and bachelor's degrees through this unique College. Most of these graduates are working adults who used to think they could never attain a college degree.

Mission: Regents College affirms that what individuals know is more important than how or where they acquired the knowledge. Regents believes that students can demonstrate their knowledge and competencies through a variety of methods. The College exists to advance the learning of students, primarily adults who, for personal, economic, family, or other reasons, cannot attend conventional colleges full-time and choose to pursue their education in a flexible, self-paced manner. While remaining open to all, the College ensures academic quality through rigorous programs, student-centered advisement, and careful assessment. By offering high-quality innovative educational opportunities to those desiring an alternative to traditional institutions of higher education, the College strives to broaden individual horizons, develop intellectual autonomy and respect for inquiry, expand career interests and options, and inspire a commitment to lifelong learning.

Regents Credit Bank

The Credit Bank is a transcript service for those who want to consolidate their academic records for employment purposes but are **not** interested in earning a Regents College degree. The Credit Bank will accept the Same educational achievements that are accepted toward the degrees, according to their same academic standards and policies.

Educational experiences accepted for the Credit Bank
- College courses from a regionally accredited college or university.
- Approved college-level proficiency examinations;
- Military education programs;
- Certain courses sponsored by business, industry, or government;
- Federal Aviation Administration Airman Fixed Wing Certificates;
- Special Assessment: an individual examination of college-level knowledge gained from experience or independent study. This is usually an oral exam and is usually administered in Albany, New York.

The University of the State of New York (USNY) Credit Bank transcript will list any of these credits from acceptable sources but will not evaluate them for duplication or for any set of degree requirements.

Individuals who have attended several educational institutions may find it more convenient to consolidate their educational accomplishments on one consistent and cumulative transcript for easy reference for themselves and for employers or college officials when applying for admission to a college or for employment.

How the Regents Credit Bank Works

1. To participate in the Regents Credit Bank, you must submit a completed enrollment form, along with the $215 enrollment fee, to the Records Office of Regents College. Members may add acceptable credits to the USNY Credit Bank transcript as long as they maintain 'active status'..

2. After receiving a letter acknowledging receipt of the enrollment form, you will be asked to have official documentation submitted for all acceptable educational experiences. This documentation **must come directly from the college agency;** student copies of transcripts cannot be used.

3. Once all transcripts are on file, they will be reviewed for acceptability, and approved credit will be placed on a USNY transcript. Only those courses or examinations that you want to have appear on the transcript will be recorded and kept on file. Please write to inform us which credits you wish to have appear. A student copy of the transcript will be forwarded to you after your initial review and after each review update.

4. As a Credit Bank member, you can request that an official USNY transcript be sent to an institution, agency, or person at any time.

5. Education that is not acceptable toward one of the Regents College degrees cannot be listed on the USNY Credit Bank transcript.

6. Regents Credit Bank members are eligible for Special Assessment examinations. For details, write directly to Regents College.

Regents College
Douglas R. Whitney, Dean of Assessment (DWhit9490@aol.com)
7 Columbia Circle
Albany, NY 12203-5159
Phone: 518-464-8778
FAX: 518-464-8777

III

Study

Research & Exploration

Part III - Research and Exploration

Study

Goals for Part III:

Educational Applications of the Internet

Identify Internet Resources for Students

This Part will outline study resources on the Internet that will assist you in making the most of your online academic experience. Government and university libraries contain vast information holdings, and new technologies are opening these to users as never before. Over the past few years many colleges and universities have installed electronic card-catalog systems that open their libraries to students and researchers. Also, numerous papers, reports and literature are available via email and ftp.

All of the resources described in Part III - Study are selected for their ability to provide the Internet student with study sources that are not available to people without computers. Through use of the tools of the Internet, this vast world of information wealth is available for use by online scholars. As was mentioned in our earlier disclaimer, no listing of resources or connections can possible be comprehensive, since new ones are coming online daily. Some of the guides published here will provide pointers to additional updated lists of information.

Research on the Internet

Telecomputing is still a new way for most people to participate in the educational processes, and thus as pioneers we are likely to be unfamiliar with most of the particulars of navigation. In order to understand which Internet tools should be used for your research projects, and to better develop strategies for data collection, these are a few basic questions to ask:

- What are your educational goals for this research? Are these goals appropriate for the course requirements, and will they further your overall academic goals?

- What is leading in your approach - are your goals designed to conform to the available technology, or is the technology being properly used to meet the goals?

- Is the Internet tool the most effective means of data searching available, or can this goal be just as effectively reached by use of local or more traditional sources?

These questions do not present a checklist for whether the Internet should be used. There is a real place for using online sources for info that is locally available. Skill-building is a necessary function, but it is easy to be seduced by the fun of the process. It is important for a development plan to include allowance for such "overhead' or you might delay your overall progress.

Building Your Internet Skills

Skill-building is a legitimate goal in itself, and is required for your long-term academic career. However, it is easy for the original point of your educational exercises to become secondary to the thrill of 'working the net'. Be sure, therefore, to keep your original study goals in mind.

Basic Internet Services and Associated Academic Resources: Remember that the basic building blocks of the Internet have been developed over the years to meet the changing needs of users, and a strong component of these early days was the activities and needs of the academic community. Because the origins of the Internet were among universities and government research facilities, there is a rich variety of educational resources within each tool's domain. These resources have been well developed over the years and are expanding dramatically as more institutions come online all the time. As you conduct your research you will pick up the techniques of these tools.

Send any updates and suggested revisions to: tellus@caso.com

✔ Review Internet's Educational Applications

The Student's Use of Email

Email is usually everybody's first use of the Internet, and in fact when you ask someone what the Internet is, the most common suggestion is that it enables people to talk to each other all over the world (email). As well as allowing 'one-to-one' communications, the use of email has been expanded through *listserv* programs to include mailing lists and journals. Also, email can substitute for many other features of the Internet through work-around techniques.

For the online student, the use of email is essential. It is the medium by which you will be corresponding with your instructor and fellow students, submitting papers and position statements, and inquiring of multiple sources for information needed in the completion of your course work. With the use of email the possibilities for distance education have been greatly expanded. Papers can be submitted and returned faster that is possible even for students who are attending on-campus.

As well, since all correspondence is held in the 'live' medium of online text, inquiries and research will be more easily introduced into writings. As we have read in some of the guest articles in this book, formulating your thoughts for email transmission will prove to be an aid in organizing your overall course work. Bringing the world of online education to a reality using nothing more than email presents the student with a tremendous opportunity.

Email Workarounds: This topic is covered extensively in the Guest Article *Accessing the Internet by Email: Doctor Bob's Guide to Offline Internet Access*, by Bob Rankin. This guide shows how to retrieve files from ftp sites, explore the Internet via Gopher, search for information with Archie, Veronica, Netfind, or WAIS, tap into the World-Wide Web, and even access Usenet newsgroups using email as your only tool. Students with the full range of Internet tools may also wish to read this article for insights on the working of the network, as well as for information on particular tools. Email workarounds Dr. Bob describes include:

- **FTP by Email**, a means of accessing files that are stored on remote computer systems ("sites"). Files at ftp sites are typically stored in a tree-like set of directories (or nested folders for Mac fans), each of which pertains to a different subject. With ftp by e-mail, the desired site is reached through a special "ftpmail server" which logs in to the remote site and returns the requested files to you in response to a set of commands in an e-mail message.

63

- **Archie by Email** - a search utility to use if you have no idea at which FTP site your desired file resides, or if you're curious to know if files matching a certain naming criteria are available via FTP. An Archie server can be thought of as a database of all the anonymous ftp sites in the world, and using Archie by email can be convenient even if your Internet connection provides ftp service, because of the extended time required for some Archie searches.

- **Gopher by Email**, an excellent tool for exploring the Internet and the best way to find a resource if you know what you want, but not where to find it. Gopher knows where things are, thanks to the many volunteers who spend time creating 'pointers', and by email the desired site is reached through a special "gophermail server".

- **Veronica by Email**, gives users access to a system that indexes the global set of Gopher menus, and by which users can search quickly for specific information. Be warned, though - due to the inherent complexity of the file structures within the Internet, these searches are often stymied and come back 'empty'.

These valuable techniques and many others are available in this article, which gives you the opportunity to turn 'simple' email into a very powerful educational tool. Even if you have full access to the Internet, you may find it expedient to use one of these workarounds on occasion.

Mailing Lists and Journals

Email is the medium of mailing lists and journals. Organized postings and automatic responses are operated by special software pertaining to specific topics of interest. Users sign on by sending coded email, and submit 'postings' also by email. Postings are returned to subscribers by email. While not an 'official' part of the Internet, these mailing lists and journals are a powerful component of it.

Mailing lists are built on the use of email. Postings to the list by the individual are sent via email, as are return postings by the list operator. Moderated lists are those where a person considers each posting and passes on only those that meet list criteria. Unmoderated lists can be a bit 'wild and wooly' in that <u>all</u> postings are automatically sent to all subscribers, leaving a high degree of responsibility in subscribers hands.

Be sure and visit The Internet University's companion website:
http://www.caso.com/
This site contains up-to-date listings and current news about online ed.

Mailing Lists for the Student

A Good Mailing List for a Beginner: Help-Net is a resource that is maintained by Temple University as a mailing list. For beginners and those wishing to 'brush up' on tools or techniques, this is an excellent resource. To subscribe to the Help-Net mailing list, send this command: SUBSCRIBE HELP-NET <YourFirstName YourLastName>; send the email to: HELP-NET@VM.TEMPLE.EDU, and you will receive an email message instructing you how to proceed, and how to utilize the list to its greatest benefit. You may post questions after observing for awhile to become familiarized with the protocols of mailing list interaction.

A Free Source of 'How-To' Information: A comprehensive document which details the commands used to subscribe, unsubscribe and search mailing list archives can be obtained by emailing the command: get mailser cmd nettrain f=mail to this email address: LISTSERV@ubvm.cc.buffalo.edu.

List 2 - Mailing Lists: While there are over 5,000 mailing lists open to the public for free subscription, we are listing a selection which may be of interest to you. People 'subscribe' to a list and then send and receive postings by email. For a good introduction to this topic, send a request HELP by email to:

LISTSERV@vm1.nodak.edu.

For a list of lists, send the command: LIST GLOBAL /<keyword>, inserting an appropriate keyword such as 'marketing' or 'economics', to the same address.

Cole's Law: *Cabbage must be thinly sliced.*

THE NATURAL LIFE CYCLE OF MAILING LISTS
a humorous but accurate assessment, by 'Anonymous'

Every list seems to go through the same cycle:

❶ *Initial enthusiasm* - people introduce themselves, and gush alot about how wonderful it is to find kindred souls.

❷ *Evangelism* - people moan about how few folks are posting to the list, and brainstorm recruitment strategies.

❸ *Growth* - more and more people join, more and more lengthy threads develop, occasional off-topic threads pop up.

❹ *Community* - lots of threads, some more relevant than others; lots of information and advice is exchanged; experts help other experts as well as less experienced colleagues; friendships develop; people tease; everyone is comfortable asking questions, giving answers, sharing opinions.

❺ *Discomfort with diversity* - the number of messages increases dramatically; not every thread is fascinating to every reader; people start complaining about the signal-to-noise ratio; person 1 threatens to quit if *other* people don't limit discussion to his pet topic; person 2 agrees with person 1; person 3 tells 1 & 2 to lighten up; more bandwidth is wasted complaining about off-topic threads than is used for the threads themselves; everyone gets annoyed.

❻ *Smug complacency and stagnation* - the purists flame every-one who asks an 'old' question or responds with humor to a serious post; newbies are rebuffed; traffic drops to a doze-producing level of a few minor issues; all interesting discussions happen by private email and are limited to a few participants; the purists spend lots of time self-righteously congratulating each other on keeping off-topic threads off the list.

- OR -

❻ *Maturity* - a few people quit in a huff; the rest of the participants stay near stage 4, with stage 5 popping up briefly every few weeks; many wear out their 'delete' key, but the list lives happily ever after.

The Student's Use of Usenet

Usenet is a globally distributed bulletin board system. This is not a 'network' in the hardware sense, but rather exists as an arrangement between thousands of computer-managers (of mainframe and mini computers) worldwide. In order to understand how the Usenet works, imagine an office bulletin board made electronic and multiplied by a factor of millions. Imagine further that this bulletin board is divided into areas of interest ('domains'). As people browse this bulletin board, they choose from among postings that are of interest to them, and leave contributions that they consider relevant.

The Usenet network is an 'intellectual connection system', where users are involved in their choice of 8000+ specialized groups discussing topics ranging from education, C++ programming, spelunking, Limbaugh or Clinton. As a real-world experiment in free speech and characterized by barely-controlled anarchy, this feature of the Internet gives the student access to many current and up-to-date information resources, all organized into specific subject areas.

The Usenet's Top-level Domains: The Usenet groups each have a unique name, and the user accesses the recent postings of each group by using the Internet provider's *newsreader*. If you are interested in learning more about adult education, for instance, you might want to observe the group `misc.education.adult`. Note that the name infers the subject matter of the group, as is the case with most Usenet group names. The first component of this name (`misc`) is the *domain* of this group, and is the initial organizing category. Here are the generally recognized primary domains:

alt	-	alternative and less formally-managed groups
bit	-	groups of Bitnet, a network which preceded the Internet
biz	-	business-related, press releases, commercial information
comp	-	covers computer science, hardware and software info
k12	-	activities and issues related to kindergarten - grade 12
misc	-	topics not easily categorized within the other domains
news	-	for distributing Usenet news and announcements
rec	-	arts, hobbies and recreation activities
sci	-	groups which address scientific issues
soc	-	groups which address issues of sociological nature
talk	-	debate-oriented sessions, similar to talk radio

Obtaining a List of Usenet Newsgroups: A frequently-updated list of available Usenet newsgroups is available free of charge on the Internet via ftp. This document consists of a current listing by newsgroup name, with a brief description of the focus of the group. The URL for this list: `ftp.uu.net:/networking/news/config/newsgroups.z`.

Learning More About Usenet: One place to learn more about Usenet, is on Usenet itself! Subscribe to the group `news.answers` for a centrally located source of FAQs (frequently asked questions) files. Browse here for a month or so and just about every question you could have about Usenet or the operations of the Internet will be answered.

Other newsgroups which have been established as sources of Internet information for the beginner or person wishing to expand his knowledge of Internet tools and techniques are:

```
alt.best.of.internet
alt.internet.services
news.announce.newusers
news.newusers.questions
news.announce.newsgroups
news.internet.services
rec.humor.oracle (just joking!)
```

Usenet Groups of Interest to the Student: While every online course a student takes has its own requirements and research will often lead to unforeseen areas, we have chosen 900+ selected newsgroups that may be of interest for your academic work. While selections for this list was of necessity somewhat arbitrary, we have chosen groups with broad interest. Take some time and browse a few that seem like they may be relevant to your needs. Post inquiries as they occur to you, and remember that while the Usenet is a bit disorganized, there are some rules to obey. In many ways Usenet is as useful to the student as the mailing list is, and it will undoubtedly evolve into one of your most effective research tools.

We have included a short list (less than 12% of available groups!) in the List section, without descriptions which you can infer from the name of the group. Take the time to browse this list and follow any of these groups that seem like they will assist you in your academic pursuits.

List 3 - Usenet Newsgroups Some of these are focal groups, and provide access to parallel groups which are more tightly focused on a more specific topic. For instance, if you read various postings to the `alt.support` Usenet newsgroup you may discover a host of similar groups, including:

```
alt.support.arthritis        alt.support.diet
alt.support.asthma           alt.support.divorce
alt.support.attn-deficit     alt.support.loneliness
alt.support.big-folks        alt.support.obesity
alt.support.cancer           alt.support.shyness
alt.support.depression       alt.support.tall
```

The Student's Use of FTP

File Transfer Protocol (ftp) is the tool which is used to copy files between computers on the Internet. With ftp you can log onto a remote computer to *download* or *upload* files, although typically it is the download procedure that we will be interested in. There are thousands of ftp sites around the world that will provide the student with access to a wealth of information.

Files that can be transferred via FTP include text files, program or application files, graphic images, sounds, files formatted for particular software programs (e.g., files with word processing formatting instructions), multimedia files, etc. After they are downloaded it is necessary to 'translate' them to useful documents at your own site - in this regard ftp is unlike Telnet which enables the user to actually implement programs resident on the remote site.

Various administrators of computer networks throughout the Internet have dedicated portions of their systems to public access, offering files stored therein for anyone on the Internet to retrieve. These sites support 'anonymous' logins; using this technique any user may have access, generally using an email address as a password. While this seems odd (using your name to access an 'anonymous' site) the use of the term comes from the fact that the user does not have to be previously known to the remote site for access to be allowed.

Finding the Right FTP Site: There is undoubtedly no one list that contains <u>all</u> the world's ftp sites, particularly since new ones are coming online all the time, and sites are often discontinued. However, a very complete list is available (via ftp, naturally) from one cᶠ these addresses:

· `rtfm.mit.edu:/pub/usenet/news.answers.ftp-list/sitelist`
· `ftp.edu.tw:/documents/networking/guides/ftp-list`
· `oak.oakland.edu:/pub/msdos/info/ftp-list/zip`

While it is possible to get these site addresses, be aware that this will be an extensive list (over 1MB in size!) and that the information describing each site will be quite limited. For real ease of retrieving a file, there is no substitute for having these three ingredients:

❶ the full address of the ftp site

❷ the full name of the directory in which the file is stored

❸ the exact name of the desired file

Help from *Archie*

Browsing' an ftp site is particularly difficult because filenames are so cryptic. Owing to the MS/DOS roots of the early days, an eight character limit is established for filenames. It is very difficult to tell what the file is from a name like this (PLG00357.JPG). Also, computer locations of files (hundreds of thousands) are impossible to guess. In the home-grown wisdom of the Internet, a utility has been written which allows you to search thousands of sites simultaneously - this is *Archie*.

Written by students and staff at McGill University in Canada, Archie is a utility that archives databases of all the files available on all of the registered anonymous ftp sites worldwide - well over two million files. The utility provides this information to any Internet user. For more information on Archie, you can access help from your Internet provider's archie server simply by typing archie help at your shell prompt.

Selected FTP Sites of Student Interest

For this book we have selected some ftp sites that the online student may find useful (see **List 5 - FTP Sites**). This is a very short list considering that there are literally thousands of anonymous ftp sites existant today, but for an introduction to the world of ftp, the student will likely find sources of interest from this list. A brief description of a few lists is offered by way of introduction.

Social Studies Research: For an example of a site that provides students with powerful research resources, visit the *Project Hermes* site (ftp: ftp.msstate.edu) where you will find a wealth of recent historical data, including archives of US Supreme Court decisions.

Music Resources: A compilation of the lyrics from many contemporary songs are available from the *Lyric and Discography* site:

ftp://cs.uwp.deu/pub/music

which will enable the student to review the give and take of the ever-changing music scene. Updated regularly, this site gives access unimaginable in the days before the technology of the Internet was introduced.

The extended list of ftp sites are all available via anonymous ftp. For the sake of information gained, as well as to explore the Internet and experience ftp, select one or more of these sites and browse the contents. This will reveal ftp to be one of the online scholar's most powerful tools.

The Student's Use of Telnet

Telnet is a service which allows the student to log on to a remote computer; this enables a user in one location on the Internet to act as a terminal on a distant computer. Once logged on, the user can use this remote system as if his computer were part of that network. Telnet is used to allow remote access to everything from library catalogs, databases, computer bulletin boards and interactive role-playing games. With Telnet the student has access to any and all services that the remote computer provides to its local terminals.

Another term for Telnet is 'remote login'. Telnet is initiated by specifying the target computer; from the time of connection everything that is typed on your keyboard is sent to the other computer as if your computer is a remote terminal of the distant computer - every character you type is sent directly over the Internet connection. Typical Telnet destinations include library catalogs and bibliographic databases, full-text databases and collections of journals and scholarly papers, data files such as census data, scientific compilations and statistical information, etc. Many Telnet sites are available free of charge, though access may be limited to certain hours of the day or number of visitors.

Selected Telnet Sites of Student Interest

For this book we are presenting Telnet addresses and passwords for various sites of interest to the student, including over 80 college and university libraries. There are literally thousands of other sites available, which you will undoubtedly find in your research. The abbreviated list of 105 Telnet sites is offered for your study. A more complete list of Telnet sites is available via, free of charge, from:

`ftp://tcet.unt.edu/pub/telecomputing-info/IRD`

Other Telnet addresses and associated login information is available via telephone or email request from the providing institution.

Be sure and visit The Internet University's companion website:
http://www.caso.com/
This site contains up-to-date listings and current news about online ed.

The Student's Use of the Web

<u>WWW</u> - brings point-and-shoot ease of use to the casual user. The Web (also known as WWW, or the World-Wide Web) is the fastest growing part of the Internet - for every user eighteen months ago there are more than 100 users today! This tremendous growth in user base is directly attributable to the development of *browsers* which enable those with no expertise in UNIX to 'surf' (cruise freely) the world's Web sites.

On the Web, users get documents or information in a of variety of formats including text, graphics, sound and video. The information is linked through *hypertext* format, which means that the information in one document can be dynamically connected to a different document. For example, while you are reading a document on Frank Zappa, it may be possible to click the mouse on a 'button' on the screen and within moments you will be able to hear a clip of his work. As well, you can click on Zappa's birth date to open a new document with his biography.

The Capstone of the Internet: The Web allows even a casual user of the Internet to be amply rewarded for invested time and energy. Information and entertainment for any interest is available entirely by mouse clicks. The point-and-click *graphical* interface ties together the text-based building blocks of the Internet, also, bringing an exciting new dimension! Here are a few examples of providers maintaining sites on the Web:

- Museums, including the Smithsonian and the Louvre, which present displays and examples of their holdings;
- Corporations, where product information and service connections are available;
- Government, providing access information, administrative reports, legislative proceedings, scientific information, census data, etc.;
- Magazines and a range of online publishers ('zines);
- Business sites, with research information about financial markets, investments, etc.;
- Hobby and recreational sites, enabling interaction with other enthusiasts and participants
- Individuals, discovering a new way to meet people.

Academic Resources: Of particular interest to the online student is the extensive list of universities and colleges contained here. It is impossible for any printed list to be complete - new additions are being made daily, but here you will find a list of hundreds of sites.

The invention of graphical Web browsers gives a boost to the beginner user analagous to the introduction of Macintosh's *graphical user interface* in the mid '80s. Everyday people are suddenly capable of working in a domain only recently populated exclusively by computer 'savvy' people, or those who had supported access through a university or corporation. Point-and-shoot interfaces are an important component of the ready use of the globe's computer network by millions of non-computer majors through the Web.

List 6 - Educational Websites: A collection of various websites that may be of interest to the online student, this list is not intended to be comprehensive in any way, but rather to 'sketch in' the wide range of educational resources available on the Web.

List 7 - College and University Websites: This list is an abbreviated collection of Websites from various international colleges and universities. Given the extreme rush to the Web, many colleges and universities have established websites. These range in complexity from extensive to 'under construction'. This list is provided for exploration - bear in mind that this is a volatile environment and that sites come and go, and undergo dramatic changes, often overnight.

Yanoff's Internet Services List

This listing one of the most comprehensive collection of Internet resources available, and is maintained by Scott Yanoff, an Internet hero and legend. This list provides Gopher and WWW addresses for a wide variety of sites. For directions on how to download this list, email to:

`yanoff@alpha2.csd.uwm.edu`

or look for it in the newsgroup `alt.internet.services`. An abbreviated roster of topics for this important Internet resource is included in the List section of this book. If something there appeals to you as relevant for your academic needs, by all means download this list and follow the address to the information source.

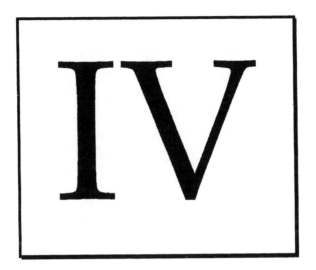

Horizons

Special Connections

Part IV - Special Connections

Horizons

Goals for Part IV:

☐ **CLEP and CEUs**

☐ **High School and Equivalency**

☐ **Personal Enrichment Courses**

☐ **Student Aid and Loans Online**

Part IV - *Horizons* - Special Connections will describe connections to specialty education resources including personal enrichment, equivalency degrees, continuing education, and non-credit courses. This section describes the tremendous variety of informational, instructional and equivalency sources 'out there' on the net. These resources are generally lower in cost than the accredited courses described in **Part II - *Sources***, and will often be more innovative and exciting in their approach.

There are many educational opportunities on the Internet other than for-credit courses. This section will address some of these in detail. Online equivalency courses give the returning student a low-cost and low-impact way of attaining credits and certification. Personal growth subjects are areas which will often utilize the greatest innovation in course delivery.

1. CLEP and CEUs

CLEP (College-Level Examination Program)

By the year 2000, three of four job classifications will require some sort of post-secondary education. To upgrade your level of certification, CLEP (College Level Examination Program) may prove to be a low-cost and high-convenience alternative. CLEP examinations are a series, each 90 minutes, that allow you to demonstrate your expertise in this wide variety of subjects:

GENERAL EXAMINATIONS

English Composition

Humanities

Mathematics

Natural Science

Social Sciences and History

SUBJECT EXAMINATIONS

American Literature

Analysis & Interp. of Literature

English Literature

Freshman College Composition

College French

College German

College Spanish

American Government

American Hist. I: Coloniz.-1877

American Hist. II: 1865-Present

Human Growth and Development

Intro. to Educational Psychology

Principles of Macroeconomics

Principles of Microeconomics

Introductory Psychology

Introductory Sociology

Western Civ. I: To 1648

Western Civ. II: 1648- Present

Calculus w/ Elementary Funct.

College Algebra

College Algebra-Trigonometry

Trigonometry

General Biology

General Chemistry

Info. Systems & Computer Apps.

Principles of Management

Introductory Accounting

Introductory Business Law

Principles of Marketing

Getting Credit for CLEP: CLEP examinations are recognized by over 2,800 colleges in the US - to determine whether the college of your choice is a participant, contact the college's admission office. These exams are held at more than 1,200 locations throughout the country, and will be arranged abroad upon request. Generally, these exams are offered according to a monthly schedule. A free booklet (CLEP Colleges) lists all the testing sites with contact information so you can ask about testing schedules, as well as determine whether your college is listed among those that award CLEP credits.

With CLEP it is possible to be awarded credit for courses you have not taken but have learned an equivalent amount of knowledge in life. CLEP thus shortens the time required to get a degree, by shortening the time of earning a credit from two to three months to a ninety minute test. As well, CLEP saves money because the courses bypassed through the tests are courses that won't have to be paid for on the way to a degree.

No prerequisites are required to take a CLEP exam: no age restriction, degree requirements (high school or postsecondary), etc. To be awarded credit for CLEP at a college, however, you must meet any specific requirements set by that institution. Again, check with participating institutions to determine your eligibility and application procedures.

To learn more, write or call:

Charter Oak College	Regents College	Thomas Edison State Coll.
66 Cedar St.	7 Columbia Circle	101 West State St.
Newington CT 06111	Albany NY 12203	Trenton NJ 08608
(203) 666-4595	(518) 464-8500	(609) 984-1150

Other colleges and universities also offer external degree programs or special weekend colleges designed for working adults. For additional information, contact the college you plan to attend or:

Center for Adult Learning and Education Credentials
American Council on Education
1 DuPont Circle
Washington DC 20036
(202) 939-9475

Information in this profile is derived from the booklet: *CLEP Colleges* is available at participating colleges, or directly from the source:

College Level Examination Program   (609) 771-7865
P. O. Box 6601
Princeton NJ 08541-6601

CLEP Courses Through the EUN (Electronic University Network)

The EUN provides CLEP preparation courses - for additional information on EUN (the Electronic University Network, on America Online) see **Part II - Sources**. The student gets credits by independently doing the course work and then taking the nationally-accepted CLEP examination. Credit is then granted by your "home" college, by an external-degree colleges, or by another CLEP-recognizing authority.

These courses are 'open entry/open exit', which means that you can enroll any time and work at your own pace. There are no set schedules; you can start when you want and finish when you're ready.

Current fees for courses using the CLEP examination programs are $345 for a 3-credit course, $630 for a 6-credit course or two 3-credit courses, and $100 per credit when you register for 9 or more credits at one time. Books and shipping vary for each course. The current examination fee for CLEP exams is $40 per course, which you pay directly at the time you register for the exam.

Call an EUN admissions counselor to register for courses or for more detailed information, costs for books and shipping, or tuition assistance applications at 1-800-225-3276.

Continuing Education Units (CEUs)

The International Association for Continuing Education and Training maintains standards for CEUs (Continuing Education Units). These are credits that professional persons often must attain as part of their continued certification requirements. In researching for this book we were able to find only three institutions that offer CEUs online, but as with all things 'Internet' this number is expected to grow rapidly. One CEU is generally defined as the equivalent of ten "contact" hours of participation in an organized continuing education experience under qualified instruction.

For additional information regarding course offering institution's procedures, fees and requirements, contact them directly. Contact information is provided.

University of Florida - 7 courses
University of Washington - 1 CEU Course
University of Wisconsin-Madison - 33 CEU Courses

University of Florida - 7 courses

University of Florida, Division of Continuing Education
Dept. of Independent Study by Correspondence & Distance Education
Accreditation by the Southern Association of Colleges and Schools

The University of Florida has been in the business of offering home study programs for over 75 years (since 1919). Last year alone, some 5,000 students from all over the world took advantage of this program. This program represents all the universities in the State of Florida and is offered by the University of Florida. Faculty is selected from any one of Florida's nine universities. It is possible to obtain either college or high school credit through this program, or a certificate in a special area. The University is currently offering several courses for CEUs. For more information, or for updated listings of their CEU offerings, contact them directly.

Joanne M. East, Ph.D., Director
Division of Continuing Education, Suite D
University of Florida
2209 NW 13th Street
Gainesville FL 32609-3498

(904) 392-1711
(800) 327-4218

University of Florida - 8 CEU Courses

Management Ethics	FLOR#MGT1	2.2 CEUs
Quality Management	FLOR#MGT2	2.2 CEUs
Managing the Problem Employee	FLOR#SUP4	1.5 CEUs
Principles of Supervision	FLOR#SUP1	1.5 CEUs
Sexual Harassment in the Workplace	FLOR#SUP8	2.2 CEUs
Supervisory Communications	FLOR#SUP2	1.5 CEUs
Supervisory Leadership	FLOR#SUP3	1.5 CEUs
Working Better with Your Boss	FLOR#SUP5	1.5 CEUs

University of Washington - 1 CEU Course

Accredited by the Western Association of Schools and Colleges

The University of Washington's Distance Learning courses are open to any high school graduate or any person 18 years or older who chooses distance learning for such reasons as remote location, full-time career, physical disabilities or educational preference. The University is currently offering one CEU course - C Programming. For additional information about their course offerings or an updated list, contact them directly:

Corliss Harmer at (206) 543-2350 or (800) 543-2320.
Email address: instudy@u.washington.edu

UW Distance Learning, GH-23
University of Washington Extension
5001 25th Ave. NE
Seattle WA 98195

(206)543-2350
(800) 543-2320

Developing a C Application (WASH#CPROG-C900)   4 CEUs

Students work one-on-one with the instructor to develop a C or C++ application which demonstrates their knowledge and skills. Participants taking this noncredit Distance Learning course prepare a proposal for an application project and develop a schedule for the project. They develop general source code, debug, improve and enhance the program, and prepare appropriate documentation to design a significant application in C or C++ in the areas of graphics, database or statistics. Participants who want to communicate with their instructors via email or need access to a C compiler receive a free six-month Uniform Access account when they register for the course. *This course is not offered for academic credit.* Prerequisite: a sequence of four C programming courses or six months of on-the-job C programming experience.

University of Wisconsin-Madison - 33 CEU Courses

Accredited by the North Central Association of Colleges and Schools.

This listing of courses in engineering, disaster management and computer science developed and administered by the University of Wisconsin - Madison, Department of Engineering Professional Development (EPD). Taking courses through EPD's Independent Study Program allows you to study when and where you choose, work at your own pace and receive one-on-one help from your instructor through the mail. You may begin your course anytime up to one year to complete it.

The Department of Engineering Professional Development is committed to providing the most rewarding and convenient continuing education possible. Our distance education courses offer alternatives to the traditional classroom and save you time and travel expenses. In addition to correspondence courses, we also offer courses by videotape, audiographic teleconferencing and satellite transmission.

Independent Study courses offered through the University of Wisconsin carry the accreditation of the North Central Association of Secondary Schools and Colleges. Named "best" in the United States for distance learning programs by the U. S. Distance Learning Association along with International School of Information Management (ISIM)

Updates of the correspondence course listing are available on the World-Wide Web and gopher, and via automated email and anonymous ftp.

WWW: `http://epdwww.engr.wisc.edu`
Gopher: `epdgopher.engr.wisc.edu`
ftp: `epd.engr.wisc.edu` - go to directory named `epdfiles`
            transfer to the file named `iscatalo`
email to: `listserv@epd.engr.wisc.edu`
            message: "`send iscatalog`"

800-462-0876
608-263-3160 fax

Tom Smith, Director of Engineering Telecommunications Programming
608-462-7426
email: smithtw@engr.wisc.edu

Judy Faber, Program Manager
608-262-1735; email: faber@engr.wisc.edu

University of Wisconsin-Madison - 33 CEU Courses

Solid Waste Landfills	2 CEUs
Solid Waste Recycling	2 CEUs
Solid Waste Composting	2 CEUs
Waste to Energy	2 CEUs
Collecting and Transporting Recyclables and Solid Waste	2 CEUs
Concrete Structures	14.4 CEUs
Elementary Surveying 1	10 CEUs
Elementary Surveying 2	10 CEUs
Photogrammetry	14.4 CEUs
Value Analysis & Engineer. for Architects, Engineers, Builders	15 CEUs
Intro. to Environmental Topics: Water Quality Management	10 CEUs
Storm and Sanitary Sewer Design	10 CEUs
Remote Sensing: Basics and Environmental Applications	10 CEUs
Basic Engineering Refresher	6 CEUs
Operations Decisions in a Production Enterprise	10 CEUs
Steam-Plant Operation	12 CEUs
Intro. to Value Analysis and Value Engineering	15 CEUs
Introduction to AutoLISP Programming	4 CEUs
Advanced AutoLISP Programming	5 CEUs
Aim and Scope of Disaster Management	2 CEUs
Principles of Management	3.5 CEUs
Natural Hazards: Causes and Effects	3 CEUs
Disaster Preparedness	3 CEUs
Damage and Needs Assessment	3 CEUs
Disaster Response	3 CEUs
Environmental Health Management After Natural Disaster	2 CEUs
Health Services Organization in the Event of Disaster	2 CEUs
Emergency Health Management After Natural Disaster	2.5 CEUs
Epidemiologic Surveillance After Natural Disaster	2 CEUs
Emergency Vector Control After Natural Disaster	2.5 CEUs
Review of Basic Calculus	6 CEUs
Review of Intermediate Calculus	6 CEUs
Review of Vector Calculus	6 CEUs

☑ High School and Equivalency

Many people are seeking alternatives to the traditional high school, whether for purposes of obtaining their diploma after going to work, or because the high school setting is not right for them. In this book we profile a few of these schools, and as in the case of the earlier descriptions persons who are interested in this subject should contact the providers directly. Institutions are profiled in alphabetical order:

1. Cyber High School (non-accredited)
2. University of Florida
3. University of Nebraska - Lincoln

Since this aspect of online education is in its virtual infancy, we strongly recommend that the student make every effort to ascertain the validity of the curriculum for his needs.

Cyber High School - Ojai CA

Cyber High School is a high school that is entirely resident on the Internet. We offer a complete curriculum and instruction and are accessible to anyone who has Internet access, anywhere in the world. CHS will commence with our first classes (just 9th and 10th grades to begin with) in Fall '95, and we are presently processing the applications of our first prospective students.

CHS is designed to operate entirely over the Internet. Lessons and tests are delivered by e-mail or on-line in real-time. Office hours and 1-to-1 conversations are conducted via "talk", and class discussions by IRC. Many of the resources used in the classes are found on the Net - from historical primary documents, to Latin texts, to scientific data, to English and American literature. Assignments and projects include using Net technologies in their presentation. As newer applications (voice, video) become more widely available to our students, they will be integrated into the programs and procedures.

As it is a new school, CHS cannot be accredited by the Western Association of Schools and Colleges until it has been educating students for a period of time. We are following the WASC and the University of California guidelines, and are working with these organizations toward full accreditation and certification, a process that, at its most accelerated, takes three years. All high schools in the western United States go through the same process and they may only seek accreditation after they've opened their doors and are teaching students.

Cyber High is not home schooling. All classes are taught by qualified teachers, and regular communication, instruction, and evaluation are integral to each course.   Cyber High is not for everyone. Because of the self-directed nature of much of the curriculum, students are expected to be at or above grade level upon acceptance.

Your APPLICATION will be reviewed by Cyber High School's Admissions Committee. All applicants considered for admission will be required to take an admissions test. Upon notification of acceptance, a nonrefundable deposit will be required to hold the student's place. The deposit will equal 10% of the annual tuition, and will be applied toward the student's tuition. Tuition for the 1995/96 school year is $5,000.

Cyber High School
P.O. Box 790
Ojai, CA   93024

John DeGrazia-Sanders
cyberhi@webcom.com
http://www.webcom.com/~cyberhi

2. University of Florida - Gainesville FL

University of Florida Independent Study by Correspondence provides high school courses which are designed to fully meet the Florida Department of Education's Curriculum Frameworks and are regionally accredited by the Southern Association of College and Schools. Our department provides all course materials and text books for each course. Each course is designed to be self directed. All assignments and exams are individually graded by qualified instructors and returned with comments to student. A typical high school course will have a mid-term and final exam.

All courses use school textbooks from national publishers. There is no attendance or other record keeping, our department provides an official grade report upon completion of each course. For credit to be accepted by a local school, a principal or counselor's signature is required on the application form. This signature is your guarantee of the local school or school board's prior approval that the course credit will be transferred. While the University of Florida does not offer a high school diploma, our high school courses may be used toward graduation requirements subject to your local school board's policies.

We are in the process of offering our courses with the option of corresponding via electronic mail (E-Mail). If you have access to E-Mail and would like to consider this option contact our department. The instructor of the course you enroll in may allow for the E-Mail option. Use of this service (where available) will not cost extra. Our Department is able, in some instances, to provide you with a temporary student E-Mail account. You will have to provide your own access to the necessary computer/terminal and software. Computer labs are often available at various community colleges and campuses and schools. You may even know of some local business or individuals who could accommodate you with access to E-Mail. Contact our office for more details.

One distinct advantage of a correspondence course is the ability to take a course <u>anytime</u> and <u>anywhere</u>. All books and materials are mailed. Completed assignments are returned via mail. High school midterms and final exams <u>must</u> be administered in the presence of a proctor (typically the high school counselor or principal).

All written assignments are individually graded by qualified instructors and returned with comments. This ensures that any questions a student may have are personally answered by the instructor.

High School tuition is $75. Textbooks and required study guides may be purchased from the Department of Independent Study Bookstore at the time of enrollment. Course Transfers are possible if a student requests in writing to change from one class to another within two months of enrollment. Written approval from the students principal or counselor is required prior to transfer. Extensions may be made if a student is unable to complete a course during the one-year enrollment time. The extension is for six months, and only one extension may be made. No enrollment may continue for more than 18 months.

University of Florida
Division of Continuing Education
2209 NW 13th Street, Suite D
Gainesville FL 32609

(904) 392-1711 ext. 201
1-800-327-4218
fax: (904) 392-6950

email: learn@nervm.nerdc.ufl.edu

Courses offered:
Accounting 1
Algebra I, II
American Government
American History
ART/2-D Comp. I, II
Business Mathematics
Economics
English I, II, III, IV
Explorations in Mathematics
Fundamentals of Environmental Science
Health I - Life Management Skills
Humanities to 1500
Informal Geometry
Peer Counseling I, II
Personal, Social, & Family relationships
Physical Science
Pre-Algebra
World Cultural Geography
World History

3. University of Nebraska - Lincoln NE

Accredited by the North Central Association of Colleges and Schools and the Nebraska State Department of Education.

The mission of the University of Nebraska - Lincoln division of Continuing Studies is to extend the resources of the University to promote lifelong learning. The UNL Independent Study High School provides opportunities for students in various circumstances to meet their educational needs. Among those served are students who:

- Are unable to attend a local school because they live in isolated areas.
- Are in other countries and are unable to obtain an accredited high school diploma from a school in the United States.
- Have dropped out of school but want to continue their education and earn a high school diploma.
- Have difficulty coping with the time and place restrictions of a classroom and want to proceed at their own pace.
- Cannot attend a local school because they are homebound.
- Want to accelerate their high school progress.
- Need basic instruction to improve their skills.
- Want a quality education in a home school setting.

A resident staff of certified teachers endorsed in their subject matter areas provides instruction to the school's global student body. the UNL Independent Study High School also has a principal who coordinates the day-to-day operations and an academic adviser who is available for assistance in planning and course selection. The high school teaching staff is available for consultation about and assistance in any course. Personal, one-on-one student attention is a priority for Independent Study High School staff members.

CARES (Computer-Assisted Response Evaluation System) enables students to respond to objective questions by marking answer sheets similar to those used for nationally standardized college entrance examination. Once completed, the answer sheets are sent to the UNL Independent Study High School where computers read them, calculate a grade based on the number of correct responses, and prepare a report to be returned to the student within 24 hours.

We offer two Internet services; electronic mail and gopher. For information inquiries and submission of course assignments, send your request to unldde@unl.edu. For course enrollments (see detailed information in the next section). To send CARES optical scan sheets via electronic mail, or to receive comments on your coursework and grades through electronic mail, you may select the new **Electronic Response Service**.

You can also connect to the University of Nebraska-Lincoln's gopher, NU Frontier. On this server you will find information on our independent study

programs and listings of the department's other programs. Using your gopher service, connect to: `gopher cwis.unl.edu`
or `gopher.frontier.unl.edu`. From the main menu, the path is:

You can also access NU Frontier via UNL's World Wide Web (WWW) server. Using a hypertext-based Internet browser program, connect to
`http://www.unl.edu/cwis.html`.
Click on the link to NU Frontier and follow the path listed above.

Tuition, course materials, handling fees, and, in some cases, sales tax and electronic response service fees are the costs attached to an independent study course.

Tuition per course: nonresident: $83; resident: $79

University of Nebraska - Lincoln
Division of Continuing Studies
33rd & Holdredge Streets, Room 269
Lincoln NE 68583-9800

(402) 472-4321
unldde@unl.edu   http://www.unl.edu/cwis/html

Courses offered:

Advanced Algebra I, II
American Government
American History I, II
Basic Grammar
Basic Mathematics I, II
Beginning Accounting I, II
Beginning Algebra I, II
Beginning Piano I, II
Biology I, II, III
Business and Consumer Math I, II
Business and International Etiquette
Business English & Communication
Business Law
Career Planning
Chemistry I, II
Civics
Economics
Effective Reader Skills
English-9; I, II
English-10; I, II
English-11; I, II
English-12; I, II
Family and Personal Etiquette
French I

General Agriculture 1, 2
General Art
General Homemaking: Home Mgt
General Literature I, II
General Mathematics I, II
Geometry I, II
Health Science I, II
Horticulture, Landscaping
Horticulture, Lawn and Plant Care
Intermediate Grammar
Intermediate Piano I, II
Introduction to Business
Latin I, II
Multicultural Literature
Office Systems
Personal Finance
Physical Science I, II
Precalculus I: Analytic Geometry
Precalculus II: Trigonometry
Sociology
Spanish I, II
World Geography I, II
World History I, II
Writing Research Papers

✓ Personal Enrichment Courses

Personal Enrichment work

For the purposes of this book, we have gathered miscellaneous, *non-accredited* course providers in this section, with the list currently acquired including these seven institutions:

American Coastline University
Athena University
Diversity University
Globewide Network Academy
Headmaster Distance Learning Service
New Frontieres courses
Virtual College of the Neighborhood

Tuition for these providers is generally lower than fees charged by the accredited course providers described in **Part II - *Sources***. Also, the student attending these courses will often find these institutions to be more innovative in their approach to the educational processes, and will find a more eclectic variety of course subject and content.

This is where the student can 'dabble' in the education process, and where you can experiment with the processes that are being developed now in the *virtual* classroom-as-laboratory. Some of these course providers are developing highly interactive courses with MOO and MUD protocols, and even provide introductory 'how to' courses designed to give the student the basic skills necessary to participate. These present the student returning to school, but who is perhaps unfamiliar with online education, with the perfect opportunity to learn some 'ropes'.

New courses and providers of this type are coming online constantly. For updated information contact the providers directly and follow the associated newsgroups and educational information resources outlined in **Part II - *Courses*** and **Part III - *Study***. Other sources of personal enrichment courses will emerge over the years, as the enhanced opportunities of online education become more understood and mastered by educational institutions.

American Coastline University

As a Research University, American Coastline functions to serve the needs of its students by providing an academic program designed to improve the student's professional communications and personal growth and instill an appreciation for individual research and lifelong learning, while recognizing individual accomplishments and ability relating to academic and professional competence. ACU's Student Handbook provides full explanation of writing requirements, research tips, and a sample research paper.

ACU offers degree programs at all levels. Most of the work can be completed on your computer and transmitted via online service or submitted on disk. The University accepts transfer credit from all postsecondary prior education. There may be limits based on the requirements of a specific degree program. All courses may be completed on paper via the mails, on computer by mailing disks, and by transferring data on-line.

On Accreditation: American Coastline University is incorporated in the State of Louisiana and registered in the State of Hawaii, and has met all reporting requirements for degree granting institutions. ACU's under-graduate and specialized training Professional Development Institute is registered with the California Council on Private Postsecondary Education. The institution is not a member of any non-governmental or private accrediting agency. The University is a member of the International Council of Universities Without Walls, Toronto Canada. Persons seeking to use the degree for credential or licensing purposes should check with that body to insure acceptability. University standards are set to equal or exceed those of comparable institutions and the Faculty welcomes review of any official agency at any time.

Degree Programs: American Coastline University offers Bachelor, Master, Doctor of Philosophy and Professional Doctorate degrees. Degree programs have been designed around a belief that intelligence is essentially the ability to solve the problems of present behavior in terms of its possible future consequences. This may relate to learning based on experience and that one's ability to solve daily problems involves both memory and foresight.

Tuition Schedule: Students have the option of requesting tuition based on the per semester hour rate. Most students enroll in a degree program for a flat tuition fee. This assumes the student will complete a degree program in three Semesters or less. An additional fee of $300.00 per semester will be charged after 12 months of full time enrollment.

Degree Programs

Application Fee	$ 100
Bachelor's	1,900
Master's	2,100
Doctorate	2,400
Full General Catalog	50
Tuition (Semester hr.)	125
Foreign Language Fee	300
General Education Package	500
Advanced Business (MBA)	450
MBA/ Computer Learning	2,400

For specific information about your own requirements send a full resume, copies of transcripts to:

American Coastline University
Professional Development Center
733 Bishop St, Ste 170
Honolulu, Hi   96813

FAX (504) 242-7708
email: acpdi@ix.netcom.com (Raymond Chasse)

Athena University

Athena University is a non-profit institution providing an integrated, interdisciplinary curriculum in the Liberal Arts. AU has an open admission policy. While ACT and SAT scores are helpful in looking at a person's past academic achievements, they are not used as the sole basis for acceptance to the School for Undergraduate Studies. The ability to achieve is determined by the ability to do the assigned academic tasks - the first semester determines whether the student can continue with AU.

Accreditation: Since Athena University is a new institution, it has not yet received accreditation from a regional accreditation body. Athena is seeking accreditation from North Central Association of Colleges and Universities and strives to ensure a high-quality program to meet those standards. Athena Administration will work with individual students who wish to transfer Athena credits to other colleges to see that coursework is given appropriate credit.

Student Services: Athena University maintains an Office of Student Services to aid the student in finding their way around an environment that may be very foreign to them. Student Services provides an ongoing orientation program to offer seminars on a virtual environment to give hands-on experience with innovative and exciting online learning.

Tuition: Since Athena does not suffer the overhead expenses of maintaining buildings and parking facilities, tuition is kept low: $100 per credit hour for undergraduate courses. Most of the courses are three-hour courses. Tuition is the same whether you are a degree-seeking student or taking a course for no credit.

For additional information, email an inquiry to either of these email addresses, or go to this website:
email: vou@delphi.com (Dolores Capps, Registrar)
    wpainter@gteens.com (William Painter)
http: //www.drag.net/~VOU/index.html

Athena University Courses Offered: At press time for this book, AU offers more than two hundred courses. This is an abbreviated list:

3D and Form
20th Century China
Absolutism
Adult Development & Learning
Adult Education & Group Process
Adult Instructional Strategies
Advance Programming of OOP Lang
Advanced Composition
Advanced Short Story Writing
Age of Augustus (Livy, Ovid, Horace)
Age of Cicero
Algorithms

American Civil War
Amer. Colonial War of Independence
American Culture
American Culture and Society
American Economic History
American Economic History I
American Economic History II
American Economic History since 1860
American Economic History to 1860
American Environment
American Foreign Policy
American Idioms for Non-Native Spkrs

American Legal History
American Lit. B: The Young Nation
American Lit. of the Great Depression
American Literature 1607-1865
American Literature 1865-1929
American Literature A: Colonial
American Literature C: Contemporary
American Literature in the War Years
American Novel
American Revolution
Analysis Managerial Decision-Making
Ancient Greek and Roman Literature
Ancient Women & Rise of Patriarchy
Application of Stats in Social Sciences
Art in Age of Digital Dissemination
Art of the Romans
Basic Grammar
British Drama A, B
British Lit. A: Before Shakespeare
British Lit. B: Shakespeare-1914
British Lit. C: Contemporary
British Lit. in the Enlightenment
British Lit. in the Romantic Era
British Novel A, B
Business Ethics
Business Planning
Business Policy & Administration
C Programming Language
Chaucer and His Age
Classical Chinese Education
Classical Civilizations
Classical Political Theory: Plato-Mill
CMC in the Humanities
Colonial Culture and Society
Commercial Revolution
Communist Societies
Comparative Management
Comparative Societies: East and West
Comparative World Religions
Computers & Software in Classroom
Concepts of Political Inquiry
Construct. of Revolutionary Societies
Contemporary Civilizations
Creative Process
Cultural Criticism: Feminist, Gender
    and Cultural Studies
Current Economic Issues
Data Analysis
Data Base Management Systems

Data Structures
Devel. of the American Constitution
Developmental Composition
Directed Readings
Directed Readings in CMC
Directed Studies
Documentation of Instruct. Software
Drawing
Early British Literature
Economic Devel. of China Since 1949
Economy and Democracy
Educational Gerontology
Educational Psychology
Electronic Journalism
Elementary Latin I, II
Elizabethan Cultural Mindset
Emergence of Sys. & Related Thought
Epigraphy
Era of Universal Education
Erasmus and Martin Luther
Erasmus and the Renaissance
Establishing & Maintaining WWW &
    Gopher Sites
Ethics in Scholarship
Evaluation of Computers & Software
Feminist Literary Criticism
Feudalism and Manorialism
Firearms and Civilization
Florence and the Renaissance
Forming of America
Foundation Studies
French Revolution
Freshling Composition
From Commune to Community
Geographic Information Systems
Global History I, II
Gothic Cathedral
Gov't, Bureaucracy, & Planning
Government Regulation of Business
Great War
Greek and Roman Mythology
Heresies of the High Middle Ages
History of Adult Education
History of American Technology
History of Music I, II, III
History of Tech. Devel. in the US
History of the City of Rome
History of the English Language
History US Foreign Rel - Pre 1920

History US Foreign Relations to 1920
How Free are Free Markets?
Humanism and Church Reform
Humanist Paradigm of Education
Humanists and Education
Humanities Senior Reading Seminar
Humanities Senior Writing Seminar
Independent Educational Projects
Independent Research in Adult Ed
Independent Study in Gender Issues.
Influence of Computers on Society
Influences of Romans on Lit. & Cult.
Inter-War Years
International Management
Intro. to Statistics in PoliSci.
Introduction to CMC
Introduction to Creative Writing
Introduction to Critical Thinking
Intro to Educational Computing
Intro to Generic Software Apps
Introduction to Hebrew Studies
Introduction to Linguistics
Introduction to Management
Introduction to Marketing
Intro - Medieval & Renaissance Latin
Introduction to OOP Languages
Introduction to Personnel Mgt
Introduction to Sociology
Intro. to Structured Program. Lang.
Intro. to Technology Assessment
Introductory Latin Prose Composition
Italian Renaissance
John Calvin and the Reformation
Latin American Wars of Independence
Latin Epigraphy
Latin III (Intro to Prose - Caesar)
Latin IV (Intro to Poetry - Vergil)
Latin Literature in Translation
Learning from Socrates to Cassiodorus
Literary Criticism I, II
Machiavelli and the Renaissance
Management Science
Martin Luther
Martin Luther and "Public" Ed
Martin Luther and the Modern State
Martin Luther and Role of Women
Martin Luther and Western Thought
Medieval Art

Medieval Civilizations
Medieval Eurasian Women
Methods of Instruction - Computer
Milton and His Age
Modeling
Modern Civilizations
Modern Europe
Myth and History
Napoleonic Europe and Romanticism
Napoleonic Wars
Nonfiction Writing Workshop
North American Colonies
Northern Renaissance Art
Novel Writing
Object-Oriented Methodology
Object-oriented Methodology and C++
Online Adult Instructional Strategies
Online Teaching Internship
Operations Management
Organizational Decision-Making
Origins of Civilization
Origins of the American Civil War
Paleomathematics & Paleoastronomy
Pathologies of History
Patterns of Prehistory
Patterns of Technics
Philosophy of Adult Education
Philosophy of History
Playwriting
Political Economy of US Trade Policy
Prehistory of Computing
Prejudice & Social Conflict in World
Problems of Development: A Survey
Problems of International Relations
Process of Creating Adult's Programs
Public Policy Analysis
Qualitative Research In Education
Quantitative Research - Social Sci
"Querelle des Dames"
Radical Reformation
Recent US History from 1919 to Date
Reformation
Reformation and Educational Theory
Renaissance
Renaissance British Literature
Renaissance Humanism
Renaissance Studies
Rise of the American State
Rise of the Universities
Risk and Risk Management

Roman Comedy (Plautus, Terence)
Roman History
Second World War
Select American Authors
Senior Reading Seminar in English
Senior Seminar
Senior Seminar in History
Senior Thesis Seminar:
Senior Writing Seminar in History
Shakespeare
Short Story Writing
Sir Thomas More and the Renaissance
Social Change
Social Conflicts and Movements
Social History of Science
Social Institutions
Sociology of Technology
Software Engineering
Special Topics
Strategic Planning
Structure of the English Language
Student Teaching in an IT Environ.
Suffragettes and Feminists
Survey of Procedural Languages
Survey of Western Lit. Pre-1400
Symbols
Systems Analysis I, II

Technical Writing
The Beats
Topics in Political Economy
Traditions of Learning
Turing's Children
United State's History Since 1865
Universal Soldier
US and Asian Relations Since 1913
Victorian British Literature
Virtual Playwriting
Visual Literacy
Wars of America since 1865
Wars of Religion
Western Art and Architecture
Western Constitutions
Witchcraft in Europe, 1300-1736
Women and Rise of the New Culture
Women in Art History
Writing about Art
Writing about Literature
Writing about Music
Writing and Culture
Writing Historical Fiction I, II
Writing in Science and Mathematics
Writing in Social Action
Writing Science Fiction I, II

Diversity University

Diversity University MOO campuses are Internet locations for serious experimentation in network-based, interactive teaching, learning and social services. Those wishing to further this community development are welcome! Online Educational Workshops is offering Basic MOO Skills Workshops and MOO Support Sessions, both held on the Diversity University MOO.

Basic MOO Skills Workshop: For two hours you will be able to learn and practice basic MOO commands to enable you to speak, move around, explore the environment, read, and handle objects. These workshops are free, but you must register ahead of time for a particular date and time. There are two reasons for this: 1) Because student participation is so important, class size is severely limited. 2) All students need at least a temporary account on the Diversity University MOO, and unless you already have one, we need a little time (and information) to set one up for you. Registration is being held real-time, online in the Online Educational Workshops office on the Diversity University MOO.

The DU administration would like to thank the many volunteers contributing time and effort to further this vision. We would also like to thank the Internet Multicasting Service, Embry-Riddle Aeronautical University (ERAU), and the Annenberg/CPB Project for their support in this venture.

If you have any questions, either drop by our MOO office (during MOO Support Session hours would be best) or write to cindy@fred.net

Cindy Bartorillo cindy@fred.net FredNet MOO: telnet fred.net 8888

Globewide Network Academy

The Globewide Network Academy is a consortium of educational and research organizations. It's mission is to create a competitive market for online courses and degree programs as well as to provide services to member organizations. GNA is organized as a non-profit corporation incorporated in the state of Texas. All corporate activities take place online and as such, GNA is the world's first virtual corporation. Services offered by GNA include mailing list support, web support, a central catalog of courses offered by member organizations, and contacts to potential volunteers, teachers, and students. Planned future services include a grant writing center, a financial administration system, a library, and a legal center.

Accreditation: GNA is a forum in which educators can offer courses and degree programs. Because it does not offer courses and degree programs directly, accreditation is not appropriate for GNA as a whole. Many of the members of GNA are accredited , and these are clearly marked as such. The Globewide Network Academy is divided between the core organization and member organizations. Each member organization is fully autonomous and determines all internal policies as well as all curriculum and course content decisions.

The GNA's Course Catalog, a listing of active and planned courses, is available from the GNA web server. Each course listing contains the email address for the instructor of the course. The catalog as well as course submission and member application forms may be found at:

http://www.gnacademy.org/

Questions and comments about this catalog or the Globewide Network Academy should be directed toward: gna@mcmuse.mc.maricopa.edu. Questions and comments about GNA member organizations and particular courses should be directed to the listed course or school contact. Also, there is a newcomer's reception held at the third Wednesday of each month at the GNA cafe at 1830 GMT. To attend,

```
telnet moo.du.org 8888
connect guest
@go #6490
```

See the following list for contact information for each of the participating institutions in the GNA.

GNA Participating Institutions

Acadia University - one of Canada's oldest universities
Division of Continuing Education, Nancy A. Van Wagoner, Director
Wolfville, Nova Scotia B0P 1X0 CANADA
email: vanwagon@max.acadiau.ca
http: //www.acadiau.ca

Athena University - an alternative virtual institution
email: vou@delphi.com (Dolores Capps, Registrar)
        wpainter@gteens.com (William Painter)
http: //www.drag.net/~VOU/index.html

College of Education - University of Oregon
email: jmour@oregon.uoregon.edu (Janet Moursund)

Ecole Superieure en Sciences Informatiques - ESSI
(School of Information Technology Engineering) - Nice-Sophia, France
email: sander@essi.fr (Peter Sander)
http: //www.essi.fr/

Front Range Community College - profiled in Part II-Sources (FRCC)
email: cgermann@csn.org (Clark Germann)
http: //mosquito.frcc.cccoes.edu

Global Electronic Multimedia University - Poland
email: slawiecd@usctoux1.cto.us.edu.pl (Dariusz Slawiecd)
http: //uu-gna.mit.edu:8001/uu-gna/schools/gemu/index.html

Heritage Institute, Antioch U - profiled in Part II-Sources (AOCH)
email: Heritage_Institute@mist.seattleantioch.edu
http: //www.seattleantioch.edu/Heritage/Heritage.html

Honolulu Community College - technical training institution
email: pete@hcc.hawaii.edu (Peter Kessinger, Provost)
http: //www.hcc.hawaii.edu/

Institute of Baltic Studies -Estonian history, culture and society
email: ibs-staff@eenet.ee
http: //www.ibs.ee/index.html

Internet Public Library - interactive Internet library experiment (MOO)
email: ipl.moo@umich.edu
http: //ipl.sils.umich.edu/

Royal Institute of Technology - Sweden; postsecondary engineering
email: Registrator@lektor.kth.se
http: //www.kth.se/

MacVicar School of Education & Tech. - computer courses & projects
    email: mset-talk@moose.uvm.edu
    http: //uu-gna.mit.edu:8001/uu-gna/schools/mset/index.html

New Frontiers Institute - (South Africa) supporting Early Education
    email: dewaal@studaff.und.ac.za (Shaun De Waal)

Online Educational Workshops - basic Internet skills workshops, MOO
    email: cindy@fred.net <Cindy Bartorillo>

Open University - UK's largest University, strong online presence
    email: M.Eisenstadt@open.ac.uk (Marc Eisenstadt, Professor)
    http: //kmi.open.ac.uk/ou/ouhome.html

Oregon State University School of Education
    email: stewarro@ccmail.orst.edu

Palm Beach Community College
    email: javier2@ix.netcom.com

Rogers State College - profiled in Part II-Sources (ROGE); EUN school
    email: RSCLayton@AOL.com

Sagacity Learning Universe - for working in structured environment
    email: tabeles@tmn.com (Dr. Tom P. Abeles)

Seattle Pacific University - Division of Continuing Studies, education
    email: rkester@spu.edu

Ta-Ming Virtual University - (Taiwan) alternative technology education
    email: leechih@peacock.tnjc.edu.tw (Richard Lee)

U Can Institute
    email: (idd@io.org) Office of the Clerk
    http: //uu-gna.mit.edu:8001/uu-gna/schools/ucan/ucan.html

University Colleges - Canada
    email: wunicols@freenet.vancouver.bc.ca

Virtual School of Manufacturing - design and mgt of manufacturing
    email: chris.thompson@gtri.gatech.edu (Chris Thompson)

Virtual School of Natural Sciences - devel. WWW & MOO courseware
    email: gna-vsns-organizers@tsun.desy.de
    http: //uu-gna.mit.edu:8001/uu-gna/schools/vsns/index.html

Virtual Schools of Library and Information Science
    email: gna-library@gna-lists.unam.mx
    http: //uu-gna.mit.edu:8001/uu-gna/schools/vslis/index.html

Headmaster Distance Learning Service

This email transmission gives some basic introductory information about the Headmaster Distance Learning Service:

```
Subj:  Re: asking info online courses

Thanks for your inquiry...          Paul Dorrance

We CREATE user adaptable software for the 21st Century and
offer Consulting & Network support. We provide HEADMASTER
Distance Learning Service!  40+ ON LINE Individual Mastery
Learning Courses!  Baud rates to 28.8K - Call 406-442-0547
with your modem, use PASSWORD: FREE!

D&S Diversified Technologies
Paul Dorrance & Ben Schmitt  | email: hdmaster@lewis.MT.net
Voice: 406-442-8656          | fax: 406-442-3357
```

Courses offered by Headmaster:

Sciences:
  Biology
  Electronics
  Physical Science
  Physics

Business:
  Accounting I-II
  Business Law
  Business Math
  DOS
  Intro to Business
  Keyboarding
  Legal Secretary
  Microsoft Works
  Office Procedures
  Pagemaker
  WordPerfect

College Credit:
  Facilitator Certific.
  Intro to Telecom
  Plains Indians Trad.

English:
  Elementary Writing
  English 9
  English 10
  English 11
  ESL
  Writing Course

Mathematics:
  Algebra I-II
  Business Math
  Calculus
  Geometry
  Math Mission (Elem.)
  Pre-Algebra

Social Sciences:
  African Culture
  Am. Indian Culture
  American Gov't
  Consumer
  Economics
  US History
  World Cultures
  World Geography
  World History

Health Services:
  Health
  Health for your Life
  Nurse Assistant

The New Frontiers Institute

From: DEWAAL@studaff.und.ac.za

The Institute believes in providing holistic education. Methods have evolved from research and practical work in the field and through keeping up to date with developments from around the world. The methods of the Institute besides being practical and oriented to development, looking at all needs of persons. The result of this investigation, research and practical work has been the development of the EDUCATION FOR LIFE PROGRAMS

The following Creative courses are offered :

Creative Poetry Writing

This is a course focusing on how to become a successful writer, how to promote oneself, one's work and attain recognition. It is divided into two parts: a skills enhancing and creativity development section of six lectures plus practical work; a success oriented section of six lectures on attaining skills, becoming successful. Tuition for those attending via email: $40.

Creativity for Success

Principles and methods for enhancing creativity, generating ideas, becoming more successful. Tuition for those attending via email: $100.

For information on New Frontier's Early Education courses, please request a mailing.

The Director, New Frontiers Institute,
11 Rayleigh, 214 Moore Road
Durban 4001, South Africa

email: dewaal@studaff.und.ac.za

Virtual College of the Neighborhood

The Virtual College of Neighborhood Study is not a school. Its credits are not, at this time, transferable to any other institution. This organization operates through the mechanism of a newsgroup. Persons who act upon any advice posted in this newsgroup do so at their own risk. The Virtual College of Neighborhood Study seeks the support of accredited schools of higher learning and organizations in this venture. Please contact the registrar with your offer of support. Additionally, individuals willing to commit to approximately 3 hours a week for a period of weeks at a time, are encouraged to apply as Trustees.

TUITION:

There are no charges or fees associated with any services of the Virtual College of Neighborhood Study.

email: sunsetrest@aol.com (SunsetRest)
voice: (718) 871-8340
US Post: PO Box 288; Brooklyn, NY 11220

HOW TO ENROLL:

1. Send e-mail to: `listserv@SJUVM.STJOHNS.EDU`
    a. Label subject as **VC: enroll**
    b. In the body of the message type:
         `ADD VIRTCOLL` <your e-mail address> <your full name>

COURSE OFFERINGS **(partial listing):**

Business Improvement Districts
Calling Your First Meeting
Evicting Drug Dealers
Fire Safety
Grassroot Fund raising
Immigration
Incorporating as a Not-for-Profit
Develop. in Non-Industrial Nations
Landlord-Tenant Conflicts
Neighborhood Newsletter Publish.
Neighborhood Park Clean-ups
Networking

Pollution
Potholes
Recycling
Rural Community Issues
Sanitation
Sidewalk Tree Planting
Traffic Congestion
Transportation Issues
Vest-Pocket Parks
Writing By-Laws

✔ Finding Financial Aid on the Internet

Completing a college education costs anywhere from $35,000 to over $100,000, assuming a four-year residency program. Costs will be less to the online student, but still significant. Many students will have tuition and other costs covered by employees, but more will have to turn to financial aid to help pay for their education.

Most students going after a bachelor's degree will spend in excess of four years, especially if they are working full-time to support themselves and their families. The average student in America will actually take five to six years or more to attain that degree. The typical online student is returning to school, which means that they will only be taking one or two courses at a time, maintaining a 'gradualist' approach ('slow and steady wins the race').

Many students turn to financial aid to help pay for their education. The college or university a student attends may be a good source of financial aid, and it is important to research this option fully. Most institutions profiled in **The Internet University** offer some financial aid - request information from the provider.

We have provided this brief summary of information for the student to research sources of online information. For a more complete assessment of the field, download the file: "FAQ: Financial Aid, Scholarships, and Fellowships" by Mark Kantrowitz, frequently posted on various Usenet newsgroups, but also available via

ftp: `rtfm.mit.edu:/pub/usenet/news.answers/`
`college/financial-aid-faq.`

For those without ftp access send email to:
`mail-server@rtfm.mit.edu`
with the messages `help` and `index` in the body on separate lines.

Some resources are focused on issues faced by lending or institutional administrations (the mailing lists `finaid-l`, `medaid-l`, `finnet-l`, `studemp`, and `dirloan2` being examples of this). Requests to these sites for assistance by the financial aid end-user are not welcomed, and are usually ignored.

Financial Aid Info Mailing Lists

There are few places on the Internet devoted specifically to the search of online information pertaining to financial aid. This scenario is likely to change over the near future, however, as interest has been expressed in many forums for a more organized approach to this subject. The few lists that our research disclosed which address the issue are described below. To complicate the issue, these are <u>two</u> mailing lists with the same name - you may wish to subscribe to both. These lists are:

☛ **grants-l** - a mailing list for announcements of grants and scholarship opportunities, with particular emphasis postdoctoral work in international education and research. To subscribe, send email to:

    `listproc@listproc.gsu.edu`

with the message `subscribe grants-l <your full name>` in the body of the transmission. For a list of archived postings send email to the same address with message `index grants-l`.

☛ **grants-l** - the other mailing list with the same name is the Grants & Contracts Bulletin Board system of the National Science Foundation. For further information on this list, contact Mary Ann Messier at (202) 357-7880 or `grants-r@nsf.gov`. To subscribe, send email to:

    `listserv@jhuvm.hcf.jhu.edu`

with `subscribe grants-l` in the message body.

Financial Aid Information on Usenet

These Usenet newsgroups are frequented by students and may contain discussions of interest to those looking for financial assistance. Topics may include discussions of available grants, scholarships, fellow-ships, loans, or updates on current changes in ongoing financial aid programs. Inquiries may be posted to these lists to ascertain the current state of affairs and levels of discussion. Also, ask about any new newsgroups established (more are every month) pertaining to the subject.

alt.college.us	misc.education
alt.education	misc.education.adult
alt.education.disabled	misc.education.medical
alt.education.distance	misc.education.science
alt.education.higher.stu-affairs	soc.college
alt.education.research	soc.college.admissions
alt.education.student.government	soc.college.financial-aid
alt.uu.future	soc.college.grad
comp.edu	soc.college.teaching-asst

Financial Aid Information Website

Described as being "the most comprehensive collection of financial aid information on the Internet" this site is maintained by Mark Kantrowitz of Carnegie Mellon University's School of Computer Science. The site includes a financial aid estimation utility that generates a picture of your academic financial needs, as well as links to:

- college and university financial aid Web and Gopher servers
- information from the US Government and other sources
- information about grants and loans
- online scholarship and fellowship databases

Also included are several resource documents, including:
- "Funding for Graduate School"
- "Annotated Bibliography of Financial Aid Resource Materials"
- The online version of the book: "Don't Miss Out: The Ambitious Student's Guide to Financial Aid" by Octameron Associates

Mark Kantrowitz's comprehensive Financial Aid Information Website is available free-of-charge at this URL:

<u>http</u>: //www.cs.cmu.edu/afs/cs/user/
mkant/Public/FinAid/finaid.html

If in your research you find any resource that is not contained at this site, the author requests that you send it on to him via <u>email</u>: mkant@cs.cmu.edu.

Financial Aid Information on Commercial Online Services

Of the online service providers, America Online seems to have the best financial aid information resources. If you are a subscriber to one of these services, seek additional info at the indicated destination:

☛ **AOL**: •College Board: [Keyword: COLLEGE BOARD]
•RSP Funding Focus: [Keyword: RSP]
☛ **Compuserve**: •College Student Forum: [GO STUFOB]
☛ **Prodigy**: •College BB: [JUMP COLLEGE BB]

Educational Grant Info from US Federal Government

Information related to Federal grant and contract opportunities is available by gopher from these sources:

marvel.loc.gov/GovernmentInformation/InformationByAgency
and
ericir.syr.edu/InternetGuides&Directories

Books on Student Financial Aid

There are many books on the subject, and indeed arranging student aid has become a growth industry in itself. All students are encouraged to beware of paying for assistance, and to ensure that any payments made to consultants or financial aid assistants come <u>after</u> you have checked the appropriate Better Business Bureau to check for negative reports. These books may assist you in your search:

<u>Scholarships and Fellowships for Math and Science Students</u>
> by Mark Kantrowitz & Joann P. DiGennaro
> pub. by Prentice Hall, Englewood Cliffs, NJ, 1993
> ISBN 0-13045-345-5 paper ($19.95) 325 pages

<u>The College Blue Book - Scholarships, Fellowships, Grants & Loans</u>
> by Huber William Hurt, Harriett-Jeanne Hurt and Christian E. Burckel
> pub. by Macmillan Publishing Company, New York, 1993
> ISBN 0-02895-004-6 ($48.00) 855 pages.

<u>Fund Your Way Through College</u>
> by Debra M. Kirby and Christa Brelin
> pub. by Visible Ink Press, Detroit, MI, 1994
> ISBN 0-81039-457-X ($19.95) 731 pages

<u>The A's and B's of Academic Scholarships</u>
> by Deborah L. Klein
> pub. by Octameron Associates, Alexandria, VA, 1992
> ISBN 0-94598-174-0 ($7.00) 139 pages

<u>Financing Graduate School</u>
> by Patricia McWade
> pub. by Peterson's Guides, Princeton, NJ, 1993
> ISBN 1-56079-147-0 ($14.95) 191 pages.

<u>Foundation Grants to Individuals</u>
> by Carlotta R. Mills
> pub. by Foundation Center, New York, 1994
> ISBN 0-87954-493-7 ($55) 538 pages

Guest Articles

The Online Classroom In Action: Some pioneering instructors and course providers are establishing these educational techniques. In this article James O'Donnell chronicles his experiences managing the virtual classroom. It is reprinted here by his kind permission.

Teaching on the Infobahn by James J. O'Donnell, Ph.D.

Our master image of the site of teaching has been for many years the classroom. Wherever teaching actually takes place, we imagine it situated within four walls, with rows of desks facing an authoritative podium of some kind. We might prefer still to think of Mark Hopkins, the student, and the log, and such personalized instruction indeed happens more often than we sometimes fear, but every September, academics drift back into thousands of classrooms to begin the year's work.

In January 1994, I broke out of the classroom and wandered out onto the information superhighway. What eventuated was the most exciting teaching I've done in years, and I now plan to spend as much time as I can out there on the highway, dodging traffic, and teaching my heart out. In doing so, I am convinced that I have blundered into the future and started to live some of the science fiction I used to consume voraciously when I should have been memorizing Greek verb forms.

I was preparing in January to teach a course I have often taught before, an introduction to the work and thought of Augustine of Hippo for advanced undergrads and especially beginning grad students. I have a great, almost patho-

logical fear of the academic tendency to repetition verging on self parody, and so I was seeking a way to renovate the course. At the same time, I was reflecting on the fact that the relatively small number of students who would take such a course at Penn (in the end, ten were enrolled) could easily be supplemented by others elsewhere who would not have many opportunities for such a relatively specialized course. I then determined, with the same easy naivete with which Mickey and Judy used to decide to put on a show in the barn, to create an email list to accompany my course, invite the world to join, and see what happened.

To my delight, it was all just as easy as Mickey and Judy made it seem. I made preliminary announcement in numerous email lists in late December, then formal announcement in early January. Over 550 subscribers from around the world, from Bangkok to Istanbul, signed up, and about 375 of them stayed the course from mid-January to early May. They included students at every college and university level, scholars of standing both in the field of patristics and in many other fields, and other internet-surfers of an immense variety.

Procedure was this: I had posted in January a variety of syllabus files,

111

suggested readings, information about myself and the course, and the like, originally to a gopher menu (later supplemented with a World-Wide Web page: see below for addresses). Sometime before the regular Monday afternoon classroom seminar, I would post some preliminary information to the list with suggested topics and the like. We met for two and a half hours on Monday afternoons for a fairly traditional seminar. One student was assigned each week to be rapporteur, and s/he posted by Monday midnight a summary of the discussion to the list as a whole; in addition, any special presentations, handouts, etc., were also posted to the list. (So when Professor Eugene Vance of the University of Washington came for a memorable lecture, the full text of his talk went to the network immediately, followed over the term by two student papers that brilliantly responded to his work.) General discussion followed. There was more discussion early in the term, and some of it ranged fairly widely as list members had topics they needed to ventilate. I see now that I could and should have done a better job of priming the pump later in the term, chiefly by making sure that there was a clear sense of a "reading assignment" for list members to follow. (Ideally, such reading assignments would be made available online, though there can of course be technical and legal problems in doing that for many things one might want to read.)

I was concerned at the outset that, especially with a topic as potentially controversial as Augustine, the list might get out of control. "Flame wars" are familiar on the internet, and with a sensitive religious topic, things could get ugly. I was prepared at a moment's notice to make the list a moderated one (where only messages that I approved would go to the group), to detach it from the classroom course (I was concerned that my paying customers at Penn get at least their full money's worth), or shut it down entirely. The question never arose. Discussion was firm, vigorous, often outspoken, but remained civil and stayed as close to topic as any reasonable classroom seminar would -- that is, it was not perfectly focused, but it responded well to nudges after I had allowed it to stray fruitfully a bit. There are clearly techniques that I am only beginning to learn for optimizing discussion and transmission of useful information in such an environment, but they are really only extensions of the traditional classroom teacher's methods. (I was also teaching during the same term an undergraduate survey course "The Worlds of Late Antiquity" where the classroom students were required to use email for discussion; they also "published" their papers to each other by email and were encouraged to write papers responding to each others' work thus turning the classroom paper exercise into a real act of communication with an audience of the students' peers. Much of what I learned in each of these courses will help me in the future in both open and closed settings.)

The diversity of participants made for a far richer course than I could ever teach myself. Take, e.g., the time our correspondent in Istanbul reported on a lecture given there on medieval Christian philosophy by a Franciscan priest to the faculty of the (Islamic) University of the Bosporus. Well and good, the faculty opined when it was over, but it's too bad Christianity is not a truly rational religion, like Islam. Leaving aside the question of comparative rationality of religions, I think it is undoubtedly good for my students at Penn, taking a course on a very traditional "western" figure, to be reminded that the whole picture looks quite differently if you happen to be in a different seat. Disciplinary specialties other than my own made for points of view closer to home but still independent of mine as well. The gopher/WWW server now contains papers written by almost a dozen people, including students in my course, faculty elsewhere, and at least one master's thesis elsewhere now getting a much wider and more serious audience than would have been the case otherwise. All the course materials (somewhat digested and indexed) will be kept on line for the next time I teach this course: in other words, a gradually richer environment for Augustinian studies on the net (soon to be enhanced by more texts and translations, e.g.) will grow where this course has planted the seed, and each successive course will be the better for it.

I am happy to say that the success of the experiment has made it possible to continue and expand what I have been doing. In the fall, I will teach a course on Boethius' Consolation of Philosophy in a similar way with one vital addition. It will now be possible for students to enroll for the course for credit from remote locations through the University of Pennsylvania's "College of General Studies". Tuition and fees will amount to about $800 for one course of grad/undergrad university credit on an official transcript. I imagine a primary audience for such a course (the text will be read in Latin by those taking it for credit) as school teachers needing to collect credits to keep up their certification or work towards degrees, but if I have learned one thing on the internet it is that you never know who the real audience is likely to be. The arrangements will be similar to those last spring except that paying customers away from Penn will have special times during the week for online conferencing (using MOO software) and will have their work evaluated, criticized, and discussed, and of course they will get grades.

The one point to emphasize above all others in this regard is this. None of what I am talking about is technology. I do not see myself as a technological specialist, nor have I any interest in becoming one. I am in many ways a traditional, tweedbacked, cottonbreasted, chalkdusted, blearyeyed academic, still fired with the passion for new and old books that drove me to graduate school, still ready and eager to pass off a lecture or start pushing students through their Socratic paces at a moment's notice. Those fundamental educational activities are what engage my spirit, and it is those activities that I now look to pursue with the exciting new tools that networked communication gives me. Email, gopher, and WorldWide Web placed in scholars' hands in 1994 a package of tools that are already stunningly easy to use and that multiply the power of the teacher to reach students and stay in touch with them far beyond what the old classroom allows. (I think it is true to say for my Penn-only course this spring, I saw fewer students in my office than in any comparable course in my career, but I had more and better contact with more of them than in any comparable course. The traditional "office hours" are in fact a painfully inefficient way to manage student contact; email chatting at midnight is far more effective. There is nothing that I describe doing here that a faculty member with the right (essentially simple) piece of equipment on her desktop could not learn to do within about an hour all told. The use of networked technology is in fact the cheapest, easiest, and most powerful enhancement to teaching that I can see

within my reach, and it will only get easier and more powerful as the years go by. I cannot imagine ever passing a semester in the classroom again without the umbilical cord to the network to energize, diversify, and deepen what we do.

The easiest way to find out more about these enterprises is to have a look for yourself on the network. If you can only use "gopher" look for the gopher at ccat.sas.upenn.edu, then choose menus in succession for "Course Materials", "Classical Studies", and "Latin 566: Augustine". With WWW access through Lynx, Mosaic, or the like, you can begin by going to this address:

http://ccat.sas.upenn.edu/jod/jod.html

and then select the item for "Augustine".

Prof. James J. O'Donnell, Coordinator
Center for Computer Analysis of Texts
Department of Classical Studies
720 Williams Hall
University of Pennsylvania
Philadelphia, PA 191046305

email: jod@ccat.sas.upenn.edu
http://ccat.sas.upenn.edu/teachdemo

> **More Info on Getting Connected**: The future of the Internet lies in the Web. In the attached article Frank Hecker chronicles his experiences getting online with the WWW. It is reprinted here by his permission.

Personal Internet Access Using SLIP/PPP:
How You Use It, How It Works

by Frank Hecker (hecker@access.digex.net)

Introduction

As the Internet has been popularized in newspapers, magazines, and books, many people are joining (or trying to join) the community of Internet users online. Some subscribe to commercial services like CompuServe and America Online that are adding some Internet-related features to their existing services. Others purchase accounts on commercial services which provide Internet access as their main offering, or are getting accounts on "Free-Nets" and other community network systems which offer Internet access as an adjunct to community information.

Finally, there is a small but rapidly growing number of people who are experiencing the joys of connecting to the Internet directly from their PCs or Macintoshes, without having to login to larger systems and put up with the hassle of UNIX commands or restrictive menus. In this paper I discuss this highest level of personal Internet access, both how you use it and how it works. I assume that you have some understanding of the Internet and the services it supports (e.g., Telnet, FTP, electronic mail, and so on), but that you know very little about TCP/IP, SLIP, PPP, and other obscure acronyms.

My goal is <u>not</u> to give you complete step-by-step directions on how you can configure your PC or Mac for connection to the Internet, but rather to provide a conceptual overview of personal Internet access without getting into too many technical details. My hope is that after you finish reading this paper you will have a good idea of how personal Internet access works, how SLIP and PPP are used in real life, and whether it makes sense for you to use them. With that end in mind I conclude the paper with some advice on where to go next for more information.

This document was originally written for the Washington, D.C., area community network CapAccess (the informal name for, and a service mark of, the National Capital Area Public Access Network, Inc.); it grew out of some thinking I did about the long-term directions for community networks and what part low-cost personal Internet access might play in their evolution. At the time I could not find any non-technical high-level explanation of the concepts behind SLIP and PPP Internet connections; as the poet Muriel Rukeyser said of her biography of the physicist Willard Gibbs, I wrote this paper in part because I needed to read it.

I'd like to thank the other members of the CapAccess organization for their comments on early versions of this paper; however the views I express herein are mine alone and don't necessarily reflect the position of Cap Access.

Why Bother?

When I first became an Internet user, I used a so-called "shell account" service provided by a local D.C.-area Internet access provider, the Digital Express Group, Inc. (It's called a shell account because you login to a central UNIX host and type UNIX commands into the UNIX command interpreter or "shell.")

I used this service much as you might use a BBS, a "Free-Net," or other UNIX-based community network systems like CapAccess (albeit with a few more functions): I would use my Macintosh and its modem to login to the central UNIX host (a Sun system), read and compose electronic mail using Pine (a UNIX email program), read and post Usenet news articles using a UNIX-based newsreader, retrieve files using FTP and then download them using Zmodem, and so on. For software I used the shareware communications program Zterm, a copy of which came with the Global Village 14.4 Kbps modem I have. (For those of you who have PCs, Zterm is a typical character-based communication program with VT100 terminal emulation and Zmodem download capabilities, comparable to Procomm or CrossTalk.)

Overall this setup worked pretty well. Why then did I decide to change it? My most important reasons were as follows:

* I was tired of using UNIX-based utilities with their different interfaces (control keys, cursor keys, command lines, and so on). I wanted to access the Internet using the same "point and click" interface I used with native Mac utilities.

* I wanted to be able to read and compose email offline, without having to stay logged into the service while I read and wrote long messages.

* I wanted to streamline the process of downloading files and avoid the need for an extra Zmodem transfer after I retrieved something using FTP.

* Finally, I wanted to be able to use new graphical Internet applications, most notably Mosaic and the WWW, which were not accessible with the traditional character-based interface I used.

Me, My Computer, and the Internet

In order to address the above issues I eventually upgraded my Internet access service to a so-called "SLIP account." SLIP or Serial Line Internet Protocol is a communications protocol that supports an Internet connection (i.e., using TCP/IP) over a dial-up line. PPP or Point-to-Point Protocol is a newer protocol that does essentially the same thing; however it's better designed and more acceptable to the sort of people who like to standardize protocol specifications. For the rest of us it's six of one and a half dozen of the other for the most part, and I'll often use the term "SLIP/PPP" to refer to them interchangeably. (Although, as I note below, PPP is likely to become better supported and more popular in the future.)

Not only was setting SLIP service up much simpler than I anticipated, it also gave me a whole new perspective on how individuals will likely use the Internet in the future. I'll get to the technical details later; instead I'll begin by describing a typical communications session:

I start with my Mac booted and its modem connected to a phone line. First, I invoke the SLIP application. (In Mac terms this "application" actually consists of an extension plus a control panel; for those more familiar with DOS, it is roughly comparable to a TSR or "Terminate and Stay Resident" utility). The SLIP software asks me for my SLIP password (which goes with my SLIP userid--more on this below), and then uses a script to dial the SLIP access number at my Internet access provider. My modem dials out, their modem answers, and then the script takes over for a few seconds until the SLIP connection is established. I then forget about the SLIP application, and often close it just to get it out of the way. (Part of it is still running "underneath," however.)

At this point I have a live connection between my Mac and the Internet. The next thing I typically do is start up the Eudora mail program, and then ask it to check for and retrieve my electronic mail. Eudora asks for my mail account password (which goes with my mail account userid). Note that these are a different userid and password than my SLIP userid and password; I discuss this in detail below.

Eudora then goes out and downloads my mail from my mailbox on the Internet access provider's mail server. This can take from a few seconds to a few minutes, depending on how much mail I've received and how big the messages are. When downloading completes I have all my new mail messages in an in box on the Mac.

I can then either read my mail or do something else. Usually I read at least a few messages that look important, and perhaps respond to a couple of them. When I respond my messages get put in an out box for later delivery; they aren't sent right away.

Suppose one of the messages is about something on another Internet-connected system, such as the CapAccess community network system. I then invoke the NCSA Telnet application and connect to CapAccess ("cap.gwu.edu") to check things out. This brings up a VT100-like screen similar to what you'd get dialing in directly, with a prompt for the login id. I give my CapAccess userid and password, and then I'm logged in as usual and can do all the standard CapAccess operations. Note that this Telnet connection isn't going through either the Internet access provider's UNIX host system or the CapAccess phone lines and modems; it's going over the Internet from my Mac to the CapAccess Sun system (with some hops along the way through IP routers, "black boxes" which pass the traffic through various networks of the Internet).

Suppose that something I read in a CapAccess forum refers to an information file that you can FTP from someplace.

Then, without closing the Telnet session, I can bring up the Fetch application, which is an implementation of FTP for the Mac. Fetch allows me to start a session to a public or "anonymous" FTP site, browse through the directories, and download files using FTP directly to my Mac; download speeds for text and binary files are comparable to those achievable using traditional communications programs and protocols like Zmodem. (They are not always quite as fast, for various reasons too complicated to go into in this paper, but they are fast enough for me.)

After finishing the FTP session I can go back to my Telnet session and continue. TCP/IP and SLIP (or PPP) can "multiplex" several connections; that is, several connections can be open at once and can be sending and receiving data, with TCP/IP and SLIP/PPP sorting it all out and transmitting and receiving that data over the single dialup connection to the Internet access provider's SLIP/PPP access point.

If the Mac had true "preemptive" multitasking (like OS/2 or Windows NT, for example), I could actually have different downloads going on simultaneously while I ran other Internet applications. As it is though, doing an FTP transfer on my Mac will pretty much kill performance on a Telnet session; however it works fine to keep multiple applications open for use but otherwise idle, and I can then switch between them as desired.

If I'm really done with my Telnet session, I'll log out of the remote system and close the link. I might then bring up NewsWatcher, a Usenet news reader for the Mac. NewsWatcher connects to the Internet access provider's Usenet news server and then presents me with a list of my currently subscribed newsgroups, together with an indication of how many postings are available in each group. I double-click on a newsgroup I'm interested in checking, and NewsWatcher downloads the list of current postings in the group, by subject. (It knows about "message threads," so if multiple postings have the same subject it only shows me one line in the listing of articles.)

I then double-click on the line corresponding to a posting (or thread) I want to read, and NewsWatcher down-loads the text of that posting and puts it on the screen in a window. More double-clicking lets me advance through the newsgroup article by article, marking articles as having been read as I download and read them. I can also compose and post follow-up articles or new articles, which are uploaded to the Usenet news server .

If I don't read all articles in a newsgroup or get through all newsgroups, I can look at them later when I next use NewsWatcher. I can also mark articles as having been read without downloading them, in case the subject line indicates that I would likely have no interest.

Thus far in this example I've discussed electronic mail (Eudora), Telnet (NCSA Telnet), FTP (Fetch), and Usenet News (NewsWatcher). I also have Turbo-Gopher, a Macintosh version of a Gopher client. TurboGopher allows me to get exactly the same information accessible via a so-called "VT100" Gopher client (as found on many Internet hosts), but with the following advantages: it gives me a point and click graphical interface; files can be saved directly to my Mac (as opposed to saving them in a host UNIX directory and then downloading them); and it doesn't require me to login to a UNIX host first.

Finally, I have the much-heralded NCSA Mosaic (the Macintosh version, of course), and can explore the World Wide Web with full access to multimedia information including formatted text, graphics, sound, etc. I must confess that using Mosaic over a 14.4 kbps dialup line is not nearly as exciting as the hype would suggest. Mosaic typically takes a minute or more just to bring up a single page of information, because of all the embedded graphics included in most WWW data. (You can tell Mosaic not to download the graphics images, but then what's the point?) I've accessed sound clips once or twice; it takes about five minutes of downloading just to hear my Mac talk to me for a few seconds. Using Mosaic over a 14.4 Kbps connection can be as frustrating as trying to eat ice cream through a straw; but it's still fun to play with, and there are many new information sources that can be accessed only through the World Wide Web and a WWW browser like Mosaic.

While all this is happening TCP/IP and SLIP are still running quietly underneath it all over the dialup link. After a while I figure it's time to save my pennies and cut the connection. (I get four "free" hours per day--i.e., included in my basic monthly rate--but these can go fast,

especially as I connect at least two or three times a day. My provider charges $1 per hour for each additional hour.) I remember I still have electronic mail messages in my Eudora out box, so I go into Eudora and tell it to send all outgoing mail. It uploads the messages to my Internet access provider's mail server, which then will take care of sending them on to their final destination.

Having finished all my online stuff, I go back to the SLIP application and tell it to disconnect. At that point I lose all the fancy functionality like Mosaic, FTP, etc. However I can still read my electronic mail in Eudora, compose replies, and queue them for delivery the next time I connect.

In summary:

* I have dialup Internet access using a special dialup number and a userid and password associated with that access.

* I can run a wide variety of applications over the dialup link to implement traditional Internet services such as electronic mail, FTP, Telnet, and Usenet news, as well as newer services like Gopher and Mosaic/WWW.

* Using some Internet services (e.g., electronic mail) requires that I have additional userids and passwords assigned to me by my Internet access provider. Others do not; that is, they are either inherently anonymous in nature (e.g., anonymous FTP, Gopher, Mosaic/WWW) or involve separate arrangements with other organizations (e.g., Telnet to a remote Internet host like CapAccess).

119

* Most of these services can only be used while the dial-up Internet connection is active. However with others (really only electronic mail, for now) you can do at least some things offline. (There's no reason in theory why some of the Usenet news reading process couldn't be done offline; however the current version of the NewsWatcher application does not implement this.)

How It All Works

Having told you how I access the Internet from my Mac, I'd like to now go into more detail about what's going on behind the scenes. My apologies for the level of technical detail; I'll try and keep it to the minimum necessary to make my points. (Though I can't resist staying with a good analogy, as you'll see.)

Let's start with what "being on the Internet" really means. For your PC or Macintosh to be "on the Internet" in the sense that I'm using the term, the following three things must be true:

* Your PC or Mac has software which can send and receive data using the TCP/IP family of communications protocols.

* Your PC or Mac has some sort of communications link to an Internet access point from which data it sends can go out over the Internet to other systems, and by which data sent from other systems on the Internet can be sent to your PC or Mac.

* When connected in this way, your PC or Mac has an identifying number (called

an "IP address") which other systems use in sending data to your PC or Mac, and by which your PC or Mac identifies itself when sending data to other systems.

For those who really want to know, "TCP/IP" stands for Transport Control Protocol/Internet Protocol (which are really two separate protocols that work together), and is a shorthand name for a specific way of packaging up data for sending it over a communications link. TCP/IP is analogous in many ways to protocols like Kermit or Zmodem which package up data for downloading or uploading over "normal" dial-up connections (e.g., to a BBS).

But you really don't need to know that, any more than you need to understand how telephone line signaling works in order to call someone. In fact, this is a good analogy if you think about what it means to be "on the public telephone network" and use local or long-distance phone service:

* You have a device (i.e., a telephone) which can send and receive data (i.e., the sound of voices) using some sort of low-level magic (which you don't really worry about).

* Your phone has a communications link (phone line) to an access point (your local telephone central office) through which your phone can connect to other phones anywhere in the world (and vice versa).

* When connected in this way, your phone has an identifying number (your phone

number) which other phones use in connecting to your phone, and by which your phone is identified when connecting to other phones (as in Caller ID).

The three elements common to both cases are thus as follows:

* you have an end-user device which has the smarts to "talk" in a certain way;

* you have a link to an access provider over which your device can "talk" with other devices; and

* your device has an identifying number or address used when your device "talks" to other devices and vice versa.

If it's that simple, why has connecting to the Internet using SLIP or PPP traditionally been so hard for individual users? Because doing it has been like try-ing to get phone service in an environment where you have to build your own phone, you have to search far and wide to find a phone company you can connect to (and may not have one at all in your area), and you have to pay a big premium for service if and when you find a service provider.

Making Your Mac or PC Internet-Capable

Let's go back and analyze what's happening when I use my Mac on the Internet. First, let's discuss what you need to make your PC or Mac Internet-capable, "building a phone" as it were (and we'll price it out to boot).

I started with a Macintosh system with a 14.4 Kbps modem. Assuming that you already have a PC or Mac, you can add a new 14.4 Kbps modem for as little as $100

to $150 (U.S.) or so, depending on the modem's brand, whether the modem is external or internal, etc. For example, I recently bought a Practical Peripherals 14.4 Kbps external modem for $140; four years ago I paid almost $500 for an earlier Practical Peripherals modem that only supported 9.6 Kbps.

To that I added the requisite TCP/IP software. For Macintoshes this comes in two parts: First comes a product called MacTCP supplied by Apple; MacTCP is the standard TCP/IP product for all Macs. Then comes software to implement either the SLIP or PPP protocols that MacTCP needs to support TCP/IP over dialup links. I use the InterSLIP software from InterCon Systems Corporation; it is freeware.

MacTCP is not freeware, but you can get it (along with InterSLIP and related stuff noted below) by buying either of the books "Internet Starter Kit for Macintosh" by Adam Engst or 'The Mac Internet Tour Guide" by Michael Fraase. Also, Apple is including MacTCP in the new System 7.5 operating system. After its release System 7.5 will be shipped with all new Macs, so at that point you'll get TCP/IP software on new Macs at no extra cost whatsoever. (You'll be able to get it for older Macs by buying System 7.5 as an upgrade, although if you don't need the other System 7.5 features you'll save money with MacTCP as part of Engst's or Fraase's books.)

For 386 or better PCs running Windows 3.1 you can get a similar combination of TCP/IP software with SLIP capability by buying Engst's or Fraase's companion volumes for Windows or similar works.

The software in this case is a entry-level version of Chameleon from NetManage. (A shareware product, Trumpet Winsock by Peter Tattam, is also available, and many people prefer it.) In the next major release of Windows (Windows 4.0 or "Chicago") Microsoft will be including TCP/IP and PPP capability in the base operating system. At that point you'll get TCP/IP software at no extra cost if you buy a PC with Windows 4.0 preloaded. (You'll be able to get it for older PCs by buying Windows 4.0 separately.)

I should add that the cheapness of (commercial) TCP/IP software for Macs and PCs is a very recent phenomenon. Traditionally TCP/IP software has been seen as of interest only to businesses running inhouse local area networks, and it cost as much as $400 or $500 per PC or Mac. TCP/IP software is still this expensive in many cases if you need true LAN capabilities, but software vendors have woken up to the rapidly growing market for individual use of TCP/IP over dial-up lines to access the Internet. Thus many commercial TCP/IP software packages have dropped in price to $200 or less, at least for basic capabilities.

As noted above, within the next year or so this cost will drop further to zero; that is, at some point TCP/IP and SLIP or (more likely) PPP capability will be bundled with the base operating system software shipped with every new Windows PC and Mac. At that point the only incremental cost to make your PC or Mac "Internet-capable" will be for the modem itself, which many if not most people who buy computers will be buying anyway for other reasons--for example, to connect to BBSs or to commercial online services such as America Online, CompuServe, or Prodigy.

Some final notes on software compatibility: There are a number of potential compatibility problems in configuring software "stacks" consisting of the base TCP/IP software, network drivers underneath, and Internet applications on top; this has been especially true when mixing and matching software from different sources. Fortunately these problems are not really an issue in the Macintosh world today, and are rapidly becoming a thing of the past in the PC world (at least for people using Windows).

As noted above, in the Macintosh world Apple is the only major supplier of the basic TCP/IP software, in the form of the MacTCP product. All Macintosh Internet applications are thus written to interface to the MacTCP software, so compatibility problems are kept to a minimum. Most of the problems that do occur are connected to the particular revision of MacTCP being used with a given application on a given Mac; almost all current Mac Internet applications work best with the current 2.0 revision of MacTCP.

In the Windows world the compatibility problem has not yet been totally solved, but has been alleviated to a great degree by the development of the "Windows Sockets" or "Winsock" stand-ard and the implementation of TCP/IP products that conform to it. The Winsock standard specifies the interface between Windows-based Internet applications (e.g., Telnet and FTP) and the TCP/IP software underneath them.

Thus for example, since NCSA Mosaic is a Winsock-compliant application, you can run it over either NetManage's Chameleon TCP/IP software or Peter Tattam's Trumpet Winsock software. Both these products provide a WINSOCK runtime library that implements the Winsock interface; the WINSOCK.DLL file is different for each TCP/IP product, but the interface provided to applications running above the TCP/IP software is always the same--at least in theory.

Connecting to the Internet

As described above, I first made my personal computer Internet-capable by installing the proper TCP/IP and SLIP software on my modem-equipped Macintosh. (I later installed comparable software on my PC as well.) Next I signed up with a service provider that could give me a connection to the Internet (in my case the D.C.-area company Digital Express Group, Inc.). My Internet access provider supplied me with at least three things (actually more, but we'll get to that): a dial-up SLIP access phone number to have my modem connect to, a personal "SLIP userid," and a personal password to go with the SLIP userid. The SLIP userid is some arbitrary string like "xx537", and the password is like a standard login password for a UNIX system or BBS.

I configured the InterSLIP software with the dial-up SLIP access phone number and my SLIP userid, and now direct the software to call up the SLIP phone

number using the Mac's 14.4 Kbps modem. The call is answered by a corresponding 14.4 Kbps modem at the other end (like the ones used by BBSs). That modem is connected to a SLIP-capable "terminal server," a black box that takes the data coming from my Mac over the dial-up line and retransmits it to my Internet access provider's local area network, which is in turn connected to the Internet using an "IP router" (another black box you don't have to worry about).

This terminal server is similar to the ones used on many college campuses and at many Free-Nets and other community networks like CapAccess to connect users from dial-up modems over a LAN into the actual UNIX host system they login to. The main difference is that the SLIP-capable terminal servers (more generally known as "remote access servers") have an extra capability which lets them pass "raw" TCP/IP data through. (Access using PPP is similar.)

In fact, when you first connect to the Internet access provider's modem and remote access server, it looks very much like logging in to a remote UNIX system, particularly if you're using SLIP. (That's if you were looking at the conversation, which typically you don't--login is normally handled by an automated script). One of the first things you would see would be a prompt for a userid, at which point you (or the script) would enter the special SLIP/PPP userid. You would see a password prompt, in response to which you (or the script) enter the SLIP/ PPP password. (The SLIP or PPP software would prompt you for your password if you hadn't supplied it with the rest of your configuration information.)

On a BBS or UNIX system you'd next see the opening screen and menu (or a UNIX prompt). However with a SLIP or PPP connection your software and the remote access server now go into a special mode where they start exchanging TCP/IP data. This is somewhat reminiscent of what happens when a communications program is in download or upload mode, and if you looked at what's actually going across the dial-up line it would look pretty much like garbage with a few recognizable bits mixed in. However you don't actually see the garbage because the SLIP or PPP software doesn't bother showing it to you; it just says "connected" and that's it.

A couple of important points to note: First, having made the SLIP or PPP "connection" you really aren't logged in to any host; you just have the capability to send data out over the Internet. To continue with our telephone analogy, you've plugged in your "phone" and have "Internet dial tone" but you haven't called anybody yet.

You might ask, why do you need a userid and password if you're not actually logging in to anything? Because my Internet access provider wants to be able to bill me for the time I spend connected to the Internet through their remote access server, and to do this they need an id of some sort to know that it's me connecting. I in turn would like a password so that no one else can connect to their SLIP/PPP

remote access server and bill time to my id. You can think of this as my "Internet calling card number" and associated Personal Identification Number or PIN.

For those really into the bits and bytes, an interesting technical question is: How does the remote access server check my userid and password and then account for my connect time? The answer is that it either checks my userid and password against an internal database held in non-volatile memory on the remote access server itself, or it sends the userid and password to a real computer system to be checked against a userid/password database on disk. (For many modern remote access servers this can be done using the "Kerberos" authentication protocol invented at MIT; Kerberos has the advantage that your password is sent over the network in an encrypted form, which decreases the likelihood that someone might intercept it and use it to gain unauthorized SLIP/PPP access.)

If the SLIP/PPP userid checks out, the remote access server (if it has this capability) then sends a "start of call" record to a real computer system to be stored in a log (many remote access servers use the UNIX "syslog" protocol for this); a similar "end of call" record is sent when the modem connection ends (i.e., the user disconnects). These two records together enable the Internet access provider to compute the time and length of the SLIP or PPP session for billing purposes. Again, this is all quite similar to the way long-distance calling cards work.

The analogy extends even further: if I

always made the connection from the same phone, my Internet access provider could theoretically use Caller ID or similar mechanisms to know it was me calling, just as I don't have to enter a calling card number to dial long distance from my home phone. However, just as I might make long distance calls while on the road, I might connect my modem to different phones (in fact I do, as my Mac is actually a PowerBook laptop); thus having a separate SLIP/PPP userid and password is necessary to handle this.

There's another crucial piece I've left out so far: my "Internet phone number," the IP address. In my case my Internet access provider assigns me my very own IP address (mine is 164.109.211.201, in case you're curious); this is the fourth piece of initial information I was given when I signed up, along with the three I've already mentioned: SLIP/PPP dial-up access number, SLIP/PPP userid, and SLIP/PPP password.

Many remote access servers also have the ability to assign callers an IP address "on the fly;" the address picked is displayed during the login sequence and the TCP/IP software on your PC or Mac then picks it up and uses it. When you dial up the next time, you might get a different IP address. This is not as confusing as you might think, as it turns out that for various reasons (touched on later) it doesn't matter what your IP address is, as long as you have a valid connection.

The theory behind doing this dynamic assignment of IP addresses is that it lets the Internet access provider use a limited-size pool of addresses to serve a much larger number of people. After all, people only need the address when they're connected to the modems and remote access server, so the access provider really doesn't need to supply any more IP addresses than it has dial-up SLIP/PPP ports.

However I prefer the way my Internet access provider does it. For one thing, it's much easier to understand, especially using the phone number analogy. For another, the IP address is often used by remote systems to identify who's connecting to them over the Internet, just as people use Caller ID to identify who's phoning them. (Using the IP address for authentication in this way is not totally secure and fool-proof, but then neither is Caller ID for that matter.) With "on the fly" assignment I might get a given IP address at one point, and after I disconnect from the service someone else could get the same address a few minutes later.

Finally, sometimes the dial-up connection will be lost during an Internet session (for example, because of line noise). Because of the nature of the TCP/IP protocols, if you have a fixed IP address you can often recover the session simply by reestablishing the dial-up SLIP or PPP link; this is not possible if your IP address changes each time you connect.

To summarize: after signing up with an Internet access provider and connecting to their SLIP/PPP terminal server we're now "on the Internet" (or we have "Internet dial tone" if you will), having fulfilled the three conditions we discussed above:

* With the help of a modem and low-cost TCP/IP software we have an "Internet-capable" PC or Mac.

* We've established a TCP/IP over SLIP (or PPP) connection to our Internet access point.

* We've got an IP address or "Internet phone number" and are ready to "make calls;" i.e., to connect to other systems and make use of Internet services.

This has been a long section and we still haven't gotten to the point of doing anything really useful. But have patience; believe me, even telephone dial-tone would seem this complicated if you really looked "under the covers." In fact, just a few years ago (before "equal access") getting long-distance phone service in the U.S. through a non-AT&T carrier such as MCI was also pretty complicated; some may remember when you always had to dial a special access number and enter your personal access code before you could dial a long-distance number using a long-distance company other than AT&T.

Using Core Internet Services

At the end of the last section I'd gotten to the point where my computer had "Internet dial tone:" it had established a TCP/IP link to the SLIP/PPP-capable remote access server of my Internet access provider, and was now ready for me to do useful work (or "make some calls," to continue our telephone analogy).

The first thing I did in my example was to check my electronic mail, and so I started the Eudora mail program. Eudora

is available for both Macs and PCs running Windows. In its first incarnation (release 1.4) it is a freeware program; I got my copy from Adam Engst's "Internet Starter Kit" book. Eudora is now also available in a commercial version (release 2.0) with somewhat more functionality (like mail filters) and official technical support; I recently bought a copy of release 2.0 for $65 from Qualcomm, the vendor that now sells and supports it.

However, before I explain how Eudora works, I have to digress for a moment and talk about Internet electronic mail. Traditionally Internet users have logged in to multi-user systems which are connected to the Internet 24 hours a day. When users send mail the messages are transmitted (almost) immediately over the Internet from the originating host ("cap.gwu.edu") to the receiving host ("agency.gov") and then are put in the mailbox for the recipient ("rroe"). (Incidentally, the low-level protocol used to send messages between Internet electronic mail hosts is called SMTP - Simple Mail Transfer Protocol.)

At some later time the recipient ("rroe") logs into the receiving mail host and then reads the mail messages out of their mailbox using a mail program such as Pine or Elm. They can also compose new messages, which are then sent to the recipient's mail host as described above. Note that the user has to stay logged in to their mail host during the entire time they're reading messages and composing new ones.

This method is the way I used to read

and compose mail using my original Internet shell account: I would login to my Internet access provider's host system ("access.digex.net") and use the UNIX-based mail program Pine to read and respond to electronic mail.

However, now that I have a computer which can be linked to the Internet more directly, I would much prefer to read and compose mail on the Mac itself and send it or receive it over the Mac's Internet connection. As in the example above, my Mac does have its own Internet address ("164.109.211.201") and even its own Internet host name ("ion.digex.net"). (I'll discuss how Internet host names work in more detail below when I talk about FTP.) Unfortunately, though, I can't use the traditional SMTP mail protocol, at least to receive mail.

Why? Because mail sent using SMTP is sent directly to the recipient host, which in this case would be my Macintosh ("ion.digex.net"), and my Mac would have to be on the Internet to receive it; otherwise the sending host would not be able to make an SMTP connection. But because I'm using an intermittent dial-up SLIP/PPP connection, there's no guarantee that my computer would be online at the exact time the sending host wanted to send the message, and thus I could end up not receiving messages sent to me.

(The sending host will in fact periodically retry sending mail messages if it cannot connect to my computer the first time. However the sending host does not retry forever, and if it cannot connect successfully within a given time period,

say three days, then it will give up on delivering the mail. If my computer is connected to the Internet only for brief periods during those three days then it is quite possible that the sending host will never be able to connect to it.)

Going back to our telephone example, sending Internet electronic mail in the traditional manner (i.e., using SMTP end-to-end) is somewhat like leaving a message for someone on their personal answering machine: you can call their phone number 24 hours a day and count on the fact that their answering machine will almost always be turned on and ready to record messages. But in my case my "Internet phone number" (IP address) is active only part of the time (when I'm connected to my Internet access provider via SLIP or PPP and have "Internet dial tone") and my "personal answering machine" (my computer) won't always be turned on and ready to receive my messages.

The solution to this problem is very simple: I'll have another Internet-connected system (a "mail server") receive my email messages for me, and then when I'm connected to the Internet I'll download my mail messages from that system to my Mac. Continuing the answering machine analogy, this arrangement is similar to what phone companies provide via services like Bell Atlantic's Answer Call; in place of your having your own answering machine, the phone company provides a voice mailbox for you somewhere in their network, and callers to your number can leave messages in that voice mailbox. You can then periodically call a special phone number associated with the voice mail-box service, punch in your access code, and listen to your messages.

In my case, rather then sending email to "hecker@ion.digex.net" (recall that "ion.digex.net" is the host name of my Macintosh), people send email to: "hecker@access.digex.net", where "access.digex.net" is the name of the mail server run by my Internet access provider; this system runs 24 hours a day and has a permanent Internet connection. Once I dial up my Internet access provider and my SLIP connection is active, I then have Eudora connect to the host "access.digex.net" over the Internet and download any messages I've received since last I connected.

The specific protocol used to do this is not SMTP, but is another protocol called Post Office Protocol or POP. In particular Eudora and the "access" system use POP3, the third and most recent version of this protocol. In technical jargon the system "access.digex.net" is thus a POP3 server.

I didn't mention it above, but I also have to supply Eudora with a userid and password, which it then passes on to the mail server when connecting to it using POP. If there were no userid or password, then anyone else on the Internet could connect to my Internet access provider's mail server and download my mail.

As it happens, my "mail userid" and associated password are the same ones I used to use when logging in to the "access" system itself as a user of an Internet shell account, namely "hecker" and the

corresponding login password. This makes for a smooth transition from the old way of doing things (using a shell account) to the new way (using SLIP/PPP): my electronic mail address is still "hecker@access.digex.net" (userid: "hecker" on host "access.digex.net") and I don't have to choose a new password if I don't want to.

Also, if I ever want or need to I can still dial up the "access.digex.net" system in the old way (i.e., using a VT100-compatible communications program instead of SLIP or PPP) and login and read my mail using Pine. (The mailbox format used by POP is the same standard UNIX mailbox format used by Pine, Elm, & other host-based mail programs.)

However, my mail userid and password are not necessarily the same as my SLIP/PPP userid and password that I've previously mentioned; this is because we are talking about two fundamentally different services provided in two fundamentally different ways. SLIP/PPP access is a low-level communications service accessed by dialing up a SLIP/PPP-capable terminal server; POP email access is a higher-level service accessed by connecting over the Internet to a POP3-capable host system (mail server). Thus if you get a new SLIP or PPP account from an Internet access provider you may well receive an email (POP) userid and password in addition to your SLIP/PPP userid and password.

There are exceptions to this. Some smaller Internet access providers do not have separate remote access servers, but rather connect modems directly to serial lines on their UNIX host systems and support SLIP or PPP access using software running on those systems. (This host-based software may be either traditional SLIP or PPP software or SLIP-derived software like the new product The Internet Adaptor; see below for more information about TIA.) In this case a user--or more correctly, their SLIP software executing an automated login script--would login to the host system using a single userid and password, and would then invoke a special SLIP or PPP command to convert the session into a SLIP or PPP connection. Eudora or other POP3 mail programs would use this same userid and password to download mail.

Some providers may also wish to provide users with the convenience of having a single password for all services. In this case they can simply arrange that the SLIP/PPP userid and password used by the remote access server be the same as the userid and password used by the POP3 mail server. For example, the national Internet access provider Netcom does this for their SLIP-based NetCruiser service.

Suppose that I had a full-time hard-wired Internet connection in my home (for example, like those starting to be provided by some cable companies in the U.S.). I could then have "Internet dial tone" all the time, and I wouldn't need a dial-up protocol like SLIP or PPP to connect. I also wouldn't need the equivalent of a SLIP/PPP userid and password; as I discussed previously, their main use is for authentication and billing for Internet access, and the cable company already has a perfectly good way to bill you for cable-based services.

However I might still want the cable company to store my incoming electronic mail messages for me; for example, I might not want to keep my computer turned on all the time. In this case I could use Eudora and POP to connect to a remote mail server, just as I do now over SLIP or PPP, and I would still have to have a mail userid and password supplied to me by the cable company in its role as an Internet access provider.

Continuing the answering machine analogy, having an electronic mailbox accessed using POP can thus be viewed as a value-added option to a basic Internet connection, just as having a voice mailbox through Bell Atlantic's Answer Call is a value-added option to a basic phone line. This also implies that email service could be "unbundled" from basic Internet service; for example, you might have a basic Internet connection but no electronic mail service, or (more likely) you might get basic Internet service from one service provider and an electronic mailbox service from another.

(As it happens, I don't know of any Internet access provider that currently unbundles POP-based email in this way. However as competition heats up in the Internet access market, some companies may choose to further break their current services down into standard and optional offerings, in order to offer the lowest entry-level price possible. There may also be a market niche for companies providing

SLIP/PPP service only, with customers expected to arrange for electronic mail service on their own; some nonprofit Internet cooperatives do business this way today.)

Back to Eudora: As I've mentioned, once Eudora has downloaded my incoming email messages to my Mac I can then read them at my leisure; I don't need to maintain the Internet SLIP connection. What about sending messages? Here again I don't need to be connected in order to compose messages, but (it almost goes without saying) I do need to be connected in order to send them.

As it turns out, for historical reasons (a fancy way of saying "that's just the way it is") the POP protocol is not used when sending electronic mail messages. Instead Eudora uses the SMTP protocol I discussed earlier, but with a twist. In "SMTP classic" the sending host (my Mac in this case) connects directly to the receiving host (say "whitehouse.gov", if I'm sending a message to Bill Clinton). However the receiving host might be down or unreachable due to some Internet problem, so that Eudora would have to postpone sending the message to a later time, say a few hours later.

But why should I have to go to all the trouble of remembering to reconnect periodically to my Internet access provider? Instead what happens is that Eudora uses the SMTP protocol to send my message to my mail server. The server then uses SMTP again to send the message on to its final destination. If the mail server can't do so right away it will keep

trying until it succeeds; meanwhile I can disconnect my Mac and not worry about it.

You may have noticed that I didn't say anything about userids and passwords when sending mail. That's because the mail server doesn't authenticate me in any way when sending mail via SMTP; I just tell Eudora to upload the message and the email server accepts it.

You might then ask, "Doesn't this mean that someone else can send fake electronic mail under your name?" For this and other reasons, the answer is yes, they certainly can. As it happens, it is almost trivially easy to send forged Internet mail, and has been ever since Internet mail began. This is why, for example, you should be very skeptical if you ever get a message purportedly from your Internet access provider telling you that you need to change your password to "k00l/d00d".

There are well-known ways to solve this problem, but they haven't been implemented because they depend on encryption and related technologies, and implementation in the Internet has been held hostage to the same sort of disputes we've seen in the infamous "Clipper chip" controversy.

(I don't want to rehash this whole issue here, but I do want to point out the basic underlying problem. In the "market" that is the Internet, the most successful "products" are based on technologies that are available world-wide and that are in the public domain or otherwise freely usable. Exporting encryption technology from the U.S. is legally restricted because of national security concerns, and "public key" encryption, the most useful type for electronic mail, is covered by a software patent in the U.S. Thus there are at least two major obstacles to creating a world-wide standard for secure Internet mail– yet another example of how once obscure policy questions can eventually come to affect all of us.)

That's about it for electronic mail. The case of Usenet news (online conferences) is somewhat similar, and worth covering at this point. Again, we need to digress for a moment and talk about how Usenet news works underneath. Usenet is not a communications network per se but rather a loosely-organized collection of host systems which exchange conference articles with each other. (In this sense Usenet is analogous to FidoNet in the PC BBS world, and in fact there are gateways between Usenet and FidoNet.)

When a conference article is submitted (or "posted") on one system it is then sent on to one or more other systems, which then send it on to others, and so on (rather like a chain letter) until all Usenet hosts receive it. Once an article is received at a host it is stored for people to read it. There are a few thousand Usenet conferences (or "newsgroups") and several thousand Usenet hosts around the world. Thus as you might imagine a lot of traffic flows through the system every day, so much so that a typical Usenet host system stores only the last few days worth of articles.

If I want Usenet access from my personal computer there are at least three possible ways to get it. First, I could have my computer be a fullfledged Usenet host and receive all conferences; this is pretty much out of the question in my case, given that it's hard to fit several gigabytes of disk space in a laptop, and I'd need a lot of connect time each day to receive all the articles. Second, I could have my computer be a Usenet host but receive only a few newsgroups; this is a much more reasonable thing to do, and you can get software for both Macs and PCs to do it, but I'd still be receiving every article in every newsgroup I chose to receive, even articles of little or no interest to me.

The third alternative is what I use with my computer: connect to a remote Internet host acting as a "news server;" this host ("news1.digex.net" in my case) receives all Usenet newsgroups and stores all articles for as long as it can without running out of disk space. Assuming that I have an Internet SLIP/PPP connection active, I then have the NewsWatcher application connect to the news server over the Internet and download the list of articles (i.e., by subject line) in each news-group. I then pick which articles I want to read and have NewsWatcher down-load only those; the rest are left unread (at least by me) on the news server.

Conceptually this process is quite similar to using a POP mail server as described above. As with mail there is a special protocol, NNTP (Network News Transfer Protocol), by which NewsWatcher and the server talk to each other.

However I don't have to supply a userid or password when reading and posting news. I do have to tell News-

Watcher my email address ("hecker@access.digex.net") because this is used to mark my posted articles as coming from me, and is also needed when I send mail to someone in lieu of posting a reply to the newsgroup. However this information is not used to authenticate me to the news server in any way.

You might ask, can anyone on the Internet then use NewsWatcher (or other NNTP client programs) to read and post articles from and to my Internet access provider's news server? There are some news servers on the Internet for which this is true; using these "public NNTP sites" anyone can read or (in some cases) post Usenet news articles. (And I might add, using these servers as well as through other means it is possible to send forged Usenet postings by another's name, similar to what can be done with Internet mail.)

However my Internet access provider's news server will not accept requests from anywhere on the Internet; it will only accept requests from IP addresses and host names that it knows about, that is, those that represent valid subscribers to the provider's SLIP or PPP service. Since my Mac has an IP address and Internet host name assigned by the Internet access provider when I signed up, the provider's news server will recognize me as a valid user. Thus IP address and host name are again used as a useful (albeit not totally secure) means of authenticating users. (Some news servers do authenticate users using a userid and password as well.)

The final point I want to make about Usenet news is that, like access to a mail server, access to a news server is a value-added service over and above basic SLIP or PPP Internet access and could in theory be unbundled as well, so that you might have a basic Internet connection with no mail or Usenet news service at all, an Internet connection and mail service but no Usenet news service, or Internet service, mail service, and news service from one, two, or even three providers. (Again, most present-day Internet access providers do not in fact unbundle services in this manner.)

Accessing Other Internet Services

With both electronic mail and Usenet news it's not enough just to have a SLIP or PPP Internet connection; you also need to have access to a special Internet host or hosts acting as mail or news servers respectively. This access is usually prearranged with some organization, typically the Internet access provider itself.

However there are a wealth of other services for which you need only a basic Internet connection. The first example is using anonymous FTP to download information files or shareware. On my Mac the Fetch program (which implements FTP) simply asks me for the name of the host I wish to connect to. Some magic then happens to convert the host name to an IP address (analogous to looking up a phone number) and a connection is made, after which I download files. The site doesn't ask for an individual password, and doesn't really care who I am.

Second, as a mild security measure many FTP sites will check to make sure that the IP address from which you're connecting (e.g., the IP address of my Macintosh) matches the Internet host name associated with the IP address. In telephone terms this is like getting the phone number of a caller via Caller ID and then looking in a reverse or "criss-cross" directory to find out their name.

This is probably as good a place as any for a brief digression on Internet host names. As implied earlier, Internet host names (like "cap.gwu.edu") are to IP addresses ("128.164.140.32") as people's names are to their phone numbers, and in fact there is a "directory assistance" service to do automatic lookups of IP addresses for a given host name and vice versa. This automated service is referred to as Domain Name Service or DNS, and is invoked by my Macintosh every time I give it an Internet host name to connect to. The lookup is done by querying an Internet host called a DNS name server; in my case this server is one maintained by my Internet access provider, and its IP address is yet another of the pieces of configuration information I got when signed up for SLIP or PPP service.

Besides letting me (or more properly, my Macintosh) look up IP addresses automatically, my Internet access provider's DNS name server also maintains entries listing the Internet host name and IP address of my Mac. This lets remote systems like anonymous FTP sites do the sort of checks I briefly mentioned above. Other than that my Mac's host name ("ion.digex.net") isn't used for much, as email for me is sent to the mail server's host name ("access.digex.net") instead.

Like directory assistance, DNS name service is essential but fundamentally uninteresting (unless you need to use it and it's not working). It is usually provided by the Internet access provider as a part of basic Internet service and is not really a good candidate for unbundling. (However many Internet access providers do provide an extra cost service whereby you can choose your own personal customized host name, like "hecker@my-company.com".)

Continuing on, Telnet from my Mac works similar to FTP: I tell the NCSA Telnet application the host name I wish to connect to, it does the silent DNS lookup to find the IP address, and then connects me directly over the Internet to the remote system. The only userid and password required is whatever the remote system might ask for; some Telnet-based services use a dummy or "guest" userid and password, or even no userid or password at all. Connecting to a UNIX system via Telnet normally looks almost exactly like connecting via dial-up.

Connecting to more exotic systems like Multi-User Dungeons or MUDs is very similar (and typically uses Telnet or a Telnet-based protocol underneath): you supply the host name you wish to connect to, you connect, you sign on in some way, you type at the system, you get responses back, you repeat until you're done, and then you logoff and disconnect. The underlying SLIP or PPP Internet connection must be active during the entire session, which may range in time from a few minutes to several hours (or even days, for enthusiastic MUD fans).

The Gopher and World Wide Web

services are a little more complicated in the way they work. When I start up either TurboGopher (for Gopher) or NCSA Mosaic (for World Wide Web) they attempt to connect initially to a preset "known host" system (or systems, if alternates have been set up); for TurboGopher these host systems are at the University of Minnesota and for Mosaic at the National Center for Supercomputing Applications at the University of Illinois Urbana-Champaign. Both TurboGopher and Mosaic can be changed to connect to other initial host systems, or to not connect to a host system at all.

Once connected to an initial host system, TurboGopher or NCSA Mosaic operate in a true "client/server" fashion: the client (i.e., the program running on the Mac) sends a request over the Internet to the server (the program running on the remote host), which in turn sends back a response. All this happens invisibly underneath using a special-purpose communications protocol (Gopher+ for Gopher and HTTP or HyperText Transport Protocol for the World Wide Web); all you see on the screen is a graphical "point and click" interface like that characteristic of other Mac- or Windows-based programs.

If you pick an item from a Gopher menu or choose to follow a hypertext link in the World Wide Web then one of three things may happen: you may get a menu ("page" in WWW jargon) on the same system, you may get a menu (page) actually stored on another system, or you may invoke an item that does something other than just go to another menu or page. The first case is not

that interesting, so we'll skip it. (It's actually a special instance of the second case.)

In the second case, for menus (pages) served by another system on the Internet, TurboGopher or Mosaic automatically reconnect to the new system and send the proper low-level commands to retrieve the menu (page) being invoked. As you browse through the menu hierarchy (or the hypertext tree) the programs automatically switch from system to system as needed, so there is no single system to which Turbo-Gopher or Mosaic remain "connected."

In the third case, when a user invokes a menu item or clicks on a hypertext link, some special action may be performed. One very common action is to initiate automatic downloading of some file. This is implemented essentially by having FTP-like functionality built into Turbo-Gopher and Mosaic, so that by invoking a Gopher or WWW item you can fetch any file retrievable via anonymous FTP. If the file is of a special type TurboGopher and Mosaic can do also something special with it. For example, if the file were a graphics image in GIF format then after downloading is complete TurboGopher or Mosaic would try to invoke a GIF viewer to show you the file. (You must already have GIF viewer software, and you must have made sure that TurboGopher or Mosaic are configured to use it.)

There are lots of other interesting features of Gopher and the World Wide Web; however, the most important thing to remember is that, unlike mail and Usenet news, you don't have to have anything to use Gopher and the World-

Wide Web except the Internet connection itself and the proper client programs.

Summary

It's been a long and tangled path thus far, and thank you for sticking with it. Here are the key points I'd like you to take away from this paper:

* You can take a Macintosh or a 386 or better Windows-based PC that already has a modem and for a relatively small one-time expenditure (as low as under $50 U.S. for TCP/IP and SLIP or PPP software) make it capable of being a full-fledged Internet node.

* For an expenditure of between $10 and $40 per month in the U.S. (depending on your location and the amount of competition in your market) you can sign up with an Internet access provider who will let you connect your PC or Mac to the Internet on an on-demand, dialup basis. What you get for your money is an Internet host name and IP address (with a directory entry for your system maintained by DNS), a number to call for SLIP or PPP access, and a special SLIP/ PPP userid and password to authenticate you and allow your connect time to be tracked. (Note that if your Internet access provider assigns IP addresses "on the fly" then you won't get a host name or IP address of your own.) Your provider should also supply you with some other miscellaneous configuration information as well, most of which is pure gobbledygook and is needed only when you first configure SLIP or PPP (but is very important at that time).

* With just the basic dial-up Internet PPP service you can use FTP clients like Fetch to download files, Telnet programs like NCSA Telnet to login to remote systems, Gopher clients like TurboGopher to access Gopher servers, and WWW clients like NCSA Mosaic to access World Wide Web servers.

* If your Internet access provider also runs a POP mail server (as almost all do), you can have the mail server receive mail for you and then use an email program like Eudora to download it when you're connected, for you to read and respond to offline. Your provider will supply you with a mail userid and password to do this (which may be the same as the SLIP/PPP userid and password); authentication is done by the mail server.

* If your Internet access provider also runs an NNTP news server, you can use a Usenet news reader such as News-Watcher to connect to the news server, select interesting Usenet news articles, and download them for reading. You can also post new articles or follow-ups to old articles. The news server will authenticate you (if necessary) based on your IP address and host name (and/or a userid and password).

* In theory electronic mail and Usenet news services could be unbundled from basic Internet access. This is rarely seen today but may become more common as the market for personal Internet access evolves.

Note that a higher-speed dedicated Internet connection, via cable for example, would work in a similar manner. The major difference would be in the first two items. First, for a high-speed connection your PC or Mac would not use a modem but rather something like an Ethernet controller board, which typically runs about $100 to $200 U.S. on up. (This might hook up to a "cable Ethernet" connection located on your set-top box.)

Second, with a dedicated connection there would be no need for an equivalent of the SLIP/PPP userid and password, as the cable company could simply bill you monthly as it does today for cable service.

Everything else would work exactly the same way, only faster; the applications software itself (e.g., Eudora, NewsWatcher, TurboGopher, NCSA Mosaic, etc.) would stay the same and would be configured the same. (Whether a TCP/IP connection uses SLIP, PPP, Ethernet, or other network technology is essentially transparent to the user application.)

I should add that typical "Internet over cable" technologies support a high "downstream" bandwidth (i.e., to the home) but a slow "upstream" bandwidth (i.e., to the cable company headend and thence to the Internet). They are thus ideally suited for applications like Mosaic, where you typically download to your PC or Mac a great deal of data in the form of graphics images, sound clips, etc., with only a few commands going in the other direction back to the World Wide Web servers. As a result, "Internet via cable" may be the next frontier for power users currently enjoying the benefits of SLIP and PPP dialup access.

Developing a New Academic Medium: The online classroom is a dynamic environment. In this article, reprinted here by his kind permission, John Gresham describes this new realm.

From Invisible College to Cyberspace College
Computer Conferencing and the Transformation of Informal Scholarly Communication Networks

by John L. Gresham, Jr., Ph.D.
Director of Library Services, Sterling College, Sterling KS
Originally published by IPCT-J Interpersonal Computing and Technology

Scholarly communication is in the midst of a technological revolution. Much has been published regarding the changes in the formal scholarly communications network that will follow the shift from print to electronic journals (Robison, 1993). Less consideration has been given to the transformation of informal scholarly communications networks through computer mediated communication. However, the impact of technology on informal networks of scholarly communication or "invisible colleges" also merits attention. In fact, the changes in scholarly communication are coming more rapidly along these informal channels. The academic community and publishing industry have been slow to replace print journals with electronic publications as a medium of formal scholarly communication, while the use of email and online discussion groups for informal scholarly communication expands with breathtaking rapidity. Informal scholarly networking is moving from physical locations in conference and research centers into "cyberspace," the virtual space created by electronic networks.

The transformation of informal scholarly communications has already begun and academia is in the initial stages of a shift from the invisible college to the cyberspace college as a new form of the informal research network. In order to analyze that shift, I begin with a brief description of invisible colleges followed by a descriptive and historical introduction to computer conferencing. Then I describe the current uses of computer conferencing within the academic community and reflect upon the present and future impact this new form of communication will have on informal scholarly networks.

Background: the Invisible College

The importance of informal networks to the growth and dissemination of scientific knowledge was noted by Price (1961, cited in Cronin, 1982) who coined the term, "invisible colleges" to describe these informal communities of scientific specialists. Since Price, informal collaboration and communication within invisible colleges is commonly viewed as an essential pre-quel to the formal publication and dissemination of advances in scientific knowledge. In a review of research on invisible colleges, Cronin concluded that such informal scholarly communication networks are the "lifeblood of scientific progress for both the physical and the social sciences" (1982, p. 225). An invisible college is a social network of generally around 100 individuals who function as the scholarly in-group within a given specialization. Most of the significant research within the specialization is usually produced by members of such an invisible college. This research is facilitated by the informal exchange of information through contacts within this social network at conferences and other forums. While these informal networks vary in structure across various research areas, they share the common functions of facilitating group identity and purpose within a research specialization and keeping participants abreast of current trends and new developments within their area of specialized interest.

These informal communication networks provide a forum for the sharing and testing of new ideas through feedback and discussion. Inter-disciplinary exchange of ideas emerges along the peripheries of interconnecting invisible colleges. Cronin points to this generation and exploration of new ideas as a key contribution of the invisible college to the expansion of knowledge, especially in the social sciences. Also, practical information about research and funding opportunities is often exchanged initially through these informal networks. Due to publication lags in the formal scholarly communication networks, the cutting edge of information in a given scholarly specialization is frequently found within these invisible colleges.

Cronin notes the following advantages of the invisible college in contrast to the more formal channels of scholarly communication: currency of information; specialization of information; opportunity for feedback and input at formative stages of idea development; and potential for interdisciplinary transmission of ideas. The disadvantages of invisible colleges as a means of scholarly communication include the elitist and restrictive nature of the networks. These colleges emerge around nuclei of major researchers, leaving many institutionally and geographically remote scholars cut off from the significant communication channels in their specialization. High costs are another disadvantage. Invisible colleges function through personal contacts and this requires funding for frequent travel to conferences. As an informal communications system, invisible colleges have the further disadvantage of disseminating large amounts of trivial and irrelevant data, along with more significant information.

In the conclusion to his review of research, Cronin notes the potential for computer conferencing to emerge as a new means of informal scholarly communication but does not foresee any drastic changes in the invisible college through the introduction of computer mediated communication. Others foresee computer networks as having a more radical impact on informal scholarly communication. In their discussion of the social impact of computer mediated communication, Hiltz and Turoff (1993) suggest that electronic networks might lead to a more open form of invisible colleges with wider participation and faster exchange of information leading to more rapid paradigm development within specialties, greater interdisciplinary communication between specialties, and an expanded rate of research breakthroughs.

Tracz, (1980) based on his experience with the EIES computer conferencing system, confidently predicts, "the old style invisible college will be easily replaced by the new style electronic college." Past experience with new technologies would suggest that Tracz may be overstating to speak of the electronic college "replacing" the invisible college. Rather than replacing print and face-to-face communications, electronic publishing and communications seem to foster a flood of additional print literature and conferences devoted toward analysis of the new media.

It is more realistic to consider the impact of computer conferencing upon invisible colleges as the emergence of a new form of informal network in cyberspace existing alongside traditional invisible colleges. The emergence of new electronic or cyberspace colleges can be traced through a review of the nature and history of computer conferencing and description of the current uses of computer conferencing in academic communication.

Intro to Computer Conferencing

Electronic conferences are known by many names and no consistent nomenclature has yet emerged. The following names for this form of communication have appeared: electronic conferences, econferences, computer conferences, mailing lists, lists, listservs, electronic forums, online discussion groups, scholarly discussion groups, special interest groups, news groups, and netgroups. Harnad (1993) creatively describes this new form of academic communication as "scholarly skywriting." All of these terms describe the special use of computer mediated communication or email for group communication. Hiltz and Turoff define computer conferencing systems as the use of the computer "to structure, store, and process written communications among a group of persons" (1993, p.7). Harnad succinctly describes econferences as "multiple reciprocal email--electronic discussion groups in which every message is immediately disseminated to all members" (1993, p.82).

There are some helpful introductions to computer conferencing (Collins, 1993; Nickerson, 1992b) but most users learn how electronic conferences work by using them. Subscription to a conference is usually accomplished automatically with an email message to the computer conferencing program. Electronic confer-

139

ences use computer conferencing software such as LISTSERV to handle subscriptions and to automatically distribute messages or "posts" to all subscribers to the online conference. E-conferences differ from other types of teleconferencing such as video- or audio- in that messages are typed and transmitted as text.

While synchronous or real-time electronic communication is possible, the most common form of current e-conference is based on asynchronous communication. Messages are instantaneously transmitted to all conference subscribers but each participant reads and responds to these postings at his or her own convenience. Several topics or conversational "threads" can proceed simultaneously, each identified by its subject heading. Subscribers can easily follow the threads of interest to them and delete the others. They can respond to postings by replying to the list (in which case the message goes out to every subscriber) or replying to one individual subscriber (via that person's individual email address.)

The person who creates an electronic conference is known as the list owner. The conferencing software makes subscribing and most other activities automated but the list owner is usually available to assist conference participants with technical questions and problems. The list owner(s) will usually send a charter or mission statement to all subscribers describing the suggested subject areas encompassed by

that particular conference and giving technical instructions for using the list. These instructions will usually include directions for searching the archives of the conference in which previous postings are filed, and sometimes other electronic documents as well. With computer conferencing software such as LISTSERV, keyword searching of these archives is possible.

On moderated lists, the listowner or designate engages in various degrees of editing or selecting what messages appear on the list and/or directing the conversation in order to keep the conference within the stated parameters of discussion. Moderators try to keep the list away from the email practice known as flaming in which discussion degenerates to ad hominem attacks rather than scholarly debate and polite disagreement.

Scholarly electronic conferences have been compared to: a library where one goes to gather information, read, and think; a seminar, conference or salon where one informally debates ideas with colleagues; a room of people or dinner party with several interesting conversations going on at once; and a newspaper (especially the editorials and opinion columns) where one simply subscribes and reads the exchange of ideas without participating in the discussion (called "lurking" on computer conferences) (Berge & Collins, 1993b). Another has compared e-conferences to the conversation in the faculty lounge: "We pose queries, ask leading questions, report on conferences, review books and articles, ask for collaborators, call for papers, invite constructive criticism of new ideas, discuss each other's work, gossip and so on (Reimer, 1993)." Such comments point to many of the ways in which academics are adopting computer conferencing as a medium for informal scholarly (and sometimes not-so-scholarly) communication. Before investigating the academic uses of electronic conferences in more detail, I will trace the history of this technological development from its roots in government research centers to its adoption by the wider academic community.

History of Computer Conferencing

The history of computer conferencing and computer networks has been traced by Hiltz & Turoff (1993), Nickerson, (1992a, 1992b, 1992c) Quarterman (1990, 1993), and Williams (1992). The first computer conference was developed by Turoff for the United States Office of Emergency Preparedness in 1970. The system was named EMISARI (Emergency Management Information System and Reference Index). EMISARI was originally conceived as a means of electronically facilitating the Delphi method of structured group communication for the purpose of collaborative decision making and forecasting. It was successfully implemented as a communications system during the wage price freeze of the early seventies when it was used to share information among the ten regional centers of the Office of Emergency Preparedness. This system

served as the prototype for Turoff's later system, EIES (Electronic Information Exchange System) developed at and operated from the National Research Foundation at NJIT.

The 1970s saw the development of a number of other conferencing systems such as FORUM and then PLANET at the Institute of the Future, CONFER at the University of Michigan, ORACLE at Northwestern University, CONCLAVE in England and others. The most significant development during this time, however, was the ARPANET wide area network created by the U. S. Defense Department agency, DARPA (Defense Advanced Research Projects Agency). Originally created to facilitate information sharing among defense research centers, ARPANET was the testing ground for the TCP/IP protocols. These protocols became the basis for the subsequent emergence of the international network of networks known as the Internet.

Interestingly enough, ARPANET's developers were primarily interested in file transmission (FTP) and remote logon (TELNET); email and computer conferencing capabilities were only added to the system as an afterthought (Quarterman, 1993). Nonetheless, by 1978 the predecessor of later online discussion groups had already emerged on the ARPANET network, the unofficial SF-LOVERS (science fiction lovers) electronic conference which flourished despite the opposition of network authorities. Whereas the earlier conferencing systems like EIES ran on one central mainframe computer which all conference participants would have to log in to, ARPANET introduced the present era of distributed networks in which email and other data flow from site to site via packet switching technology. By 1986, ARPANET was replaced by NSFNet (National Science Foundation Network), the major backbone for the Internet, network access was expanded beyond defense research to the wider scientific and academic research communities, and the stage was set for the present explosion of scholarly electronic discussion groups on the Internet.

While the Internet is the major carrier of electronic conference email today, the significant developments in computer conferencing in the 1980s took place on other networks. The largest electronic conferencing network had its beginnings in 1979 when two Duke University graduate students took advantage of the networking capability of the new UNIX mainframes to write software for a UNIX Users network called Usenet. By 1984, the network included 150 e-conferences or "newsgroups" distributed to 2000 sites. By 1992, there were more than 15,000 sites and over 2,000 newsgroups on Usenet. While Usenet rapidly developed into a forum for online discussion groups on an incredible number and variety of topics, the scholarly use of this medium remained unrealized. With the exception of some of the computing technology and other scientific newsgroups, most Usenet newsgroups had the often deserved reputation of being "mostly havens for under informed students and dilettantes rather than respectable scholarly forums for learned societies" (Harnad, 1993, p. 82).

A significant variety of scholarly e-conferences first emerged on the BITnet network. BITnet began as a network connecting Yale University and City University of New York in 1981 and rapidly grew to connect 500 colleges and universities. BITnet's acronym was originally explained as meaning "Because its there" with the explanation that the network emerged for no other reason than that the technology was available to network university IBM mainframes together and it was done. Later, the acronym was reinterpreted to mean, "Because it's time." Through links to other networks such as EARN in Europe and ASIANET in the Far East, BITnet provided connections to over 2000 sites by the early nineties. BITnet provided fertile ground for the development of scholarly electronic conferences for two reasons--first and obvious was that it was a network of institutions of higher education; and second it offered only limited file transmission (FTP) capabilities, leaving email and computer conferencing as its basic services.

The proliferation of electronic conferences on BITnet was facilitated by Eric Thomas' development of LISTSERV computer conferencing software for IBM mainframes in 1986. This software has proven so popular that "LISTSERV" is often used as a generic term for electronic conferences/ discussion groups and the software has recently been made available in UNIX and VMS formats. By the early 1990s, over 900 electronic conferences were carried on BITnet.

The growth in scholarly or academically oriented electronic conferences and discussion groups on Internet and BITnet in the early nineties can be traced through the various editions of The Directory of Scholarly Electronic Journals Newsletters and Academic Discussion Lists. The first edition (1991) listed 517 academic discussion lists, the second edition (1992) listed 769, the third edition (1993) listed 1152 (Strangelove & Kovacs, 1993). The current situation is such that with gateways between networks the distinctions between Internet, BITnet and even Usenet mean little to most e-conference participants. Most scholarly discussion groups have both Internet and BITnet addresses and many of the conferences have Usenet feeds which allow them to be accessed as Usenet newsgroups as well. What is of most interest to the scholarly participant in electronic conferences is not the networking technology which supports the discussion group but the content of the discussion itself. How are scholars actually using electronic conferences for research and communication?

Academic Computer Conferencing

Little research and reporting has appeared on the uses of computer mediated discussion groups or conferences in the academic community. Hiltz (1984) surveyed participants in four scientific conferences on the EIES system which included scholars doing research on futurology, social networks, general systems theory and devices for the disabled. According to the survey, the results of participation in these four conferences included clarification of theoretical controversies, expanded networks of professional contacts, greater awareness of information sources and scholarly activity in the subject areas, and increased communication both within specializations and across disciplines. In another study, Freeman (1984) pointed to the EIES conference as an important factor in the emergence of Social Networks Analysis as a new scientific specialty.

Based on a survey of participants in communications and psychology e-conferences, Schaefermeyer and Sewell (cited in Kovacs & Kovacs, 1991) noted that for these network users, email had begun to replace telephone, postal mail, and face-to-face communications as a preferred means for the scholarly exchange of information concerning research and instructional interests as well as for social communication.

Kovacs & Kovacs (1991) surveyed a number of subscribers to ARACHNET, an e-conference for e-conference moderators and e-journal editors. Their survey included 20 moderators of e-conferences in the subject areas of computer science,

143

English, ethnomusicology, labor economics, library and information science, literature, history, philosophy, physics, political economy, postmodern culture, psychology, southeast Asian studies, and text processing. These moderators observed the following uses of e-conferences as a research tool: establishment of collaborations, information exchange/confirmation, maintaining current awareness, development of research ideas, medium of publication. Many moderators noted that email was replacing postal and phone communication among scholarly colleagues. These activities correspond almost identically to the informal communication exchanges described in earlier research on invisible colleges, illustrating the movement of the invisible college into cyberspace.

Berge and Collins (1993a) also observed the use of computer conferencing to augment personal and professional networks, noting that "coauthors for articles and books have been discovered, researchers with similar projects have been found, employment, funding and research opportunities have been turning up regularly through computer conferencing." In a later article, Berge and Collins (1994) provide a more qualitative report on electronic conferencing. They provide several quotes from an e-conference discussion on the potential social impacts of computer mediated communication to illustrate the quality of scholarly debate and discussion possible in an electronic conference.

In order to get a more detailed picture of how scholars within a particular discipline are using electronic conferences for scholarly communication, I subscribed to a number of religious studies conferences for a few months in Winter 1993-1994 to observe the interactions and to query participants. Religious Studies provides a helpful case study because of its interdisciplinary character. The discipline encompasses historical, philosophical, literary and social scientific approaches dispersed among a number of sub-disciplines such as Biblical studies, historical, comparative and social scientific study of religions, archeological studies, and theological/ philosophical studies. The variety of religious studies oriented e-conferences reflects this. I subscribed to lists for historical and comparative study of religions (RELIGION), study of Greco-Roman Judaism and related religious movements and religious texts of the time (IOUDAIOS), social scientific study of religion (SSREL-L), study of new religions (NUREL-I), Archaeology (ARCH-L), history of American evangelicalism (HISTEC-L), history of American Catholicism (AMERCATH), and constructive theology (THEOLOGOS).

I posted queries to several of these lists asking religious studies scholars to tell how they were using the Internet, and especially e-conferences to facilitate research and instruction. I received 20 responses describing a variety of uses of e-conferences. Based on these responses and my own observation and participation in these and other e-conferences, I have learned that scholars are using e-conferences to :

1. Communicate with an international community of scholars (especially useful to geographically remote scholars);

2. Communicate with scholars sharing common interests, subject specialties;

3 Ask questions of scholars in fields outside one's specialization;

4 Track down sources, texts and other bibliographic information;

5. Discuss, review and debate new publications in the field;

6. Meet and interview experts for research;

7. Exchange and critique pre-publication papers;

8. Do collaborative research and writing;

9. Share teaching tips: syllabi, text-books, etc.;

10. Seek advice for research and field-work from more experienced scholars;

11. Gather advice & bibliographic suggestions for dissertation research;

12. Observe, participate in discussion beyond academia (Usenet groups);

13. Read up-to-date accounts and evaluations of new discoveries, publications;

14. Learn about relevant resources on the Internet and other electronic resources;

15. Learn about research opportunities; calls for papers, reviews, job openings;

16. Get feedback on new ideas;

17. Maintain and continue relationships with distant colleagues;

18. Chat;

19. Make new friends;

20. Become part of a virtual community.

These uses of e-conferencing reinforce earlier observations concerning electronic networks becoming a communications medium for informal scholarly networking. In addition to describing how they were using computer conferencing, several of the religion scholars who responded to my queries also noted some of the advantages of this communications medium. Several scholars noted the geographic access provided by the Internet. Religious scholars in Hong Kong, Saskatchewan, Canada and Fort Worth, Texas noted how e-conferences enabled them to overcome their remote locations and maintain scholarly communication with other specialists in their areas of interest. Another scholar, teaching in a small religion department with little opportunity for ongoing dialogue with other scholars in his particular specialization, expressed a similar appreciation for the ability to transcend geographic barriers through e-conferencing. Not only geographical, but other barriers to access were overcome via e-conferencing.

Graduate students, who might otherwise find it very difficult to break into the old style invisible colleges note the ease by which they gain access to a variety of scholarly experts in their area of study with whom they may discuss their dissertation research. The speed and currency of information was noted in one response which described the reporting and analysis of a recent archeological discovery weeks before its reporting in print and at least months before its analysis in the scholarly literature. A couple of respondents commented on the benefits of participation in e-conferences in areas beyond their specialty. This suggests that the value of invisible colleges for the interdisciplinary and cross-disciplinary exchange of information is also enhanced by computer conferencing.

The only significant negative comments on e-conferencing related to the great amounts of trivial and irrelevant information exchanged and problems of information overload. The first problem, irrelevant information, seems intrinsic to informal communication. The same problem was noted as a weakness of invisible colleges as an information system. The second problem, information overload, is a persistent feature of electronic communication. However, as scholars use computer mediated communication they learn techniques to overcome these problems. One scholar who responded to my survey noted how he sought to overcome these problems by using the LISTSERV software to receive e-conferences in a digest format in order to quickly skim messages and save only those of interest and relevance to him.

From Invisible Colleges to Cyberspace Colleges

From this survey and earlier studies, it is evident that the kinds of informal scholarly communications that characterized those social networks known as invisible colleges are now increasingly taking place across computer networks. Moreover, computer conferencing is transforming and improving the invisible college. One of the most significant transformations will involve the size and scope of informal scholarly networks. The fairly localized and limited invisible college of about 100 or so individuals will expand into huge international electronic networks of scholars. Rossman (1992) refers to the "global enlargement" of the scholarly network and Quarterman explains how the "global matrix of interconnected computer networks facilitates the formation of global matrices of minds" (1993, p.56). This global expansion in size will be accompanied by an equally significant increase in the speed of information exchange. Harnad argues that computer conferencing "promises to restore the speed of scholarly communication to a rate much closer to the speed of thought" (1993, p.85). Thus, the expenses of travel and the limitations of time and space which hampered the effectiveness of the invisible college will be overcome by CMC.

Of equal importance, the elitism of the old scholarly networks will be overcome. Electronic conferences tend to be interesting and illuminating mixes of teachers and students, academics and non-academics, graduates and under-graduates, theoreticians and practi-tioners with all having equal access to contribute to and learn from the ongoing conversations. For those with access to the electronic networks, entrance into these scholarly discussion groups comes quite easy. (Hopefully, access to the networks will become more and more universal as well.). More resistant barriers of race and gender prejudice which had the potential of forming invisible colleges along the lines of "old boys networks" are overcome through the text based medium of commu-nication. Communicating textually, postings are more easily judged by their content than the by the physical characteristics or appearance of the poster (Rheingold, 1993).

The textual record leads to certain other improvements over the old style invisible college, as well. The elusive and ephemeral nature of information in verbal networks is overcome because computer conferencing creates a written and searchable record of previous information exchanges. While the problems of information overload and irrelevant information which hamper-ed the usefulness of the invisible college will remain and may be intensified in the cyberspace college, the format of the information as electronic text allows for alleviation of the problem through the use of technology to store, organize, search and retrieve needed information. Thus, many of the weaknesses of the invisible college such as limitations of size, geography, and access, social barriers to access, and problems in managing the flow of information will be overcome by computer mediated communication.

The introduction of a new communication medium not only impro-ves invisible colleges, it transforms them into something new-- "cyberspace colleges." The textual basis of e-conferencing coupled with the speed and interactivity of electronic communi-cation creates a hybrid form of communication. Yates (1993) demons-trated the hybrid nature of computer conference posts by applying a measurement known as "lexical density" which has been used to describe differences between speech and text. Yates measured the lexical den-sity of computer conferencing messages to show how they range across the spectrum of lexical differences between speech and writing. With charact-eristics of both speech and writing, com-puter conferencing represents a new and evolving form of media communication.

Levinson (1990) sees computer conferencing as a natural evolution in the history of media communication. That history is characterized by the development of means (such as written, and later, printed text) to escape the limitations of face-to-face communi-cation followed by subsequent attempts

147

to recover the interactivity and immediacy of pre-technological communication through development of new communications media (such as telecommunications). Computer conferencing represents a further step toward recovering the interactivity of face-to-face communication while maintaining the gains in permanency afforded by textual communication. Harnad (1993) ranks this new communications medium as the fourth major revolution in the history of communication following the beginning of human speech, the development of writing, and the invention of the printing press. He emphasizes that each of these revolutions has impacted both the processes and contents of human thought and this latest revolution will have similar far reaching impacts. The invisible college, as it moves into cyberspace via computer mediated communication, will not remain unchanged.

Since computer conferencing is a new form of communications media, its full impact on the informal scholarly networks cannot be fully predicted. Nonetheless, some potential impacts of this communications medium on informal scholarly networking can be predicted by relating the purposes of the invisible college to the capabilities of computer conferencing. The old style invisible college was based on the free exchange of information among persons in the social network, even though this form of exchange did not carry the tangible recognition and rewards of actual publication in the formal communications network represented by journals and monographs. Does computer conferencing foster this free exchange of information in the absence of the social contacts available in the old style invisible colleges? According to Sproull and Kiesler, (1991) computer conferencing actually enhances such information exchanges. Noting the high rate of response to queries broadcast over computer networks despite the absence of personal contact, Sproull and Kiesler suggest that the ease of responding to information requests in a computer conference fosters a form of "electronic altruism" which stimulates the free exchange of information in this environment.

In a discussion of online education, Harasim (1990) has outlined several more aspects of computer conferencing which suggest the potential for this medium to enhance intellectual collaboration. The textual basis of computer conferencing fosters the reflective and analytical cognitive skills associated with the task of expressing ideas in written form. The asynchronous flow of information encourages fuller group participation by giving all participants opportunity to add to the conversation at their own pace. The opportunity for feedback and ongoing discussion makes computer conferencing an ideal active learning tool.

Harasim finds computer conferencing especially effective in the area of idea generation. Harasim's focus is on the use of computer conferencing as an educational tool utilized by teacher and students, but her comments are quite relevant to the use of this medium for collaborative research among scholars. As was noted above, research on the invisible colleges suggested that a chief value of the informal scholarly networks for the expansion of knowledge consisted in the generation of new ideas, precisely the area of intellectual activity Harasim finds most augmented by computer conferencing. Thus, we find a convergence of form and function as the cyberspace college uses computer conferencing to generate and explore new ideas through collaboration and free exchange of information. Due to the unique features of computer conferencing, the role of the informal scholarly communication network in the expansion of knowledge should be enhanced by the shift from invisible college to cyberspace college.

Trends and Future Developments

Current trends and future developments in computer conferencing includes:

1. Clarification of questions of intellectual ownership and copyright in relation to electronic conference postings: The similarities of these postings to verbal conversation has led to some loose practices in regard to quoting, disseminating and otherwise reusing other's postings, but the textual character of these postings is now leading toward the development of more careful practices of attribution and permission for such reuse.

2. The proliferation of paired e-conferences and e-journals: This is a current trend in which e-conferences emerge as companions to e-journals, providing a virtual meeting spot for discussion and debate of the journal contents, and e-journals emerge as outgrowths of e-conferences, providing a forum for more formal and lengthy articles and reviews to complement the conference discussion. This may lead to merging and overlap between the two media such as is the case now in the highly interactive e-journal PSYCOLOQUY. These developments will lead toward the growth of "virtual research institutes," such as the Institute for Research on Virtual Culture, in which interrelated e-journals, e-conferences, electronic archives and other forms of computer mediated communication will support larger scale coordinated collaborative research and study over electronic networks (Stepp, 1993).

3. Multimedia: Computer conferencing itself will be transformed as network hardware and software continues to become more supportive of the transmission of multi-media information. E-conferences of the future may carry graphics, sound, and video as well as text, moving computer conferencing into the realm of virtual reality (Sinclair & Kearns, 1993). The cyberspace college will be succeeded by the "virtual college."

149

Conclusion

Technology will transform the future of scholarly communication. Just as the formal scholarly communication network will be impacted by the e-journal, even so shall the informal networks of scholarly communication known as invisible colleges be impacted by the e-conference. Computer conferencing is leading toward a new form of informal scholarly communication I have described as cyberspace colleges. The significance of cyberspace colleges is suggested by Rossman's claim that, "the primary importance of computer tools for the electronic university lies not in machines that will think for scholars but in scholars using such tools to amplify 'collective intelligence,' bringing many minds together for more effective collaborative research" (1992, p.58). The cyberspace college represents such use of computer technology to expand and enhance the human element in research by facilitating larger and more effective networks of scholarly communication.

REFERENCES

Berge, Z. L. & Collins, M. P. (1993a). Computer conferencing and online education. The Arachnet Electronic Journal on Virtual Culture [Online], 1 (3). Available FTP: byrd.mu.wvnet.edu Directory: pub/ejvc File: BERGE V1N3.

Berge, Z. L. & Collins, M. P. (1993b). The founding and managing of IPCT-L: a listowners' perspective. Interpersonal Computing and Technology: an Electronic Journal for the 21st Century [Online], 1 (2). Available e-mail: LISTSERV@guvm.georgetown.edu Message: Get BERGE IPCTV1N2.

Berge, Z. L. & Collins, M. (1994). Life on the net. Educom Review, [Online], 29, (2). Available e-mail: editor@educom.edu.

Collins, M. P. (1993). Computer networks and networking: a primer. Interpersonal Computing and Technology: An Electronic Journal for the 21st Century [Online], 1(1). Available email: LISTSERV@guvm.georgetown.edu Message: Get COLLINS IPCTV1N1.

Cronin, B. (1982). Progress in documentation: invisible colleges and information transfer, a review and commentary with particular reference to the social sciences. Journal of Documentation, 38, 212-236.

Freeman, L. (1984). The impact of computer-based communication on the social structure of an emerging scientific specialty. Social Networks, 6, 201-221.

Harasim, L. M. (1990). Online education: an environment for collaboration and intellectual amplification. In L. M. Harasim (Ed.), Online education: perspectives on a new environment (pp. 39-64). New York: Praeger.

Harnad, S. (1993). The post-Gutenberg galaxy: The fourth revolution in the means of the production of knowledge. In Mason, R. (Ed.), Computer conferencing: the last word (pp. 77-89). Victoria, B.C.: Beach Holme Publishers. (Originally published in The Public Access Computer Systems Review, [Online], 2 (1). Available e-mail: LISTSERV@uhupvm1 Message: Get HARNAD PRV1N2.)

Hiltz, S. R. (1984). Online communities: a case study of the office of the future. Norwood, NJ: Ablex Publishing.

Hiltz, S. R. & Turoff, M. (1993). The Network nation: human communication via computer. Rev. Ed. Cambridge: MIT Press.

Kovacs, M. J. & Kovacs, D. K. (1991). The state of scholarly electronic conferencing. Electronic Networking, 1(2), 29-36.

Levinson, Paul. (1990). Computer conferencing in the context of the evolution of media. In L. M. Harasim (Ed.), Online education: perspectives on a new environment (pp. 3-14). New York: Praeger.

Nickerson, G. (1992a). Computer mediated communication on BITnet. Computers in Libraries, 12(2), 33-36.

Nickerson, G. (1992b). Listservers. Computers in Libraries, 12(3), 13-18.

Nickerson, G. (1992c). Usenet. Computers in Libraries, 12(4), 31-34.

Quarterman, J. S. (1990). The matrix: computer networks and conferencing systems worldwide. Burlington, Ma.: Digital Press.

Quarterman, J. S. (1993). The global matrix of minds. In Harasim, L. M. (Ed.), Global networks: computers and international communication (pp. 35-56). Cambridge: MIT Press.

Reimer, D. (1993). Ioudaios e-manual [Online]. Available email: dreimer@ox.ac.uk.

Rheingold, R. (1993). Virtual communities. In Mason, R. (Ed.), Computer conferencing: the last word (pp. 103-108). Victoria, B.C.: Beach Holme Publishers. (Originally published in Whole Earth Review, Winter 1988).

Robison, D. F. W. (1993). Bibliography on electronic journal publication and publishing. In Strangelove, M. & Kovacs, D. Directory of electronic journals, newsletters, and academic discussion lists (pp. 27-38). Washington, D.C.: Association of Research Libraries.

Rossman, P. (1992). The emerging worldwide electronic university: information age global education. Westport, Ct.: Greenwood Press.

Sinclair, G. & Kearns, L. (1993). From text to multimedia: computer mediated communication in the 80's and 90's. In Mason, R. (Ed.), Computer conferencing: the last word (pp. 251-261). Victoria, B.C.: Beach Holme Publishers.

Sproull, L. & Kiesler, S. (1991). Computers, networks and work. Scientific American, 265 (3), 84-91.

Stepp, E. (1993). Virtualization of institutes for research. The Arachnet Electronic Journal on Virtual Culture [Online], 1 (6). Available FTP: byrd.mu.wvnet.edu Directory: pub/ejvc File: STEPP V1N6

Strangelove, M. & Kovacs, D. (1993). Directory of electronic journals, newsletters, and academic discussion lists. Washington, D.C.: Association of Research Libraries.

Tracz, G. (1980). Computerized conferencing: an eye opening experience with EIES. The Canadian Journal of Information Science, 5, 16-20.

Williams, B. (1992). Directory of computer conferencing in libraries. Westport, Ct.: Meckler.

Yates, S. (1993). Speech, writing and computer conferencing: an analysis. In Mason, R. (Ed.), Computer conferencing: the last word (pp. 37-56). Victoria, B.C.: Beach Holme Publishers.

BIOGRAPHICAL SKETCH

John L. Gresham, Jr. (jgresham@acc.stercolks.edu)
is Director of Library Services at Sterling College, Sterling Kansas. He received a Ph.D. in Religious Studies from Baylor University and a Master of Library Science from University of North Texas. He is author of a guide to Religious Studies resources on the Internet entitled "Finding God in Cyberspace".

Workaround Techniques From a Master: Some people have access only to **email**, and may feel that the rest of the Internet will be denied them. In this comprehensive article by Bob Rankin, **workaround** methods are outlined that work to overcome this limitation. The article is reprinted here by the author's kind permission.

Accessing the Internet by Email
Doctor Bob's Guide to Offline Internet Access
by Bob Rankin

Summary: This guide will show you how to retrieve files from FTP sites, explore the Internet via Gopher, search for information with Archie, Veronica, Netfind, or WAIS, tap into the World-Wide Web, and even access Usenet newsgroups using E-MAIL AS YOUR ONLY TOOL.

How to Access Internet Services by Email

If you don't have direct access to the Internet through your BBS or online service, you're not alone. About half of the 150 countries with Internet connections have only email access to this world-wide network of networks. But if you think that sounds limiting, read on. You can access almost any Internet resource using email. Maybe you've heard of FTP, Gopher, Archie, Veronica, Finger, Usenet, Whois, Netfind, WAIS, and the World-Wide Web but thought they were out of your reach because you don't have a direct connection.

Not so! You can use simple email commands to do all of this and much more on the Internet. And even if you do have full Internet access, using email services can save you time and money.

If you can send a note to an Internet address, you're in the game. I encourage you to read this entire document first and then go back and try out the techniques that are covered. This way, you will gain a broader perspective of the information resources that are available, an introduction to the tools you can work with, and the best methods for finding the information you want.

FTP BY EMAIL

FTP stands for "file transfer protocol", and is a means of accessing files that are stored on remote computer systems. In Internet lingo, these remote computers are called "sites". Files at FTP sites are typically stored in a tree-like set of directories (or nested folders for Mac fans), each of which pertains to a different subject. When visiting an FTP site using a "live" internet connection, one would specify the name of the site, login with a userid & password, navigate to the desired directory and select one or more files to be transferred back to their local system. Using FTP by email is very similar, except that the desired site is reached through a special "ftpmail server" which logs in to the remote site and returns the requested files to you in response to a set of commands in an email message.

Using FTP by email can be nice even for those with full Internet access, because some popular FTP sites are heavily loaded and interactive response can be very sluggish. So it makes sense not to waste time and connect charges in these cases. To use FTP by email, you first need a list of FTP "sites" which are the addresses of the remote computer systems that allow you to retrieve files anonymously (without having a userid and password on that system).

There are some popular sites listed later in this guide, but you can get a comprehensive list of hundreds of anonymous FTP sites by sending an email message to the internet address:

```
mail-server@rtfm.mit.edu
```

and include these lines in the BODY of the note.

```
send usenet/news.answers/ftp-
   list/sitelist/part1
send usenet/news.answers/ftp-
   list/sitelist/part2
    ... (lines omitted for brevity) ...
send usenet/news.answers/ftp-
   list/sitelist/part18
```

You will then receive (by email) 18 files which comprise the "FTP Site List". Note that these files are each about 60K, so the whole lot will total around a megabyte! This could place a strain on your system, so first check around to see if the list is already available locally, or consider requesting just the first few as a sampler before getting the rest.

Another file you might want to get is "FTP Frequently Asked Questions" which contains lots more info on using FTP services, so add this line to your note as well:

```
send usenet/news.answers/ftp-
   list/faq
```

After you receive the site list you'll see dozens of entries like this, which tell you the site name, location and the kind of files that are stored there.

```
Site     : oak.oakland.edu
Country: USA
Organ    : Oakland Univ.
           Rochester, MI
System : Unix
Comment: Primary Simtel
           Software Repos.
Files    : BBS lists; ham
           radio; TCP/IP;
           Mac; modem
           protocol info;
           MS-DOS; Windows;
           PC Blue;
           PostScript;
           Simtel-20; Unix
```

If you find an interesting FTP site in the list, send email to one of these ftpmail servers:

```
ftpmail@sunsite.unc.edu
ftpmail@decwrl.dec.com
bitftp@pucc.princeton.edu
ftpmail@census.gov
```

It doesn't really matter which one you choose, but a server that is close may respond quicker. In the body of the note, include these lines:

```
open <site>
*use "connect <site>" for dec.com
sites
dir
quit
```

This will return to you a list of the files stored in the root directory at that site. See the figure below for an example of the output when using "oak.oakland.edu" for the site name.

```
+---------------------------------------------------------------+
| -r--r--r-- 1 w8sdz     OAK     1255 Nov  9 16:32 README        |
| drwxr-xr-x 3 w8sdz     OAK     8192 Feb 25 05:17 SimTel        |
| d--x--x--x 3 root      system  8192 Jan 19 20:26 bin           |
| d--x--x--x 5 root      system  8192 Dec 30 05:15 etc           |
| drwxrwx--- 2 incoming  OAK     8192 Feb 25 11:05 incoming      |
| drwxr-xr-x 3 w8sdz     OAK     8192 Jan 30 17:37 pub           |
| drwxr-xr-x 2 jeff      OAK     8192 Apr 17  1994 siteinfo      |
+---------------------------------------------------------------+
```

In your next email message you can navigate to other directories by inserting (for example)

```
chdir pub
```

before the "dir" command. (The "chdir" means "change directory" and "pub" is a common directory name, usually a good place to start.) Once you determine the name of a file you want to retrieve, use:

```
get <name of file>
```

in the following note instead of the "dir" command. If the file you want to retrieve is plain text, this will suffice. If it's a binary file (an executable program, compressed file, etc.) you'll need to insert the command:

```
binary
```

in your note before the "get" command.

Tip: Many directories at FTP sites contain a file called 00-index.txt, README or something similarly named which

gives a description of the files found there. If you're just exploring and your "dir" reveals one of these filenames, do a "get" on the file and save yourself some time.

OK, let's grab the text of The Magna Carta. Here's the message you send to ftpmail@census.gov (or another ftpmail server):

```
open ftp.spies.com
    (The name of the FTP site)
chdir Gov/World
    (The directory where the file lives)
get magna.txt
    (Sign here please, John)
quit
    (Bring it on home)
```

Here are the commands you would send to to get a file from the Simtel Software Repository that was mentioned earlier.

```
open oak.oakland.edu
```

155

(The name of the FTP site)
`chdir SimTel/msdos/disasm`
(The directory where the file lives)
`binary`
(Because we're getting a ZIP file)
`get bubble.zip`
(Sounds interesting, anyway...)
`quit`
(We're outta here!)

Some other interesting FTP sites you may want to "visit" are listed below. (Use these site names on the "open" command and the suggested directory name on your "chdir" command, as in the previous examples.)

`ocf.berkeley.edu`
   Try: pub/Library for documents, Bible, lyrics, etc.
`rtfm.mit.edu`
   Try: pub/usenet/news.answers for USENET info
`oak.oakland.edu`
   Try: SimTel/msdos for huge DOS software library
`ftp.sura.net`
   Try: pub/nic for Internet how-to documents
`quartz.rutgers.edu`
   Try: pub/humor for lots of humor files
`gatekeeper.dec.com`
   Try: pub/recipes for a cooking & recipe archive

Remember you can't just send email to ftpmail@<anysite>, rather you send the "open <site>" command to one of the known ftpmail servers.

You should note that ftpmail servers tend to be quite busy so your reply may not arrive for several minutes, hours, or days, depending on when and where you send your request. Also, some large files may be split into smaller pieces and returned to you as multiple messages.

You'll need to scrounge up a version of the "uudecode" program for your operating system (DOS, OS/2, Unix, Mac, etc.) in order to reconstruct the file. Most likely you'll find a copy already at your site or in your service provider's download library, but if not you can use the instructions in the next section to find out how to search FTP sites for a copy.

One final point to consider... If your online service charges you to store email files that are sent to you and you plan to receive some large files via FTP, it would be wise to handle your "inbasket" expeditiously to avoid storage costs.

ARCHIE BY EMAIL

Let's say you know the name of a file, but you have no idea at which FTP site it might be lurking. Or maybe you're curious to know if files matching a certain naming criteria are available via FTP. Archie is the tool you can use to find out.

Archie servers can be thought of as a database of all the anonymous FTP sites in the world, allowing you to find the site and/or name of a file to be retrieved. And using Archie by email can be convenient because some Archie searches take a LONG time to complete, leaving you to tap your toes in the meantime.

To use Archie by email, simply send an email message to one of the following addresses:

```
archie@archie.rutgers.edu
archie@archie.sura.net
archie@archie.unl.edu
archie@archie.doc.ic.ac.uk
```

To obtain detailed help for using Archie by mail, put the word

```
help
```

in the subject of the note and just send it off. You'll receive email explaining how to use archie services.

If you're the "just do it" type, then enter the command:

```
find <file>
```

where "<file>" is the name of the file to search for, in the BODY (not the subject) of the note.

This will search for files that match your criteria exactly. If you want to find files that contain your search criteria anywhere in their name, insert the line

```
set search sub
```

before the "find" command. Some other useful archie commands you might want to use are:

```
set maxhits 20
```
(limit output, default is 100 files)
```
set match_domain usa
```
(restrict output to FTP sites USA)
```
set output_format terse
```
(return output in condensed form)

When you get the results from your Archie query, it will contain the names of various sites at which the desired file is located. Use one of these site names and the directory/filename listed for your next FTP file retrieval request.

Now you've learned enough to locate that uudecode utility mentioned in the last section. Let's send email to archie@archie.rutgers.edu, and include the following lines in the message:

```
set match_domain usa
```
(restrict output to FTP sites in USA)
```
set search sub
```
(looking for a substring match...)
```
find uudecode
```
(must contain this string...)

Note: You'll be looking for the uudecode source code, not the executable version, which would of course be a binary file and would arrive uuencoded - a Catch 22!

Now you can use an ftpmail server to request "uudecode.bas" (if you have BASIC available) or "uudecode.c" (if you have a C compiler) from the `ftp.clarkson.edu` site.

It should be noted that the latest version of uudecode can be found at the SimTel repository. Send email to listserv@SimTel.coast.net, including any or all of these commands in the BODY of the note, and the requested files will be returned to you by email.

```
get uudecode.bas
get uudecode.c
get uudecode.doc
```

GOPHER BY EMAIL

Gopher is an excellent tool for exploring the Internet and is the best way to find a resource if you know what you want, but not where to find it. Gopher systems are menu-based, and provide a user-friendly front end to Internet resources, searches and information retrieval. Gopher knows where things are, thanks to the many volunteers who spend time creating pointers to useful collections of 'Net resources. And Gopher takes the rough edges off of the Internet by automating remote logins, hiding the sometimes-cryptic command sequences, and offers powerful search capabilities as well.

When visiting a Gopher site using a "live" Internet connection, one would specify the name of the site, navigate through a series of hierarchical menus to a desired resource, and then either read or transfer the information back to their home system.

Using Gopher by email is very similar, except that the desired site is reached through a special "gophermail server" which gophers to the remote site on your behalf and and returns the requested menu, submenu or file to you in response to a set of commands in an email message.

Although not every item on every menu will be accessible by "gopher-mail", you'll still find plenty of interesting things using this technique. Down to brass tacks... send email to:

```
gophermail@info.lanic.utexas.edu
```

You can optionally specify the address of a known gopher site on the Subject line to get the main menu for that site instead. Here are some interesting gopher sites you may like to explore at your leisure.

```
cwis.usc.edu
gopher.micro.umn.edu
english-server.hss.cmu.edu
```

Let's be bold and skip the HELP stuff for now. Fire off a note to one of the gophermail servers and specify

```
Subject: cwis.usc.edu
```

You'll get a message back from the server that looks something like the text in the figure below.

To proceed to a selection on the returned menu just email the whole text of the note (from the menu downwards) back to the gopher server, placing an "x" next to the items(s) you want to explore. You'll then receive the next level of the gopher menu by email. Some menu choices lead to other menus, some lead to text files, and some lead to searches. In the example above, let's select

```
x 9. Other Gophers & Info Resources
```

and mail the whole shebang right back at the gophermail server. You should then get a menu with a number of interesting selections including "Gopher Jewels". You'll find a LOT of good stuff along that path. The Gopher Jewels project is probably the best organized collection of Internet resources around.

```
Mail this file back to gopher with an X before the items you want.

    1. About USCgopher/
    2. How To Find Things on Gopher/
    3. University Information/
    4. Campus Life/
    5. Computing Information/
    6. Library and Research Information/
    7. Health Sciences/
    8. Research and Technology Centers/
    9. Other Gophers & Info Resources/

You may edit the following numbers to set the maximum sizes after
which GopherMail should send output as multiple email messages:

Split=27K bytes/message <- For text, bin, HQX messages
Menu=100 items/message <- For menus and query responses
#
Name=About USCgopher
Numb=1
Type=1
Port=70
Path=1/About_USCgopher
Host=cwis.usc.edu
# ... (some lines deleted) ...
Name=Other Gophers and Information Resources
Numb=9
Type=1
Port=70
Path=1/Other_Gophers_and_Information_Resources
Host=cwis.usc.edu
```

If a menu item is labelled "Search" you can select that item with an "x" and supply your search words in the Subject: of your reply. Note that your search criteria can be a single word or a boolean expression such as:

```
document and (historic or
    government)
```

Each of the results (the "hits") of your search will be displayed as an entry on yet another gopher menu!

Note: You needn't actually return the entire gopher menu and all the routing info that follows it each time you reply to the gophermail server. If you want to minimize the size of your query, you can strip out the "menu" portion at the top and include only the portion below that pertains to the menu selection you want.

Just remember that if you use this approach, you must specify "get all" on the Subject line. (Exception: for searching, specify only the search terms on the Subject line.) The example below is equivalent to selecting "option 9" as we did earlier.

```
Split=OK bytes/message
Menu=0 items/message
#
Name=Other Gophers
Numb=9
Type=1
Port=70
Path=1/Other_Gophers_and_
   Information_Resources
Host=cwis.usc.edu
```

If this looks like nonsense to you, here's a human translation:

Connect to PORT 70 of the HOST (computer) at "cwis.usc.edu", retrieve the sub-menu "Other Gophers", and send it to me in ONE PIECE, regardless of its size.

Note: Sometimes gophermail requests return a blank menu or message. This is likely because the server failed to connect to the host from which you were trying to get your information. Send your request again, it'll probably work.

VERONICA BY EMAIL

Speaking of searches, this is a good time to mention Veronica. Just as Archie provides a searchable index of FTP sites, Veronica provides this funct-ion for "gopherspace". Veronica will ask you what you want to look for (your search words) and then display another menu listing all the gopher menu items that match your search. In typical gopher fashion, you can then select one

of these items and "gopher it"!

To try Veronica by email, retrieve the main menu from a gophermail server using the method just described. Then try the choice labelled "Other Gopher and Information Servers". This menu will have an entry for Veronica.

You'll have to select one (or more) Veronica servers to handle your query, specifying the search words in the Subject of your reply. Here's another example of where using email servers can save time and money. Often the Veronica servers are very busy and tell you to "try again later". So select 2 or 3 servers, and chances are one of them will be able to handle your request the first time around.

A Gophermail Shortcut: The path to some resources, files or databases can be a bit tedious, requiring several email messages to the gophermail server. But here's the good news... If you've done it once, you can re-use any of the email messages previously sent in, changing it to suit your current needs. As an example, here's a clipping from the Veronica menu you would get by following the previous instructions. You can send these lines to any gophermail server to run a Veronica search.

```
Split=64K bytes/message <- For
text, bin, HQX messages  (0 = No
split)
Menu=100 items/message <- For menus
and query responses (0 = No split)
#
Name=Search GopherSpace by Title
word(s) (via NYSERNet)
Type=7
```

```
Port=2347
Path=
Host=empire.nysernet.org
```

Specify the search words in the Subject line and see what turns up! You can use boolean expressions in Veronica searches. For a guide to composing Veronica searches, send these lines to a gophermail server:

```
Name=How to Compose Veronica
  Queries
Path=0/veronica/how-to-query-
  veronica
Host=veronica.scs.unr.edu
```

USENET BY EMAIL

Usenet is a collection of over 5000 discussion groups on every topic imaginable. In order to get a proper start and avoid embarrasing yourself needlessly, you must read the Usenet new users intro document, which can be obtained by sending email to:

```
mail-server@rtfm.mit.edu
```

and include this line in the BODY of the note:

```
send usenet/news.answers/
  news-newusers-intro
```

To get a listing of Usenet newsgroups, add these commands to your note:

```
send usenet/news.answers/
  active-newsgroups/part1
send usenet/news.answers/
  active-newsgroups/part2
send usenet/news.answers/
  alt-hierarchies/part1
send usenet/news.answers/
  alt-hierarchies/part2
```

To get the FAQ (Frequently Asked Questions) file(s) for a given newsgroup, try a command like this:

```
index usenet/<newsgroupname>
```

(Substitute dots for dashes if they appear in the newsgroup name.) If any FAQ files are available, they will be listed in the returned info, and you can request them with a command like:

```
send usenet/<newsgroupname>/
  <faqfilename>
```

Once you've handled the preliminaries, you'll need to know how to read and contribute to Usenet newsgroups by email. To read a newsgroup, you can use the gophermail service discussed earlier in this guide.

To obtain a list of recent postings to a particular newsgroup, send the following lines to one of the gophermail servers mentioned previously. Specify "Subject: get all" and include only these lines in the message body.

(You must replace "<newsgroup>" below with the name of the Usenet newsgroup you wish to access. eg:

```
    alt.answers,
    biz.comp.services,
    news.newusers.questions, etc.)
```

```
------- begin gophermail message
    (do not include this line)
    Name=<newsgroup>
    Type=1
    Port=4320
    Path=nntp ls <newsgroup>
    Host=gopher.ic.ac.uk
------- end gophermail message
    (do not include this line)
```

If this doesn't work, you can try another Host by substituting one of the lines below.

```
Host=infopub.uqam.ca
   (limited coverage)
Host=teetot.acusd.edu
   (sometimes works)
```

Note that many of these sites carry only a limited range of newsgroups, so you may have to try several before finding one which carries the newsgroup you're looking for. When the newsgroup does not exist, gophermail sends something like "'nntp ls <newsgroup>': path does not exist". When a site does not accept outside requests, gophermail sends something like "Sorry, we don't accept requests outside campus".

If successful, the gophermail server will send you a typical gopher menu on which you may select the individual postings you wish to read.

Note: The gophermail query in this example is the greatly edited result of many previous queries. I've pared it down to the bare essentials so it can be tailored and reused.

If you decide to make a post of your own, mail the text of your post to:

```
group.name@pubnews.demon.co.uk
group.name@dispatch.demon.co.uk
group.name@bull.com
group.name@cass.ma02.bull.com
group.name@paris.ics.uci.edu
group.name@crs4gw.crs4.it
group.name@berlioz.crs4.it
group.name.usenet@canaima.
   Berkeley.EDU
group.name@charm.magnus.acs.
```

```
ohio-state.edu (???)
group.name@undergrad.math.
   uwaterloo.ca (???)
group.name@nic.funet.fi (???)
```

(For an updated list send e-mail to mg5n+remailers@andrew.cmu.edu)

For example, to post to
`news.newusers.questions`
you might send your message to:

```
news.newusers.questions@
   pubnews.demon.co.uk
```

Be sure to include an appropriate Subject: line, and include your real name and e-mail address at the close of your note.

WAIS SEARCHES BY EMAIL

WAIS stands for Wide Area Information Service, and is a means of searching a set of over 500 indexed databases. The range of topics is too broad to mention, and besides, you'll soon learn how to get the topic list for yourself.

I recommend that you send email to "waismail@sunsite.unc.edu" with HELP in the body of the note to get the full WAISmail user guide. But if you can't wait, use the info below as a quickstart.

A list of WAIS databases (or "resources" as they like to be called) can be obtained by sending email to the waismail server with the line

```
search xxx xxx
```

in the body of the note. Look through the returned list for topics that are of interest to you and use one of them in the next example.

OK, let's do an actual search. Send email to:

```
waismail@sunsite.unc.edu
```

with the following commands in the note body:

```
maxres 10
search bush-speeches lips
```

This will tell WAISmail to search through the text of the "bush-speeches" database and return a list of at most 10 documents containing "lips".

A successful search will return one or more "DOCid:" lines, which identify the location of the matching documents. To retrieve the full text of a matching document, send one of the returned "DOCid:" lines (exactly as is) in the body of your next message to WAISmail.

(**Note**: The WAISmail server at "quake.think.com" is defunct. The server listed above still had a few bugs as of this writing, so if it doesn't work, try the WAIS via gophermail method described next.)

A list of WAIS databases can also be obtained by sending email to gophermail@calvin.edu with
  "Subject: get all"
and these lines in the message body:

```
Type=1
Name=WAIS Databases
Path=1/WAISes/Everything
Host=gopher-gw.micro.umn.edu
```

```
Port=70
```

Look through the returned list for topics that are of interest to you and select one to search. Specify your search term(s) on the Subject line, and clip out just the section of the returned gopher menu that corresponds to your target database. For example:

```
Type=7+
Name=bush-speeches.src
Path=waissrc:/WAISes/
   Everything/bush-speeches
Host=gopher-gw.micro.umn.edu
Port=70
```

You will (hopefully) receive a gophermail menu in response listing the matching "documents". To retrieve the full text of a matching document, just make a selection from the returned gopher menu, and the referenced file will be sent to you.

In my testing, WAIS by gophermail was not reliable. Often a blank menu was returned but repeated attempts did eventually meet with success.

WORLD-WIDE WEB BY EMAIL

The World-Wide Web is touted as the future of Internet navigational tools. It's a hypertext and multimedia system that lets you hop around the Net, read documents, and access images & sounds linked to a source.

Have you ever heard someone say, "Wow, check out the cool stuff at http://www.somewhere.com/blah. html" and wondered what the heck they were talking about? Now you can retrieve WWW documents by email using the Agora WWW-mail server in Switzerland.

All you need to know is the Uniform Resource Locator (or URL, that long ugly string starting with "http:", "gopher:", or "ftp:") which defines the address of the document, and you can retrieve it by sending email to:

    agora@www.undp.org

In the body of your note include one of these lines, replacing "<URL>" with the actual URL specification.

    send <URL>

This will send you back the document you requested, with a list of all the documents referenced within, so that you may make further requests.

    deep <URL>

Same as above, but it will also send you the documents referenced in the URL you specified. (May result in a LOT of data coming your way!)

To try WWW by email send the following commands to agora@mail.w3.org :

    www send http://www.w3.org

You'll receive in due course the Agora help file and the "WWW Welcome Page" from Cern which will include references to other Web documents you'll want to explore.

Note: The URL you specify may contain only the following characters: a-z, A-z, 0-9, and these special characters /:._-+@%*()?~

As mentioned earlier, you can also get Usenet postings from the WWW mail server. Here are some examples:

    send news:comp.unix.aix
    (returns a list of recent postings)
    deep news:comp.unix.aix
    (returns the list AND the postings, this can be a LOT of data!)

There is another WWW-mail server whose address is:

    webmail@curia.ucc.ie

This server requires commands in the form: go <URL>

Note: The WWW-mail servers are sometimes unavailable for days (or weeks) at a time without explanation. If you get an error or no reply, retry in a day or so.

WWW SEARCH BY EMAIL

There's a lot of great stuff out on the Web, but how do you find it? Well, just like Archie and Veronica help you search FTP and gopher sites, there are several search engines that have been developed to search for information on the Web. But until now, you had to have direct Internet access to use them.

After a bit of research, I have found that it is possible to use several WWW search mechanisms by email. Here are some sample queries that you can use to search via Lycos, WebCrawler and the CUI W3 Catalog. Any of these lines can be sent to the agora@mail.w3.org address to perform a search. If you're not interested in spam or frogs, then by all means feel free to use your own search keywords.

For Lycos, append a dot to your keywords to force an exact match, or you will get a substring search by default. Separate words with a "+" sign.

```
http://query1.lycos.cs.cmu.edu
  /cgi-bin/pursuit?spam
http://query1.lycos.cs.cmu.edu
  /cgi-bin/pursuit?spam.
http://query1.lycos.cs.cmu.edu
  /cgi.bin/pursuit?frog.+dissection.
```

For WebCrawler searches you must separate words with a "+" sign. All searches are exact, no trailing dot required.

```
http://webcrawler.cs.washingto
  n.edu/cgi-bin/WebQuery?spam
http://webcrawler.cs.washington.ed
  u/cgi-bin/WebQuery?frog+dissection
```

For CUI W3 Catalog searches you must separate words with "%20" as below. All searches are exact, no trailing dot required.

```
http://cuiwww.unige.ch/
  w3catalog?spam
http://cuiwww.unige.ch/
  w3catalog?frog%20dissection
```

MAILING LISTS

There are literally thousands of discussion groups that stay in touch using email based systems known as "mailing lists". People interested in a topic "subscribe" to a "list" and then send and receive postings by email. For a good introduction to this topic, send

email to:

```
LISTSERV@vm1.nodak.edu
```

In the body of your note include only this command:

```
GET NEW-LIST WOUTERS
```

Finding a Mailing List

To find out about mailing lists that are relevant to your interests, send the following command to the same address given above.

```
LIST GLOBAL /keyword
```

(Of course you must replace "keyword" with an appropriate search word such as Marketing, Education, etc.)

Another helpful document which details the commands used to subscribe, unsubscribe and search mailing list archives can be had by sending to:

```
LISTSERV@ubvm.cc.buffalo.edu
```

In the body of your note include only this command:

```
get mailser cmd nettrain
f=mail
```

New in These Parts?

If you're new to the Internet, I suggest you subscribe to the HELP-NET list where you're likely to find answers to your questions. Send the command:

```
SUBSCRIBE HELP-NET
  <Firstname Lastname>
```

in the BODY of a note to LISTSERV@VM.TEMPLE.EDU, then email your questions to the list address:

165

`HELP-NET@VM.TEMPLE.EDU`

FINGER BY EMAIL

"Finger" is a utility that returns information about another user. Usually it's just boring stuff like last logon, etc., but sometimes people put fun or useful information in their finger replies. To try out finger, send email with

```
Subject: FINGER
jtchern@headcrash.berkeley.edu.
To: infobot@infomania.com
```

You'll receive current sports standings! (The general form is FINGER user@site.)

Just for kicks, try finger using a combination of gopher and WWW. Send this:

```
send
gopher://<site>:79/0<user>
```

to the WWWmail server mentioned earlier.

"DIRECTORY ASSISTANCE" BY EMAIL

"WHOIS" is a service that queries a database of Internet names and addresses. If you're looking for someone or you want to know where a particular Internet site is located, send email with

```
Subject: whois <name>
To: mailserv@internic.net
```

Try substituting "mit.edu" or the last name of someone you know in place of "<name>" and see what comes back!

Another alternative name looker-upper is a database at MIT which keeps tabs on everyone who has posted a message on Usenet. Send email to "mail-server@rtfm.mit.edu" and include this command ONLY in the BODY:

```
send usenet-addresses/<name>
```

Specify as much information as you can about the person (lastname, firstname, userid, site, etc.) to limit the amount of information that is returned to you. Here's a sample query to find the address of someone you think may be at Harvard University:

```
send usenet-addresses/
    Jane Doe Harvard
```

NETFIND is another more powerful search engine that uses a person's name and keywords describing a physical location to return a bunch of info about the person (or persons) who fit the bill.

Let's say we want to find someone named Hardy at the University of Colorado in Boulder. Our Netfind query will be addressed to

```
agora@mail.w3.org
```
and will contain the only line:

```
gopher://ds.internic.net:4320/7net
find%20dblookup?hardy+boulder+colora
do
```

Netfind works in two phases. First it displays a list of internet domains that match your keywords, then it looks for the person in the domain you select. Netfind by email is very similar, in that you'll receive a listing of matching domains from which you must make one or more selections.

Each selection is numbered and there are corresponding "gopher://" commands at the bottom of the listing. Let's pick the selection for

```
cs.colorado.edu computer science
dept, university of colorado,
boulder
```

which means that our next command to agora@mail.w3.org will be:

```
gopher://ds.internic.net:4320/0netfi
nd%20netfind%20hardy%20cs.colorado.e
du
```

If all goes well, you'll receive a list something like this:

```
full_name: HARDY, JOE
```
   (not a real person)
```
email: CrazyJoe@Colorado.EDU
phone: (303) 492-1234
address: Campus Box 777
department: COMPUTER SCIENCE
```

Note that if you know the person's domain name already, you can jump right in with a query like the latter one above.

You can also try the "Four11 Online User Directory", a free directory of users and their email addresses. Send email to info@four11.com for details on how to search the Four11 directory.

ADDRESS/NAME SERVER INFO BY EMAIL

This is a little on the technical side, but anyway the Mail Name Server (dns@grasp.insa-lyon.fr) offers some useful services by email. Some of the commands you can send in the BODY of your note are:

```
help
```
   (full details)
```
ip host.foo.bar
```
   (get host's addresses)
```
name ip#
```
   (get host name from address)
```
ns host.foo.bar
```
   (get host's name servers)

TELNET BY EMAIL

Sorry, it can't be done. Actually it CAN be done, but apparently nobody has done it. I'd love to be proven wrong on this!

A FEW NET-GOODIES

Here are some other interesting things you can do by email. (Some of them are accessible only by email!)

• THE USENET ORACLE: A cooperative, anonymous and humorous exchange of questions and answers. Send email to oracle@cs.indiana.edu for more info.

• ALMANAC, WEATHER & THE SWEDISH CHEF: Infomania offers a bunch of other services by email! Almanac (daily updates), Weather, CD Music Catalog, etc. Send email to infobot@infomania.com with subject HELP for full details.

• SENDING A FAX BY EMAIL: Free faxing via the Internet? You bet. For details, send the line below to mail-server@rtfm.mit.edu (in BODY of note)
```
send usenet/news.answers/
   internet-services/fax-faq
```

• U.S. CONGRESS AND THE WHITE HOUSE: Find out if your congressman has an electronic address! Email to the address congress@hr.house.gov and you'll get a listing of congressional email addresses.

You can also contact the President (president@whitehouse.gov) or V. Pres. (vice.president@whitehouse.gov), but don't expect a reply by email. Messages sent to these addresses get printed out and handled just like regular paper correspondence!

• OTHER SOURCES OF US GOV'T INFO: Send the lines below to mailserver@rtfm.mit.edu (in BODY of note)
send usenet/news.answers/us-
    govt-net-pointers/part1
send usenet/news.answers/us-
    govt-net-pointers/part2

• INTERNET PATENT NEWS SERVICE: Send email to patents@world.std.com for more information on this service.

• THE INTERNET MALL: To get a copy of this long list of net-connected businesses, send email to taylor@netcom.com
with Subject: send mall

• FINDING EMAIL ADDRESSES: For a guide to finding someone's email addresses, send this line to mailserver@rtfm.mit.edu (in BODY of the note) send usenet/news.answers/
    finding-addresses

• SENDING MAIL TO VARIOUS NETWORKS: For a guide to communicating with people on the various networks that make up the Internet, send the line below to mailserver@rtfm.mit.edu
(in the BODY of the note)
send usenet/news.answers/
    mail/inter-network-guide

• SENDING MAIL TO FAMILY MEMBERS: Family Internet MailCall is a fee-based service that helps you keep in touch via a private mailing list. Details:
family-info@mailcall.com.

• USENET SEARCHES: A new service at Stanford University makes it possible to search USENET newsgroups for postings that contain keywords of interest to you. You can even "subscribe" and receive a daily list of newsgroup postings that match your search criteria. Send mail to
netnews@db.stanford.edu
with HELP in the body of note for full details.

• MOVIE INFO: To learn how to get tons of info on movies, actors, & directors, send mail to
movie@ibmpcug.co.uk with HELP in the body of the note.

• STOCK MARKET QUOTES: If you want to get a current quote for just 1 or 2 stocks, you can use the QuoteCom service. They offer this free service along with other fee based services. For details, send email to
    services@quote.com
with a subject of HELP.

• ANONYMOUS EMAIL: The "anon server" provides a front for sending

mail messages and posting to Usenet newsgroups anonymously, should the need ever arise. To get complete instructions, send email to
`help@anon.penet.fi`

• NET JOURNALS LISTING: I highly recommend 'The Internet Press - A guide to electronic journals about the Internet". To get it, send email with Subject:
`subscribe to ipress-request@northcoast.com`

• MUSI-CAL: Send email to `concerts@calendar.com` to retrieve a help message that tells how to use the Musi-Cal online concert calendar service.

• ASK DR. MATH: Have a math question? No problem's too big or too small for The Swat Team. Write to `dr.math@forum.swarthmore.edu`

• SCOUT REPORT: Scout Report is a weekly featuring announcements of new and interesting resources on the Internet. To subscribe, send email to `majordomo@is.internic.net` with "Subscribe scout-report" in body.

CONTACTING THE AUTHOR

"Doctor Bob", also known as Bob Rankin, welcomes your feedback on this guide and can be reached at the following addresses. Send corrections, ideas, suggestions and comments by email. I'll try to include any new email services in future editions of this guide.

Internet: `bobrankin@mhv.net`

MORE PUBLICATIONS FROM DOCTOR BOB!

"100 COOL THINGS TO DO ON THE INTERNET!"
"Doctor Bob's Internet Business Guide"

Send just $5 each (cash, check or money order) plus a SASE to:

```
--> DOCTOR BOB
--> PO BOX 39, DEPT U4
--> TILLSON, NY 12486  USA
```

Note: For email delivery (preferred) you can skip the envelope but make sure to send your email address along with your order.

Student Reactions to Online Education: Perceptions by participants of educational CMC are important indicators for appropriate development of methodology. Professor Mary McComb's assessment of her experiences is reprinted here by her permission.

Augmenting a Group Discussion Course with Computer Mediated Communication in a Small College Setting

by Mary McComb, Assistant Professor of Communication Arts
Marist College, Poughkeepsie, New York
Originally published by IPCT-J Interpersonal Computing and Technology

INTRODUCTION

In this case study, I will report on how students and I used computer-mediated communication (CMC) in a group discussion course at a small college. First I will describe the course and its objectives, including details on how CMC augmented the classroom and office-hour communication among the professor and student groups. Next I will review the advantages of using CMC to augment instructional communication, drawing on pertinent literature, as well as my own experience as both teacher and former student in CMC-augmented courses. Finally, I will report on students' responses to a survey about their attitudes about CMC in the group discussion course.

Course Description

The course, Group Discussion Skills (GDS), was for junior or senior students. It was offered as a Special Topics course and was also an IBM Showcase project--to demonstrate how Marist College is using the IBM mainframe for instruct-ion. Course design was similar to that of a Pennsylvania State University group discussion course in which I was involved for seven semesters as a graduate teaching assistant. That course has been previously described (Phillips, 1989; Santoro & Phillips, 1989; Santoro, Phillips, & Kuehn, 1988). One of the reasons for augmenting the Penn State course was to make it possible for instructors to teach more students per semester for the much-in-demand group communication course. That rationale does not apply to Marist, with a total enrollment of about 4200 and maximum class sizes in the Communication Arts program of about 30 students. Marist has a tradition of intense student-teacher contact. Faculty are required, for example, to schedule eight office hours a week, and Marist students use those office hours. Marist students seem to value face-to-face contact with faculty, so I wondered whether they would resist CMC. One of my concerns in augmenting classroom communication with CMC was that students might think it extraneous. Would they would take advantage of this novel communication channel?

Course objectives included teaching students a procedure for group problem-solving, called "Standard Agenda", as well as communication skills for leadership, conflict resolution, cross-gender communication, and general participation in problem-solving groups. (See Phillips, 1989, for a theoretical basis for this type of course design.) The course was designed as a corporate simulation, with students assigned to their working groups for the entire semester. Working in semester-long groups allows students to experience the maturation and growth that take place in long-term groups, and duplicates real-life situations in which work group members must communicate with colleagues over time.

For their final project, groups were charged with completing a professionally-written proposal, an action plan to educate people to be discerning media audience members. Interim group assignments took students through the Standard Agenda phases, allowing me to ascertain that they were understanding and following the procedure. I didn't grade these assignments; rather I commented on what needed to be fixed, and asked them to revise the work until it was evident that they had fulfilled the requirements of that particular Standard Agenda phase. An outside evaluator and I graded the final group projects. I awarded two A's, one B, and one C. The outside evaluator awarded

one A (we agreed on the top project), one B, and two C's.

As instructor, I acted as a supervisor, consultant, coach, and, finally, evaluator. In class sessions, I briefed the students on the goals and necessary action for each Standard Agenda phase, and offered practical, skills-based instruction in effective group communication behaviors in the areas of leadership, conflict management, and cross-gender communication. Formal classes met according to need, but fairly infrequently -- 17 class periods out of a possible 28 in a 15-week semester. Ten class periods were left open for groups to work together. During these group work sessions, I was available in my office for consultation. I coached students through the process when they requested my help, either in class, during office hours, or via electronic mail. I also guided them in comments on their interim assignments. More consultation was provided as we monitored group communication patterns through the use of SYMLOG, a method of evaluating group interaction developed by Robert Bales and colleagues (Bales, 1970; Bales & Cohen, 1979). SYMLOG helped students to diagnose and solve problems within their groups. (For a thorough description of SYMLOG use in group discussion courses, see Kelly, Kuehn, & McComb, 1989.)

This pattern of meeting infrequently in classroom meetings, groups working independently, and consulting with the

171

instructor on as as-needed basis, attempted to duplicate, within an academic setting, the activities of a real-life work group. In most small group courses, groups meet under the instructor's eyes, at designated times and places. However, in this course, groups were in charge of when and where they met, an arrangement that more closely resembles group work in an organization, in which the supervisor would not hover over the group, but would expect it to function autonomously. Like a supervisor, I tracked group progress by asking for and evaluating their work, requiring regular progress reports, and meeting with the groups occasionally for SYMLOG evaluations or when they requested consultations. I expected the groups to contact me when they needed clarification or assistance. CMC was the medium that enabled students to work independently, yet keep in touch with me and with each other.

CMC AUGMENTATION

Marist assigns each incoming student a mainframe computer account. Although all Marist students must take a required Introduction to Computers course, not all the students had done so prior to my course, so I held a simple training session at the semester's beginning. Only two students from each of the four groups, however, were required to use the computer system. They were designated the group's official "Communicators" and were responsible for computer liaison between their

group and myself. Nineteen students actually used the computer during the course; only five never logged on.

Each student could send and receive private electronic mail, (email) and had a private online "file cabinet" to store mail and other course materials, and had a simple online text editor. Each student also had access to a read-only online file library containing course documents--syllabus, assignment outlines, lecture outlines, grading criteria, bibliographies, and other material--that would otherwise have been provided as handouts. Finally, all students were able to read and post to a private class "bulletin board" on which I posted schedule or requirement changes and other important class announcements.

The computer system was used for the following interactions in the course:

1. Students submitted their group assignments to me. I inserted my comments in capital letters under the pertinent text in their work, asked them to resubmit until the work was "good enough" to continue, and send the assignments back.

2. Students or groups sent questions or concerns to me or to other students as private mail.

3. I sent instructions, questions, directions, guidance, etc. to groups or individuals as private mail.

4. Groups sent me weekly group process reports as private email. I responded to problem areas or

issued praise in return mail.

5. Students wrote and edited their assignments online using the text editor.

6. Some groups wrote their assignments on a word processor, uploaded them and sent them to me.

7. I posted class announcements on the bulletin board.

8. Students posted messages (although not too many) on the bulletin board.

9. I made course materials that would otherwise have been handouts available on the library disk.

10. Through Internet, students had access to other resources, such as Comserve discussion groups, as well as an outside grader for the final project.

ADVANTAGES OF CMC

A brief review of literature on CMC-augmented instruction indicates that its advantages are a result of three characteristics: a) asynchronicity, b) efficient information access, and c) increased social distance. In the following discussion, I will talk about benefits of CMC that accrue from these characteristics.

Asynchronicity

This characteristic means that people don't have to be logged onto the computer system at the same time in order to communicate. Asynchronicity frees students and teachers from time and distance limitations. It also allows either reflective or spontaneous inter-

action (Harasim, 1986, p. 66). GDS students, for instance, could send me a question during a late-night meeting. The next morning when I logged on, I could respond to their note, which they could then read next time their official communicator checked the mail.

Benefits that emerge from asynchronicity include convenience, more contact among class participants, more control of communication for students, and the necessity to communicate in writing.

Convenience

CMC as an adjunct to classroom instruction allows both students and teachers more convenient communication. Course participants don't have to wait until class, office hours, or to connect via a telephone call to communicate with each other. This timeliness means that students can get questions answered quickly (Kuehn, 1988), and that communication can be continuous (Phillips & Santoro, 1989). Stranded at home in a snowstorm this winter, I was still able to communicate via CMC with my students 15 miles away.

Another convenient factor of CMC is the ability to communicate directly with a particular sub-group or audience within a larger class. Instructors can respond to students' particular questions and needs, without taking up class time to work on a problem affecting only one group (Phillips & Santoro, 1989, p. 160). Most email systems make it possible for users to pre-set "bulk" mailing lists. For instance, I had mailing lists set up for each group. By typing "mail Bruin" I could then compose a note that, when sent, would automatically reach the six Bruin group members. I also had a pre-set list of all group communicators. By typing "mail allcoms" my note would reach all eight communicators. CMC's convenience can make more contact possible among course participants, as I will discuss next.

More Interaction

Another benefit of freedom from spatio-temporal limitations is more interaction and more flexibility in communication among class members and thus potentially more exchange of ideas, increased participation and variety of interchange.

To faculty teaching some 200 undergraduates in the Penn State group communication course, the main advantage of the move to CMC-facilitated instruction was increased student-teacher contact (Phillips, Santoro, & Kuehn, 1988). In one semester, the senior instructor received and responded to 3,169 messages. In a subsequent semester of the same course, he handled more than 5,500 separate transactions. Students handled an average of 35 transactions each, with group communicators handling an average of 400 each (Phillips & Santoro, 1988). A Canadian continuing education course also had similar high rates of participation. During the 12-week course, there were 3,312 conference items and about 4,475 personal notes. This averaged to about

85 conference submissions and 120 personal notes per person (Harasim, 1986, p. 62).

In the 24-student GDS course I read and responded to 59 student notes (not including my comments on each group's 15 weekly reports) and sent 17 additional messages to groups or individuals. I posted 36 messages on the class bulletin board. Only one student posted a message. I also engaged in synchronous "TELL" communication, (single line messages, interactively exchanged), when students and I were logged on at the same time, although I did not tally the number of these conversations, nor did I tally the number of face-to-face conversations I had with individuals or groups.

Increased Control

Another advantage of CMC is that it turns more of the control over the instructional communication over to students. The Brazilian educator Paulo Freire (1983) uses the term "banking education" to describe traditional instruction in which the "all-wise" professor pours knowledge into the empty vaults in the students' heads. The instructor distributing materials to the waiting students, or lecturing them, or calling on them in class discussions are instances of the active instructor-passive student dichotomy. CMC, however, allows students to initiate communication with the instructor without waiting for permission to talk. Students can read or print online materials that they feel they need, instead of having to wait until class to get materials. If they lose the documents, they can simply print another or consult copy online. Both the frequency and immediacy of communication, as well as the option for the students, to initiate contact--aspects that give the students more control over the educational transaction (Garrison & Baynton, 1987)--exist in the CMC environment. On the other hand, instructors lose some control. You can encourage a response in the classroom, but when you make a query on email you can't force an answer.

Having class materials on the mainframe encourages student initiative and responsibility. With online handouts, students must be responsible for getting their own materials, instead of waiting passively for the instructor to hand them out. Mainframe communication can also encourage students to seek consultation or help more assertively. In a classroom, a good instructor will monitor students' nonverbal behaviors. If she sees grumbling or scowling faces, for instance, she can tease out the questions, concerns, or problems. Again, the instructor is doing most of the work here. With part of the instructional dialogue taking place on the computer, students must take initiative to write the instructor with their problems or concerns.

Communication in Writing

A final benefit of asynchronicity is the need to communicate in writing. The limitation to written communication

encourages a clearer and more organized articulation of ideas, which fosters critical thinking habits. The permanence of retrievability of CMC communications may also encourage careful critical thought. According to Hernandez, Mockus, Granes, Charum, & Castro (1987)

The responsibility involved in writing is... much more serious than that involved in the spoken word. What is heard from the living voice can be modified by passing from one hearer to the other, be adapted to situations, be forgotten. The written word remains. (p. 68)

In spoken communication, the hearer can immediately interrupt for clarification when the speaker's meaning is unclear or confusing, or the speaker will see from the hearer's facial expression that he is confused, and then can clear up the confusion. Spoken ideas need not be perfectly articulated because of this opportunity for instant feedback. But a reader's questions or misunderstandings cannot be cleared up as he or she happens upon them. So a writer must make ideas, questions, direction of thought, bases for claims, and so forth, completely explicit. Writers using CMC must work for explicitness and clarity. Writing forces them to think their ideas through in order that they be understood, thus the necessity to write sharpens one's critical thinking abilities.

But CMC also gives participants time to compose their thoughts carefully. The time for reflection and the distance of the written interaction allow the slow thinker or shy person opportunity to interact just as much as the quicker or bolder person, who can, however, still interact at his or her own pace without having to wait for permission. CMC "can provide the experience of learning from each other to students who would be too shy or lacking in self-confidence to make a presentation in front of a face-to-face group or are simply unprepared at the time to speak off the cuff..." (Mason, 1988, p. 38). A participant in a Canadian CMC class reported, "the nature of conferencing allows an individual to finish her thoughts without fear of being interrupted by a keen, more outgoing colleague. I feel this is a great equalizing force in a group" (Harasim, 1986, p. 66).

EFFICIENT INFORMATION ACCESS

The second set of benefits from CMC results from easily accessible online information. Course materials can be provided online; messages sent and received can be automatically filed away for future reference; the Internet allows access to a wealth of information.

Online Course Materials

Using CMC, instructors can put materials online which would other-wise need to be photocopied, collated, stapled, and distributed. This elimin-ates last-minute rushes to printers or to the campus copy center. I don't have to wait until class time to make resources available to the students but can post handouts at any time. Also solved is the problem of students losing handouts. They simply print out another one.

Automatic "Paper Trail"

Most email systems allow users to automatically save copies of messages sent and received. For instance, I save all correspondence for each group in what our computer system calls a notebook. These "paper" trails make it easy for me to track a group's problem areas, or refer to how other groups and I handled problems. File and mail management systems allow easy callup of all correspondence and assignments for a particular semester, invaluable when grading time comes around. Online storage also aids face-to-face meeting with groups. Sitting around a computer, teachers and students can easily refer to the assignment they are discussing (Kuehn, 1988). Students can also compare their assignments with those of other student groups (Phillips & Santoro, 1989).

Access to the Internet

Finally, through campus mainframes that are connected to the Internet, students and faculty have access to information from literally the entire world. Negotiating the Internet isn't necessarily straightforward, but more and more documentation and instruction is available on using the Internet to gather information and communicate with others worldwide. In GDS, I communicated with an outside evaluator on the Internet; he sent his grading criteria online to me and I posted it for my students. I forwarded the students' final projects online for him to grade; he sent his rankings back. In a senior thesis course at Marist that also uses the computer system, some groups have subscribed to COMSERVE hotlines as part of their fact-finding effort.

Increased Social Distance

The final set of benefits that accrue from CMC are a result of the increased social distance of this communication medium. CMC lacks visual and auditory cues, an absence that some users regard as an inadequacy (Hiltz, 1978, p. 160), that can result in a "sense of depersonalization" (Hiltz, 1986, p. 96). "Social interaction online does not seem 'natural' at first" (Hiltz, 1986, p. 100). But Feenberg (1987) reports that

CMC users often feel they gain a more immediate access to each other's thought processes, undistracted by the status signaling and social games that are played simultaneously with speech in face-to-face encounters.... ordinary individuals possess the 'literary' capability necessary to project their personalities in written texts. The loss of the interlocutor's bodily presence does not signify impersonality, but freedom from undesirable social constraints. (p. 174)

Students who might be too shy to speak to the instructor or other students face to face might find it easier to communicate online. Phillips & Santoro (1989) report

students could argue and disagree without involving excessive emotions or personalities. Shy students were at no disadvantage. They had opportunities to enter discussions which would have intimidated them had they been conducted face to face. Even though the groups met regularly, individuals could make their comments on the system and have them automatically included on the agenda without having to fight their way into the discussion"(p. 160).

In an essay on student help-seeking in computer conferences, Karabenick (1987) speculates that students would find it easier to ask help via CMC than in person, because of CMC's greater interpersonal distance. Phillips & Santoro (1989) did find that "students could ask questions without publicly embarrassing themselves" (p. 159-60).

In this brief review, I've discussed the advantages of CMC-augmented instruction. Asynchronicity provides more convenience for participants, the potential for more contact, more control for students, and the necessity to communicate in writing. Computer systems' storage and communication capabilities means easy access to course materials, "paper trails" of assignments and messages, and contact with information resources worldwide through the Internet. Finally, CMC's increased social distance might encourage shy people to communicate and ask questions without embarrassment, as well as encourage discussion of ideas rather than personalities.

GDS SURVEY

I wanted to find out how students felt about using CMC in the GDS course. I limited the survey to the advantages that result from the characteristic of asynchronicity--convenience, control, and written communication. Specifically, I wanted to identify a) what advantages in communication they identified in the CMC-augmented class versus a regular class, and b) whether they regarded CMC as making the class more rewarding than non-CMC-augmented classes. I also wanted to compare differences in responses between the 19

students in the class who used CMC and the five students who didn't use the computer system.

All 24 students completed a survey on course evaluation day. I instructed students not to write their names on the surveys. The forced-choice survey also had adequate space for students to explain their answers. Below I report: a) student perceptions about how CMC improved communication with the instructor and with other groups, compared to non-CMC-augmented classes, b) student reports on whether their groups ever avoided communicating with me using CMC, and c) comparisons between CMC users and non-users about the bulletin board, career utility of learning CMC, and rewards of CMC.

RESULTS

Table 1 - Students' attitudes on CMC advantages for group communication with the instructor, compared to other classes.

Item	Students (n=24)	
1. Instructor answered our notes quickly	21	88%
2. Group could initiate communication with instructor	21	88%
3. Group could communicate with instructor without waiting for class or office hours	21	88%
4. More detailed instructor comments on assignments	20	83%
5. Able to turn in assignments or reports at any time	20	83%
6. Communication with instructor could occur any time	19	79%
7. Quicker turnaround time on assignments	19	79%
8. More frequent communication with instructor	17	71%
9. Seeing our instructor's thoughts in writing helped us understand her thoughts	13	54%
10. Having to express our ideas in writing helped clarify our thoughts	11	46%

Nineteen students explained their answers either in the space provided or elsewhere on the survey form. These comments did not fall neatly into easily recognizable categories. Students would write about more than one advantage, or mention advantages in other sections of the survey. I sorted the comments in terms of their "gist," the advantages that their comment reflected most clearly and directly. Five students commented on several advantages. One student said,

This way of communicating was beneficial to all of us because we could get quick responses to ?'s w/out having to play "phone tag." We also followed the instructor's advice/criticism/comments to help us get our assignments done quickly.

Another said,

Through the computer, the group was able to type in questions at any time. This was especially useful when we were all in a group meeting & we all had various questions. We were able to ask the questions as a group as opposed to separately. It saved time. In addition, we were able to get our assignments back quicker & able to do rewrites on the original copy instead of having to rewrite the whole assignment.

A third remarked,

We could talk to the instructor as often as we needed to and at any given time. Our answers always came within hours. Her responses

were more helpful because she gave examples and detailed notes in the actual assignment. Convenience played a big role.

Convenience, time factors, and improved access to the instructors were advantages most often written about. For example,

It was nice if we had a problem we could send it over the computer and in turn we would get a very rapid response. Communication over the computer saves a lot of time!

Nine comments stressed improved access to the instructor. For example,

It's convenient because professors are not always in their office and I found that our professor answered EMAIL quicker than phone mail.

And,

I felt that using the computers gave our group better access to the professor.

Four students commented on the usefulness of having comments in writing. For example,

Having communication access with the computer allowed for a more understandable way of expressing our thoughts & ideas as well as interpreting the instructor's.

And:

Having Mary's comments written out whenever she saw a problem was quite advantageous for us & showed

179

us exactly where we went wrong or if we were exactly right.

Two students appreciated the ability to communicate either as individuals or as a group. For example,

Our group could communicate with the instructor at any time without the hassle of dealing with office hours. An individual group member or the whole group could communicate with the instructor in a detailed, convenient fashion.

I did not survey the students about advantages from increased access to resources or social distance. However, students did recognize social distance as a characteristic of CMC. Two students emphasized the need for face-to-face communication in addition to the computer. For example,

Communication was higher but the actual 1-1 talking cleared up confusion more.

One student did say, however, that CMC "made me feel more comfortable in approaching teacher for help on questions or problems with assignments."

I was also curious if CMC ever inhibited students' communication with me. So one survey question asked, "Were there any times that your group hesitated to contact your instructor over the computer system?" Table 2 presents the results.

Table 2 - Student hesitation to contact instructor via CMC

Q. Were there any times that your group hesitated to contact your instructor over the computer system?		5 YES	19 NO
Reasons			
1. Students (n=24) who checked item			
2. Preferred talking to her by phone or in person		3	
3. Were not sure she would answer our note		0	
4. Hard to put our question or concerns in writing--easier to talk than write		2	
5. When we had questions, we weren't near a computer terminal		0	
6. We thought she would disapprove if we asked questions or were confused--that our group's reputation would fall in her eyes		2	
Other			
1 ("needed immediate attention and couldn't wait for a computer response--- knew she was in the office")			

Explanations included, "group decided it might be quicker to call our professor"; "usually wanted to 'figure out our problems' alone." Comments in this section again indicated social distance was a concern for two students:

One said,

I found that a face to face meeting was more beneficial than one over the computer.

Another said,

We used the computer very often because it was more efficient. It was better than running around looking for Professor McComb. The only time we did not use the computer is if we had a major problem and felt it would be more effective to talk to her in person.

Although course design did not require that each student log on to the computer, I had noticed that most students were doing so. I wanted to know if students perceived any advantages for student/student communication in the class. Table 3 presents students' attitudes about CMC advantages for communicating with fellow group members.

Table 3 Students' attitudes on CMC advantages for group communication w/ fellow group members, compared to other classes.

Item	Students (N=24)	
1. Able to edit pieces of assignments together	18	75%
2. Communication with group members could occur at any time	16	67%
3. Able to work faster	14	58%
4. Group could initiate communication with each other	11	46%
5. Seeing group members' thoughts in writing helped us understand their ideas	8	33%
6. More frequent communication with group members	7	29%
7. Having to express our ideas in writing helped clarify our thoughts	5	21%
8. Group members answered our notes quickly	3	13%

As Table 2 indicates, fewer students were convinced of CMC's advantages for student to student communication than were convinced of improved student-instructor communication. Perhaps this was because only 19 out of the 24 students used the computer.

Four students complained about non-users. For example,

The use of computer was beneficial to see if computer will become a part of the classroom of the future. The only problem is a lot of people are not computer literate-leaving the burden to us "computer geeks" to do assignments.

Another said,

Only 2 or 3 of us were regularly checking our E-mail, so it was not used to its full potential.

Typical comments from those who

recognized benefits to group work included:

For those who used the computer - it improved communication. -Notes could be sent whenever. - Asgs were emailed in if they could not attend a meeting.

And,

Each group member would work on a section individually and then the whole group's work would be put together. This was more convenient and less time consuming. Also, members could communicate with one another at anytime, which was also convenient.

Finally,

If we were supposed to meet in the computer center and one of us couldn't make it or we moved to the library it was easy to just send a quick note on mail to another member. This was more reliable than using a phone.

I wanted to know if there were any differences in attitudes about the class between computer users and computer non-users. Table 4 presents differences in attitudes between computer users and non users.

Table 4 - Differences in attitudes between computer users and non-computer users

Item	Computer users (n=19)	Non-computer users (n=5)
Computer bulletin board helped group keep informed of class announcements and other information, compared to other classes	18(95%)	3(60%)
Learning to use computer electronic mail will benefit you in your career	17(89%)	1(20%)
Would be inclined to take other classes taught in a similar manner	16(84%)	1(20%)
Group use of the computer in this class has made the experience more rewarding	16(84%)	1(20%)

It is clear that computer users were more enthusiastic about CMC than the non-users. One CMC user said that the class was rewarding

Because it wasn't only a communication class-- it was a class learning about using a tool to communicate with others.

Another said,

it helped me communicate using the computer - which supposedly is the wave of the future!

One student said rewards arose because the computer "gave us a sense of accomplishment outside the assignment." The computer was also rewarding, said one student, because "it made it more of a professional atmosphere and gave us the feeling of greater success." Another said, "it was more challenging to learn this method of class work and communication." One student found it rewarding to "help each other learn skills needed."

Computer nonusers were less enthusiastic about the computer aspect of the course. Only one of five nonusers felt that using electronic mail would help them in their careers. One of five nonusers expressed interest in taking a similar course. And none of the nonusers and 12 of the nineteen users felt that the computer made the class more rewarding than non CMC courses.

DISCUSSION

This short survey focused on advantages that come from CMC's asynchronicity--convenience, opportunity for more contact among instructors and students, more control over communication, and the necessity to communicate in writing. Students recognized how quick, convenient communication at times of their choosing could be advantageous for interaction with the instructor, and, in some cases, for interaction among students. Fewer students recognized the usefulness of communicating in writing as an aid to expression and clarification of thoughts.

Students were less convinced of CMC's advantages for student-student communication. These results might reflect that fact that course design did not require that each student log onto the computer system. Groups varied in their members' use of the computer. Some students who did use the computer expressed dissatisfaction with student underutilization of the system.

There were only two negative comments about the computer system. One student disliked the lack of an automatic word wrap on the online text editor. Although he checked six advantages of using CMC, another nonuser, "very uncomfortable" with the computer, qualified his answer by commenting, "I think the computer system would have been more helpful or 'user-friendly' if it was modern...these mainframes are completely obsolete." Another non-user checked six advantages of using the computer to communicate with the instructor, but in a final comment downplayed the computer system's part in the course's success:

The class as a whole was very interesting. The computer aspect was difficult to handle at first, but once the initial fear was overcome, it proved to be somewhat beneficial. However, I don't feel that the computer system was a large deciding factor in the course's success.

Another said that the final project alone was what made the course rewarding.

The survey did not attempt to question students on the advantages of social distance or access to resources.

However, students did address the issue of social distance. Some pointed out the need for face-to-face interaction in addition to CMC, especially for major problems. One did say that CMC made it easier to contact the instructor with questions. Future surveys should explore the social distance characteristic of CMC, as well as its potential for improving access to resources.

Suggestions for CMC Use

Survey responses reflect that CMC's advantages accrue only for instructors and students who log on regularly. The quick responses that students value so highly occur only if the instructor answers mail regularly. I did not keep a record of my exact time online, but I logged on at least once Mondays through Thursdays (but usually two or three times), and at least once from Friday through Sunday (barring weekends away). CMC is not convenient for students unless instructors log on outside their office hours. Survey comments also remind instructors that they must write their online comments and notes clearly, for them to be useful to students.

Instructors using CMC also need to be aware that learning-disabled students might experience few or no advantages from CMC. A learning disabled student in the GDS course reminded me that some learning disabled students find it difficult to read or type online. This student told me that she could read my assignment remarks if I doublespaced them, which I did in corresponding to

them. Instructors who use CMC to augment their courses must be aware of the needs of learning disabled students, especially if CMC usage is required in a course. Faculty who want to use CMC should work with whatever campus facility exists for learning disabled students, to see if staff there might assist learning disabled students to read or write email messages, as they currently help such students to edit and proofread term papers, or provide facilities for untimed exams.

Although five students complained about group members not taking advantage of the computer, I am hesitant to require that all students log on. In a course of this type, CMC is not used for lengthy discussion of ideas. Those dialogues take place in the classroom, in office visits, and, I hope, in student groups. CMC is mainly used, with some exceptions, to pass information from group to instructor and back. So, it is not necessary that each individual log on. Nonusers seemed satisfied with their group communicators' liaison as they passed on computer bulletin board information to the group (see Table 4). One of my course objectives was for students to use initiative in seeking out and using available resources for problem-solving. So I left it up to the groups to discover and explore the potential of CMC for their group process. They seemed to do so. With four groups, only eight students (two per group) were required to learn CMC. Yet 19 students used it. This figure indicates that groups educated themselves about this important resource.

CONCLUSION

CMC definitely has advantages for the instructor. Instructors can be available to students whenever they log onto the computer as well as in class and office hours. Marking assignments online goes quickly and avoids unwieldy piles of paper and potentially lost assignments. Faculty can mark assignments whenever they have computer access--day or night-- without carrying stacks of work between school and home. They can easily review a group's progress by browsing through their assignments or mail files. CMC provides instructors an online "desk," for notes, handouts, and other materials, making it possible to reduce desktop clutter. Instructors and students can access these materials from home or school. Faculty can avoid delays at the copy center, or crisis rushes to the program photocopier. Online archives make updating next semester's courses easy. It's also easy to send materials to other colleagues online, for their suggestions or comments. And Internet makes a world of resources available. Instructors can provide students materials from such services as Comserve, or train students to browse the Internet themselves. I felt rewarded to see that my students recognized many of CMC's advantages. My concerns that students at a small campus would not appreciate or use CMC were unfounded. CMC has benefits other than making larger class enrollments possible--one of the original justifications used at Penn State for incorporating CMC into a popular group discussion class. Thus it can make sense to use CMC at a small college, or in a small class.

Although I did not keep counts, I noticed that more Marist students and groups did visit me in my office compared to students in the similar Penn State class. I attribute this to Marist's size, its tradition of student-teacher contact, and the location of my office in the Communication Arts building, where most communication classes are held. I also hold more office hours than I did at Penn State. Yet, despite my availability for face-to-face communication, the survey results indicated that students liked the convenience of augmenting their communication with me by using email. CMC was not an "extra" complicating factor for my students, but an added useful dimension to the course.

BIOGRAPHICAL NOTE: Mary McComb is Assistant Professor of Communication Arts at Marist College in Poughkeepsie, New York. Her Ph.D. in Speech Communication and M.Ed. in Adult Education - Distance Education are from The Pennsylvania State University. She has taught small group discussion, computer literacy, and senior thesis courses augmented by computer-mediated communication, and is developing an introductory film course using CMC to extend classroom discussion.

WORKS CITED

Bales, R.F. (1970). Personality & interpersonal behavior. Holt, Rinehart & Winston

Bales, R.F., & Cohen, S.P. (1979). SYMLOG: A system for the multiple level observation of groups. New York: The Free Press.

Feenberg, A. (1987). Computer conferencing and the humanities. Instructional Science, 16, 169-186.

Freire, P. (1983). Pedagogy of the oppressed (M.B. Ramos, Trans.). Continuum.

Garrison, D.R., & Baynton, M. (1987). Beyond independence in distance educat.: The concept of control. The American Journal of Distance Education, 1(3), 3-15

Harasim, L. (1986). Computer learning networks: Educational applications of computer conferencing. Journal of Distance Education, 1(1), 59-70.

Hernandez, C.A., Mockus, A., Granes, J., Charum, J., & Castro, M.C. (1987). Lenguaje, voluntad del saber y calidad de la educacion [Language, the will to know, and quality of education]. Educacion y Cultura, 12, 60-70.

Hiltz, S.R. (1978). Computer conference. Journal of Communication, 28(3), 157.

Hiltz, S.R. (1986). The 'virtual classroom": Using computer- mediated communication for university teaching. Journal of Communication, 36(2), 95-104.

Karabenick, S.A. (1987, June). Computer conferencing: Its impact on academic help-seeking. Paper presented at the Second Symposium on Computer Conferencing and Allied Technologies, Guelph, Ontario, Canada.

Kelly, L., Kuehn, S.A., & McComb, M.E. (1989). Evaluating how individual performance affects group outcomes. In G.M. Phillips (Ed.), Teaching how to work in groups(pp. 66-83). Norwood, NJ: Ablex.

Kuehn, S.A. (1988, April). Discovering all the available means for computer assisted instruction. Presented at annual meeting of the Eastern Communication Ass'n.

Mason, R. (1988). Computer conferencing and the university community. Open Learning, 3(2), 37-40.

Phillips, G.M. (Ed.). (1989). Teaching how to work in groups. Norwood, NJ: Ablex.

Phillips, G.M., & Santoro, G.M. (1988, July). Solving a problem-solving problem via CMC. In M.G. Moore (Ed.), Discussion papers, The American Symposium on Research in Distance Education.

Phillips, G.M., & Santoro, G.M. (1989). Teaching group communication via computer-mediated communication. Communication Education, 38, 151-161.

Phillips, G.M., Santoro, G.M., & Kuehn, S.A. (1988). The use of CMC in training students in group problem-solving. The American Journal of Dist. Ed., 2(1), 38-51.

Course
Catalog

Course Catalog

Course Index by Category

Course Descriptions by Provider

Course Catalog - This section provides the information that most people will have purchased this book for. It includes descriptions of more than 700 courses that are offered by more than thirty providers. The section opens with a listing of the providing institutions which has a four-character identifier code, the institution's degree provisions, number of online courses in the catalog, and page number for your reference. If you are interested in a particular university or college, consult this list for their location in the catalog.

Four Character Identifier - Each provider has been issued a four-character identifier code to assist you in navigating this book. With this code you may readily identify the provider for any course by checking the first four characters of the course number. For instance, consider this course listing from the index:

Concepts in Design: Digital Photography   **MASD**#PHO1   277

From this entry we can see that this particular course is offered by the University of Massachusetts - Dartmouth (MASD) and that the course description is located on page 277. All course providers have a similar four-character code, listed in Provider Index on page 191. Consider the entry for MASD:

University of Massachusetts - Dartmouth	**MASD**	272	12

This entry shows that further information on that university is available on page 272, including that there are 12 courses following the institutional profile.

Course Index Categories - Following the provider list on page 191 is a comprehensive index with all of the courses in this catalog organized by the following categories:

1. Arts	13. Humanities
2. Aviation	14. International
3. Business	15. Languages
4. Communications - Interpersonal	16. Legal
5. Communications - Online	17. Literature
6. Composition	18. Management
7. Computers	19. Mathematics
8. Economics	20. Miscellaneous
9. Education	21. Municipal
10. Government	22. Psychology
11. Health Sciences	23. Science
12. History	24. Sociology

Please note that these categories are of necessity somewhat arbitrary; some subjects could rightly appear in more than one category. We have elected to list each course in one category only, so be sure to check related categories if the course you want is not listed where you first check.

Following the Course Index are the course descriptions. These are organized by course provider, and in each case the listing of courses is prefaced by a brief profile of the providing institution. We have included in each of these descriptions the required contact information for you to initiate discussions and connections necessary to sign up for your courses. Please note that this is an extremely volatile field and that all course offerings and descriptions are subject to change. Contact the organization directly for up-to-date information.

We hope that this course index is very helpful to you in your search for academic success. If you find any courses that are discontinued or which have been revised, please contact us by email to: tellus@caso.com. We are also interested in your experiences if you have participated in any online course.

When contacting any organization mentioned in this book please tell them that you learned about their services in Cape Software's book:

THE INTERNET UNIVERSITY - COLLEGE COURSES BY COMPUTER

Catalog of Available Courses

The Course Providers of The Internet University:

Institution	Code	Page	A	B
Antioch University	AOCH	213		7
Brevard Community College	BREV	216	√	10
California Institute of Integral Studies	CIIS	219	√	n/a
City University	CITY	221	√	11
University of California-Dominguez Hills	DOMI	225		5
Edgewood College	EDGE	227		3
Embry-Riddle Aeronautical University	ERAU	230		14
University of Florida	FLOR	235		46
Front Range Community College	FRCC	243		17
Heriot-Watt University	HERI	247	√	12
Western Illinois University	ILLW	253		26
University of Iowa	IOWA	258		5
Internat'l School of Information Mgt.	ISIM	261	√	33
Int'l Society for Technology in Ed.	ISTE	268	√	16
University of Massachusetts - Dartmouth	MASD	273		12
New School for Social Research	NEWS	278	√	53
Norwich University	NORW	293		2
Nova Southeastern University	NOVA	295	√	57
New York Institute of Technology	NYIT	307	√	106
Pennsylvania State University	PASU	324		14
University of Phoenix	PHOE	327	√	60
Rochester Institute of Technology	ROCH	336	√	72
Rogers State College	ROGE	348	√	33
Salve Regina University	SALV	356	√	12
Thomas Edison State College	THOM	360	√	9
University of Washington	WASH	364	√	75
Webster University	WEBS	374		3
University of Wisconsin - Madison	WISM	375		12
University of Wisconsin - Stout	WISS	384		6

KEY:
A=Degree or certificate availability via Internet
B=Number of courses available via Internet

Course Index:

Communications - Interpersonal

Computers

Economics

Education

Government

Management

Mathematics

Be sure and visit The Internet University's companion website:

http://www.caso.com

This site contains up-to-date listings and current news about online ed.

<u>Tell us what we missed - Win a free book:</u>

If you know of an educational resource available on the Internet and it is not listed in this book, please notify us via email and we will include it in subsequent editions. The person who provides us with the most useful tip each month will be awarded a free copy of the most recent edition of:

The Internet University - College Courses by Computer

All suggestions for changes in content or additional resources should be sent to the following email address:

tellus@caso.com

The field of online education is changing so quickly that nobody can possibly contain the entirety of the field in one book. We at Cape Software are working to catalog these resources and with your assistance we will be better able to carry out our aims. Thank you for your inputs!

Course Descriptions

Course Providers of The Internet University:

Institution	Code	Page
Antioch University	AOCH	213
Brevard Community College	BREV	216
California Institute of Integral Studies	CIIS	219
City University	CITY	221
University of California-Dominguez Hills	DOMI	225
Edgewood College	EDGE	227
Embry-Riddle Aeronautical University	ERAU	230
University of Florida	FLOR	235
Front Range Community College	FRCC	243
Heriot-Watt University	HERI	247
Western Illinois University	ILLW	253
University of Iowa	IOWA	258
Internat'l School of Information Mgt.	ISIM	261
Int'l Society for Technology in Ed.	ISTE	268
University of Massachusetts - Dartmouth	MASD	273
New School for Social Research	NEWS	278
Norwich University	NORW	293
Nova Southeastern University	NOVA	295
New York Institute of Technology	NYIT	307
Pennsylvania State University	PASU	324
University of Phoenix	PHOE	327
Rochester Institute of Technology	ROCH	336
Rogers State College	ROGE	348
Salve Regina University	SALV	356
Thomas Edison State College	THOM	360
University of Washington	WASH	364
Webster University	WEBS	374
University of Wisconsin - Madison	WISM	375
University of Wisconsin - Stout	WISS	384

Be sure and visit The Internet University's companion website:
http://www.caso.com/
This site contains up-to-date listings and current news about online ed.

Antioch University - 7 courses

Accredited by the North Central Association of Schools and Colleges

Antioch University
2607 Second Ave.
Seattle WA 98115

Antioch University is a national university founded in 1852. In addition to the main Yellow Springs, Ohio campus, Antioch has campuses in New England, southern California and Seattle. Heritage Online is directly affiliated with Antioch's Seattle campus.

All Heritage Online courses are available for Antioch University credit. Antioch offers quarter credits (3 quarter credits=2 semester credits) on a Credit/No Credit system only. While letter grades are not issued, credit granted at the 400 Level is equal to a "C" or better and at the 500 Level is "B" or better. Antioch University credits are acceptable in many states toward educator re-certification and within school districts for salary advancement.

All courses are self-paced and may be started at any time. Upon enrollment, you'll receive by mail the software you will use to obtain easy email access to instructors, ease in sending and receiving documents as well as browsing of course message boards, attending live classroom conferences and private dialog with other students. One year is allowed from the registration date to complete a course. Extensions are allowed up to one quarter beyond the quarter in which the course is to be completed for an additional fee.

Distance Courses for Teachers: Enroll in any of seven distance courses designed especially for teachers in subjects at the leading edge of educational change. Courses earn Antioch University credit, are offered by instructors with classroom teaching experience, and involve 'hands-on' learning applicable to classroom teaching.

Tuition is $80 per credit at the upper division (400 level) and $90 per credit for graduate (500 level) credit. Tuition payment is due at the time of registration. Courses may also be audited for a somewhat lower fee.

Antioch University
2607 Second Ave.
Seattle WA 98115
email: deans@cloud.seattleantioch.edu

Antioch University Course Descriptions

Exploring Models of Teaching Excellence (AOCH#ED406N)   3 credits

Are you in search of excellence in your teaching? Broaden your horizons by exploring in this study your own mental guides for teaching and what really matters to you as a teacher. This study will immerse you in exploring models of motivation theory, learning styles, lesson designs, TESA and cooperative learning, and in examining both real teachers as well as fictional teachers from film who sometimes portray teaching in unrealistic ways. This course is an excel-lent way to expand your working knowledge of leading edge theory and practice.

School Restructuring in the '90's (AOCH#ED406O)   5 credits

This course is designed for the many educators in America today who are involved in school-wide improvement, immersing them in the national dialogue on restructuring, the stages of educational change and obstacles to improvement efforts. This course will cover effective problem-solving approaches, elements of successful school improvement and how educators can become effective agents of change.

Teaching & Learning Thru Multiple Intelligences (AOCH#ED406P)5 credits

In this course, educators will expand opportunities for student success and learn both the theory and practice of multiple intelligence instruction in order to reach students according to their innate learning abilities. Participants will listen to a taped lecture of Dr. Howard Gardner of Harvard University who explains his theory on linguistic, mathematical, kinesthetic, visual, musical, interpersonal and intrapersonal forms of human competence. A text, "Learning and Teaching Through Multiple Intelligences" will guide participants through 20 or more different teaching strategies for each intelligence. This course allows in-depth practice in teaching according to varying student abilities from classroom teachers with lots of experience in this area.

Whole Language in Practice (AOCH#ED406Q)   5 credits

Participants in this course will learn how to make the whole language approach really work in their teaching situation. A course workbook and Regie Routnam's book **Invitations: Changing as Teachers and Learners K-12** will immerse participants in the instructional theories and methods of whole language covering reading, spelling, writing, oral sharing, vocabulary and phonics. Participants will articulate their own philosophy of learning and develop a plan of teaching practices that incorporate the whole language approach.

The Internet as a Teaching Tool (AOCH#ED406G)   4 credits

Don't miss out on this exciting opportunity to renew student enthusiasm in any subject area by learning how to use the Internet as an instructional tool. This course provides educators guidelines for exploring the most fun and user-friendly part of the Internet, the World-Wide Web (WWW) and for developing lesson plans which use WWW pages as part of the instructional plan. The course will use **Netscape**, cited by many as the best WWW software program. A manual including several lesson plan examples as well as an on-line cross-curriculum resource page will give participants a head start in developing their own lessons including WWW pages. Whether on computers in class or the school lab, kids will love learning through WWW.

Using Museums as a Model for Learning (AOCH#ED406M)   3 credits

Learn how to develop and use the classroom 'museum' as a class project for team building, to reach different learning styles and to have a 3-D portfolio to share the best student work. In this course, you can visit museums anywhere and use them as case studies in learning about heroes, values of different cultures and the fun of collecting and sorting information to develop classroom displays on any subject.

Creating and Learning with the Internet (AOCH#ED400F)   3 credits

Imagine teachers and their students learning together how to publish their own pages on the Internet, creating online forms for surveys or conducting discussions across classrooms, and in virtually all curricular areas. This course will enable regular classroom teachers with ambition but only limited Internet experience to create projects using the most user-friendly aspects of the Internet, the World-Wide Web (WWW) which has graphics and sound, as well as text capability. This course covers the skills of HTML (a language used in creating WWW pages) to assemble text, pictures and multimedia materials as ways to organize and motivate student learning in any subject area. How about doing a science study on wolves where the teacher and class together learn how to publish WWW pages including wolf pictures and sounds, online student papers on wolves and links to many other pages in cyberspace on the subject? Or how about a social studies project where your classroom designs an online survey to collect attitudes about school from students in Japan, Sweden and Australia? You'll be surprised how easy these projects can be particularly when you learn with and from your students.

Brevard Community College - 10 courses

Electronic University Network
1977 Colestin Rd.
Hornbrook CA 96044

800-225-3276

Now you can earn one of eleven degrees, ten of them in technology fields with great career opportunities now and in the future! Brevard Community College is a highly-respected, accredited public college located in the heart of the Florida Space Coast and known around the world for its outstanding technology education. Through its new online campus, BCC now offers you the opportunity to earn a degree entirely online, on your own schedule, at your own location, in the company of other online students and your instructors.

All the degrees require 60 semester credits. Of these, 45 may be transferred from other schools, and 15 are to be earned from BCC Online. In addition, you will need to satisfy the specific course requirements of the degree you want. Most degrees BCC offers online prepare you for a bachelor's degree earned from an accredited senior university. For example, City University offers several bachelor's degrees that build on the BCC programs. The Brevard Community College associates degrees are in:

Associate in Arts (AA) in General Studies: This degree prepares you for upper-division (3rd-4th year) study and completion of a bachelor's degree in a large number of fields, including business, computer science, liberal arts, and technical fields.

Associate in Science (AS) in these fields:

Criminal Justice: Designed not only for men and women preparing to enter the fields of law enforcement, corrections, private security, etc. but also for already-employed professionals seeking incentive benefits or career enhancement.

Fire Science Technology: Prepares men and women to be firefighters, and qualifies fire personnel for career advancement. Courses satisfy the Bureau of Fire Standards and Training requirements for Fire Officer I Certification Exam and Fire Inspector Certification Exam.

Hazardous Materials Technology: Challenges students to prepare for an exciting and critically important career in the field of environmental protection. Students learn current scientific trends and policies related to hazardous materials control and disposition as they reach into 21st-century goals to aid in managing our delicate ecosystem.

Legal Studies: Prepares men and women to join the legal team and handle varied responsibilities. Graduates work in law firms, corporations, banks, title companies, and government agencies.

Solar Energy Technology: Prepares women and men to work in the fast-growing field of solar energy. Provides theory and technical training to accelerate job-finding and career growth.

Electronic Engineering Technology: Program prepares studenst for employemnt as electronic technicians, in advanced technology companies, and space industries.

Drafting & Design Technology: This curriculum provides competency for students who desire employment in the design fields. Technical drafters translate ideas, sketches, calculation and specification into completel, accurate working drawings used in manufacturing.

International Business: Prepares students for initial employment with business and industries engaged in international commerce and trade. Students analyze the theoretical aspects of international trade, its relationship to the American economy and operational aspects of exporting and importing.

Marketing Management: The cornerstone of business activities for both profit and not-for-profit organizations, the marketing curriculum prepares students for careers in advertising, research, distribution, packaging, production, and manufacturer's representative. Demand for employees and opportities for advancement to management areas in all business fields is vast in this career field.

Radio & Television Broadcast Programming: This program prepares the student for employment in radio and television fields running the gamut from technical basics to advanced production methods. The curriculum includes wrtiting for the electronic media, broadcast news production, media issues, and advertising.

Tuition & Fees: BCC's moderate costs make an online college education affordable: they are the same low fees as those paid by on-campus students. The fee for a non-Florida resident for a 3-credit course is $455 when videotapes are required, and $405 when they are not. Other fees and charges may apply.

Courses start at the first of each month. The courses last 16 weeks from your starting date. The courses can all be taken to meet degree requirements at Brevard or another college; to increase job skills; and/or to help you grow intellectually. The courses, along with brief descriptions, are listed below. If you want to take courses, but haven't decided to seek a degree, in one of these growing fields, you may register for individual courses.

Brevard Community College Course Descriptions:

Financial Accounting (BREV#ACG2021)　　　　　　　3 credits
Financial accounting for service and merchandising enterprises organized as sole proprietorships, partnerships, and corporations. Emphasis on the accounting cycle, financial statements, receivables/payables, inventory costing, depreciation and disposal of plant assets, corporate stock and bond issues.

Managerial Accounting (BREV#ACG2071)　　　　　　　3 credits
Accounting as it applies to managerial theory and practice; cost accounting concepts and relationships; forecasting and budgeting; business information requirements.

Microcomputer Applications Processing (BREV#CGS1530)　　　3 credits
An introductory course in the application of commercially available software for microcomputers - topics include: word processing, electronic spreadsheets, data base management, computer graphics and key pad.

Communications I (BREV#ENC1101)　　　　　　　　3 credits
The first of two writing courses which teaches principles of pre-writing, organizing, revising, and editing essays. Includes basic research and documentation methods.

Communications II (BREV#ENC1102)　　　　　　　3 credits
A continuation of ENC 1101 with emphasis on writing about literature using different rhetorical strategies. Selections from the areas of the short story, essay, novel, poetry, or drama provide the basis for advanced essay writing, research, and practice in literary analysis.

Legal Assisting - Contracts (BREV#PLA1423)　　　　　3 credits
This course introduces the student to laws involving contract information and terminology.

Introduction to Astronomy (BREV#AST1002)　　　　　3 credits
A study of the solar system, stars, galaxies, and cosmology. An elementary survey of astronomy as both a human activity and a physical science. Primarily for non-science majors.

Introduction to Environmental Science (BREV#EVR1001)　　　3 credits
A survey of basic chemical, biological, and physical principles of environmental science and ecology and the application of these principles to current political, scientific and economic issues.

Survey of Human Anatomy/Physiology (BREV#BSCC1092)　　　4 credits
Includes terminology; chemistry; cell biology and cellular respiration; tissues; survey of all organ systems.

Engineering Graphics I (BREV#EGSC1110)　　　　　　4 credits
Beginning course in drawing, involving lettering, sketching, orthographic projection, dimensioning, sections, pictorials, threads and fastener, charts and graphics, and a study of points, lines, and planes.

California Institute of Integral Studies

Accredited by the Western Association of Schools and Colleges.

Electronic University Network
1977 Colestin Rd.
Hornbrook CA 96044

800-225-3276

The California Institute of Integral Studies is a nonprofit, nonsectarian graduate school located in San Francisco. The school was founded in 1968 by Haridas Chaudhuri and was originally known as the California Institute of Asian Studies. In 1980 the name was changed to the California Institute of Integral Studies to indicate the Institute's commitment to a unifying vision of humanity, nature, world and spirit.

The central, distinctive mission of the Institute is to provide an environment, facilities and guidance for systematic, disciplined study and re-search in the integration of Eastern and Western worldviews, philosophies, healing and spiritual practices, and cultural traditions. The approximately 800 students enrolled in Institute programs are committed to the concept of lifelong learning. They seek an education which has personal as well as vocational value.

THE SCHOOL FOR TRANSFORMATIVE LEARNING

In Fall, 1992, the School for Transformative Learning was established within the California Institute for Integral Studies to define, research and promote integral approaches to learning and creative social change. The school's programs are a response to the crises facing the planet and our cultures -- crises created by lack of meaning, the disintegration of inherited institutional forms, and violence done to our fellow humans and to our natural environment. The human community has created these dilemmas, and we need to resolve them. Since our inherited ways of thinking and responding to such dilemmas themselves are part of the problem, we are convinced that we need to learn our way out of these dilemmas -- we need to discover how to transform the ways we perceive the world, the ways we imagine the future, and the ways we work together. And we need to discover how to facilitate such learning within individuals, groups and institutions.

All of the School's programs embody an integral vision which respects the spiritual dimension of experience, incorporates diverse ways of knowing, and exposes learners to the texture, feel and worldview of diverse cultures. The School applies the principles of integral philosophy to the design of our degree programs, focusing on learning which permits learners simultaneously to develop the intellect, the spirit and the

219

imagination, and to incorporate affective and experiential as well as conceptual learning. All programs encourage students to bring an integral worldview to explore diverse cultural stories, worldviews or paradigms, to understand the divisions and transitions within the larger culture, and to plan and carry out practical action in the world.

(1) THE ADVANCED STANDING Ph.D. - 90 to 105 units, depending on the program option; prerequisite is an MA from an accredited graduate school.

(2) THE STRAIGHT-THROUGH Ph.D. - 130 to 145 units, depending on the program option; prerequisite is a BA or BS from an accredited school, and evidence of substantial advanced learning and professional achievement.

CURRICULUM DESCRIPTION: The four areas are: (1) Learning & Change in Human Systems; (2) Foundations; (3) Conduct of Inquiry; and (4) Integrative Seminar.

Electronic Network Support: The doctoral program is supported by an interactive electronic network. The online 'virtual campus' provides an environment for all ISD students to interact with one another and with the faculty and staff. The online network also enables members of the learning community to address issues of common interest. For distance learners, courses are taught online. The exchange between students and faculty, and among students, is lively, challenging, and personally supportive. In addition to seminars, online activities include exchanging papers, discussing issues in private forums, sharing resources, receiving information and updates on Institute activities, and participating in topical discussions with guest presenters and faculty.

For further information and an application packet, contact:
Gail Jones, Program Coordinator via email: STLGail@aol.com, or call:
415/753-6100, ext. 223.
fax 415/753-1169

City University - 11 courses

City University
Office of Admissions & Student Affairs
919 W. Grady Way
Renton WA 98055

City University is a private, non-profit institution of higher education based in Bellevue, Washington. Founded more than two decades ago, the University operates with the mission of making education available to all who desire it. Primarily, City University was founded to serve working adults who want to build on their experience through education but cannot interrupt their careers to become full-time students. City University serves more than 14,000 students and employs hundreds of staff and faculty members to deliver its programs worldwide.

City University's Distance Learning program enables students to complete an entire degree outside the classroom, which makes it possible for thousands of people annually to meet their educational goals--without interrupting other commitments to work and home. City University is proud to announce its latest effort to connect adult learners with quality education: EDROADS (Education Resource and Online Academic Degree System). EDROADS takes the concept of Distance Learning to an exciting next step, via the cutting edge technology of the Internet. Through City University's World Wide Web site, students use Web browsers such as Netscape, and Telnet to apply to the university, register for courses, and complete course work electronically.

Similar to the standard Distance Learning format, students who complete courses online use a variety of printed materials. They are welcome to communicate with their instructor or advisor via traditional mail systems, telephone, or fax. However, online students may also use the Web site to send questions and assignments via email. They can participate in specialized live forums at the program and course level, many of which may feature guest experts. They can tap into info folders which offer a running dialog about program and course information, generated by faculty and students alike. And, they can conduct guided research using the wealth of resources available on the Internet.

Currently, City University offers the core series of courses for its Master of Business Administration program available online. This is one of the university's most respected, well-established programs and consists of a dozen specialty areas. The university is working to bring its MBA specialty courses and additional programs online in the near future. Be sure to visit Programs Available Online to stay up-to-date. City University offers Bachelors Completion programs through America Online's Electronic

University Network. Students who enroll for courses through EUN will have access to communication features similar to those offered for City University's Internet courses, as well as a variety of research tools available on America Online.

TUITION: Students who enroll at City University assume responsibility for the payment of tuition and fees, in accordance with the financial policies set forth in the City University catalog. All tuition and fees are due at the time of enrollment. Students who fail to pay tuition and fees upon enrollment are subject to a late payment fee. This applies to all courses. Students are responsible for purchasing course materials and textbooks separately, as well as for the cost of postage where necessary. In addition, students are responsible for costs associated with their online service provider.

The following tuition rates are effective through August 31, 1995. These rates apply to courses offered to Distance Learning and online students, and classroom-based courses.. For additional information on tuition for courses conducted outside the United States, please contact an advisor by phone (1-800-426-5596 or 206-637-1010, ext. 3393), by fax (206-277-2437), or by email.

Regular Graduate per Credit..... $244
Undergraduate, Regular
Upper-Division per Credit..... $176
Undergraduate, Regular
Lower-Division per Credit..... $62

City University
Office of Admissions & Student Affairs
Jennifer Boudart, Director of Media Relations (x3852)
919 W. Grady Way
Renton WA 98055

206-637-1010, 1-800-426-5596
206-277-2437 fax
e-mail: info@cityu.edu

City University Course Descriptions

Management Accounting (CITY#MC500)   3 credits

Measurement is a key requirement for successful Information Age organizations. In managing strategic systems, accounting measures are critical in managerial decision-making. The influence of accounting practices on resource allocation; the reporting, control and analytic environment in which the manager and the accountant function; budgeting, cost concepts, and responsible accounting systems.

Organizational Behavior (CITY#MC519)   3 credits

Within the strategic systems model, learning is an organizational imperative. This imperative poses a unique challenge as managers and stakeholders work within the human systems of the organization. This course focuses on human resources and understanding of individuals, groups and organizational dynamics that are essential to effectively supporting continuous improvement and organizational learning. The exploration includes the key issues of individual differences, individual and organizational learning, motivation, team effectiveness, and organizational change.

Quality Management & Statistical Methods (CITY#QM500)   3 credits

From a Strategic Systems perspective, an organization's long-term success results not from products and services but from the processes that create them. Quality management and the concept of continuous improvement are key to understanding and managing successful organizational systems in the information age. This course focuses on the tools necessary for gaining knowledge of systems and processes; minimizing mistakes and defects in systems and processes; reducing process complexity; stabilizing systems and processes; and, ultimately, to improving processes and systems to benefit customers and stakeholders.

Managerial Communications & Research Methods (CITY#MC511)   3 cr.

Central to managing strategic systems are vision, teamwork and information based decision making. Each of these elements is dependent on effective communications. This course examines various forms of organizational communications and provides practical experience in writing for a variety of communication situations (e.g., business letters, memoranda, case studies, proposals, and analytical reports). Emphasis is on the way learners can develop a strategic understanding and control over their writing process and product. The course focuses on analysis of audience and situations under which communication is intended.

Managerial Economics (CITY#MC514)   3 credits

Organizations of the future must be able to adapt rapidly to a dynamic and ever changing economic environment. Strategy, stakeholders, and information-based decision making are the most important elements of managerial economics in a strategic systems organizational environment. Within this context, the course will provide an in-depth analysis of demand and supply market pricing and customer behavior. Topics will include: estimating production costs and profit maximization in different market environments; fundamentals of project analysis; how customers choose goods and services; and strategies for hiring, pricing, production, advertising etc.

Management Information Systems (CITY#MC516)   3 credits

The roles of information and information processing in supporting the organization's strategic systems will be explored. Students will develop a manager's view of information systems purchase or development that is based on user requirements. The focus is on information based decision making and managing information technology with the goal of continuously improving effectiveness, efficiency, and/or profitability of the organization.

Organization & Management (CITY#MC535)   3 credits

Old systems must be transformed if organizations are to survive the rapid changes of today's global economic environment. Central to this transformation is the need for a whole systems approach to organization and management. Specifically, this course will cover organizations and organization theory from a traditional and transformational view thus describing the transition from the industrial age to the information age. New perspectives, contexts and processes of organization will be explored.

Marketing Management (CITY#MB545)   3 credits

A key strategic system within modern organizations is the system of service/product promotion. Today's global economic environment has forced all organizations, public or private, profit or non-profit, to effectively communicate with their customers regarding their products and/or services. This course will review various applications of marketing concepts based on an organization's finite resources and continuously changing environment.

Operational Management (CITY#MC550)   3 credits

Techniques and models designed to manage strategic systems in manufacturing and service operations. Using case analyses and application of decision models, emphasis on problem identification, model selection, and results or computerized solution interpretations; inventory planning and control models, activity based accounting, facilities layout, scheduling and work force planning models, productivity improvement, and quality assurance.

Principles of Finance (CITY#MC553)   3 credits

Strategic is the operational term when it comes to financing modern organizational systems. The principles of finance explores strategic financial management as ideas and principles that work together in the decision-making process. Financial markets and interest rates, financial statement analysis, valuation of the firm, risk and return, capital structures, costs of capital and dividend policy are covered in this course.

Legal Systems in a Global Economy (CITY#MC555)   3 credits

The shift to a global economic environment has created a variety of challenges for modern organizations. As competition increases in established markets, developing new markets overseas has become a strategic alternative for many organizations. The challenges of such a strategy are many, not the least of which are the legal challenges. Legal Systems in a Global Economy is designed to explore the legal content of multinational business operations; comparative law and regulation as established in the United States and abroad; and legal liability in global commerce.

California State Univ.-Dominguez Hills - 5 courses

Accredited by the Western Association of Schools and Colleges

Humanities External Degree Program
1000 E. Victoria SAC2-2126
Carson, CA 90747 US

The Master of Arts in the Humanities offers a broad interdisciplinary exposure to all of the areas of the Humanities - history, literature, philosophy, music, and art - and the establishment of an integrative perspective among them, with emphasis on their interrelating effects and influences. The student is provided with the opportunity to specialize in a particular discipline of the Humanities, or in specific cultural thematic areas which could be traced across all of the humanities disciplines.

The Master of Arts Degree is offered as an external degree program for anyone presently holding a Bachelor's Degree, who prefers an individualized approach to advanced education rather than traditional classroom courses on college campuses. Achievement of the degree emphasizes independent study guided by qualified faculty. Credit earned at California State University are transferable to other member institutions.

Students are now given the option of communicating with instructors and/or taking selected courses by computer via email and conferencing. This is an alternative mode of delivery to the current curriculum delivery system. Students with access to a personal computer and modem or other telecommunications linking device may use the system to: contact instructors; send assignments; receive course guides and materials, instructions, advising or comments; converse with fellow students; do online research; as well as participating in several other activities.

California State University - Dominguez Hills -
Humanities External Degree Program
1000 E. Victoria SAC2-2126
Carson, CA 90747 USA

Email: huxonline@dhvx20.csudh.edu
World Wide Web: http://dolphin.csudh.edu/~huxindex.html

Voice: (310) 516-3743 - M-F, 8am - 4pm PST
FAX: (310) 516-4399 - 24 hours/day

California State Univ. - Dominguez Hills Course Descriptions

Defining the Humanities: History (DOMI#HUX501)   2 credits

Advanced study of the nature of history through examination of historical method and its application to a history book of the student's choice.

Defining the Humanities: Literature (DOMI#HUX502)   2 credits

Advanced study of the nature of literature by examination of images of self in selected poems and novels.

Defining the Humanities: Music (DOMI#HUX503)   2 credits

Advanced study of music, focusing on concepts of meaning and form in music at a philosophical rather than theoretical level. The ability to read music is not required.

Defining the Humanities: Art (DOMI#HUX504)   2 credits

Advanced study of key concepts in art by focusing on aesthetics and art theory.

Defining the Humanities: Philosophy (DOMI#HUX505)   2 credits

Advanced study of key concepts of Philosophy by focusing on contemporary issues and conflicts and their analogies in traditional philosophical readings.

Edgewood College - 3 courses

Electronic University Network
1977 Colestin Rd.
Hornbrook CA 96044

800-225-3276

Edgewood College combines natural lakeside beauty and the advantages of a small private college with the colorful and cosmopolitan atmosphere of a university-oriented city. The result is a stimulating learning environment where students and faculty share ideas and where concern for others is emphasized. Founded as a Catholic college by the Dominican Sisters of Sinsinawa in 1927, Edgewood sponsors an ecumenical program involving people of many faiths. A collaborative program with the University of Wisconsin-Madison means that students have access to courses, facilities and study resources not usually available at a private college of Edgewood's size.

A program in human issues offers courses for credit toward a degree or noncredit learning experiences. Instituted as a way to increase the immediacy and relevance of education to our global society, students select topics of broad human significance and develop a program of practical study and/or research to produce a final report. Edgewood also offers a variety of opportunities for international study, from two-week study tours to a semester abroad. Students may enhance their Edgewood College studies by choosing to enroll in specialized classes at the University of Wisconsin under Edgewood's tuition. One University class per semester may be taken, and all students have access to the University library system, art museum, geological museum, and other educational resources.

Through a Weekend Degree program, non-traditional students may obtain bachelors' degrees in accounting, business, computer information systems, criminal justice, English, religious studies, or RN degree completion. Three-hour classes meet two weekends a month on a regular semester basis. Coursework is concentrated, but the academic quality and content are not compromised. The College offers alternative routes to credit for its degrees through the American College Testing Program's Proficiency Examination Program (PEP), the College-Level Examination Program (CLEP), the College Board's Advanced Placement program (AP), retroactive credit for foreign language proficiency, and Credit for Prior Learning (CPL). Noncredit classes, including one-day programs or short-term courses (day or evening) of contemporary interest, are offered each semester through the Continuing Education Office. At the graduate level,

Edgewood offers programs leading to an MBA or an MA in education, educational administration, or religious studies.

Edgewood College is offering three management courses online. Each course provides 4 semester hours of credit and may be taken individually or as part of a 12-credit certificate. When you have completed the 12 credits, you will receive a Certificate in Management or a Certificate in Leadership Studies. You may choose the certificate you wish to receive based on your career and personal needs and preferences; those employed in or seeking management positions may wish to choose the Certificate in Management. Others, especially those working in nonprofit organizations, education, and the arts may choose the Certificate in Leadership Studies.

The fee for each 4-credit course is $600. This fee covers tuition, instruction, the course teleguide, orientation, and technical support. Textbooks and shipping for each course are extra.

Edgewood College, Director of Admissions
855 Woodrow Street
Madison, WI 53711
Telephone: 608-257-4861
Toll Free: 800-444-4861

or contact:
Electronic University Network
Attn: Edgewood College Admissions
1977 Colestin Road
Ashland, OR 97520
(800) 225-3276

Edgewood College Course Descriptions

Management Concepts (EDGE#BUS235)   4 credits

This course is designed to familiarize you with the principles and theories of management. To give you universally applicable techniques in this field, the format will include four basic functional areas: planning, organizing, activating and controlling. To give you added insight in order to enhance your administrative effectiveness and leadership potential, these areas will be supplemented by a study of organizational behavior. Leadership, motivational theory, communication, decision making, implementing change, and conflict resolution will be among the topics discussed.

Psychology of Management (EDGE#BES335)   4 credits

This course will explore the structure and functions of formal organizations, their characteristics, dynamics and processes. This will be done from the perspective of current psychological thought on personality, group interaction, and systems theory. Organizational issues examined will include conflict resolution, leadership roles and characteristics and constructive use of power and authority. The goal of the course is to provide you with a knowledge of the theory and practice of the psychology of management and leadership in such a way that will allow you to directly transfer classroom experience into work-related leadership skills. Prerequisite: Management Concepts (EDGE#BUS235)

Advanced Leadership Seminar (EDGE#EUN435)   4 credits

As an organizational philosophy is created and priorities are established, it is important to have a component dealing with leadership. Leaders are not born, they are developed by knowledge, experience, guidance, seasoning and integrity. Leadership is not related to any exclusive trait. It not particularly complicated. It is a community open to anyone possessing drive, passion, character, curiosity and a sense of herself or himself. In today's organizations, there are many average leaders doing a good job and making a substantial impact. There are several competent leaders who are doing a great job and whose path is evident by their considerable influence and tremendous output. And then, there is that rare and precious treasure, the Legendary Leader. In addition to their extraordinary expertise, they possess tremendous personal power. The sources of that power are what confer the Legendary status. The sources are the respect, admiration, affection, esteem and honor coming from those they lead. Prerequisite: Management Concepts (EDGE#BUS235)

Embry-Riddle Aeronautical University - 14 courses ERAU

> Embry-Riddle Aeronautical University
> Department of Independent Studies
> 600 South Clyde Morris Blvd.
> Daytona Beach FL 32114-3900
>   Attn: Jim Gallogly

Embry-Riddle Aeronautical University is prepared to meet your graduate level educational goals with Master of Aeronautical Science (MAS) degree with Aviation/Aerospace Management or Operations Specialization.

The Master of Aeronautical Science program, with Aviation/Aerospace Management or Operations Specialization is fully accredited by the Commission on Colleges of the Southern Association of Colleges and Schools. The programs were designed to enable the aviation/aerospace professional to master the application of modern management concepts, methods, and tools to the challenges of aviation and general business. The special intricacies of aviation are woven into a strong, traditional management foundation and examined in greater detail through the wide variety of electives. A total of 36 credit hours are required for the program. A course catalog which clearly defines all requirements will be provided once you are selected for admission.

INDEPENDENT STUDIES PROGRAM

Embry-Riddle provides you an excellent opportunity to earn an accredited aviation-orientated Master's Degree in the privacy of your own home. Using state-of-the-art instructional methods and techniques students interact electronically with faculty, staff, and fellow students. The University has established a private forum on Compuserve to facilitate communications between faculty/students and student/student. You can connect to local node when using the electronic communications system. This will, in most cases, alleviate your having to access long distance telephone numbers.

COST: Tuition is established at $285.00 per semester hour. Each course is three credit hours for a total tuition of $855.00 per course. Textbooks, case studies, and shipping fees will vary from course to course. Total cost per 3 credit hour course should range between $900.00-$975.00. To access the ERAU forum, there is a one time program fee of $20.00 for the CompuServe software.

1-800-866-6271 anytime; or (904) 226-6263, M-F from 0800 - 1700 EST

Email: galloglj@cts.db.erau.edu

MASTER OF AERONAUTICAL SCIENCE CURRICULUM

Advanced Aviation/Aerospace Science Core (all MAS students):

MAS 602 The Air Transportation System	3 cr.	
MAS 603 Aircraft and Spacecraft Development	3	
MAS 604 Human Factors in the Aviation/Aerospace Industry	3	
MAS 605 Research Methods and Statistics	3	12

MANAGEMENT SPECIALIZATION
(students must complete any 4 of the following courses):

ABA 521 Management Information Systems	3	
ABA 632 Aviation Labor Relations	3	
ABA 645 Airport Management	3	
MAS 636 Aviation/Aerospace Planning Systems	3	
MAS 640 Supply & Distribution in Aviation/Aerospace Industry	3	
Any combination to equal		12

ELECTIVES:

ABA/MAS (500-600 Level) Electives	9	
MAS 690 Graduate Research Project	3	12

Total Required: (At least 18 credit hours must be MAS courses)   36

OPERATIONS SPECIALIZATION (students must complete all courses):

MAS 606 Aviation/Aerospace Communication/Control Systems	3	
MAS 608 Aviation/Aerospace Accident and Safety Systems	3	
MAS 620 Air Carrier Operations	3	
MAS 622 Corporate Aviation Operations	3	12

ELECTIVES:

ABA/MAS (500-600 Level) Electives	9	
MAS 690 Graduate Research Project	3	12

Total Required: 36

Embry-Riddle Aeronautical University Course Descriptions:

The Air Transportation System (ERAU#MAS602)   3 credits

A study of air transportation as part of a global, multi-modal transportation system. The course reviews the evolution of the technological, social, environmental, and political aspects of this system since its inception at the beginning of the century. The long-term and short-term effects of deregulation, energy shortages, governmental restraints, and national and international issues are examined. Passenger and cargo transportation, as well as military and private aircraft modes are studied in relation to the ever changing transportation requirements. Prerequisites: Demonstrated knowledge of aviation rules and regulations, and economics.

Aircraft and Spacecraft Development (ERAU#MAS603)   3 credits

This course is an overview of aircraft and spacecraft development. Included are vehicle mission, the requirements directed by economics, the military and defense considerations, and the research and developmental processes needed to meet the vehicle requirements. Aviation and aerospace manufacturing organizations and techniques are addressed to include planning, scheduling, production, procurement, supply, and distribution systems. The course studies the aviation and aerospace maintenance systems from the built-in test equipment to the latest product support activities. Prerequisites: Demonstrated knowledge of college-level mathematics and economics.

Human Factors in the Aviation/Aerospace Industry (ERAU#MAS604) 3cr.

This course presents an overview of the importance of the human role in all aspects of the aviation and aerospace industries. It will emphasize the issues, problems, and solutions of unsafe acts, attitudes, errors, and deliberate actions attributed to human behavior and the role supervisors and management personnel play in these actions. The course will study the human limitations in the light of human engineering, human reliability, stress, medical standards, drug abuse, and human physiology. The course will discuss human behavior as it relates to the aviator's adaptation to the flight environment as well as the entire aviation/aerospace industry's role in meeting the aviator's unique needs. Prerequisite: Demonstrated knowledge of behavioral science.

Research Methods and Statistics (ERAU#MAS605)   3 credits

A study of current aviation research methods that include techniques of problem identification, hypothesis formulation, design and use of data gathering instruments, and data analysis. The interpretation of research reports that appear in professional publications are examined through the use of statistical terminology and computations. A formal research proposal will be developed and presented by each student as a basic course requirement. Prerequisites: Demonstrated knowledge of college-level math, including introductory statistics, and basic computer operations.

Aviation/Aerospace Comm./Control Systems (ERAU#MAS606)   3 credits

A detail analysis of current and future development and trends in the control of air traffic that includes the evolution of current national policies, plans and their objectives. The most recent planned improvements for each major component of the ATC system are examined individually and as part of the system as a whole. Prerequisites: Demonstrated knowledge of flight rules and regulations and basic navigation.

Aviation/Aero. Accident Invest. & Safety Systems (ERAU#MAS608)   3cr.

A critical analysis of selected aircraft accidents and an evaluation of causal factors. Particular emphasis is placed on the study of human factors connected with flight and support crew activities in aviation operations. Identification and implementation of accident prevention measures are stressed as integral parts of the development of a complete safety program.

Air Carrier Operations (ERAU#MAS620)   3 credits

A study of air carrier operations systems from the viewpoints of the groundbased dispatch, operations specialists, managers, and the cockpit flight crew. Topics include advanced flight planning, aircraft performance and load considerations, impact of weather conditions, and routing priorities. Prerequisites: Demonstrated knowledge of flight rules and regulations, basic meteorology, basic navigation, and basic aircraft performance.

Corporate Aviation Operations (ERAU#MAS622)   3 credits

The establishment and operations of a corporate flight department are examined along with the procedures and techniques generally accepted as standards by professional corporate fight operations. Included is a practical view of the corporate aviation mission of management mobility and use of the resources available to accomplish it. Prerequisites: None listed.

Advanced Aviation/Aerospace Planning Systems (ERAU#MAS636)   3cr.

Planning and decision-making techniques and strategies used in the aviation industry are emphasized. The types and sources of data needed for decisions about route development and expansion, fleet modernization and new markets are examined. The methods of collecting, analyzing and applying the data through computer applications, modeling, heuristic, value theory, and payoff tables are studied. The limitations and problems associated with strategic planning are discussed. Prerequisites: Demonstrated knowledge of management principles and economics. Prerequisites: Demonstrated knowledge of management principles and economics.

Supply & Distrib. in Aviation/Aerospace Industry (ERAU#MAS640)   3cr.

A study of the elements of physical distribution that includes the structure of supply organizations, priority systems, cost categories, inventory control, and the applications of electronic data processing. Case studies are employed to present issues, problems, and analyses of supply systems in terms of customer satisfaction relative to costs incurred. Prerequisites: Demonstrated knowledge of management principles.

ABA 521 Management Information Systems (ERAU#ABA521)   3 credits

A study of general systems concepts, purposeful systems within aviation organizations, decision and information systems, planning and control systems, and project management and evaluation systems. Prerequisites: Knowledge of principles of management, and introduction to computers.

Aviation Labor Relations (ERAU#ABA632)   3 credits

An introduction to labor law as applied to the aviation industry. Topics include labor union organization and constituency representation, the collective bargaining process, typical labor contract terms and provisions, grievance, mediation, and arbitration procedures, contract administration, labor actions, restrictive employment practices, Title VII of the Civil Service Reform Act of 1978. Prerequisites: Demonstrated knowledge of principles of management.

Airport Management (ERAU#ABA645)   3 credits

A study of the major airport management functions, especially planning, development, and operations. The management of on-site activities by airport tenants and their relationship with the airport operator are analyzed. The current problems confronting airports in areas such as regulation, financing, revenue generation, cost control, establishment of rent and user charges, safety, security, and the socioeconomic relationship of the airport to the community it serves are explored. Prerequisite: Demonstrated knowledge of principles of management.

Graduate Research Project (ERAU#MAS690)   3 credits

A written document on an aviation/aerospace topic which exposes the student to the technical aspects of writing. This course is included in the ABA curriculum to provide the student with the opportunity to pursue a project of special interest, but not to the level of a thesis. This is a required course for those students who choose not to write a thesis. Prerequisite: ABA 522 or MAS 605.

University of Florida - 46 courses

University of Florida, Division of Continuing Education
Dept. of Independent Study by Correspondence & Distance Education
Accreditation by the Southern Association of Colleges and Schools

University of Florida
2209 NW 13th Street
Gainesville FL 32609-3498

The University of Florida has been in the business of offering home study programs for over 75 years (since 1919). Last year alone, some 5,000 students from all over the world took advantage of this program. This program represents all the universities in the State of Florida and is offered by the University of Florida. Faculty is selected from any one of Florida's nine universities. It is possible to obtain either college or high school credit through this program, or a certificate in a special area.

University courses are numbered using Florida's common course numbering system and are easily translated into degree program requirements at any of Florida's nine state universities or twenty-eight public community colleges. Every institution sets its own rules for the number of credits that may be transferred as well as the courses that may be applied toward its undergraduate degrees. It is the student's responsibility to ensure that the credit earned from any institution will be accepted in the program of the college he or she is attending. Florida's program provides courses in a non-traditional medium; **it does not offer degrees by correspondence**.

The content of a college-level course is, as nearly as possible, the same as the equivalent course given on campus. Independent Study courses should be considered equivalent to courses of the same number of campus. If you are interested in applying courses to a degree program, you should understand that each college and university has its own rules on the amount of independent study credit that may be applied. Some state institutions in Florida permit up to twenty-five percent of degree requirements to be met by correspondence study. **It is your responsibility to obtain counseling from the university where your credit is to be applied and to meet its deadlines for course completion**.

A maximum of one year is allowed for completion. The minimum time for course completion is one month. Some courses have restrictions on the rate at which written assignments may be submitted; if there is no restriction cited in your study guide, a maximum of **six written assignments** per week may be submitted for college courses.

Examinations: Most courses consist of a midterm and a final examination. These examinations are administered by a proctor at universities, community colleges, high schools and educational training offices everywhere. Some courses use open-book examinations to summarize the course content and may be taken at home without proctoring.

A proctor may be a special faculty member, a principal, or librarian. An armed forces education officer is an acceptable proctor if you are in the military. Any other proctor must be approved by our office. To maintain the validity of the examination, no student, relative of the student, or non-designated person will be allowed to proctor an examination. You are responsible for any fees charged by the proctor.

Tuition for university courses is as follows:

Florida Resident Tuition:
2-Semester Hour Course:	$113.64
3-Semester Hour Course:	$170.49
4-Semester Hour Course:	$227.32

Non-Florida Resident Tuition:
2-Semester Hour Course:	$440.48
3-Semester Hour Course:	$660.72
4-Semester Hour Course:	$880.96

Joanne M. East, Ph.D., Director
Division of Continuing Education, Suite D
University of Florida
2209 NW 13th Street
Gainesville FL 32609-3498

(904) 392-1711
(800) 327-4218

University of Florida Course Descriptions

American Federal Government (FLOR#POS2041)   3 credits

Basic principles of the Federal Constitution; civil rights; political parties and the electoral process. Structure and machinery of the federal government, Congress, the President, and the Judiciary. Seventeen assign'ts, one exam.

Ancient and Medieval Civilizations (FLOR#EUH2100)   3 credits

Provides a survey of Western traditions from the beginnings through the end of the Middle Ages. Emphasis is on patterns of thinking and on those institutions most distinctive to Western tradition. Twelve assign'ts, 3 exams

Basic Marketing Concepts (FLOR#MAR3023)   3 credits

Gives the student an understanding of the decision areas and the ability to utilize marketing concepts to make business decisions. A required prerequisite for all marketing courses. Twenty assignments, one exam.

Biological Anthropology: Human Evolution (FLOR#ANT3511)   3 credits

Human evolution and contemporary variation. Relationship with other primates. Human genetics; anthropometry. Population differences, distribution, and history. Course does not incorporate a laboratory; accordingly it does not meet the UF general education requirement in biological sciences. Eighteen written assignments, two examinations.

British Authors: Beginnings to 1790 (FLOR#ENL2011)   3 credits

Survey of English masterworks. Intended for students in liberal studies and those exploring a literature major. Includes authors such as Chaucer, Marlowe, Shakespeare, Jonson, Milton, Dryden, Congreve, Swift, Pope, Johnson, and Boswell. Fifteen written assignments and one exam.

British Authors: Early Romantics (FLOR#ENL2020)   3 credits

Survey of English masterworks. Intended for students in liberal studies and those exploring a literature major. Includes authors such as Blake, Coleridge, Wordsworth, Mill, Browning, Wilde, Shaw, Conrad, Woolf, and Eliot. Fifteen written assignments, one examination.

Concepts of Management (FLOR#MAN3010)   3 credits

Intro to the nature and process of management, with emphasis upon management of physical and human resources. Not required for management or human resource management majors. Twenty assignments, 2 exams.

Contemporary Health Science (FLOR#HSC2100)   3 credits

A comprehensive approach to health concerns and problems in contemporary society, including methods of assessing individual health needs. Sixteen written assignments, two examinations.

The Courts (FLOR#CCJ3200)   3 credits

Jurisdiction, policies, and procedures of courts in the administration of criminal justice. Ten written assignments, two examinations.

Criminology (FLOR#CCJ3011)   3 credits
An examination of the field of criminology, including its theories, basic assumptions and definitions. Eleven written assignments and 2 exams.

Educational Psychology (FLOR#EDF3210)   3 credits
An introduction to the application of psychology to the problems of education in a variety of educational settings. It examines the theoretical and applied aspects of learning, motivation, human development, personality, and measurement and evaluation. Seventeen written assign'ts, 2 exams.

English Grammar (FLOR#LIN2670)   3 credits
The basics of traditional English grammar. Designed to complement composition and creative writing courses, as a review for those students who will take preprofessional examinations, and as a basic course for students interested in improving their knowledge of English. Twenty written assignments, one examination

Exploring Geological Sciences (FLOR#GLY1000)   3 credits
Selected topics in the geological sciences for those not majoring in science. Twenty written assignments, 1 examination.

History of Russia 1825 to Present (FLOR#EUH3572)   3 credits
Examination of the social, economic, cultural, and political development of Russia from the reign of Tsar Nicholas I to the present day. Although internal history is stressed, appropriate attention will be paid to Russia's role in international relations. Fourteen written assignments, two exams.

Hitler's Third Reich (FLOR#EUH4465)   3 credits
Deals with the background and nature of the Nazi Regime, the character of Hitler's dictatorship, and th origins and course of WW II in its European context. It also examines National Socialism's impact on German institutions and racial consequences. Fourteen written assignments, two examinations.

International Relation (FLOR#INR2001)   3 credits
The nature of international relations; nationalism, imperialism, militarism, armaments, history of international relations, foreign policies, functions and problems of democracy; international organization, and the United Nations. Sixteen written assignments, one examination.

Introduction to Agronomy (FLOR#AGR3005C)   3 credits
Introduction to the principles and practices of field crop production. Thirteen written assignments and one examination.

Introduction to Criminal Justice (FLOR#CCJ2020)   3 credits
Designed to provide freshman and sophomore students with knowledge of terminology, classification systems, trends, and theories of criminal justice. Fourteen written assignments, two examination.

Introduction to Philosophy (FLOR#PHI2010)   3 credits
Systematic introduction to the range of problems philosophy deals with and the variety of methods and styles with which they can be approached. Fifteen written assignments, no examinations.

Introduction to Public Relations (FLOR#PUR3000)   3 credits

The nature and role of public relations, activities of public relations professionals, major influences which affect organizational behavior, the ethics and professional development of public relations professionals. Twenty-one written assignments, one examination.

Language: Humanities Perspective (FLOR#LIN2000)   3 credits

The nature of human language, and its relationship to thinking. Fifteen written assignments, one examination.

Law Enforcement (FLOR#CCJ3101)   3 credits

An advanced survey of law enforcement concentrating on the police, with emphasis on functions (law enforcement, order maintenance, public service) and responsibilities (e.g., preservation of constitutional rights, community relations), including organizational and management aspects. Thirteen assignments, 2 examinations.

Marriage and Family (FLOR#SYG2430)   3 credits

Development of masculine and feminine roles. Recent changes in premarital interaction, dating, sexual involvement, coed dorm living, and living together. Mutual adjustment and parenthood. Alternative live styles including group marriage, communal living, and open marriage. Seventeen assignments, 2 exams.

Measurement and Evaluation in Education (FLOR#EDF4430)   3 credits

The basic principles and methods of measurement, evaluation, and test construction. Prerequisite: permission of department representative. Thirteen written assignments and one examination.

Nineteenth Century Europe: A Survey (FLOR#EUH3004)   3 credits

European history from the close of the Napoleonic Wars to the turn of the century, a period in which Europe was at the height of its wealth and power. Particular attention is paid to the major powers. Fourteen written assignments, two examinations.

Personality (FLOR#PPE4004)   3 credits

Methods and findings of personality theories and an evaluation of constitutional, biosocial and psychological determinants of personality. Seventeen written assignments and two examinations.

Principles of Macroeconomics (FLOR#ECO2013)   3 credits

The nature of economics, economic concepts and institutions; emphasis on the accounting, analytical, and policy aspects of national income and product, as well as public finance, money and banking, and international trade. Twenty-two written assignments, one examination.

Principles of Microeconomics (FLOR#ECO2023) 3 credits

Theories of production, determination of prices and distribution of income in regulated and unregulated industries. Attention is also given to industrial relations, monopolies, and comparative economic systems. Twenty-two written assignments, one examination.

Public Administration in American Society (FLOR#PAD3003) 3 credits

A general introductory course in public administration. Management of large-scale government bureaucracies, including organization, career systems, and financing. The role of bureaucracies in modern society in the formulation of public policy. Eleven assignments, two exams.

Quality Mgt.: What, How & Why of Team Work (FLOR#MGT2) 2.2 CEUs

This is a course for current and future managers who want to know more about how organizations can empower their workforce to improve products and services in order to increase customer satisfaction. A quality-driven organization is characterized by three dimensions: total involvement, process involvement, and customer service. Following an ingroductory lesson, each of these dimensions - implemented through principles, policies, and practices - is examined in a separate lesson. One written assignment may be submittedper week. Four written assignments, one exam.

Religion in America (FLOR#REL2120) 3 credits

Examination of the scope and nature of religious movements and institutions in America. Twenty written assignments and one examination.

Risk Management and Insurance (FLOR#RMI3011) 3 credits

An introduction to the principles of risk management and insurance and their application to personal and business pure risk problems. Prereq.: Fundamental Business Statistics or permission of instructor. Twenty-two written assignments and one examination.

Social Foundations of Education (FLOR#EDF3604) 3 credits

An examination of the current educational system in the United States. The analysis draws on the disciplines of philosophy, sociology, history, anthropology, political science, and psychology in order to foster critical thinking about prevailing practices and beliefs. The aim of the course is to deepen awareness of the role schools do and can play in a democratic society. Satisfies the general education requirement for the College of Education, the College of Health and Human Performance, and the College of Fine Arts. One written assignment may be submitted per calendar week; fifteen assignments and one examination.

Survey of Mass Communications (FLOR#MMC1000) 2 credits

Introduction to the various mass communication media, with special emphasis on the roles and responsibilities to society and the public. Five written assignments may be submitted for grading per calendar week. Fifteen written assignments, one examination.

The English Novel: 20th Century (FLOR#ENL3132) 3 credits

Includes works by Conrad, For, Lawrence, Joyce, Forster, Woolf, Murdoch, Amis, and Fowles. Eighteen written assignments, no examinations.

The Modern World Since 1815 (FLOR#WOH1030)   3 credits

The origins and development of political, economic, social, and intellectual developments in the modern world since 1815. Eighteen written assignments, three exams.

The Modern World to 1815 (FLOR#WOH1023)   3 credits

The origins and development of political, economic, social and intellectual antecedents of the modern world from the end of the Middle Ages to 1815. Eighteen written assignments, three examinations.

Twentieth Century Europe: A Survey (FLOR#EUH3005)   3 credits

European history from the turn of the century through the two world wars. Particular attention is paid to the major powers in this period when Europe declined from it preeminent position. Fourteen assignments, two exams.

Writing for Mass Communication (FLOR#MMC2100)   3 credits

A preprofessional course designed to provide fundamental instruction and practice in writing as a basis for Upper Division courses in advertising, journalism, and public relations. Stresses the basic similarities in writing for all mass media. Nineteen written assignments, no examination.

Management Ethics (FLOR#MGT1)   2.2 CEUs

This is a beginning course for business or government managers designed to provide a basic understanding of the many conceptual, individual and organizational issues surrounding business ethics. While the individual is ultimately responsible for his or her own actions, institutions often control the situations in which many ethical decisions are made. Although generally exploratory in nature, this class provides managers (and future managers) with some background information and basic tools, as well as provides some critical standards for approaching and evaluating ethical questions in the work place. Four written assignments, one examination.

Managing the Problem Employee (FLOR#SUP4)   1.5 CEUs

Focuses on the theory and practical skills required for effective supervision of problem employees. Contributes to supervisor's ability to maintain a productive working environment. Teaches how to recognize the problem employee, as well as provide strategies for managing and dealing with the problem employee. Six written assignments may be submitted for grading per week. Ten written assignments and one exam.

Principles of Supervision (FLOR#SUP1)   1.5 CEUs

Helps to prepare individuals for first-line supervision. Topics include delegating, decision-making, planning, time management, organizing, staffing, directing, controlling, and labor relations. Content can be applied in all supervisory activities; course does not center on any specific occupation. Ten written assignments, one examination.

Sexual Harassment in the Workplace (FLOR#SUP8)   2.2 CEUs

This is a beginning course for current and future managers that provides a basic understanding of the many conceptual, individual, and institutional issues that surround the subject of sexual harassment in the workplace. The course deals with such issues as changing cultural attitudes at word; the

241

evolution of the subject; its personal, corporate, and societal ramification; profiles of typical victims and perpetrators; the changing legal definitions of harassment; and preventive measures to be taken by both individuals and organizations. Four written assignments and one examination.

Supervisory Communications (FLOR#SUP2)   1.5 CEUs

Improves the supervisor's communications, motivation, group communications and barriers, written communications, and speaking. Six written assignments may be submitted for grading per week. Ten written assignments, one exam.

Supervisory Leadership (FLOR#SUP3)   1.5 CEUs

Developing and applying effective supervisory leadership skills are major tasks in every organization. Course includes study of the leadership role and the need to develop power and influence within that role. Different leadership approaches, skills, and styles are considered from the standpoint of understanding motivation and communication with subordinates. Relationship between effective leadership and organizational change is explored. Four written assignments may be submitted for grading per week. Ten written assignments, one exam.

Working Better with Your Boss (FLOR#SUP5)   1.5 CEUs

Deals with an important yet often very difficult relationship by just about everyone who works in an organization: getting along with the boss. This relationship can be managed, shaped and influenced, by the subordinate.

242

Front Range Community College - 17 courses ┌─────┐ FRCC └─────┘

Accredited by the North Central Association of Colleges and Schools

```
Front Range Community College
3645 West 112th Avenue
Westminster  CO  80030
```

Front Range Community College has recently started giving online access to eighteen courses, a number that is expected to increase as demand allows. The computer online courses bring you credit classes via email and the Internet. Using any computer with a modem and communications software, computer course students will dial into the Internet for assignments, lecture notes, and discussions with the instructor and other students.

Exams will be given over the Internet or through a prearranged proctor. Essays, lecture notes, and all other materials will be exchanged by computer. You can take the course from home, from work, or from anywhere in the world where you can access the Internet. The content and requirements for online courses are the same as for the courses taught on campus - only the delivery method is different. They will be graded and transcripted the same as any other courses - and, of course, are fully transferrable to other colleges and universities.

Attendence in the CyberClassroom: Students are expected to check their email daily for lecture notes, assignments, and communication from their CyberFaculty. In addition, students may be placed in online 'teams' and be required to work with other students on specific projects.

Student Services: now online to answer your questions about academic advising, career counseling, financial aid, testing center, and other topics. Address your inquiries to: FR_Susan@Mash.Colorado.edu.

How do these courses differ from conventional (on-campus) courses, and how do they transfer? The only difference between Special Delivery and traditional courses is the method of delivery. As with any credit course, you must complete reading assignments, take tests, and participate in other activities. The video or audio program (included in some courses) is really just the "lecture" part of the regular class.

All students must complete an application for admission to the college. FRCC requires all new students to participate in a basic skills assessment, which is used to assure proper placement. The assessment can be waived if the new student can demonstrate sufficient academic proficiency to successfully participate in the courses; waivers can be arranged with the course instructor or Student Services.

For additional information: Call or visit the Distance Learning Office ((303)466-8811 ext.554 or 513) for general information or mailing of packets and material. Call or email the instructor for information about specific courses, or send email to: wwwadmin@mosquito.frcc.cccoes.edu or Gertrude@mash.colorado.edu.

Tuition is the same for distance learning courses as for all other credit courses - request the current semester schedule for tuition rates. Fees vary, depending on the type of class and where it is held. A $15 producer's fee and a $10 broadcast fee will be charged for telecourses; a $15 fee is charged for college-by-cassette courses and online courses; a $5 fee is charged for audio courses; and student fees are charged for on-campus courses. The registration processing fee ($9 per student per semester) applies as well, along with course fees as applicable.

Front Range Community College
Distance Education
3645 West 112th Avenue
Westminster CO 80030
(303)466-8811 cxt.554

Front Range Community College Course Descriptions

English Composition I (FRCC#ENG121)   3 credits
Emphasizes the planning, writing, and revising of compositions, including the development of critical and logical thinking skills. Includes a minimum of five compositions that stress analytical, evaluative, and persuasive/argumentative writing.

English Composition II: Research Paper (FRCC#ENG122)   3 credits
Expands and refines the objectives of English Composition I. Emphasizes critical/logical thinking and reading, problem definition, research strategies, and writing analytical, evaluative, and/or presuasive papers that incorporate research. Prerequisite FRCC#ENG121.

Unix OnLine Course (FRCC#CIS175)   3 credits
This course is an introduction to the Unix operating system. It includes an introduction to the Unix file system and utilities, shell programming, Sed and Awk, and an overview of Unix system administration. Prerequisite: one programming language or permission of instructor.

C Language Programming (FRCC#CSC230)   4 credits
Students are introduced to the C programming language, which is a 'mid-level' language whose economy of expression and data manipulation features allow a programmer to deal with the computer at a 'low level'. Prerequisites: CSC150 Pascal Programming, CSC160 Computer Science, MAT121 College Algebra, or permission of instructor.

DC Fundamentals I (FRCC#ETE101)   3 credits
Students study, construct, and evaluate series and parallel DC resistive circuits to show the relationships of voltage, current, resistance, and power, utilizing formulas and common test instruments, emphasizing standard safety practices.

DC Fundamentals II (FRCC#ETE102)   3 credits
Students, study, construct, test, troubleshoot and evaluate combination resistive, magnetic, R-C and R-L circuits and describe the properties of magnetism, induction, utilizing fromulas, and common test instruments. Emphasis is on standard safety practices.

AC Fundamentals I (FRCC#ETE103)   3 credits
Students study, construct, test, troubleshoot and evaluate combination resistive, magnetic, R-C and R-L circuits and describe the properties of magnetism, induction, utilizing formulas, and common test instruments. Emphasis is on standard safety practices. Prerequisite: DC Fundamentals I.

AC Fundamentals II (FRCC#ETE104)   3 credits
Students study, construct, and evaluate series and parallel resistive-reactive circuits, with sine wave, pulse, and square wave sources, utilizing formulas and common test instruments. Emphasis is on standard safety practices.

US History I (FRCC#HIS201)   3 credits

Examines the major political, economic, social, diplomatic, military, cultural and intellectual events in American History from the first inhabitants through the Civil War/Reconstruction.

US History II (FRCC#HIS202)   3 credits

Examines major political, economic, social, diplomatic/military, cultural & intellectual events in American History from Reconstruction to the present.

Human Biology (FRCC#BIO116)   3 credits

This course is an introduction to human anatomy and physiology for students who have little or no background in science. It does not substitute for a year-long Anatomy and Physiology course with a lab. Topics covered are atoms, molecules, cells, energetics, genetics, and a vrief survey of systems.

Pathophysiology (FRCC#BIO216)   3 credits

This one semester course focuses upon the functions of the human body systems with emphasis on their interrelationships in adaptation to stress and disease.

Language Fundamentals (FRCC#ENG060)   3 credits

This course will advance the student from sentence to paragraph structure. Critical thinking skills through formulation of topic sentences and effective paragraph development will be incorporated. The course will emphasize writing as a process, including prewriting and revision activities, and will review grammar, usage, and punctuation.

Technical Writing (FRCC#ENG131)   3 credits

This course develops proficiency in technical writing, emphasizing principles for organizing, drafting, and revising a variety of documents for industry, business, and government.

Western Civilization I (FRCC#HIS101)   3 credits

This course explores the major political, social, diplomatic, military, cultural, intellectual and economic aspects of European history from prehistory to the seventeenth century.

General Psychology I (FRCC#PSY101)   3 credits

Scientific study of behavior including motivation, emotion, physiolgical psychology, stress and coping, research methods, consciousness, sensation, perception, learning and memory.

General Psychology II (FRCC#PSY102)   3 credits

Scientific study of behavior including cognition, language, intelligence, psychological assessment, personality, abnormal psychology, therapy, life span development and social psychology.

Heriot-Watt University - 12 courses

> Heriot-Watt Admissions Department
> Electronic University Network
> 1977 Colestin Rd.
> Hornbrook CA 96044
>
> 800-225-3276

Heriot-Watt University encompasses a great range of technological, professional, and vocational studies and provides a stimulating environment for creative study to the highest level. As a modern technologically based University, it gives priority to areas of study of direct industrial, commercial, and social relevance.

The same impetus is evident throughout its history. Granted its Royal Charter as a University in 1966, Heriot-Watt traces its origins back to 1821 and the foundation of the Edinburgh School of Arts, at that time a pioneering institute for the advanced education of working people in the applied arts and sciences. Subsequently becoming the Watt Institution and School of Arts and, from 1885, Heriot-Watt College, its record is of longstanding, close, and effective collaboration with industry in education, training, and innovative research in the sciences, engineering, and management.

The University's intriguing name commemorates James Watt (1736-1819), the developer of steam power and universally recognized master technologist of the first industrial revolution, and George Heriot (1563-1623), financier to King James VI of Scotland and I of England, who bequeathed a considerable fortune for educational purposes in his native Edinburgh. So, it can be said, the University links technology, business, and communication.

The University's technological base and Business School -- the Faculties of Science, Engineering, and Economic and Social Studies -- are located on a single campus at Riccarton, about eight miles west of the center of Edinburgh, Scotland. It is a modern environment of sleek, low-lying buildings, closely integrated into the existing environment -- a splendid old estate of park land landscaped in the 18th century. The custom-built and equipped University buildings, and a comprehensive range of facilities, are conveniently grouped and continuously interconnected, making this a tranquil and self-contained place for study and research, while still very much a part of the Scottish capital city.

The international character of the University is fully evident at the level of postgraduate study and research, both in the many links, partners, and sponsors in teaching and research programs -- which include individual governments, major companies from the U.S.A. and many countries of Europe as well as the U.K., a very significant level of support from European Community research, development, and training programs, ongoing involvement with many United Nations agencies, not to mention ties to a host of individual universities, research institutes, and international scientific bodies -- and in the student population.

Heriot-Watt enjoys a long tradition of welcoming students from overseas who on average make up 15% of the total student population, and a significantly higher number at the postgraduate level. Currently some 80 different nationalities are represented in the University.

INSTRUCTOR-GUIDED STUDY: The fee is $935. This fee includes all the study materials, personal guidance, feedback and support from the instructor, problem solving in all areas of the course subject material, evaluation and feedback on the practice examination, as well as technical support services regarding communications and software.

INDEPENDENT STUDY: The fee is $735. The fee includes all of the study materials for independent study of the subject and preparation for the examination.

The initial registration fee for Electronic University Network students is $75. This fee is paid only once as long as the student continues enrollment in at least one course per year.

If you are interested in the online MBA program, send email to Cathy Council (EUNCouncil@aol.com). When you write, please tell us something of your background and the nature of your interest in graduate business study. Include your name, address, and telephone number if you would like to receive a complete package of information on the Heriot-Watt University MBA.

Heriot-Watt University Course Descriptions

Accounting - (HERI#01)

Accounting is often described as the language of business. It is con　　　 with the gathering, ordering, checking, presenting and communication of financial data so that informed decisions can be made. Decision makers are positioned both outside and inside an organization. Outsiders include shareholders who want information to help them decide whether to buy or sell shares, tax authorities who require information on profits as a basis for taxation, and creditors who need to assess the organization's ability to pay its debts. Insiders are the organization's directors and managers who need information to allow them to make many crucial decisions, for example, in the areas of pricing, product performance, resourcing of raw materials, production resourcing and capital spending. Employees need to assess their organization's capacity to provide them with a long term career.

The thrust of the Accounting course is managerial in nature. A successful manager needs to cut through the information system to reach the accounting numbers that really matter, i.e., those that could influence a decision. But first the manager must understand how these numbers are put together before being in a position to spot which ones are critical. This course will provide you with both the background and the cutting tools. The mystiques surrounding accounting will be removed.

Decision-Making Techniques - (HERI#02)

The fundamentals of good decision-making are, first, a clear understanding of the decision itself and, second, the availability of properly focused information to support the decision. Decision-making techniques help with both of these problems. Their value has been greatly increased in recent years through micro-computers which have made the power of the techniques available to general managers. However, the techniques should be thought of as aids to decision-making and not substitutes for it. The course deals with the following main areas: decision analysis, advanced decision analysis, linear programming, simulation, project planning, and computers and decisions.

Economics - (HERI#03)

The objective of the microeconomics section is two-fold: to spell out the strengths and weaknesses of the free enterprise system in a politically unbiased fashion and to highlight the economics principles and tools essential for rational decision making in a company. Major microeconomics topics include: economic concepts, issues and tools; the price mechanism; demand; productivity, costs and supply; markets; economic efficiency; organization of industries; public goods and externalities; income distribution; international trade and exchange rates.

The objective of the macroeconomics section is to clarify the national and international economic environment within which firms operate. It is concerned with inflation, unemployment, exchange rates and the potential, real and money gross national product; fiscal policy and the multiplier; investment expenditure and the rate of interest; money, banking and monetary policy; stabilizing a dynamic economy; the balance of payments and international finance.

Finance - (HERI#04)

The course starts with a description of the participants in financial markets, the decisions they must take and the basic processes which are common to all financial decisions. The basic quantitative tools of financial evaluation are developed at the outset, and are used throughout the course. The analyses then move on to the incorporated firm, introduce the important distinctions between making financial decisions as individuals and making such decisions in complex organizations. This leads on to the relationships between accounting measures of performance, such as "profits," and the financial cash flows necessary for valuation. Company investment decision making is then extended to the more realistic context of companies with complex capital structures, i.e. those financed with both debt and equity capital. The tools of capital budgeting are developed, to deal with situations where there are budget constraints.

A company's working capital is its short term investment in cash, marketable securities, receivables (debtors) and short term financing, bank loans and payables (creditors). Because of the short term nature of these assets and financing, an entirely different set of financial management techniques is used in dealing with them. More and more companies are expanding their operating environments to the international scene. Financial managers must be educated in at least the basics of such markets and transactions.

Government & Industry - (HERI#05)

The objective is to make you aware of the important influence exercised by government on the actions of companies. The course is designed to explain what happens when a government deliberately and systematically tries to alter the behavior of companies. It performs this task by using a framework derived from economic analysis in which the government is the "principal" and the companies are its "agents." The principal has certain policy aims and tries to induce the agents to conform to these aims. The conventional analysis of the government-industry interface usually assumes that the government's aims can be clearly defined and that all the government has to do is to select the appropriate policy instrument, for example, taxation, subsidies or regulation of some kind. In practice it is found that the fulfillment of these assumptions is the exception rather than the rule, and the framework of analysis has changed. Instead of companies adjusting passively to government policy instruments, they are often in a position to bargain with government about the application of policy instruments. An important reason for this is that the government has to rely on companies as the main source of information on which its policies are based. The course explores in detail the main elements in the bargaining relationship.

International Trade & Finance - (HERI#06)

International economic influences are becoming increasingly important to companies in all countries. Obviously companies involved in exporting and importing goods and services operate within the international marketplace. However, companies attempting to raise finance or under-take investment decisions are also exposed to international influences.

The objectives of this course are:
-- To explain why and how international trade takes place
--To examine the financial implications of an international economy
--To discuss the technical questions which managers must face

The course combines technical and descriptive material with analysis of managerial decision-making problems.

Marketing - (HERI#07)

The focus of the course is the marketing management process itself. Thus, it is structured around the steps in the analytical and decision-making process involved in formulating, implementing and controlling a strategic marketing program for a given product-market entry.

It deals with customer characteristics, competitive and environmental analysis, market segmentation, market targeting, competitive positioning, the major marketing action program variables (produce, price, promotion and distribution), implementation and control. It also deals with the tools of marketing research, demand estimation, and industry analysis. Specific applications of the tools are identified and discussed.

The intent throughout is to analyze the major issues, concepts and techniques relevant to the marketing of goods and services, while avoiding encyclopaedic lists and arcane models of limited use. In brief, the course should provide you with a solid foundation of knowledge about what is involved in developing and implementing strategic marketing programs. The course consists of a text book supplemented by specially written, complementary distance learning material, and is structured around five major sections which follow the steps in the marketing management process.

Negotiation - (HERI#08)

Management requires negotiating skills. Suppliers, customers and colleagues are unlikely to forego their own interest merely because someone else thinks that they ought to. Nor are important decisions likely to be agreed upon without some form of negotiation between those able to influence the shape of the decisions or their impact. Negotiation is one of several means available to managers to assist in the making of decisions. It is neither superior nor inferior to other forms of decision-making -- it is appropriate in some circumstances but not in others. Deciding when it is appropriate to turn to negotiation, or away from it, is only part of the complexity of management.

The course provides a thorough grounding in the science and practice of negotiation. Various academic disciplines (economics, psychology, sociology, politics, anthropology and mathematics) have researched negotiation from their particular standpoints and much of this material forms the basis for the scientific analysis of negotiation. On the practical side, the course covers material drawn from a range of behavioral studies. It covers work by various authorities who consult and train in negotiation. The normative methods advanced by the Harvard Negotiation Project and the vast US literature, which regards negotiation as a series of tactics and ploys, are explained and evaluated.

Organizational Behavior - (HERI#09)

The Organizational Behavior course brings together the most recent developments in the understanding of human behavior in organizations. The modules are designed to combine theoretical knowledge and practical managerial prescriptions. The objective of the course is to provide students with an understanding of the importance of individual differences; work attitudes and their antecedents and consequences; and the role of process and content theories of employee motivation and performance. These are the fundamental aspects of human behavior in work settings.

Quantitative Methods - (HERI#10)

Statistics can be divided into two parts. The first part, "descriptive statistics," handles the problem of sorting a large amount of collected data in ways which enable its main features to be seen immediately. It is concerned with turning numbers into real and useful information. It includes ideas such as organizing and arranging data so that its patterns can be seen, summarizing data so that it can be handled more easily, and communicating data to others. It also includes the important area of handling business statistics generated by MIS.

The second part can be referred to as "inferential statistics." This is concerned with the problem of how a small amount of data which has been collected (called a sample) may be analyzed to infer general conclusions about the total amount of similar data which exist uncollected in the world (called the population). For example, opinion polls use inferential statistics to make statements about the opinions of the whole electorate of a country, given the results of a few hundred interviews.

Strategic Information Systems - (HERI#11)

The course examines what general managers require to know about Information Systems, both to help exploit potential opportunities and to avoid potential disasters. This is a management and not a technical course. It will show managers how the exploitation of Information Systems is now an important managerial role in order to achieve a wide range of business benefits. However, it will also show technical Information Systems managers how their roles must expand to incorporate strategic business issues.

Strategic Planning - (HERI#12)

Strategic Planning is the process of setting company objectives, choosing among alternative courses of action, allocating resources and evaluating outcomes. The objective of this course is to incorporate the transferable management skills developed in the compulsory discipline courses into a decision making structure. In business schools planning is usually taught using the case approach in an interactive class environment. This course is different in that it is designed around Stratplan, a computer simulation. Stratplan was developed using the concepts of economics, marketing, finance, accounting and quantitative methods. It provides you with an opportunity to experience the problems of running a company, and to identify the relevance of the concepts developed in the other compulsory courses.

Western Illinois University - 26 courses

Accredited by the North Central Association of Colleges and Schools.

> Western Illinois University
> Educational Broadcasting and Extended Learning
> 401 Memorial Hall
> 1 University Circle
> Macomb IL 61455

Western Illinois University offers you the opportunity to earn undergraduate credit while studying in your home at a time convenient for you. Independent study courses are offered during all terms. You begin your courses at the start of the term and have six months to complete your course work. Independent study courses are taught by WIU professors and duplicate as nearly as possible the content of courses as offered in the regular WIU classroom setting. This type of study challenges you to develop initiative, persistence, and the ability to pace your study.

Examination Request Forms for all required examinations are included in the course study guide. Mail the request form to us two weeks before the date you wish to take the examination. Acceptable proctors include testing center personnel of community colleges and universities, school superintendents, high school principals and counselors, education offi-cers of military personnel, and education officers of correctional facilities.

Graduate Students: Students who have earned a bachelor's degree may register for independent study courses to meet specific individual needs. If you are registering with WIU for the first time but are not interested in becoming a degree candidate, you must request that the college or university granting your highest degree furnish a statement of degree showing the date it was conferred.

Tuition: The following rates are current; however, tuition is subject to change without notice.

- $82.00 per semester hour for those without a bachelor's degree
- $86.50 per semester hour for those with a bachelor's degree

Email to: IS-Program@wiu.edu
URL: http://www.ecnet.net/users/miebis/index.html

Phone: 309-298-2496   Fax: 309-298-2133

Western Illinois University Course Descriptions

Advanced Fire Administration (ILLW#LAW481)   3 credits

Offers an overview of organization and management in the modern fire service. Topics include management of equipment and personnel, fire department functions, planning, resource development, labor relations, communications, financial management, and community relations.

Analytic Approaches to Public Fire Protection (ILLW#LAW482)   3 credits

Gives a broad understanding of the characterstics of systems analysis and of its uses and limitations in fire protection and other problem areas. The course is illustrated with case studies and models using the systems approach to fire supression and prevention.

Biology of Aging (ILLW#ZOOL420G)   3 credits

Explore the nature and theories of aging. Study the processes involved at the molecular, cellular, organ, and organismal levels of development and the changes that occur with time. In vitro aging is discussed in detail Examine aging in respect to each human organ system: muscular, nervous, digestive, nutritional, excretory, endocrine, and reproductive. Relationships between aging and immunity, neoplasia, and geriatric medicine are considered.

Child Nutrition and Health (ILLW#SCI303)   3 credits

This course discusses nutritional needs and problems of infants and preschool children. the course covers the development of food service and nutrition components in infant and preschool programs. Useful for anyone concerned with child nutrition and health, this course meets the teacher certification requirement for a course in child nutrition and health.

Consumer Economics (ILLW#FCS331)   3 credits

Explore such topics as consumers in a global economy; protection for consumers - rights and responsibilities; rational decision making; budgeting; consumption patterns; financial management; risk management; and retirement planning.

Elementary Spanish I: Destinos (ILLW#SPAN121)   4 credits

Develop the four basic skills - listening, speaking, reading, and writing. This telecourse makes the Spanish culture and language come alive through video episodes of a mystery that help develop basic language skills and an understanding of gestures and cultural clues that enrich communication.

Fire Dynamics (ILLW#IND444)   3 credits

A study of fire propagation phenomenon in both fuel and air regulated pahses. Variables in pre- and post-flashover fire development are discussed. The study of geometric, material, gaseous, fluid flow, and thermodynamic parameters enhances the course.

Fire Protection Structures and Systems Design (ILLW#IE&T443)   3 cr.

Study the design principles involved in the protection of the structure from fire, the empirical tests and prediction procedures, control detection and suppression system design practices, and fundamentals of the hydraulic design of sprinkler and water spray systems.

Fire-Related Human Behavior (ILLW#PSY481)   3 credits

Examines human behavior in fire incidents. The course discusses occupant behaviors, fire setting, public education and fire prevention, eyewitness reports, and post-fire interviewing; it also looks at aspects of building design as related to evacuation, communication, and safety in fire situations.

Human Biology (ILLW#BIOL304)   4 credits

Human Biology includes topics on human evolution, behavior, ecology, and physiology in detail. Human genetics, including inheritance of chromosomes, sex determination, molecular genetics, mutations, and genetic engineering are also developed.

Incendiary Fire Analysis and Investigation (ILLW#LAW486)   3 credits

Examines the procedures and techniques for the collection, comparison, and analysis of the physical evidence relative to the area of fire origin. Also studied are principles of evidence of ignition phenomenon and propagation variables; legislative, economic, psychological, and sociological variables of the incendiary fire; the role of insurance and government programs; and data analysis and prediction techniques, including pattern analysis

Introduction to Nutrition (ILLW#FCS109)   3 credits

Good nutrition is vital to all people. Learn basic nutrition concepts and ways to apply your nutrition knowledge to everyday living. This course also examines world food problems.

Labor institutions and Public Policy (ILLW#ECON340)   3 credits

Provices a broad perspective on the role of 'labor institutions' in modern industrialized society, particularly the United States. The topics in the course are organized in three general areas: 1) the institution - the structure and growth of labor organizations, the evolution of public policy toward unions in the United States, and an international comparison of labor movements; 2) an economic analysis of trade unions - sources of economic power, impact on relative wages and overall inflation; and 3) a focus on some contemporary issues - public sector unions and antidiscrimination policies.

Literature of the Americas (ILLW#ENG400)   6 credits

Deepen your understanding of what constitutes American literature through an exploration of Spanish-American, African-American, and French- and English-Canadian fiction. The novels and short stories illuminate the themes common to all four cultures - the nature of myth and history, the dilemma of the intellectual, the clash of cultures, the war of the sexes - all dramatized in very different ways.

Management in Organizations and Behavior (ILLW#MGT349)   3 credits

Gain the necessary information to enhance your ability to perform effectively in a managerial position. This comprehensive and integrated introduction to the principles of management emphasizes the management functions of planning, organizing, and control as well as such behavioral processes as communication, leadership, and motivation.

Management and Society (ILLW#MGT481)   3 credits

A contemporary study of relationships between the business institution and government, this course deals with the social responsibility of business, societal forces exerted, external environmental factors, and the individual company as part of the economic system.

Managerial Economics (ILLW#ECON332)   3 credits

Focus on the application of economic principles that business firm managers use for making decisions. This course covers topics such as demand, revenue, produc-tion, costs, supply, pricing, and competition. You will learn how decision affect profits and will study the tools and concepts necessary to maximize these profits.

Marketing and Finance (ILLW#FIN321)   3 credits

In the United States, the total combined value of real estate exceeds that of all stocks, bonds, savings, and currency. This course stresses the personal aspects of decision making about home ownership, apartment rental, or selection of a condominium or mobile home. Real estate careers and those in brokerage, property management, appraising, investment counseling, and mortgage lending are introduced and reviewed. Other important topics deal with the current status of land use controls and zoning, mortgages, and financing, private property rights, and real estate contracts. This is a survey course of basic real estate principles.

Marketing Principles (ILLW#MKTG327)   3 credits

What activities, people, and institutions are involved in getting goods from producer to consumer? Course objectives include developing your ability in problem-solving concepts, using models in the marketing field, and evaluating decision-making techniques in marketing management and planning.

Modern Drama (ILLW#ENG360)   3 credits

Survey of some of the masterpieces of drama beginning with the plays of August Strindberg and Henrik Ibsen. The course traces various elements of theater through the works of several established playwrights, including Oscar Wilde, Lady Gregory, John Synge, George Bernard Shaw, and Arthur Miller. In addition to reading several dramas, you will have the opportunity to view and listen to a play.

Moral Philosophy (ILLW#PHI330)   3 credits

This course presents a broad treatment of the central problems of moral philosophy. The course is organized around major topics such as the nature of morality, theories of values, varieties of egoism, theories of obligation, and views about rights and justice. The contributions of classical philosophers such as Plato an Aristotle are studied, along with the views of contemporary thinkers. The practical implications of various theories are explored.

Music in World Cultures (ILLW#MUS394)   3 credits

Survey the music in three world areas - India, Africa, and Latin America - with emphasis on the relationship between music and other aspects of culture, such as ethnic identity, religion, gender, and aesthetics. After a unit on the elements of music, the music in each of the three regions is explored with guided listening activities, discussions of the cultural contexts of musical performance, and comparisons of the music of different areas (drawing on the music of other world areas covered in the text).

Organization and Admin. in Criminal Justice (ILLW#LEJA306) 3 credits

Focus on the analysis of organizations, organizational theory, motivation, organizational rewards and discipline, stress, group behaviors, power, leadership, communication, decision making, human resource management, and legal aspects of public organization administration. This course increases your understanding and your ability to apply the basic ideas related to the management of public organizations and helps you to develop self-awareness about feelings and attitudes in relation to organizations.

Personnel Management for the Fire Service (ILLW#LEJA483) 3 credits

Investigate personnel practices and management procedures, including collective bargaining, binding arbitration, applicable legislative procedures, and administrative and supervisory procedures.

Religion in America (ILLW#REL301) 3 credits

Investigate American religions from an historical perspective, from pre-colonial Native American cultures to the present. Particular attention is given to the impact of religion on the development of the cultural core of the United States, the relationship between religion and politics in American social experience, popular religion, and the great religious Awakenings that helped American citizens redefine the identity and purpose of the nation in the face of cultural changes and challenges.

Shakespeare (ILLW#ENG412) 3 credits

Survey the works of the greatest and most influential writer in English literature. The course covers eight representative plays (1 history, 3 comedies, 3 tragedies, and 1 romance) that span the length of Shakespeare's career - from one of his early works , *A Midsummer Night's Dream*, to one of his last plays, *The Tempest*. During the course you will view video versions of five plays and listen to audio tapes of other plays and additional material.

University of Iowa - 6 courses

Accredited by the North Central Association of Colleges and Schools.

> University of Iowa
> Guided Correspondence Study
> 116 International Center
> Iowa City, IA 52242-1802

The University of Iowa has long been among the nation's leading educational institutions. A member of the Association of American Universities, The University of Iowa has been accredited by the North Central Association of Colleges and Schools since that organization began in 1913. Individual colleges and schools within The University of Iowa are members of various accrediting associations in their respective fields.

Guided Correspondence Study provides year-round opportunities for students anywhere to earn university credit. Because correspondence courses are self-paced and self-contained, they are free of the constraints of class location and semester scheduling. Increasingly, this flexibility appeals to adults whose jobs or family responsibilities preclude attending classes on campus and to traditional students who wish to supplement their schedules.

Enrollment in a Guided Correspondence Study course does not require admission to the University and is possible throughout the year, by phoning 1-800-272-6430 or by contacting the address listed below. Tuition is the same for undergraduate and graduate students and for in-state, out-of-state, and international students.

Qualified high school and home schooled students may enroll in lower-division Guided Correspondence Study courses, provided they have written permission. Since many of the courses in this catalog fulfill collegiate general education requirements, some high school students use Guided Correspondence Study to get a head start on their college careers.

You may begin GCS courses at any time and are allowed nine months to complete your work. If two or more assignments in a course have been submitted prior to the nine-month expiration date, your enrollment may be extended an additional three months, upon payment of a $25 fee. Any course may be taken for no credit; as a student registered for no credit, you must complete all course work except examinations. Whether you take a course for credit or not, the fee is the same.

Up to 30 semester hours of GCS courses may be applied toward an undergraduate degree at The University of Iowa, with the approval of the dean of your college. Application for and acceptance of such credit toward a degree is subject to the college and curriculum requirements in force at the time you apply for your degree. Bachelor of Liberal Studies (BLS) can apply an unlimited number of GCS hours to their degree requirement. The BLS is a liberal arts external degree sponsored by the three Iowa Regents Universities: Iowa State University, the University of Northern Iowa, and the University of Iowa. There are no residence requirements for this degree program.

Tuition and Fees: For resident and nonresident students, the tuition for credit and non-credit courses is $71 per semester hour. There is a non-refundable $15 enrollment fee per course. Costs of textbooks and other supplies are in addition to tuition.

Students can also read the GCS catalog online, if they have access to Gopher or Telnet. Telnet or point your Gopher to panda.uiowa.edu. Select University of Iowa information from the opening menu; then select Guided Correspondence Study information from the second menu.

Kristin Evenson Hirst
The University of Iowa, Guided Correspondence Study
116 International Center
Iowa City, IA 52242-1802

800-272-6430
fax: 319-335-2740
email: credit-programs@uiowa.edu

Leonard Kallio, Director
Guided Correspondence Study
Division of Continuing Education
116 International Center
Iowa City IA 52242-1802

University of Iowa Course Descriptions

Science Fiction (Historical Survey) (IOWA#8:182)   3 credits

Brief historical survey of science fiction, beginning with Mary Skelley's *Frankenstein*, a gothic precursor, and following with H. G. Wells, one of the 'fathers' of the genre, and moving, then, into a look at the genre as it has existed over the past 50 years. The course is primarily governed by theme, not time, for ideas are at the heart of science fiction.

Writing for Practical Purposes (IOWA#8W:15)   3 credits

Designed for those who are now, or will be, required to write at work. The course takes a practical approach to work-related writing projects and provides an introduction to technical writing. Early assignments help you plan and organize a project by reducing a large writing task to several smaller ones. You will be asked to write with your audience as a primary consideration, and to consider purpose, pertinent information (written and graphic), persuasive strategies, organization, and clarity of prose. You'll firm up evaluating, editing, reviewing, and revising skills. While there are no official prerequisites, it is recommended that you have successfully completed a freshman composition/basic writing course or equivalent.

Writing for Business and Industry (IOWA#8W:113)   3 credits

Using a case study method, this course explores a range of situations and problems encountered when one writes in a business and professional setting. Each assignment is based on a specific set of hypothetical circumstances that challenge students to think strategically about writing. Assignments should help students to confront future professional writing situations with confidence. Students should not count on being able to complete the course in less than 24 weeks from submission of first assignment to last. While there are no official prerequisites, you should have successfully completed a freshman composition/ basic writing course or equivalent.

The First World War (IOWA#16E:185)   3 credits

This course examines the First World War from military, cultural, and social points of view, and assess the impact of the war on diverse groups of people and on Western culture. You will read a variety of texts to assess the origins of the war, the course of the war, the experience of the war for men and women who were participants on the war front and the home front, the conclusion of the war, and significance of the war.

Introduction to Sociology (IOWA#34:1)   3 credits

Examination of how individuals are organized into social groups, ranging from intimate groups to bureaucracies, and how these influence individual behavior; nature and interrelationships of basic social institutions such as family, education, religion and economy.

Internat'l School of Information Mgt. - 7 courses

Accreditation: Distance Education and Training Council

International School of Information Management
P.O. Box 470640
Aurora CO 80047

Our degree programs for individuals include a Master's in Business Administration (MBA) and a Master's in Information Management (MS). Regardless of which program you choose, ISIM will teach you to respond to the rapid technological changes affecting your business and your career. In addition, ISIM offers an award-winning online instruction program. Along with the University of Wisconsin - Madison, Department of Engineering, Professional Development, ISIM was named "best" in the United States for distance learning programs by the U. S. Distance Learning Association.

The same quality that earned ISIM this award ensures that all our students receive education that is current, comprehensive, and useful. Whether you study through our online interactive program (electronic classroom) or our guided self-study program (print-based materials), your course work from ISIM will deliver state-of-the-art understanding and know-how. And that makes an advanced degree from ISIM a sound foundation for your success in tomorrow's marketplace.

As a distance learning institution, ISIM caters to adult learners - professionals with enough discipline and motivation to complete self-study programs. Our online classes let you plug into an electronic classroom from anywhere - 24 hours a day, seven days a week. Because classes form every 10 weeks, most online students can complete a degree within two years. Online instruction comes to you over ISIMnet, an electronic network for computer conferencing. That means you'll work and learn with students and faculty around the world. You'll even receive the full text of public exchanges among students and instructors in your courses to use as a resource in the future.

ISIM is part of a triad of education-oriented companies founded in 1953. They include ABC-Clio, an award-winning publisher of reference books, serials, and CE-ROM products; Intellimation, a multimedia educational publisher; and ISIM itself. All three companies are educational innovators. ISIM builds on the publishing expertise of its sister company, ABC-Clio. By combining mainstream publishing expertise with the latest information-dissemination technology, ISIM creates top-quality course materials.

Instruction is delivered through ISIMnet, an educational computer conferencing environment. Students use a personal computer to connect to ISIMnet three or four times a week, at their own convenience. Students interact with one another and with their instructors online by posting and receiving messages on ISIMnet, their "virtual classroom". Use of a common integrated software package makes it possible for students and instructors to exchange ideas and information in graphic, word processor, database, and spreadsheet form. ISIMnet also provides Email for private messages.

Mr. Timothy M. Adams, Director of Admissions
International School of Information Management
P.O. Box 470640
Aurora CO 80047

800-441-4746v
303-752-3752v
303-752-4044f
email: admin@isim.com

International School of Information Management Course Descriptions

Database Searching Online (ISIM#802)   5 credits

Remote databases provide a rapidly expanding source of information on every imaginable topic. This course allows participants to tap into this valuable resource by introducing the process of conducting online searches. Participants learn to define, narrow, and/or expand search criteria, and they practice conducting online searches through online service providers.

Navigating the Internet (ISIM#804)   5 credits

The Internet is a vital link in today's digital communications chain - the on ramp to the information superhighway. This course uses a simulation tool to demystify the Internet and teach students the skills they need to navigate the Internet with confidence.

Essentials of Object-Oriented Technology (ISIM#830)   5 credits

Object-oriented design can help programmers create applications faster than other design methods, and the resulting products are often of higher quality. This course teaches tools to identify projects that lend themselves to object-oriented technologies. It enables participants to strategize long-term software solutions that are multipurpose, cross-platform, and focused on the needs of the end-user.

C++ Programming (ISIM#848)   5 credits

This course transitions programmers from the traditional, structured approach to sofware development to the multipurpose, flexible environment that characterizes object-oriented design. Participants learn the principles, techniques, and tools of object-oriented programming through a simulated product development process. This course provides a working model for product development and prepares each participant to handle real-world projects as a level one C++ programmer.

Advanced Project Management (ISIM#902)   5 credits

Designed for people who manage projects as an integral part of their jobs, this course teaches participants to be informed and systematic managers in control of projects from start to finish. Participants learn to develop workable project plans using breakdown structures and task dependability networks. With an eye on problem prevention, this course also teaches techniques for risk analysis and leadership of project team members.

Project Management for Business Professionals (ISIM#906)   5 credits

Participants learn how to plan, estimate, schedule, organize, and track projects. Along with comprehensive project-planning techniques, participants explore project projection schedules using PERT and Gantt charts. The course also teaches participants how to implement project-management metrics as well as how to review project progress and take timely, corrective actions.

Managers Orientation to Process Reengineering (ISIM#924)   5 credits

Understanding precedes action in effective process reengineering. That's why business process modernization is necessary and how managers can best facilitate the transformation. This course introduces underlying concepts and fundamental elements of process reengineering. It also gives usable tools and techniques to implement process improvement.

Twenty Techniques for Process-Improvement (ISIM#926)   5 credits

The application of proper process-improvement techniques can make or break a project. This course presents 20 of the most useful techniques available to process-improvement teams. Participants learn how, when, and where to apply each technique and gain practical experience using the techniques through case studies and exercises.

Managing the Paradigm Shift (ISIM#932)   5 credits

Information technology is undergoing a paradigm shift brought about by world economic and political changes, increased competition in the marketplace, the new enterprise, and recent technological advancements. This course examines the new developments that are critical to understanding the reality of today's business operations. By demystifying the changes occurring in technology, the course helps participants adapt to them.

Managing in an Age of Info. Technology Change (ISIM#410)   5 credits

This course sets the stage for ISIM's Master of Science degree program by addressing the need for organizations to respond efficiently to technological changes. Students examine management techniques for fostering a corporate culture that facilitates innovation. Also discussed are the dynamics of growth and change and their impact on the success of a technology intensive business.

Technology, Ethics, and Social Responsibility (ISIM#430)   5 credits

Information systems often present ethical challenges such as the privacy issues inherent in sophisticated consumer databases. This course explores the social issues affecting business and professional decisions while it examines the relationship between the individual, the firm, society, and the implementation of new technology.

Information Systems Strategic Planning (ISIM#440)   5 credits

These systems are an integral part of corporate operations. This course examines guidelines for developing an information systems plan, selecting systems projects, assessing current systems, and planning future systems expansion that supports organizational growth.

Telecommunications (ISIM#450)   5 credits

This course provides a brief history of telecommunications, a look at the field's structure and regulation, information networks and telecommunications services, the basics of traffic engineering, and an introduction to primary data communications systems. The underlying functions and principles of telecommunications management are also introduced.

Emerging Technologies (ISIM#460)   5 credits

Through this course, students explore state-of-the-art and emerging technol-ogies in information processing. The class includes a survey of recent advances in software development, hardware, and computer networking strategies.

Information Systems in Business (ISIM#470)   5 credits

This course reviews information technology and how it is used in the business environment. It presents an introduction to the strategic and operational issues in the field of technology management and examines product life-cycle dynamics and critical success factors in managing technology. Students learn strategies for nurturing technological innovation within their organizations. (Guided self-study program)

Organizational Behavior (ISIM#480)   5 credits

Today, business run on hardware, software, and human capital. This course focuses on people in the organization and how they work and behave in the work environment. It examines the behavior of individuals, the dynamics of teamwork, the processes of small groups, decision-making, problem-solving, conflict management, and ways to eliminate barriers to effective communications within the workplace.

Customers, Markets and Technology (ISIM#510)   5 credits

The relationship between technology-based products and the consumers of these products comes under investigation in this course. This course also teaches methods for designing, developing, and delivering technology-base products that solve real-world problems.

Information Systems Policy (ISIM#520)   5 credits

Designed to provide an understanding of the overall information needs of an organization and the role of computer-based information systems, this course covers management of computer centers and technical personnel, systems development management, and enterprise analysis.

Planning for Information Networks (ISIM#530)   5 credits

This course presents a methodology for planning telecommunications networks from the perspective of a technical manager. General planning principles are covered, and during the course students develop a general model based on structured analysis techniques. Related topics of network architectures, risk analysis, and disaster recovery are discussed.

Technology and the Global Environment (ISIM#540)   5 credits

How does globalization relate to and affect technology innovation? That's the question this course is designed to answer. Students interpret technological activities of organizations and analyze the likely impact of them on technological choices and opportunities affecting their businesses.

Data Communications (ISIM#610)   5 credits

This course develops students' essential skills and knowledge for designing communication systems. Students examine network protocols, and wide- and local-area networks are covered in detail. topics include the seven layers of the OSI model, client-server technology, and comparison of different network architectures.

Systems Design (ISIM#620)   5 credits

This course reviews efficient processes for information systems analysis and development. It also covers state-of-the-art techniques for information systems specifications and design. Other topics covered include real-time structured analysis and design, and object-oriented analysis and design.

Telecommunications Policy (ISIM#630)   5 credits

AT&T and the Baby Bells operate within a strictly regulated environment. this course introduces students to regulatory limitations, rate structures, and tariffs. It also covers wireless technologies and related policy issues, and current issues in telecommunications.

Telephony (voice/data systems) (ISIM#640)   5 credits

Voice/data systems are becoming increasingly sophisticated. Students learn about characteristics of speech, customer premises equipment, transmission systems and impairments, multiplexing, signaling, altering and supervision, traffic engineering, and switching fundamentals. This course also examines network hierarchy and optimization.

Management (ISIM#210)   5 credits

Management provides a solid foundation for facing the challenges of a rapidly changing and highly competitive business environment. This course introduces the fundamental management functions of planning, decision-making, organizing, leading, and controlling, as well as the tools and techniques of managing people, processes, projects, and the work environment. Students explore current issues in management and gain insights into how successful organizations operate.

Accounting (ISIM#220)   5 credits

The language of business, accounting, provides crucial decision-making information to business organizations. This introduction to financial and managerial accounting prepares student to construct and interpret financial statements, generate budgets, and use accounting data for strategic and management purposes with emphasis on profitability. Legal and ethical issues in accounting are also discussed.

Quantitative Analysis (ISIM#230)   5 credits

Quantitative analysis is a valuable process for decision-makers and professionals who are responsible for guiding their organizations in today's dynamic business environment. This course provides the necessary quantitative tools for analyzing data, modeling problems, and making informed decisions. The focus is on construction of models, interpretation of results, and critical evaluation of assumptions.

Marketing Management (ISIM#240)   5 credits

Marketing is the epicenter of an organization's strategic and operational life. This course presents marketing management within the broader context of the organization's strategies and operations. Students discover the benefits of market research and analysis, and develop effective marketing strategies through segmentation, targeting, and positioning.

Managerial Economics (ISIM#250)   5 credits

Microeconomics (managerial economics) form the overall theory and foundation for the workings of a corporation. This course deals with applying microeconomics theory to the management of the firm by focusing on the use of microeconomics to enhance decision-making. By exploring the complex relationships between a manager's decisions and the resulting impact of those decisions on the demand for the company's products and the profitability of the firm, students come to understand the economic environment in which the firm operates and learn how to think strategically within this environment.

Finance (ISIM#260)   5 credits

This introduction to corporate financial management and investments provides the framework, concepts, and tools for analyzing financial decisions by applying the fundamental principles of modern financial theory. Major topics include the time value of money and capital budgeting.

Business Ethics in a Global Environment (ISIM#270)   5 credits

An organization's ethical policies affect everything from morale and product-ivity of individual workers to marketing strategies. This course explores contemporary issues in business ethics and social responsibility, especially as they relate to the broadening markets in the global business community.

Strategic Planning (ISIM#280)   5 credits

This course is designed to help students effectively guide an organization toward a profitable and dynamic future. This course provides students with a formal method of defining the organization's purpose and aligning the entire business to achieve corporate goals. It also examines emerging technologies in information processing as an important element of strategic planning.

Strategies for Change (ISIM#290)   5 credits

Today's rapid-fire changes in technology demand that business people learn to adapt quickly. This course teaches students to identify significant changes in information technology and adjust work processes to profit from them. Course participants also learn to develop strategies for managing change in their own work environments.

Int'l Society for Technology in Ed. - 16 courses   ISTE

> International Society for Technology in Education
> 1787 Agate Street
> Eugene OR 97403

The **International Society for Technology in Education** (ISTE) in conjunction with the **University of Oregon** and the Oregon State System Office of Independent Study located at **Portland State University**, Portland, Oregon, offer graduate-level *Distance Education* courses.

The purpose of these courses is to provide staff development and leadership training for educators who do not have local access to world-class leaders and staff development opportunities in computers-in-education. Educators will correspond with heir instructor as they complete each lesson. These courses are designed to meet or exceed the standards of typical computer-in-education courses offered by the college of Education at the University of Oregon. That is, if you do the work of a course and learn the course materials, you will have gained knowledge and skills comparable to what students at the University of Oregon gain by taking a similar course.

Graduate Credit: Credit for ISTE *Distance Education* graduate courses is granted in one of two ways. You may elect to receive credit through the University of Oregon in Eugene, Oregon, or receive credit through Portland State University in Portland, Oregon. Transcripts will be issued by the Registrar's Office of the university you select.

Typical Course Requirements: Although the assignments for each course vary, the following description gives the flavor of typical requirements. The *Planning for Technology in Schools* course consists of eight required assignments. (There are no midterm exams and no final exam.) The first seven assignments are associated with the written material provided with the course. These assignments are designed to require about 12-15 hours to complete. The eight assignment (the course project), counts as 30% percent of the course grade. Students are expected to spend a minimum of 40 hours on this project. It is intended to be a major and comprehensive assignment. We advise students to start it early in the course.

Course Costs: The three quarter-hour graduate level tuition is $405, and the four quarter-hour graduate level tuition is $540. For non-credit, tuition is reduced. The tuition covers the costs of instruction, the lesson guide, and other materials supplied by ISTE *Distance Education*. In addition, students are required to purchase textbooks for courses. The required text titles and the costs are listed under each course on the registration form. You may order them from ISTE or purchase them locally if correct editions are available.

International Society for Technology in Education Course Descriptions

ClarisWorks for Educators (ISTE#EDUC508K)   4 credits

This eight-lesson course is designed to provide a significant introduction to the *ClarisWorks* application. The course is offered in two versions: IBM and Macintosh. Students will learn to use the word processing, drawing, database, spreadsheet, and communications components. The Macintosh version of this course will also cover the painting component of the application. Students are provided with a number of articles that provide some background on the use of the *ClarisWorks* application in the classroom. One lesson involves the design of a major project that requires the integrationof the components of *ClarisWorks*.

Learning Linkway/Linkway Live (ISTE#EDUC508L)   4 credits

This eight-lesson course is designed to provide a significant introduction to *Linkway/ Linkway Live*. Students will learn to create *Linkway/Linkway Live* folders. They will use the built-in programming ability of *Linkway* to extend their products past the elementary level provided by the immediate features of the program. Students will be assisted in developing an understanding of the elements of an effective interface design for their products. In addition, students will read about the history, issues, and current research surrounding the use of hypermedia in education and will have the opportunity to see some examples of hypermedia on videotape. Assignments involve creating folders of the student's choice that demonstrate mastery of new ideas in each lesson. In addition, students will be expected to write about their experiences while working with *Linkway/Linkway Live* and to write a number of short papers based on the reading assignments. One lesson involves the opportunity to consider the issues of evaluation of hypermedia products.

Exploring the Internet (ISTE#EDUC508M)   4 credits

This course will cover a variety of topics from the world of the Internet. The course includes a brief discussion of the history of the Internet and issues to consider before connecting to the network. You will also cover vocabulary, software and hardware considerations, email, listservs, bulletin boards, FTP, and using the Internet for educational purposes. This course is suitable for K-12 educators who have minimal telecommunications experience.

Introduction to Logo for Educators (ISTE#EDUC510C)   4 credits

Introduction to Logo for Educators has two goals. First, students will become knowledgeable users of the Logo programming language through writing Logo programs and developing curriculum-oriented Logo projects. Second, students will examine some of the important issues surrounding the use of Logo: discovery learning, research, evaluation, the Logo philosophy, and more. The course is specifically designed for pre-college level educators who have had a reasonable amount of teaching experience. The ONLOGO video tapes from Media Microworlds, Inc. (MMI), are available on loan.

Telecommunications & Information Access (ISTE#EDUC510E)   4 credits

This course explores electronic mail, conferencing, distance education, and information access using CompuServe Information Service (CIS). It identifies ways these tools can be used for classroom and personal use. Topics covered include:

1. Exploration of the network and the information age.
2. Uses of electronic mail
3. Conferences for educators and students
4. Beyond penpals: Curriculum-based telecommunications projects
5. Distance education: Current status and information
6. Remote database searching

Learning HyperCard and HyperTalk (ISTE#EDUC508T)   4 credits

This eight-lesson course is designed to provide a significant introduction to *HyperCard*. Students will learn to create *HyperCard* stacks using the menus in the program. They will then move on to learning to program in the HyperTalk programming language that is built into *HyperCard*. In addition, students will read about the history, issues, and current research surrounding the use of hypermedia in education and will have the opportunity to see some examples of hypermedia on videotape. Assign-ments involve creating stacks of the student's choice that demonstrate mastery of new ideas about *HyperCard* and HyperTalk. In addition, students will write about their experiences while working with *HyperCard* and write short papers based on the reading assignments.

Planning for Technology in Schools (ISTE#EDUC507B)   4 credits

This course provides school leaders with information and guidelines for doing long-range strategic planning for technology in schools. Computers have a major and continuing impact on our schools, but how can we plan the impact that we wish the computers to have on the curriculum? *Planning for Technology in Schools* addresses how we can best move our schools into the information age. Each participant actually completes a substantial part of a long-range plan for technology in the school, a school unit, or classroom. At the end of each of eight lessons, you will have completed a portion of the plan.

Fundamentals of Technology in Education (ISTE#EDUC510B)   4 credits

This course offers an overview of computer applications in the elementary and secondary curriculum and focuses on how computers might impact schools in the coming years. Among the many topics covered are the evaluation and selection of educational courseware, keyboarding, word processing, database management, spreadsheets, teacher tools, graphics, Logo, telecommunications and networking, and social issues of computing. *Fundamentals of Technology in Education* is specifically designed for educators at the precollege level who are interested in examining a variety of ways in which computers can enhance the teaching and learning process.

Computers and Problem Solving (ISTE#EDUC507A)   4 credits

Problem solving is an important part of every academic discipline. Helping students become better at problem solving is one of education's goals. This course examines the topic of problem solving in curricular areas and the roles of computer in problem solving. It is based on the research-supported belief that specific instruction and practice in problem solving lead to improved problem-solving skills. Through this course, teachers can make a significant contribution to helping students become better problem solvers. Participants will gain a number of ideas on how to increase their emphasis on problem solving in the classroom. A number of course assignments require that you try out materials and ideas with students and report on the results. This course is specifically designed for precollege educators who have had a reasonable amount of teaching experience. It does not assume any specific mathematics background and you are not asked to solve any mathematics problems.

AppleWorks for Educators (ISTE#EDUC508A)   4 credits

This course is particularly beneficial for educators who want to learn how they can use the computer as a personal tool as well as a classroom tool. The course provides guided practice in the use of a database, word processor, and spreadsheet, and in the transfer of data between them. Students will also examine articles demonstrating classroom uses of the different applications and will submit several essays in response to the readings. After learning to use each application and reporting on each use, participants design a project implementing their new knowledge. This is a beginner's course for educators at the precollege level who have had some teaching experience. Students who have significant *AppleWorks* experience may take this course. It provides a model for teaching *AppleWorks*, and allows teachers to discuss in depth the integration of computers in the K-12 curriculum. However, the *AppleWorks* content itself is basic, and this course is not a substitute for an advanced *AppleWorks* class.

Pagemaker for Educators (ISTE#EDUC508R)   3 credits

This distance education course is specifically designed for educators and administrators in K-12 and higher education. Journalism and yearbook teachers who wish to investigate desktop publishing for their schools will find this course particularly helpful. You learn effective graphic design and desktop publishing as you learn the capabilities and features of Aldus *Pagemaker*. Participants do both assigned and self-selected projects, such as a classroom handout, school newspaper or yearbook, or a district budget report.

Computers in Composition (ISTE#EDUC510G)   4 credits

This course integrates software tools such as word processors, spelling and grammar checkers, outliners, and graphics programs into the teaching of writing. Course content is based on recent writing theory and research, with particular emphasis on the writing process. A basic belief is that writing should be taught across the curriculum. Teachers and teacher trainers in any content area can benefit from *Computers in Composition.*

Computers in Math Education (ISTE#EDUC510A)   4 credits

This *Distance Education* course is specifically designed for K-12 mathematics educators. The emergence of calculators and computers as useful mathematical tools has caused mathematics educators to carefully consider the role technology should play in school mathematics education. In this course, students consider unique classroom applications of technology, teaching strategies, and questions about the future of mathematics education. Students review software, apply problem solving models, and design and evaluate lessons for their students.

Instructional Use of Computers (ISTE#EDUC510H)   4 credits

This course is designed to help you learn more about how to design, conduct, and evaluate an inservice. A strong and growing foundation of research and theory strongly suggests that educators know how to improve curriculum and instruction. The problem facing education is how to appropriately implement practices that will lead to better educators of students. The goal of *Effective Inservice* is to improve education through improving the knowledge and skills of educators who will provide inservice staff development in the field of instructional uses of computers. This course is suited to teachers at all levels and in all disciplines. It is also suitable for computer coordinators and practicing inservice providers.

Introduction to Microsoft Works for Educators (ISTE#EDUC508G)4 credits

This *Distance Education* course is particularly appropriate for educators who want to learn to use the computer as a personal tool as well as a classroom tool. One part of each lesson is devoted to learning the *Microsoft Works* program; the other part is devoted to applying what you have learned to the classroom. You learn to use *Works* by doing hands-on guided workbook activities. You learn to apply the concepts by examining and critiquing articles modeling the use of word processing, database, and spreadsheets in the classroom. After learning to use *Works* tool and reporting on its use, participants design a project implementing their new knowledge. This is a beginning *Microsoft Works* course for educators at the precollege level who have had some teaching experience.

Software Sampler I (ISTE#EDUC508B)   4 credits

In this unique course, you will be provided with access to software and current theories on evaluating and integrating software into the curriculum. Participants will design, teach, and evaluate lessons using software of potential interest. Alternatively, participants may use and evaluate personal productivity software in performing teacher tasks such as creating tests or student reports. The software list includes new and well-established programs by Sunburst/Wings for learning, MECC, Tom Snyder Productions, Brøderbund, Teacher Support Software, The Learning Company, and others. You will be loaned the software you select from ISTE's software library. We have over 50 software titles to choose from. For some lessons, you may use software from your district if you wish. This course is appropriate for K-12 educators, computer coordinators, and inservice providers.

University of Mass. - Dartmouth - 12 courses

University of Massachusetts-Dartmouth
North Dartmouth, Massachusetts 02747-2300

E-Mail@UMassd.edu
URL: http://www.umassd.edu/
508-999-8605 Admissions

What is CyberEd? CyberEd is a means of delivering quality education from our desktop to yours! CyberEd is a selection of standard, full-credit University courses being offered to the global audience of the Web through the UMass Dartmouth Division of Continuing Education. CyberEd classes are kept to a size where professors can provide the same level of personal interaction as in the traditional classroom. We use the WWW, email, and perhaps other Internet resources, to provide plenty of opportunities for meaningful student-to-faculty and student-to-student interaction.

Our objective is to create a distance learning environment that rivals the traditional classroom environment in the quality and content of the learning experience we can provide. We believe the communications options provided by the Internet, and especially the World Wide Web, offer many new opportunities for meaningful interaction between faculty and students, as well as between students and other students in the same course. To this end we are taking twelve courses and making them available to students from around the globe over the Internet.

The courses will also make use of the Web's strong interactive capabilities provided in forms. While most communications with students will be asynchronous - that is, students will write something at one time and will receive a response at some later point - some of the courses may also make use of communications tools that allow for rapid exchanges in a brief time frame, much like a live conversation.

Other Internet communications tools, such as email, mailing lists, and Usenet News, will be employed where these are the most effective means for the task at hand. All of the courses take place within the framework of a single semester. While students will not be required to "attend" a particular class at a particular time or place, they will be expected to keep pace with the instructional program and complete assignments within the time frames provided by the instructor.

Tuition and Fees: Most courses are three credits and cost $365 each. In addition, while we will use Web resources as much a possible, you may have to purchase books or other course supplies by mail through our Campus Store or another source of your choice. Other fees may apply, although general University fees are waived for these courses.

273

University of Massachusetts - Dartmouth Course Descriptions

Principles of Project Engineering (MASD#ECE592)   3 credits

This course provides the student with a broad view of engineering project management and studies both the classical sequential project management and contemporary concurrent project management approaches. The life-cycle phases of research, development, and projects are studied and analyzed with an emphasis on the methodologies that lead to successful management of such projects. Included in this analysis is an introduction to the financial and economic aspects of successful engineering project management. Principles of software project management are highlighted to expose the student to the complexities of managing projects which involve developing software for embedded computer systems. In parallel with the formal study of engineering project management,a virtual work environment is created through the formation of project teams and the assignment of real engineering management tasks of contemporary interest. The student teams conduct these tasks under the supervision of the instructor, and evaluation of the student's progress and performance is conducted in a manner similar to that which can be expected in a real work environment. Case studies and other practice are also included in this course. Prerequisites: Open to upper division engineering and management students, and to others with permission of the instructor.

References: B. Blanchard and W. Fabrycky, Systems Engineering and Analysis, Prentice-Hall, 1981. Q. C. Turtle, Implementing Concurrent Project Management, PTR Prentice-Hall, 1994. Instructor-supplied/identified case studies and notes. Other: Use of Project Scheduler 6 for windows, Software from Scitor Corporation,1995.

Technical and Business Writing (MASD#ENL 600)   3 credits

This graduate-level course introduces students to the many purposes, audiences, forms, and formats of technical documents written for lay audiences. Since this is an on-line course, most assignments will focus on writing and formatting technical information for Internet and World Wide Web audiences or for audiences who want to learn about these resources. By using World Wide Web and hypertext links, students will interact with the instructor and other members of the course and peer edit each other's work. Prerequisites: B.S. or B.A. degree, or permission of the instructor RDumont@UMassd.edu. If requesting permission, include a writing sample (or samples). This sample should be at least 1000 words.

Theory & Practice in Teaching Literature (MASD#ENL684)   3 credits

This course is designed for advanced undergraduate and graduate literature majors as well as for (prospective) teachers of literature, grades 9-12 and college-level. It seeks to reconcile the theoretical, objective analysis of literature and the subjective reponse to literature by providing you with the necessary instruments of reference--namely, the constituent elements of poetry, prose, and drama--and model texts and essays illustrating recent trends in literary theory and analysis. The course aims to study and determine the quality of literature and literary theory in their ability to convey the traditional literary values of form, meaning, and symbolism, and the applicable value of literary theory as an interpretative mode of criticism that probes how we read, make sense of experience, and produce meaning. In the process, the course seeks the heightened appreciation of literary texts and theories, their intellectual, moral, and aesthetic features, the relationships amongs stylistic devices, central motifs, organic structure, and effectiveness in revealing and communicating the author's and reader's purpose and motivation and imagination and psychology. Comments or questions for the instructor? Send e-mail to LKamm@umassd.edu

Intro to Statistics for the Chem Laboratory (MASD#CHM167)   1 credit

Students in laboratory courses in experimental sciences such as chemistry, physics, and biology need an elementary background in statistics to enable them to interpret the data they obtain in the lab in an appropriate way. This course treats statistics at an introductory level as applied to experiments in a college freshman level chemistry laboratory. Topics covered include: the nature of distributions of data, histograms, basic statistical calculations, the normal distribution, t-distributions, statistical tests appropriate for small samples of data, criteria for rejection of data, analysis of data and reporting of results, and an introduction to propagation of errors. Prerequisites: One year of high school chemistry or one semester of college chemistry; three years of college preparatory high school mathematics including trigonometry. Comments or questions for the instructor? Send e-mail to MMandrioli@umassd.edu

Personal Finance (MASD#FIN 320)   3 credits

An introduction to the personal financial planning process of setting goals, developing action plans, creating budgets and measuring results. The student will become familiar with the techniques of financial analysis necessary to make choices when considering housing, insurance, retirement plans, borrowing and other personal finance issues. There will be an emphasis on investing in stocks, bonds, and mutual funds. The Internet/Web will be used to study financial planning issues and to communicate with the instructor. No prerequisites. Direct comments or questions about this course to: mgriffin@umassd.edu

Human Resource Management (MASD#HRM 462)   3 credits

In U.S. businesses today there is much confusion and misunderstanding about the concept of teams. Managers are trying to, using Peter Drucker's language, develop tennis doubles teams while behaving as baseball coaches. Team members get confused. TQM has moved from being a managerial panacea for what ails business to being a pariah in the eyes of organization members. In the middle of this muddle enters a technology that poses both a threat and opportunity for developing teams, whichever kind of team one wants. The purpose of this course is twofold: to explore the concept of team development in U.S. organizations today--the approaches, successes and failures of team development efforts; and to examine the current uses, successes and failures of electronic media, such as the World Wide Web, to develop and grow teams of people working at a distance. By the end of the course students will have developed: a theoretical and practical understanding of the skills and abilities necessary to develop and grow teams through Web site visits, Web conference attendance, and discussions with people; a network for discussing ideas and analyzing/solving problems related to team development,through the interactions with other members of this class. Direct comments or questions about this course to RDorris@UMassD.edu.

MIDI Composition: Creative Sequencing (MASD#MUS322)   3 credits

This course will explore a rich variety of procedures for developing and modifying sequences to create richer, more musical sequences. The work will be based on material from the instructor's Electronic Music Composition, published by William C. Brown. Participants will have the opportunity to share their work in progress with their colleagues, as well as their comments and suggestions. Stylistic and musical diversity are encouraged.Topics to be covered include regional editing procedures, MIDI file formats, General MIDI, pitch, duration, texture, tempo and meter, timbre/pitch change, and volume versus velocity. Prerequisites: Some familiarity with basic MIDI concepts; access to and understanding of a basic MIDI facility. Participants are expected to have MIDI hardware (at minimum, some form of MIDI input device and sound card/tone generation module) and computer-based sequencing software. Direct comments or questions about this course to RAdams@umassd.edu

Introduction to Astronomy (MASD#PHY152)   3 credits

A descriptive introduction to the planets, stars, galaxies, and general concepts of astronomy for the non-science major. Topics will include brief historical glimpses of the earliest concepts of the universie, contributions of Galileo, Newton and others. Following topics will include the nature of the earth and moon, the physical enviornments of selected planets, moons, comets, and asteroids. The general nature of the stars and stellar evolution will also be investigated. Direct comments or questions about this course to gstone@umassd.edu

Introduction to American Politics (MASD#PSC101)   3 credits

This course offers students a broad introduction to American politics, with a particular emphasis on understanding the relationship between Congress and the Presidency. The study of American politics in a presidential election year provides students with many opportunities to apply the theories and models we discuss in class to current political issues. The Internet offers political science students a stunning array of resources; over the course of the semester, we'll learn to track legislation, visit the home pages of presidential candidates, members of Congress, and key interest groups, and explore the dynamics of the 1995-96 Supreme Court term as its unfolds. By semester's end, you'll have a better understanding of why so few Americans vote, how citizens choose among candidates, successful and unsuccessful campaign strategies, the role of the media in contemporary American politics, and how the public evaluates elected officials. We'll also discuss how the organization of Congress, the executive branch, and the Courts affects public policy choices. While students will be asked to complete a core set of assigned readings, material available at various Web sites will provide the principal "text" for the course. Direct comments or questions about this course to rhackey@UMassD.edu.

Politics and the New Media (MASD#PSC 215)   3 credits

This course will investigate the use of the Internet and the World Wide Web as a means of networking, organizing and marketing issues and ideas. The course will examine how electronic communication via the Internet/WWW is changing the current theory and practice of defining, shaping and influencing issues. Prerequisite: Students should have a political science background or a stong interest/experience in activism, grassroots organizing,issue campaigns, etc.

Concepts in Design: Digital Photography (MASD#PHO1)   3 credits

This course will address concepts and techniques in field and studio digital photography. It will examine the practice of digital photography using the computer, the Internet, and the print as output media. Discussions will include how the computer functions as a darkroom and as a printmaking and dissemination tool. Topics will include advanced issues in resolution, image quality, calibration, compression, camera types and archiving. The course will actively analyze the digital image and its role in mass communication, in ethics and copyright issues, and will regard manipulation techniques relating to truth and history. Included will be consideration of electronic photography as a teaching tool and replacement for traditional chemical processes. Through on-line readings, discussion, critiques and references students will study digital photography both in concept and practice. Student work will be posted using a graphical browser, with the final goal being the creation of an on-line gallery of digital photographs open to the public. Prerequisites: Each student should own or have access to a digital camera. (point and shoot type OK..) Each student should own or have access to Adobe Photoshop on a computer with enough RAM and speed to run it. Previous experience or classes in Photography is recommended but not mandatory.

Web Craft: Creating Your Own Web Pages (MASD#WEB1)   0 credits

This seven-week, non-credit course is designed to introduce the beginner to HTML, Web Craft, and Web Style. Topics covered will include related software tools for Macintosh and Windows; the basics of HTML through to the more advanced features of Netscape and HTML 3.0; as well as an introduction to the fundamentals of Web style. Students will learn from online resources, and will carry out a series of progressively more complex assignments. Their work will be reviewed by the instructor who will be available to answer questions both by email and real-time Chat. There will also be opportunity for peer review and exchange of ideas among students in the class. The specifics of this course will attempt to adjust to the rapidly changing Web development environment. The basic goal remains the same: Help people create useful collections of Web pages of their own. Scripting and other skills tied directly to operating servers will not be covered.

New School for Social Research - 53 courses

New School for Social Research - Distance Learning Program
Accredited by the Middle States Association of Colleges and Schools, and
is chartered as a university by the Regents of the State of New York.

> New School for Social Research
> DIAL Program
> 66 West 12th Street
> New York NY 10011

The New School for Social Research was founded in 1919 as a center
for "discussion, instruction and counseling for mature men and women."
It has remained since then America's first university for adults. Over the
years, the university has grown into an accredited degree-granting
institution. It has always nurtured the widest possible range of thought
and opinion. Retaining that distinction today, the New Schools sustains a
full spectrum of academic, social, cultural, political, educational and
economic programs. As a major urban university, the New School draws
upon and contributes to the rich resources of New York City. Some 40,000
students come to its six divisions annually, enriching the university with a
variety of cultures, perspectives, aspirations, priorities, interests and
talents.

The New School's distance Instruction for Adult Learners (DIAL)
program provides an opportunity for students to take New School courses
at their own convenience. Using various media (interactive computer
conferencing, video and audio tape, as well as conventional reading
matter), students receive instruction, ask questions of the instructor or
each other, discuss issues and actively participate in the class - all from
their homes or offices, at any time.

DIAL Academics: Each semester, the number and variety of courses being
offered through the New School's Distance Learning Program grows. In
the spring of 1995, courses are being offered in the social sciences,
humanities, foreign languages, English, writing, communication, music,
business, teacher education, and computer instruction. Specific course
listings, including descriptions and faculty information, are listed in this
brochure. Each DIAL course is taught by a distinguished New School
faculty member. Courses reflect the traditions of the New School's broad-
based and responsive curriculum. Requirements for successful completion
of any DIAL course are similar to other courses you may have taken. In
addition to reading and writing, you may be asked to review works in
other media - video, film,. audio tape, photography etc.

General Credit Students: (Tuition: $450 per credit; registration fee: $15) If
you are a degree candidate at another college or university or if you have

not yet completed an undergraduate degree but would like to earn college credit, you should consider registering for general credit. As a general credit student you earn academic credit but are considered non-matriculated - not part of a degree program at the New School. You receive a grade in each course and may request a transcript of grade in each course and may request a transcript of record. Students currently enrolled in degree programs outside the New School should make a formal request to transfer credits earned through DIAL at their home school prior to registration.

Non-Credit: (Tuition: variable; registration fee: $15) If you do not need to earn academic credit or a grade, you may elect to take DIAL courses on a non-credit basis. The University does not maintain a permanent record of non-credit enrollment although you may request a 'Record of Attendance' should verification of your participation in a class be necessary. The record of attendance must be requested during the term in which the course is offered for a nominal fee.

Matriculated Students: (Tuition: $375 per credit (if registering for 6 or more credits; registration fee: $60) If you are an undergraduate degree candidate at The New School, the academic credits you earn upon successful completion of a DIAL course are counted toward your degree requirements. Degree students should consult with their educational advisor for course approval.

If you have any questions about DIAL or would like to know more about the distance learning environment, please call the DIAL office at 212-229-5880. If you have any additional questions about DIAL ACADEMICS, please call our Office of Educational Advising and Admissions at (212) 229-5630.

Mr. Peter Anspacher, Director
New School for Social Research - Distance Learning Program
DIAL - Distance Instruction for Adult Learners
66 West 12th Street
New York NY 10011

212.229.5880v
212.239.5852f

New School for Social Research Course Descriptions

Joseph Beuys and the Artistic Center (NEWS#DIAL0102)   3 credits

After a general introduction to the life and work of Beuys, we examine the development of his career as an artist by studying such sources as the popular press, art periodicals, and catalogs of group and solo exhibitions. Beuys called his political activism "social sculpture" and declared that "everyone is an artist" and that only through art could a radical transformation of society be accomplished. His gaunt face and uniform of felt hat and hunter's vest is arguably his most successful 'artwork', and the story of his plane crash and rescue by Tartars in Crimea during World War II is more famous than his oeuvre. Rather than accepting Beuys's history at face value, our discussions focus on his critical reception and his own role in forming it. The goal is to show how reception by the critics and public recognition are equal factors in the making of an artist. Comparisons are made to other artists' careers, and topics include analysis of the main venues of reception and how they are used in the construction of a successful career.

Postmodernity: Society at the Millennium (NEWS#DIAL0202)   3 credits

The intellectual roots of social theory are found in the writings of Marx, Durkheim, Nietzsche, and Weber, which reflect a range of views on the human condition. We examine the cultural concerns and critical implications of these canonical authors and see how their ideas are faring in the postmodern age. We read in four areas of contemporary social thought; symbolic interactionism, feminism, critical theory, and postmodernism. Topics include identity and subjectivity, the politics of language and perception, social construction of life-world experiences, and politics and progress in a technocratic age. Theoretical readings are supplemented by contemporary broadsides selected from magazines, videos, films, and monographs.

Discourse and Psychology (NEWS#DIAL0213)   3 credits

Contemporary American psychology has to a great extent been deprived of its psyche (soul) as well as its logos (discourse) by favoring models biased toward biological, behavioral, and psycho-social methods. This course focuses on the phenomenon of 'psychology' and what it has to say about itself. What are the discourses of the psyche? How does the phenomenon of psychology begin to take shape when we engage those discourses? Is the psyche univocal or polyphonic? How do we valuate the various 'stories' or the psyche? By engaging with analytic, literary, poetic, and philosophical texts and with some films as well, we begin to explore how the psyche speaks, lucidly or obliquely, through multi-discourse.

Introduction to the Information Millennium (NEWS#DIAL0219)   3 credits

Drawing on books, magazines, film, TV, computer software, interactive multimedia, and gleanings from the Internet, this course examines the growing prevalence and importance of digital information in our society. It maintains an interdisciplinary perspective, incorporating research, theory and readings from sociology, anthropology, economics, political science, media studies, and computer science. The goals are: 1) to analyze the function of digital information in the world today; 2) to explain the technologies by which this information is collected, processed, analyzed and disseminated; 3) to explore how information technologies affect economies, construct culture, and influence politics and to dissect their impact on ethical issues and social controversies; 4) to consider how various trends in digital information might affect society in the near and more distant future.

Censorship and the First Amendment (NEWS#DIAL0309)   3 credits

The requisite constitutional background is provided for our examination of some current First Amendment issues: 'hate speech' on the college campus and in the community; pornography and the women's movement; protection of symbolic speech; public funding of the arts; censorship in wartime (with case study of the recent Persian Gulf war); and the Religious Right and censorship. We also take a look at new questions being raised by the growth of the Internet: government regulation and censorship, 'wire-tapping' on the Internet; 'flaming', etc. Major recent Supreme Court cases are analyzed.

Identity: Modular Construction of Personality (NEWS#DIAL0334)3 credits

Who am I, and how have I come to be this way? These questions are central to any debate about human nature and identity. Just as they currently preoccupy post-modern theorists, artists and writers (Foucault, feminist theory, the 1973 Whitney Biennale, *The Crying Game*, etc.), these questions were at the heart of Plato's thinking. How is a sense of self formed, and how does it change? What important factors (e.g., race, gender, class, age, ethnicity, religion, physical ableness) contribute to one's sense of self? We examine the development of identity in today's world, where social roles and national boundaries are constantly being redefined and where the globaliz-ation of knowledge has put us all in the same village; to know oneself today is a true intellectual challenge. The class reads three modern classics that examine what we mean by a self, how we come to know who our selves are, and what conditions allow us to change our selves or identities.

Ethics and the Family (NEWS#DIAL0343)   3 credits

We examine such questions as: What is meant by a well-functioning family? Who is to say what is right or wrong, given that some degree of quirkiness exists in every family? When should there be intervention, and by whom? Drawing on works of literature, we examine many different family situations such as discord between the parents in Josephine Humphries' *Dreams of Sleep* and D. H. Lawrence's *Sons & Lovers*; divorce as in Sue Millers's *The Good Mother*; children brought up by guardians as in Marilynne Robinson's *Housekeeping*; familial stress as in William's *The Glass Menangerie* and Miller's *Death of a Salesman*; and obsessive behavior as in Jeanete Winterson's *Oranges Are Not the Only Fruit*.

How Consciousness Matters (NEWS#DIAL0407)   3 credits

Why are we conscious? New theories are now developing around this question, and science is entering a paradigm shift in which creative self-organizing processes are central. Can it be that it is through conscious awareness that the most complex levels of order are always arising? We consider these questions: What's the purpose of consciousness? Does it have an adaptive function? What's the distinction between conscious and subconscious motivation? What is our inner freedom - how can we reconcile our increasing knowledge of mechanism that govern our behavior with our experience of free choice? What are the roots of violence in our culture? We explore current theories of consciousness and consider their scientific, social and personal implications.

Introduction to Social Psychology (NEWS#DIAL0416)   3 credits

This course focuses on the nature of social behavior and the principles involved in the social construction of the person. Foundations of social perception are presented as are the topics of prejudice, aggression, social influence, attitude change, communication and persuasion, and interpersonal attraction, Students are introduced to the foundations of social theory and the range of social research conducted by the contemporary social psychologist. Mainstream social cognition, information processing, psychoanalytical and social behaviorist models of social psychology are presented as well as new research influenced by contemporary work in narrative psychology, critical theory and hermeneutics.

Rites of Passage in Fiction and Film (NEWS#DIAL0432)   3 credits

Explores the timeless rites of passage from childhood to adulthood, the ways in which tribal, ancient, and modern societies have initiated their young into manhood or womanhood. We probe works as diverse as *Huckleberry Finn, Member of the Wedding,* and *Boyz N the Hood* as chronicles of the struggle of coming of age. In addition to reading fiction ranging from Ovid to Joyce, we examine the psychology, mythology and anthropology of rites of passage as investigated by Freud, Jung, Eliade, and Van Geneep.

Creating the Self (NEWS#DIAL0447)   3 credits

Creativity is both a universal goal and an imponderable challenge for most of us. We struggle with our inner thoughts as we strive to put forth in the world the best images possible of ourselves. Our most challenging creation is our own self, a work in progress that is never completed. In this course, we examine theories of creativity and explore various issues related to creating the self. Topics are diverse: Jung's theory of synchronicity, Winnicott's theory of play, Einstein's theory of time, as well as intuition, trust, commitment, language and others.

Foundations of Feminism (NEWS#DIAL0461)   3 credits

Taking their cue from Simone de Beauvoir's seminal study *The Second Sex,* contemporary feminists here and abroad have questioned and impugned traditional female roles in a patriarchal society. From Betty Friedman and Kate Millett to Carolyn Heilbrun and Marilyn French, feminist theoreticians have proposed radically reconstructing society in order to accommodate women's search for selfhood. In examining female creativity and critical attitudes, we read Virginia Woolf's *A Room of One's Own,* excerpts from *The Second Sex,* Kate Millett's ground-breaking *Sexual Politics,* Helen Cixous' manifesto of French feminism, *The Laugh of the Medusa,* Elaine Showalter's comprehensive anthology of feminist writing, *The New Feminist Criticism,* and Marilyn French's searing *The War Against Women.* Our purpose is to examine the ways in which feminists have deepened awareness of the female condition and the measures they stipulate to effect fundamental and permanent change.

Exploring Women's Lives (NEWS#DIAL0476)   3 credits

How often do we take for granted letters, diaries, lists, memoirs, and other accounts of daily life, without regarding them as treasure houses of detailed information about the people who wrote them and the world in which they lived. When one writes, one must describe what one wishes to communicate or remember. The descriptions in journals, diaries, personal accounts, and letters are often rich in details that would otherwise be forgotten. By analyzing this personal writings of several historical and contemporary women, we explore the complexities of life as they perceive it. We learn about their values, habits, and social positions; we even learn about the political agendas some wished to promote. The goal of this course is to 'read between the lines' of a number of published personal accounts of daily life by women. In the details of these works, we explore the intricacies of their authors' lives and the ways in which they developed and maintained their own social and family networks. We learn much about the social construction of specific segments of women's culture, such as women's military culture. Additionally, we create and analyze daily accounts of our own and discuss the relative strengths and weaknesses of different forms of keeping or conveying personal accounts, including the use of email.

Difference and Identity (NEWS#DIAL0589)   3 credits

What is the real impact of mulitculturalism? At the end of this century, our notions of community and identity are challenged daily at the level of statehood, ethnicity, race, class, gender and sexual orientation. This is an introduction to contemporary articulations of 'difference' - what Cornel West calls "the new cultural politics of identity." Readings include seminal essays by Freud, Foucault, and Beauvoir, but primary focus is on texts by a younger generation of cultural critics such as Cornel West, Judith Butler and bellhooks. These authors, from a variety of perspectives, address the novel social experiences that result from the breaking up of once stable social orders. the aim of the course is to make the theory accessible, encouraging students to respond on a personal level and engage in an ongoing dialogue. The online 'classroom' provides a forum for exchanging ideas and drawing connections between the readings and our individual experiences.

Emerson, Whitman and Thoreau (NEWS#DIAL0604)   3 credits

"We have been listening too long to the courtly muses of Europe," Emerson told America in 1837, encouraging his young contemporaries to put aside the conventions for the past and trust themselves as powers "new in nature." This course examines some of Emerson's key essays, *Nature, The American Scholar, Self-Reliance, the Poet* and their relationship to the writings of two men inspired by his philosophy: Henry David Thoreau, who expressed his American individualism alone "in the woods, a mile from any neighbor," and Walt Whitman, who answered Emerson's call for a poet who could sing the vast carnival of American life. Emerson's *Essays*, Thoreau's *Walden*, and Whitman's *Leaves of Grass* are discussed in the light of their impact on American writers who followed and their relevance to American society today.

Gender in Science Fiction (NEWS#DIAL0654)   3 credits

Science and fantasy fiction exist on the borderline between today's reality and tomorrow's potential. And these 'voyages out' are paradoxically 'voyages in' - into our own psyches. Today's scientists talk about manipulating genetic codes to create new life forms. At the same time, evolving lifestyles are expanding the forms of sexual 'difference', while traditional sex roles at home and in the workplace are changing rapidly. What would we like the future of 'female' and 'male' to be? This course examines how writers of science fiction and fantasy literature have approached this question. The class reads both male and female authors and examines their structurings of gender via analogy, metaphor, symbolism, characterization, plot, story development, dialogue, point of view, style, and syntax. Traditional philosophical dualisms inscribed in sci-fi from the early 20th century (self/other, human/animal, known/alien, outer/inner, superior/inferior, male/female) are contrasted with the multiplicities of being and gender described in contemporary science fiction and fantasy. Readings of short stories and novels are supplemented by feminist analysts and critiques of the genre.

Great Women Artists (NEWS#DIAL0736)   3 credits

There have been great women artists throughout history but nobody talks about them. Discover what our standard art history texts leave out. We journey from the beginnings of visual time to the present to discover what social, cultural, economic, and religious conditions shaped the creative lives of women and gave them opportunities to make art. We find out who they were, and when, where, and under what conditions they worked. This often provocative and always fascinating survey begins at the mysterious Caves of Lascaux and takes us to the ancient Egypt, Mesopotamia and the golden island of Crete, to classical Greece and Rome, to the Medieval and Renaissance worlds, to 19th- and 20th-century France, Germany and Russia, through the World Wars to New York, the hub of the international art world today. We explore what still needs to be done to insure that women art makers take their legitimate and long overdue place in the history of art. All lectures are fully illustrated. A reading list is provided.

Nietzsche's Concept of Poetry (NEWS#DIAL0832)   3 credits

The philosophy of Friedrich Nietzsche is fundamentally linked to poetry. This course examines that link and also explores more generally the relation of philosophy to poetry, of conceptual to metaphoric language, of science to art. Nietzsche wrote in *The Birth of Tragedy*, "Let anyone have the ability to continually see a vivid play, and living constantly surrounded by spirits, he will be a poet," and in *Thus Spake Zarathustra* he insisted, "I love only what a man has written with blood. Write with blood and you will experience that blood is spirit. Without living among spirits one can cultivate literature but not *poesis* (Greek not just for poetry, but for making - creativity in all arts, in life). One can compose verse but cannot create spirit or affirm life. In four stages, tragedy, truth and falsehood, style and tempo, and finally, eros and the Eternal Return - we explore how poetry as a visionary creativity holds the key to what is original in Neitzsche's philosophy and how it joins conceptual understanding to metaphoric invention, to a philosophy of the future, to a self-overcoming, and to what Neitzsche calls 'amor fati' - the affirmation of one's own fate.

The Nature of Physics (NEWS#DIAL0918)   3 credits

Nature is both beautiful and economical. It is held together by just four forces, and most of its behavior can be summed up in two laws. Physics allows us to explain the world around us with mathematics and to understand nature in basic terms. This course is designed for anyone who feels that physics is too difficult or complicated to learn. In this course you learn in simple and easy terms how to analyze and understand motion, torque, momentum, radiation, sound and how math can be used for something more interesting than just mathematics. You learn the ins and outs of friction, projectile motion, collisions, and more. After this course, you have a better understanding of the world around you and how it works. Physics opens your eyes and mind to the true physical world. All the mathematics used in this course is reviewed as we proceed.

Business Chinese (NEWS#DIAL0982)   non-credit

An introductory course in Mandarin Chinese with emphasis on communicative sills required for trade, banking, investment, negotiation and other dealings   Previous work in Chinese is desirable, but not required. Materials are presented in business and related contexts, and classwork is supplemented by video presentations and business texts.

Doing Business in the Czech Republic (NEWS#DIAL1005)   non-credit

No prior knowledge of the Czech language is required for this introductory course, which provides basic vocabulary, everyday expressions and cultural orientation instrumental to conducting business in the Czech Republic. Essential linguistic skills are taught with emphasis on standard situations in the developing business climate. Newspaper articles, business magazines, and brochures as well as video materials are used in class for the discussion of Czech society and its current economic and political realities.

Women in French Literature and Film (NEWS#DIAL1068)   2 credits

This advanced-level course, conducted in French, explores the extent women depicted in 18th-, 19th- and 20th-century French literature either accepted or transgressed the boundaries of stereotypical images. Students read excerpts from such works as Laclos, *Les Liaisons Dangeureuses*; *Diderot, La Religieuse*; *Stendahl, Le Rouge et le Noir*; *Flaubert, Madame Bovary*; and *Duras* and *L'Amant*. We also view films based on these literary sources.

Graduate Reading: German Level I (NEWS#DIAL1092)   2 credits

This course is designed for graduate students preparing for the reading examination and others who would like to read books and articles in German. The essentials of German grammar are covered, and students practice reading and translating various kinds of texts. This course is open to students with no previous knowledge of German.

Italian Culture: Importance of Being Sicilian (NEWS#DIAL1162)   2 cr.

This interdisciplinary course combines literature, film and opera to explore the quality of being Sicilian. Beyond stereotypes, the course unveils an unprejudiced and earnest portrait of the yet mysterious entity we call 'the Sicilian people.' Texts are read in Italian. Discussion is in both Italian and English, depending on the difficulty of the topic.

Hispanic Culture: Latin Music (NEWS#DIAL1282)   non-credit

This intermediate-level course is designed to improve students' Spanish through listening to and discussion of popular songs of Spain and Latin America from the sixties to the present. Flamenco, Andean music, Tango, New York Salsa, the 'Nueva Cancion' movement, Afro-Caribbean jazz and Punta are explored, including records by Serrat, The Gypsy kings, Rosa Leon, Mercedes Sosa, Inti Llimani, Ruben Blades, Tito Puente, Henry Fiol, Fernando Solana, Silvio Rogriguez and others.

Tutoring Workshop (NEWS#DIAL1337)   non-credit

This workshop is for persons who have never taught ESL and is designed to prepare them for their first few tutoring sessions. They learn to analyze the needs of the people they are tutoring, determine their level of fluency, and select materials to help them progress in English. This is a practical introduction to the tutoring process; it is *not* a complete course in how to teach English.

Principles of Language Learning and Teaching (NEWS#DIAL1346)2 credits

A teacher needs a personal philosophy of how language is acquired and how people learn. This course looks at different theories of second language acquisition and how the application of these can affect methodology and learning style.

Business Success With Better Communi. (NEWS#DIAL1444)   2 credits

Starting from the premise that ineffective writing hurts the bottom line by slowing down decision making, this workshop can help anyone hoping to advance a business career develop a forceful and positive business writing style. By working on real-world assignments, you learn how to produce dynamic and effective letters, memos, reports, and business proposals, whether your purpose is to inform, persuade, present complex information, or inspire action.

Open Imagination: A Prose Poetry Workshop (NEWS#DIAL1551)3 credits

Just what is a prose poem? What makes one different from a poem or different from a story? What happens when a poem or a story gets carried away with itself and breaks through normal boundaries? Is the prose poem a unique species of written art? Out of what traditions has it developed? Through class members' writing and discussing their own poems, we examine how the imagination uses expressions to shape itself into many different and powerful forms. We focus on how the imagination is free to use imagery, rhythm, metaphor, narrative, voice, plot, and character in new combinations in prose poetry. Through reading the work of such writers as Louis Bertrand, Charles Baudelaire, Arthur Rimbaud, Russell Edson, Nancy Lagomarsino, Michael Benedikt, Diane Williams, Laura Chester, John Yau, Lawrence Fixel, and Charles Simic, we explore the development and rich diversity of prose poetry.

Poetry and Politics: A Workshop (NEWS#DIAL1566)   3 credits

This workshop was first offered in 1984 as part of the Poetry Project at St. Mark's in the Bouwerie Church. A poetry of opposition, especially to the blind anti-communism of the Cold War, was examined, and poets such as

286

Pablo Neruda, Audré Lorde, June Jordan, Ernesto Cardenal, Pier Paolo Pasolini, Ezra Pound and Allen Ginsberg were studied. Ten years later, Communism is dead. The Cold War is over. The election of Bill Clinton has brought a sense of cautious hope to American life - poetry included. It is time to look anew at the relationship of politics and poems. What then is the role of political poetry when the pure opposition of the '80s is unnecessary? New ways of illuminating the human condition are examined, and the students write poems on political subjects. At term end, new poems are published in magazine form.

Fiction Writing: Memory, Imagination, Desires (NEWS#DIAL1580)3 credits

Fiction, though we write it to share with the world, comes from a place within us that is the antithesis to the world, a private, interior alembic, in which memory and imagination, heated by desire, mix. We help students discover this special place, and the voices that rise from it, and to learn how to draw these voices into a well-written story. We ponder the essential mystery by which we put words on paper - how to discover material, conquer initial confusion or lack of confidence, and proceed with discipline. Basics are stressed - character, story, point of view, voice, style - as well as rhythm, pacing, psychological subtlety, development, imagery, color, tone, and the power of what's not stated but nonetheless made clear. Students' stories are discussed, as well as classics by authors such as Chekhov and Joyce. Assignments are given to students who need a gentle goad. Each story is individually critiqued, and marketing advice given. Professional writers and editors may join us on occasion.

The Great American Short Story (NEWS#DIAL1592)   3 credits

Whether taking a single moment and expanding it or taking a lifetime and condensing it, the short story writer creates a world. Because a short story is just that, short, each element used to create that world is crucial: point of view, voice, characterization, dialogue. In this workshop, students present stories in progress for class critique. We also use writing exercises to hone particular skills, try tricky techniques to open up stories that are stuck, and read published stories that do marvelous things with craft. The goal: writing stories that work and understanding why they do.

'Zine Workshop (NEWS#DIAL1668)   3 credits

This course is designed for students who want to study the modern phenomena of underground fanzines - 'zines as they are known - with the goal of creating one of their own. Beginning with an overview of the recent history of fanzines and their origins in punk rock's do-it-yourself credo, we look at how 'zines have moved into the world of illustrated non-fiction: some 'zines, such as D. Price's *Moonlight Chronicles*, are really just informally-published artist's sketchbooks. We also study comic book artists whose work has pushed the non-fiction envelope, including Robert Crumb, Joe Matt, and Julie Doucet. Group critique in this course is focused on strengthening student writing, with particular attention to clarity and the encouragement of an authentic 'voice'. The relationship between image and text is also discussed at length. This is not an illustration class, but issues of printing and distribution are considered. Students receive individual critique from the instructor.

Writers in the Planetary Garden (NEWS#DIAL1695)   3 credits

Teachers and researchers in the life sciences, environmental studies, and related fields learn how to write incisively and expressively about environments under stress. The course method is based on a unique post-hurricane seminar developed by the instructor and the science staff of the Fairchild Tropical Garden in Miami. In our time, natural science suggests a disturbed field, made poignant by a sense of imminent loss. As issues of endangerment touch a popular nerve, the authority of personal writing by professionals who are field workers, not deskbound, might help to focus public concern. A biocentric view of the world needs to be articulated convincingly. The writing process taught in this course is organic. It begins with methods for gathering and structuring information: quotations, events, experiences thoughts and images. As the intersection of professional work and personal experience is explored, simple notations and sketches evolve toward the goal of an original and publishable essay. Use of irony is explored. There is also emphasis on developing convincing metaphors, for instance, the 'tending' that many plants require from animals and/or humans suggests a strategy of intention. Such metaphors can throw light on human culture as well: the biological notion of diversity, translates into social values that writers can try to make explicit. The instructor works closely with each student to produce a singular essay for a broad audience.

Philosophical Dilemmas of a Hi-Tech Society (NEWS#DIAL1725) 3 credits

Unique cultural, social, and ethical issues have emerged in an increasingly technological society. This cross-disciplinary study examines a variety of methodological approaches appropriate to the field including technological determinism, Marxism, feminism, and postmodernism. The core of the course is a series of case studies. Topics may include technology and the environment (preservation vs. development of natural resources); technology and biology (medical ethics, genetic engineering, public health); technology and conflict (weapons proliferation, terrorism, ethnic and racial conflicts); technology and the public (media and politic, news and information processing and dissemination); and technology and education (literacy vs. secondary orality, new educational media, and distance learning. Readings include Ellul, *The Technological Society*, Kennedy, *Preparing for the Twenty-first Century*, Petroski, *The Evolution of Useful Things*, Postman, *Technopoly*, and Mitcham, *Thinking Through Technology*.

Before and After the Info Superhighway (NEWS#DIAL1727)   3 credits

With public attention drawn to the 'information superhighway', camcorders, multimedia, and a host of other information technologies, it is apparent that a revolution in communications is underway. We examine this transformation, using postmodernism and contemporary media theory. We look at both past and future, ranging from the beginnings of radio and TV to the 'transparent' virtual reality of the next millennium. This course offers a brief (non-technical) overview of the technologies involved in the new modes of communication and entertainment, and the actual content of these modes is presented, including the newest forms of subjectivity and personal communication such as computer bulletin boards. Issues of space and time in virtual reality are also considered. Other topics include digital versus analog communication, the Internet, the 'new information order', gender and communications, postmodern geography and telecommunications, the emergence of new 'languages' of expression, camcorder ethics and aesthetics (issues of privacy, sexuality, oral history, and personal expression), and multi-media for home and business.

Writing for Magazines (NEWS#DIAL1734)   3 credits

This workshop is for people who have writing skills and want to break into magazine journalism. Business aspects of journalism, such as how to pitch a story, are discussed, but emphasis is on developing an idea into a publishable article. We explore the five basic types of magazine articles - reviews, essays, investigative stories, profiles, and how-to pieces - and examine the writing, reporting and analytical techniques each requires. Students are given assignments, and work is critiqued - not criticized - in class. We also review different specialties, such as entertainment, political and business journalism. Editors and writers from national magazines are occasional guests.

Screenwriting II (NEWS#DIAL1768)   3 credits

This workshop focuses on methodology: enhancing original characterization, plot development, conflict, story pacing, dramatic foreshadowing, the element of surprise, text and subtext, act structure, and visual storytelling. Each student is expected to complete an extended treatment or synopsis and begin a script. Current marketplace requirements and the basic steps in making a sale are discussed in detail. A successful major script is used as a basic text for analysis. Prerequisite: Screenwriting I or the equivalent.

It's Only Rock n' Roll: Music + Controversy (NEWS#DIAL1928)   3 credits

From the provocative, sexy lyrics of the first R&B crossover hits to 'gangsta' rap's in-your-face disdain, popular music has been caught up in social movement, and certain styles in particular have had explosive social effects. This course points out certain moments in the history of rock n' roll when a powerful music - early rock n' roll, folk revival, San Francisco (or acid) rock, heavy metal, punk rock, rap - coincided with social issues. We consider what the music represents, what social groups feelings it expresses, and what effect it had on American popular culture. We climb back into each music by recreating its context, opening up what all the excitement was about. Readings and audio/video footage help us explore each music's style, its makers, its political and cultural associations, and how people saw and heard it. Our goal is to demonstrate the vividness and immediacy of music as social expression with social consequences.

Listening Into the 21st Century (NEWS#DIAL1956)   3 credits

As we approach the 21st century, we still speak of the music of the 20th as 'new', and for many of us, this rich and varied music of our time remains unknown. This course is guaranteed to open your ears, introducing you to the vast wealth of fascinating music produced in America over the past fifty years. We discuss issues such as musical experimentation, improvisation, the composer-as-performer, and hyper-intellectualism in contemporary classical music, and we examine a range of styles and genres including avant-jazz, cross-over, rock-influenced and world musics, electronic and computer music, and mixed media. Among the composers whose work we listen to are John

Cage, Morton Feldman, Pauline Oliveros, Philip Glass, Ornette Coleman, Laurie Anderson, Muhal Richard Abrams, Leroy Jenkins, Robert Ashley, Milton Babbitt, Cecil Taylor, Terry Riley, and Annea Lockwood.

Playwriting (NEWS#DIAL2351) 3 credits

An introduction to the basics of drama, including story, character, conflict, scene construction, and overall plotting. Students also consider such issues as drama as metaphor, realities of staging, and production problems. The course is geared to the theatrical experience of each individual student, with readings and writing exercises suggested as appropriate. Feedback from classmates approximates an audience experience, and the instructor provides detailed responses to all work submitted. Students should be expected to complete at least 20 pages of script by the end of course.

Theater Criticism (NEWS#DIAL2354) 2 credits

Based on the concept of the 'informed and experienced critic', the course is designed to help the student gain a working and practical knowledge of the theater artist's craft, the history and literature of the theater, and an awareness of the 'publicly personal' dynamic of theater criticism. Students study the writing of distinguished critics, along with specific techniques used by contemporary playwrights, actors, directors, and designers. Established artists from New York City theaters are invited to the class, students observe plays in rehearsals, and tour a working theater. In the second half of the course, students attend at least three performances after which they write critical pieces in a format suitable for publication or broadcast.

Business Ethics (NEWS#DIAL2904) 3 credits

Study both the theoretical and the practical aspects of ethics, and put its power to work in your career. Learn how to recognize and decide difficult ethical questions, how to structure deals and other business situations so other people will treat you fairly, how to use the strongest arguments from over 2,000 years of ethical thought on your side in business negotiations and disputes, and why modern research indicates that a cooperative strategy and a commitment to objective principles can be the most profitable policy in business.

Supervisory Skills Workshop (NEWS#DIAL2915) non-credit

An employee's most important contact with management is with the front-line supervisor. The achievement of organizational goals is most influenced by front-line supervisors. The course is basic training for the front-line supervisor. Topics include span of control, use of Work distribution Charts, employee training for results, delegation, responsibility and accountability, discipline, leadership, time management, problem solving, communication and self development. Students work on real case studies in this highly interactive workshop.

Marketing and Promoting a Small Business (NEWS#DIAL2943) 0 credits

In small business, increasing your profits requires increasing your sales and increasing your sales requires getting the attention of potential clients. Figuring that much out is easy, but figuring out how to do it is not so easy. The workshop offers practical advice based on real-life business situations.

Learn how to: identify your markets and match your competition; obtain appropriate mailing lists, put together direct mail packages and follow up on responses; organize and publicize promotional special events. Students are encouraged to develop projects for their own businesses.

Advanced PC Topics (NEWS#DIAL3173) 3 credits

The concept of the computer as a business tool is changing. Will the computer of tomorrow be a telephone, a calculator, a television, or a hybrid of these media? To keep up to date in this swiftly moving field, we need to know how to investigate and what questions to ask. Covering user, technological and marketing trends, this lecture course takes a look at new developments and important issues in the industry. Prerequisite: MS-DOS Introduction, or equivalent working familiarity with PC computers.

The UNIX Operating System: Introduction (NEWS#DIAL3176) 2 credits

A foundation lecture course in UNIX, probably the most powerful and easy-to-use operating system for all types of computers, micro to mainframe. Students learn about multiprocessing, file structure, and real-time computing. All standard features of any UNIX system are covered: common file commands, file filters, shell programming, text editors/formatters, and communications. Prerequisite: familiarity with another operating system - DOS, VMS, JCL.

C Language Programming (NEWS#DIAL3170) 3 credits

C is a system programming language that combines the flexibility and complexity of Assembly language with the programming ease and readability of high-level languages like ADA. C is the only high-level language used successfully in constructing operating systems. This course covers all of its language constructs, data structures and operators. Standard i/o routines and the C Preprocessor (for macros) are discussed, as are differences among various compilers for small computers and C's relation to the UNIX operating system. Borland C is used. Prerequisite: familiarity with at least one other programming language.

Introduction to C++ (NEWS#DIAL3182) 3 credits

C++, a superset of the C programming language, is becoming the most widely used programming language for developing operating systems and object-oriented applications for Microsoft Windows. This is a beginner's course. Working with Borland C++, students learn fundamentals of C++ programming, including preprocessor directives, operators, program flow control, functions, data structures, array processing, and pointers. Prerequisite: familiarity with one other programming language.

Introduction to WordPerfect; 6.0 for Windows (NEWS#DIAL3225)0 credits

This course begins with an overview of the Windows environment, including the common menu items between the program. It then covers the basics of creating, editing and printing documents while using control keys or mouse to access the menu options. Students learn how to work with up to nine documents simultaneously. Topics include creating and using button bars, editing options such as Copy, Move and Undo, and changing page layout including tabs, margins and paper size. Prerequisite: Intro. to the PC and compatibles or equivalent experience.

Restructuring Education: Learning to Lead (NEWS#DIAL0000) 3 credits

The culture of the traditional school asks teachers to implement rather than lead. In restructured schools and schools in transition, teachers are being asked to take on new roles and responsibilities, often with little or no support. Classroom teaching provides all teachers with a wealth of knowledge in new ways. In this course, teachers learn about the social, organizational, and political issues that inform leadership in schools. They explore a variety of perspectives in order to build models of how to lead change. *Graduate students only.* Call (212) 229-5881.

Functions of Human Resources Management (NEWS#DIAL8357) 3 credits

This course serves to acquaint students with the primary functional areas within the profession. As the field has become more complex, many human resources professionals are choosing to focus their expertise in one or more of these areas. Topics covered include human resources planning, job analysis and design, recruitment and selection, training and development, career planning, compensation and benefits, and employee relations. For rates and registration information, please call the Human Resources Department, 212-229-8969.

Computer Management Information Systems (NEWS#DIAL8592)3 credits

Examining the capabilities and limitations of computer-based management information systems, this course provides students with a conceptual understanding of computer systems, including hardware, software, operating systems, data bases, decision support systems, and the procedures involved in systems development. Students select and define an application appropriate to their field of interest. Prerequisite: some experience with microcomputers. This course is available for graduate credit only. For tuition rates and registration information, please call the Human Resources Department, 212-229-8969.

Norwich University - 2 courses

Accredited by the New England Association of Schools and Colleges.

Norwich University
9 Linden Street
Brattleboro VT 05301

Vermont College of Norwich University, with campuses in Montpelier and Brattleboro, offers one of the nation's oldest and most respected mentor-based programs. Undergraduate academic areas include Writing and Literature, Business and Management, Psychology and Counseling, Art, Holistic Studies, and Teacher Licensure for early childhood, elementary and secondary education. The Adult Degree Program was recently featured on national Public Radio's Morning Edition.

Begun in 1970, the Graduate program pioneers the concept of independent study graduate education for working adults. The Graduate program is one of the most highly respected non residential schools in North America and has served as a model for the development of similar programs around the country.

Our students earn a Master of Arts through a program of mentor-guided study. Some areas of study include psychology, counseling, organizational development and leadership, education, adult education, literature and writing, history, gender studies, multicultural studies, international relations And others. Created for working adults who wish to advance their education without putting the rest of their lives on hold, the Graduate program's unique learning model enables students to pursue their studies while continuing to fulfill work, family and community commitments.

TUITION & FEES: Tuition for each course is $130 per credit or $390 total. You may register online by email. The registration form to send is included on this menu. For questions about how to email your registration, please send an email request to Cathy Council (EUNCouncil@aol.com).

For more information contact: Tom Yahn, Norwich University - Brattleboro Center, 9 Linden Street, Brattleboro, Vermont 05301, Tel/Fax (802) 257-9411.

Norwich University Course Descriptions

Introduction to Transformative Learning (NORW#ED 510)   3 credits

Description and Objectives: Transformative learning embraces those approaches to knowledge and action that simultaneously enhance creativity, cognitive learning, emotional development and, in a non-sectarian sense, spiritual awareness. The goal of this course is to explore the nature of transformative learning, personally and globally. Using collaborative strategies, we will look at basic concepts, models and themes in the process of transformative learning. We will examine the following questions:

-- What does it mean to be in transition?
-- What is transformative learning?   ...transformative process?
-- In what ways does transformative change take place?
-- Through the window of paradigm shifts, how does the pace of cultural change
     affect education?
-- What is the value of questioning in transformative learning?
-- What skills are cogent for facilitating transformative process?

Dialogue as Inquiry (NORW#ED 520)   3 credits

Description and Objectives: Through the collaborative work of J. Krishnamurti and physicist David Bohm, who was influenced by psychiatrist Patrick de Mare, dialogue is re-emerging as a foundational approach to explore meaning. Bohm explained that dialogue is "a stream of meaning flowing among and through us and between us....out of which will emerge some new understanding." Dialogue holds the potential for releasing old patterns in the development of community and communication. This course is an introduction to dialogue as a process of inquiry. The curriculum is generated from the following questions:

-- What is dialogue and in what ways can it be considered transformative
     process?
-- What is a learning community?
-- How might an understanding of dialogue enhance our ability to build learning
     communities?
-- What role do our underlying assumptions play in transformative process; and
     how does dialogue reveal those assumptions?
-- How can dialogue create a space for co-creativity?

Nova Southeastern University - 57 courses

Accredited by the Southern Association of Colleges and Schools

> Nova Southeastern University
> School of Computer and Information Sciences
> 3100 SW 9th Avenue
> Fort Lauderdale FL 33315

The School of Computer and Information Sciences (SCIS) at Nova Southeastern University (NSU) offers programs leading to the degree of master of science in computing technology in education, computer science, computer information systems, and management information systems. At the doctoral level, it offers programs leading to the Ph.D. or Ed.D. in computing technology in education, and the Ph.D. in computer science, information systems, and information science. Also available are courses approved for Florida teacher certification or recertification in computer science. Combined master's/ doctoral programs are available.

SCIS is dedicated to providing rigorous programs that are timely yet provide the student with an enduring foundation for future professional growth. It has been awarding graduate degrees since 1984. For the last several years the School has had an annual growth rate of at least 10% and now has over 600 graduate students from throughout the US and a variety of other countries.

Originally *Nova University*, NSU is the 47th largest independent academic institution in the United States and the largest in Florida. NSU has a 250-acre campus in Fort Lauderdale, Florida with about 10,000 students on campus and 4,000 students in programs elsewhere in Florida, in 24 other states, and in several foreign countries. In addition to the School of Computer and Information Sciences, the University has graduate schools of law, medicine, clinical psychology, education, business, oceanography, and social and systemic studies. Since 1977, NSU has enjoyed full accreditation by the Commission of Colleges of the Southern Association of Colleges and Schools (SACS) which is recognized by the US Department of Education as the regional accrediting body for this region of the United States. The Southern Association is known nationally for imposing very high educational standards on its institutions.

NSU is, for the most part, a traditional institution. On campus it has an undergraduate school and graduate programs in disciplines such as law, medicine, psychology, business, oceanography, and computer and information sciences. In addition, NSU championed the concept of distance education - a concept that enables professionals to earn master's or doctoral degrees without interrupting their careers. The concept is realized through a combination of approaches: *clusters*, *institutes* and *online formats*.

Library Services: The Einstein Library, on the main campus, houses the University's major collection of books and journals in the humanities and sciences. The library can be searched through the computer catalog which is considerably more sophisticated than the traditional card catalog. Also, more than 25 specialized indexes in CD-ROM format are available as is dial-up access to the online catalog. The library is a member of SEFLIN and FLIN, cooperative library networks that speed access to materials from other institutions throughout Florida. The Einstein Library has also been named a cooperating library of the Foundation Center in New York, giving students access to a special collection for grants and foundation research.

School of Computer and Information Sciences
Nova Southeastern University
3100 SW 9th Avenue
Fort Lauderdale FL 33315

email. flightv@alpha.acast.nova.edu

Nova Southeastern University Course Descriptions

Assembly Language and Architecture (NOVA#MCIS500)   3 credits

A comprehensive examination of the fundamental concepts and architectural structures of contemporary computers. Complex instruction set architectures (CISC) and reduced instruction set architectures (RISC) will be studied from programming and structural viewpoints.

C++ Programming Language (NOVA#MCIS501)   3 credits

In-depth study of the C++ programming language. Principles of the object-oriented paradigm. Object-oriented programming theory and practice.

Mathematics and Computing (NOVA#MCIS502)   3 credits

Graphs theory, lattices and boolean algebras, state models and abstract algebraic structures, logical systems, production systems, computability theory, recursive function theory.

Data Structures and Algorithms for CIS (NOVA#MCIS503)   3 credits

Sorting and searching, algorithms for tree structures, advanced data structures, graph algorithms, complexity, dynamic programming, optimization problems.

Data and File Structures (NOVA#MCIS610)   3 credits

Data and file structure concepts, data record format and file organization, sequential vs. random file access methods, tree-based file structure and search techniques, indexing and data clustering, multiway sort/merge and sort algorithms, input/output blocking and buffering, and advanced secondary storage technology for multimedia binary large objects.

Programming Languages & Operating Systems (NOVA#MCIS611)3 credits

Organization and types of programming languages. Analysis of imperative, object-oriented, and declarative language paradigms. Higher-level languages. Comparative analysis of languages used in development of computer information systems. A survey of contemporary operating systems and their role in computer information systems development, operation, and evolution.

Computer Information Systems (NOVA#MCIS620)   3 credits

Covers major concepts of architecture of computer information systems, including information concepts; information flow; types of information systems; the role of information in planning operations, control, and decision making; integrated information systems across a range of functional elements. Computer information systems in organizations.

Information Systems Project Management (NOVA#MCIS621)   3 credits

Life-cycle models/paradigms. Project planning and risk analysis. Project control including work breakdown structures, project scheduling, activities and milestones. Software cost estimations techniques/models. Software quality assurance and metrics for software productivity and quality. Inspections, walkthroughs, and reviews. Approaches to team organization. Configuration management. Automated project management tools. Software maintenance. Information system security. Procurement of software services and systems. Management of operational systems. Legal/ethical issues associated with CIS and software.

Office Automated Systems (NOVA#MCIS622) 3 credits

This course focuses on strategies for utilizing technology to handle the information used in the office to improve the quantity, content, and format of work performed. Topics include the design and implementation of an office automation system; strategies for successful end-user computing; OA applicat-ions including electronic mail and voice mail; windowing; multitasking; computer conferencing; computer supported cooperative work; project management software; and decision support programs. The impact of ISDN on the office environment will also be examined.

Legal and Ethical Aspects of Computing (NOVA#MCIS623) 3 credits

This course focuses on issues that involve computer impact and related societal concerns. Topics covered include transitional data flow; copyright protection; information as a source of economic power; rights to access to computer systems; computer crime; data privacy; establishing national priorities in the technical and social aspects of computing; current and anticipated uses of computer prediction; and protection of personal ethical concerns. National computer policies of Japan, France, Great Britain, and the European Economic community and the status of regulation and emerging standards also will be examined.

Computer Integrated Manufacturing (NOVA#MCIS624) 3 credits

This course provides a framework for understanding how functional organization structure impacts the design of a management information system in a manufacturing setting. Special emphasis will be on marketing, manufacturing, and financial information systems. Topics covered include the product life cycle; production scheduling and capacity requirements planning; techniques for using MIS to make plant location and inventory management; layout decisions quality control; and internal accounting and funds management. Planning strategies for forecasting services, developing requirements and specifications, writing requests for proposals, and project management will be examined within the context of functional information systems.

Computer Graphics for Information Managers (NOVA#MCIS625) 3 credits

presents computer graphics as an aid to information managers who need a clear means of presenting the analysis of information. Topics include basic graphic techniques (e.g. histograms, bar charts, pie charts), the theory of graphic presentation of information, desktop publishing software, presentation software, graphics monitors (EGA, CGA, VGA, RGB, composite), laser printers, computer screen projection systems, and standards.

Database Systems (NOVA#MCIS630) 3 credits

The methodologies and principles of database analysis and design are presented. Topics include conceptual modeling and specifications of databases, database design process and tools, functional analysis and methodologies for database design, entity-relationship model and advanced semantic modeling methods. The auxiliary concepts and theories of database systems will also be discussed in this course. These include the architectures of database systems, logical and physical database organizations, data models for database systems (network, hierarchical, relational and object-oriented model), relational algebra and calculus, query languages, normal forms, null values and partial information, relational database design utilizing dependencies, view design and integration, concurrency control, query optimization, client/server database applications, distributed databases, object-oriented databases, and the current research and development trends of database analysis, design, modeling, and applications.

Database Systems Practicum (NOVA#MCIS631)   3 credits

The techniques of database management systems are applied to practical projects. Prerequisite: Database Systems (NOVA#MCIS630).

Distributed Database Management Systems (NOVA#MCIS632) 3 credits

Students will study information storage and retrieval in a distributed environment. Topics also include distributed processing networks; degrees of distribution; approaches to distribution - multiple unduplicated/duplicated and centralization/decentralization issues; management concerns and criteria; and technical developments in office systems (digital voice communications, LANS, electronic mail, decision support systems, etc.), and alternatives for distributed processing. Prerequisite: Database Systems (NOVA#MCIS630).

System Test and Evaluation (NOVA#MCIS623)   3 credits

An analysis of the verification and validation process. Methods, procedure, and techniques for integration and acceptance testing. Reliability measurement. Goals for testing. Testing in the small and testing in the large. Allocation of testing resources. When to stop testing. Test case design methods. Black box software testing techniques including equivalence partitioning, boundary-value analysis, cause-effect graphing, and error guessing. White box software testing techniques including statement coverage criterion, edge coverage criterion, condition coverage criterion, and path coverage criterion. Test of concurrent and real-time systems.

Data and Computer Communications I (NOVA#MCIS650)   3 credits

A course on the fundamentals of data communications and data communication networking. topics include data transmission and encoding, digital data commun-ication techniques, data link control, multiplexing, switched communications networks, circuit-switched networks, packet-switching techniques and systems (ARPANET/DDN, TYMNET, SNA, X.25 standard), local area networks, metropolitan area networks, optical fiber bus and ring topologies, the Fiber Distributed Data Interface (FDDI) standard, and the LAN/MAN standards such as IEEE802.

Data and Computer Communications II (NOVA#MCIS651)   3 credits

Communications protocol concepts, the open systems interconnection (OSI) model, the TCP/IP protocol suite, systems network architecture (SNA), internet-working, transport protocols, ISO transport standards, XTP transfer protocol, OSI session services and protocol, presentation concepts, Abstract Syntax Notation One (ANS.1), encryption, virtual terminal protocols, distributed applications including network management

(SNMPv2), file transfer (FTAM), and electronic mail (X.400). The integrated services digital network (ISDN) architecture and services, broadband ISDN, and the impact of frame relay and cell relay technologies on network design.

Computer Security (NOVA#MCIS652)   3 credits

This course provides a foundation for understanding computer and communications security issues and a framework for creating and implementing a viable security program. Topics covered will include hardware, software, and network security; the regulatory environment; personnel considerations; protective measures against a variety of potential threats including hackers, disgruntled insiders, and software viruses; and techniques for responding to incidents not prevented.

Applications of the Internet (NOVA#MCIS654)   3 credits

Enterprises thrive on information, and telecommunications is now viewed as an efficient means of disseminating and receiving information. The Internet has emerged as the dominant server for national and international data communications between commercial, government, military, and academic organizations and network hosts. This course will study the structure, organization, and use of the Internet. Internet tools and their potential application are examined including Telnet, anonymous FTP, Usenet News, Finger, Internet Relay Chat, Alex, Archie, Gopher, Hytelnet, netfind, Prospero, Veronica, WAIS, WHOIS, and WWW. Students will be able to use the UNIX operating system and the Internet to successfully manage the efficient transfer of information to distant clients.

Systems Analysis and Design (NOVA#MCIS660)   3 credits

Analysis of requirements for information systems. Elicitation/fact-finding, problem analysis, decomposition, and the requirements document. Concepts, methods, techniques, and tools for systems analysis, modeling and simulation, and prototyping. Structured and object-oriented analysis. Role of the systems analyst in the organization. Gaining user commitment and fulfilling user needs. Concepts, tools, and techniques for systems design. Design methods such as object-oriented and function-oriented design. Comparison of analysis and design techniques.

Object-Oriented Applications for CIS (NOVA#MCIS661)   3 credits

Principles of the object-oriented paradigm. Application of object-oriented methods in computer information systems. Object-oriented languages and design methods for class creation. Study of the use of object-oriented techniques in applications such as user interfaces, graphics, database systems, visual programming, hypermedia, office automation systems, and decision support systems. Techniques for software reuse.

Artificial Intelligence and Expert Systems (NOVA#MCIS670)   3 credits

This course will include an introduction to artificial intelligence as well as historical and current trends and characterization of knowledge-based systems. Search, logic and deduction, knowledge representation, production systems, and expert systems will be examined. Additional areas include architecture of expert systems and criteria for selecting expert system shells, such as end-user interface, developer interface, system interface, inference engine, knowledge base, and data interface. The student will use a commercial shell to build a working expert system.

Decision Support Systems (NOVA#MCIS671)   3 credits

This course will examine concepts of decision support in both a non-automated and automated environments. Emphasis will be placed on structures, modeling, and the application of various decision support systems in today's corporate environment. Additional emphasis will be placed on the use of executive information and expert system applications. Case studies will be used to look at existent applications of each of these types of technology.

Computer-Aided Software Engineering (NOVA#MCIS672)   3 credits

Computer-Aided Software Engineering (CASE) is a technique in which the path between initial systems analysis and the final coding of programs can be at least partly automated. Topics include a critical comparison between CASE and 4GLs (Fourth-Generation Languages), upper CASE (analysis/design), lower CASE (code generation and testing), took kits, workbenches, methodology companions, platforms, completeness and consistency checking.

Human-Computer Interaction (NOVA#MCIS680)   3 credits

this course focuses on the dynamics of human-computer interaction (HCI). It provides a broad overview of HCI as a sub-area of the computer sciences and offers specific background relating to user-centered design approaches in information systems applications. Areas to be addressed include the user interface and software design strategies, user experience levels, interaction styles, usability engineering, and collaborative systems technology. Students will perform formal software evaluations and usability test.

Multimedia and Emerging Technologies (NOVA#MCIS681)   3 credits

Recent advances in high performance computing and computer networks and their impact on network-based applications and work-group productivity are examined. New developments in optical storage technologies, imaging systems, computer architectures, communications services, and graphical user interfaces are delineated. Trends in the development and the use of multimedia. Tools, techniques, and guidelines facilitating the planning, design, production, and implementation of multimedia products.

Information Systems Project (NOVA#MCIS682)   3 credits

Students are assigned a project that involves part of all of the system development cycle. Students will gain experience in analyzing, designing, implementing, and evaluating information systems applications. Prerequisite: prior consent of instructor and program director.

Data Center Management (NOVA#MCIS683)   3 credits

This course stresses information center methods for building systems between users and analysts. The traditional life-cycle will be reviewed. The role and services of the information center will be discussed within the context of these issues: user support, goals in terms of user education and training, promoting systems support and development services, and promulgating and monitoring use of standards for software and for protection of data resources. Other topics in this course include principles of application generators, prototyping, user and provider roles in an information center. Students will be able to identify strengths and limitations of the information center approach.

Special Topics in Information Systems (NOVA#MCIS691)   3 credits

This seminar will focus on the professor's current research interests. Prerequisite: prior consent of instructor and program director.

Structured Programming in Pascal and Logo (NOVA#MCTE610) 3 credits

Data and file structure concepts, data record format and file organization, sequential vs. random file access methods, tree-based file structure and search techniques, indexing and data clustering, multiway sort/merge and sort algorithms, input/output blocking and buffering, and advanced secondary storage technology for multimedia binary large objects.

Online Information Systems (NOVA#MCTE615)   3 credits

Internet and other online information systems associated with the evolving information super-highway will soon have a dominant role in how information is organized and retrieved. Consequently, educators must have fundamental knowledge of the many online information systems available if they hope to expose their students to the full range of available reference sources. The emphasis for this course will be place on developing effective online skills so that bibliographic, full text, and numerical information can be gained in an efficient manner.

Computer Literacy and Educational Reform (NOVA#MCTE620)   3 credits

This course emphasizes that computer literacy will continue to become an essential skill in a society where information is a valued commodity. This course emphasizes technological equity among students; the role of technology in an information society; community support for computing across the curriculum; state and federal legislation related to funding for computing in education and educational reform; computer literacy and global challenges to productivity; and new models of teaching that emphasize problem-solving, higher-order thinking, and team interaction.

Survey of Courseware (NOVA#MCTE625)   3 credits

Students will explore various types of computer-based courseware. Macintosh and PC Computer-Assisted Instruction applications using hypertext, frame based and multimedia formats are evaluated for appropriateness for the intended learning audience. Characteristics of tutorials, drill and practice, instructional games, simulations and tests are surveyed.

Authoring Systems Design (NOVA#MCTE626)   3 credits

Functionality and characteristics of PC and Macintosh authoring systems, frame-based, multimedia, and hypertext are explored in this course. Instructional systems design methodology in conjunction with authoring tools is examined and critiqued.

Database Systems (NOVA#MCTE630)   3 credits

Included are fundamentals of database architecture, database management systems, and database systems. Principles and methodologies of database design, and techniques for database application development.

Computing Technology Facilities Planning (NOVA#MCTE640)   3 credits

Issues presented in this course include establishing computer laboratories and enhancing classroom facilities by incorporating computer. An investigation of computer laboratories designed for faculty use, training, and support. topics presented include establishing the computer laboratory and selecting hardware; types of software; physical layout of the laboratory; printers; networking possibilities; considerations of to the physical environment; and scheduling methods.

Computer Networks (NOVA#MCTE650)   3 credits

This course is focused on the following areas: fundamental concepts of computer network architecture and topologies, open system interconnection models and standards, analysis of transport protocol specification, network program interface, network management, and emerging computer network applications. An area that is covered in detail includes network standards that determine how data are transferred: Ethernet, token ring, and Fiber Distributed Data Interface. Attention will also be directed toward issues affecting operating peripherals, including CD-ROM drives and printers.

Multimedia and Emerging Technologies (NOVA#MCTE660)   3 credits

Recent advances and future trends in learning technology and future trends in educational computing are examined. Innovations in teacher and student workstation technology are reviewed. Emphasis is placed on an examination of audio/video and computer-based tools currently in use in schools and training centers. Special attention is given to CD-ROM technology and laser disk technology. Guidelines for selection of instruction technology and design and implementation of multimedia projects are presented.

Learning Theory & Computer Applications (NOVA#MCTE670)   3 credits

Students will explore learning theories and how learning is achieved when instruction is presented from a computer-based paradigm. The course will emphasize the computer as a learning device that can be used in effective manner to model learning theories associated with behaviorism, cognitivism, and human information processing.

Human-Computer Interaction (NOVA#MCTE680)   3 credits

This course explores the emerging field of human-computer interaction. Emphasis is placed on how software design practices are integrated with human factors principles and methods. Other issues presented in the course include: user experience levels; interaction styles; usability engineering; interaction devices and strategies; user-centered design; human information processing; social aspects of computing; and computer-supported cooperative work.

303

Computer-Based Statistics (NOVA#MCTE690)   3 credits

This course is an introduction to statistical analysis and decision making. Close attention is paid to data types, data contributions, the identification of variables and descriptive data presentation techniques. Students are introduced to both parametric and non-parametric data analysis procedures including independent and dependent sample t-tests, chi-square analysis and simple analysis of variance. A significant amount of this is centered around hypothesis testing and the use of statistical software packages.

Directed Study in Training and Learning I (NOVA#MCTE698)   3 credits

Development of readings, research, practical implementation, or other form of study as arranged between student and instructor.

Directed Study in Training and Learning II (NOVA#MCTE699)   3 credits

Development of readings, research, practical implementation, or other form of study as arranged between student and instructor.

Computer-Based Research and Statistics (NOVA#DCTE710)   3 credits

An in-depth treatment of the research and evaluation process including design, measurement, and statistical analysis is provided. Techniques for planning, designing, and conducting research and evaluation projects and collecting and analyzing data using various statistical techniques are examined. Special emphasis is placed on the selection of appropriate methodologies for a variety of problem-solving situations. Software programs for performing statistical procedures are reviewed.

Management of Computing Resources (NOVA#DCTE610)   3 credits

New developments in information technology management are examined. Practical techniques and methods for managing hardware, software, communications, distributed. Guidelines for creating an environment that integrates next generation computing components for maximum information accessibility are introduced. Various approaches to project planning, managing change and innovation, and facilitating computer and communications security are reviewed.

Human-Computer Interaction (NOVA#DCTE720)   3 credits

Techniques facilitating effective human-computer interaction are presented. Basic elements, procedures, tools, and environments contributing to the development of a successful user interface are explored. Design principles, guidelines, and methodologies for building, installing, managing, and maintaining interactive systems that optimize user productivity are reviewed. Topics include the multidisciplinary dynamics of human computer interaction, current and projected developments in HCI research, computer supported cooperative work, and strategies for implementing and evaluating human-computer dialogues.

Authoring Systems and Curriculum Design (NOVA#DCTE735)   3 credits

American education has become increasingly dependent on computer-mediated instruction. To meet this need for good software that matches instructional tasks to instructional media, many educational practitioners are turning to authoring systems. This course will stress the capabilities of authoring systems, both hypertext and frame-based paradigms. Students in this course will explore the use of authoring systems as tools for the curricular design of tutorials, drill and practice activities, instructional games, and simulations.

Telecommunications and Computer Networks (NOVA#DCTE740) 3 credits

Recent advances and new applications in the expanding field of telecommunications and computer networks are examined. The technical fundamentals, architecture, and design of computer networks are described. Strategies, tools, and techniques for network planning, implementation, management, maintenance, and security are delineated. Topics include ISDN and B-ISDN, the OSI Model, transmission media, network operating systems, topologies, configurations, protocols, and performance characteristics. Trends in standardization, internetworking, downsizing, and the development of local area networks (LANs), wide area networks (WANs), metropolitan area networks (MANs), and enterprise-wide networks are examined.

Multimedia and Emerging Technologies (NOVA#DCTE745)   3 credits

Recent advances in high performance computing and computer networks and their impact on network-bases applications and workgroup productivity are examined. New developments in optical storage technologies, imaging systems, computer architectures, communications services, and graphical user interfaces are delineated. Trends in the development and use of multimedia to support instruction, learning, and research are described. Tools, techniques and guide-lines, design, production and implementation of multimedia projects.

Computer Application of Learning Theory (NOVA#DCTE747)   3 credits

Computing machinery and other forms of high technology are assuming an increasingly dominant role in instructional delivery and school management. Many states are investing considerable resources on studies related to technology and student learning. this course will examine the complexity of learning and behavioral change, with emphasis placed on how computing machinery can be used effectively in the learning process.

Applied Database Management Systems (NOVA#DCTE750)   3 credits

Techniques for determining database requirements and managing organizational data resources are examined. Strategies for designing database management systems applications that satisfy specific requirements are presented. Components and architecture of the relational data model are analyzed. Methods for creating and implementing object-oriented inform-ation systems are explored. Topics include object-oriented languages, user interface, database & expert systems, distributed computing, advantages and drawbacks of commercially available DBMS tools and products.

Courseware & Educational Programming (NOVA#DCTE610)   3 credits

This course is an indepth exploration of the basic concepts, principles and methods of software design, including methodologies, the software product life cycle, levels of design, design presentations, design documentation, and design practices and techniques found in instructional software. The student will develop competencies in analyzing and synthesizing design for courseware using on-line tools such as C-Pilot and Writers Workbench, offline tools such as Hypercard, ToolBook, and Linkway Live, and other tools incl. authoring systems, structured programming and educational languages.

Artificial Intelligence and Expert Systems (NOVA#DCTE760)   3 credits

Principles underlying basic AI research and their applications in practice are introduced. Key AI concepts including knowledge representation, natural language processing, machine learning, and heuristic search techniques are examined. Special emphasis is placed on examining the characteristics, attributes, conceptual design and structure of expert systems. An in-depth analysis is presented of the tools, techniques, methods, and processes involved in building, implementing, and maintaining expert systems that comply with specific needs and requirements.

Systems Analysis for Educational Computing (NOVA#DCTE610) 3 credits

An in-depth study of techniques, methods, and tools for the analysis and specification of requirements for educational computing systems. Topics include: the requirements definition process including fact-finding, problem/needs analysis and decomposition, and the requirements document; system life-cycle models; application development strategies; feasibility assessment; logical specification of planned system; behavioral specification; the role of prototyping; structuring and modeling techniques for requirements definition and behavioral specs including object-oriented techniques; overview of design, implementation, verification and validation; and techniques for project management.

Computer Networks (NOVA#DCTE790)   3 credits

The technical fundamentals, design, configuration, and implementation of computer networks are described. Networking applications that are revolutionizing information access and delivery are examined. Strategies, tools, and techniques to expedite network planning, management, maintenance, and security are reviewed. Topics include information communications, the OSI Mode, ISDN and B-ISDN, transmission media, network architecture, operating systems, topologies, protocols, and performance characteristics. Trends in standardization, internetworking, downsizing, and the development of local area networks (LANs), wide area networks (WANs), metropolitan area networks (METs), and enterprise-wide networks are delineated.

Telecommunications (NOVA#DCTE795)   3 credits

An introduction to key aspects of the telecommunications from fundamental communications concepts and principles to new directions in formation transfer and delivery is presented. Methods, tools, and techniques for telecommunication planning, forecasting services, developing requirements and specifications, and project management are described. Strategies for integrating communication elements into computer networks are delineated. Topics include communications media, services, architectures, protocols, and standards. new applications in voice, video, data, and image communications are discussed. Recent developments in data communications and distributed networks, satellite communications, fiberoptics, are examined.

New York Institute of Technology - 106 courses NYIT

Accredited by the Middle States Association of Colleges and Schools.

New York Institute of Technology
Online Campus, Office of Admissions
P. O. Box 9029
Central Islip NY 11722-9029

Welcome to the On-line Campus (OLC) of the New York Institute of Technology. If you want to complete a college degree but cannot attend conventional college classes on a traditional campus because of obstacles such as time, geography, dependent children or work conflicts, we have a distance learning program tailored just for you.

We offer you the opportunity to earn degrees in Business Administration, Behavioral Science, and Interdisciplinary Studies. You can earn your degree entirely on-line, and you can transfer credits in from other colleg-es. Other options such as credit for prior learning are also available. To earn an NYIT degree, you must take at least 30 credits with NYIT.

The On-Line Campus makes college courses possible for students who choose not to attend classes on a conventional campus. The communication between students and faculty takes place entirely over a computer conferencing network, so that the course work is done by students and faculty exchanging text messages on computer screens. No one has to be logged on to the system at the same time. In order to access NYIT's TechNet, you must have a personal computer either at home or the office, a modem, and software for telecommunications and word processing.

The OLC/NYIT offers the following degrees:
Bachelor of Arts in Interdisciplinary Studies
Bachelor of Science in Interdisciplinary Studies
Bachelor of Professional Studies in Interdisciplinary Studies
Bachelor of Science in Business Administration (Management Option)
Bachelor of science in Behavioral Sciences (Options: Psychology, Sociology, Community Mental Health and Criminal Justice)

Overview: The OLC offers 6 overlapping terms each year, and we offer academic advisement at any time. When you call us at 1-800-222-6948, we can describe our program, explain the options, and help you choose your area of study. We can give you an informal evaluation of your prior collegiate and non collegiate learning, and we can also provide information regarding financial aid, course registration, computer conferencing and other features of the program.

Computer Conferencing: CoSy computer conferencing organizes users into groups ('conferences') so that the student in a course and their instructor are the addressees of a 'course conference'. In your course conferences you will find detailed course outlines and you will join in a conversation with your instructor and other students about the course work. You will upload your work directly to the course conference. You will even have direct access to NYIT's library staff on CoSy.

Curricula: As with many other colleges, our degrees require completion of a Core Curriculum. The Core serves students by insuring that their educational experience, while focused, doesn't overlook the reality that we all have a responsibility to be informed members of our community. Our Core included courses in mathematics, English, philosophy, economics, and government.

New York Institute of Technology On-Line Campus
TUITION
Per Credit - $278
Per Semester - $4,170 if full-time (full-time requires 12-16 credits)

System Time
Telecommunications - $11 per hour for CoSy computer conferencing, billed monthly. The average monthly cost for CoSy use is $15.

New York Institute of Technology
Online Campus, Office of Admissions
P. O. Box 9029
Central Islip NY 11722-9029

Phone: 800-222-6948

New York Institute of Technology Course Descriptions

Law of Evidence (NYIT#BES2300)   3 credits

An explanation and analysis of the rules of evidence. The course treats recent US Supreme Court decisions concerning the rights of the citizen against unreasonable search and seizure, and the rules of giving testimony and the protecting and safeguarding of evidence. In addition to instruction in the law of evidence, time is devoted to visiting court and to demonstrations of proper and improper presentation of evidence.

Criminal Law and Proceeding (NYIT#BES2301)   3 credits

A study of the elements of the Penal Law particularly relevant to police officers, including a review and analysis of major criminal offenses with consideration given to the available defenses and judicial interpretations.

Police Administration (NYIT#BES2305)   3 credits

An introduction to the organization and structure of a police department. Topics include an overview of the police departments, an analysis of the police function, tables of organization, chains of command and lines of authority, division of labor, and the informal police organization Attention centers on typical problems of police administration and the coordination of police services.

Patrol Function (NYIT#BES2310)   3 credits

A course devoted to an analysis of the objectives and functions of the uniformed police. Emphasis is placed on detailed examination of many typical patrol problems and consideration of both the sociological and psychological factors which facilitate or impede effective performance.

Introduction to Criminal Justice (NYIT#BES2316)   3 credits

An introduction to the contemporary American criminal justice system. discussion of the role of police, courts and prisons. Also examined is the juvenile justice system. General issues considered include: police discretion, due process and change as an integral element of the American criminal justice system.

Forensic Technology (NYIT#BES2317)   3 credits

An introduction to problems and techniques of scientific criminal investigation. Emphasis on various scientific aids to the investigator. Included are such topics as fingerprint identification, lie detector usage, hypnosis, blood typing, hair analysis, DNA typing and crime scene analysis.

Criminal Investigation (NYIT#BES2318)   3 credits

Introduction to criminal investigation in the field. Analysis and explanation of conduct at the crime scene, strategies for interviewing and interrogating witnesses and suspects, techniques of surveillance and preservation of evidence for presentation in court.

Modern Police Management (NYIT#BES2319)   3 credits

The essentials of personnel management and fundamentals of supervision and leadership as applied to the administration of police organizations. The course will examine such issues as the decision making processes, leadership styles, budgetary and union problems, motivation, discipline, public policy, performance management, and organizational development.

Police and Community Relations (NYIT#BES2320)   3 credits
This course analyzes the complex relationship between police and community, community attitudes toward police, the efforts of the police organization to create a more favorable public image, the emergence of a civil rights and civil liberties movement, and the contribution of the individual police officer to police-community relations.

Crisis Intervention for Public Safety Personnel (NYIT#BES2325)   3 cr.
Examines the concepts and techniques used by criminal justice practitioners in handling crisis situations. The focus of the course will be the development of skills to intervene effectively with specific types of crises, thereby diffusing the immediate conflict situation. Topics to be covered include: landlord/tenant disputes, family fights, suicide attempts, civil disorder and demonstrations, labor/management relations, and common crises occurring at institutional and corporate sites.

Probation and Parole (NYIT#BES2350)   3 credits
An examination of organization and management in probation and parole systems. Topics include: distinctions between probation and parole in terms of organizational function and types of clients served; client relationships and interactions with other social control agencies; case loads, case work methods, and case supervision; problems in pre-sentence investigation; and job requirements and performance standards for probation and parole officers with particular emphasis on recruitment, training and assignment. Prerequisites: NYIT#BES2401 and NYIT#BES2411.

Introductory Psychology (NYIT#BES2401)   3 credits
An introduction to selected concepts, methods, and vocabulary of psychology. Focus of study will be on the individual and the conditions that influence behavior. Topics that will be covered include: growth and development, learning and thinking, emotions and motivations, personality and assessment, maladjustment and mental health, groups and social interactions, and social influence and society.

Anthropology (NYIT#BES2405)   3 credits
An introduction to the study of ancient man and primitive cultures. Major topics include: the origins and evolution of man; the evolution of different cultural forms in terms of craft and technology, magic, religion, and gov't.

Introduction to Sociology (NYIT#BES2411)   3 credits
An analysis of the social and cultural forces which govern human behavior. The principal topics include: social interaction and organization, socialization processes, primary groups and the family (associations, bureaucracy, and other social institutions), collective behavior, population, and ecology.

Physiological Basis of Behavior (NYIT#BES2412)   3 credits
A basic course to familiarize students with the bodily processes involved in various aspects of human behavior. Physiological psychology studies the

biological basis of psychological functions such as sleeping, emotions, motivations, perceptions, learning, memory, and problem solving. the two major biological systems most relevant to psychology are the nervous system and the glandular system. Prerequisite: NYIT#BES2401.

Learning Theory (NYIT#BES2413) 3 credits

Learning theory is a fundamental science course. The student is asked to trace the emergence of modern cognitive learning theory (neo-behaviorism) from the original works of Pavlov, Thorndike, and Watson through the 'blackbox' Skinnerian school of thought. The course emphasizes theoretical rather than methodological issues and, as such, is designed to give the student a firm grasp of the conditions under which permanent behavior change occurs. Prerequisite: NYIT#BES2401.

Social Psychology (NYIT#BES2415) 3 credits

An analysis of the structures and properties of human groups. Topics include group formation, development of role relationships, intra-group intergroup conflict, factors influencing group effectiveness, the role of motivation, and attitudes in group processes. Prerequisite: NYIT#BES2401.

Measurement Concepts (NYIT#BES2421) 3 credits

The construction, validation, and interpretation of test results. Group and individual tests of aptitude, intelligence, and personality are analyzed. Each student will develop and administer a measure for a specific diagnostic or research purpose.

Statistical Analysis (NYIT#BES2422) 4 credits

Covers descriptive and inferential statistics, frequency distributions, percentile rank, measure of central tendency and variability, correlation and regression and tests of significance. Using computer software students will directly apply these statistics to specific problems common to the behavioral sciences.

Educational Psychology (NYIT#BES2423) 3 credits

Emphasis on human learning. consideration of concepts of readiness, individual differences, motivation, retention, transfer, concept development, reasoning, mental health, and measurement as related to learning. Psychological principals of teaching-learning technology are examined. Prerequisite: NYIT#BES2401.

Marriage and the Family (NYIT#BES2425) 3 credits

This course covers historical changes in family patterns, contemporary family life in different cultures and subcultures, evolution of the American family pattern, functions of the family, the family as a primary group, kinship patterns, and nuclear and extended families. Other topics include: dating, mate selection, family disorganization, and marital success.

American Urban Minorities (NYIT#BES2435) 3 credits

An in-depth analysis of the diverse ethnic structure of the urban community. Major attention is given to black, Puerto Rican, and Mexican groups. topics include: a survey of each group's social and economic structure, an examination of ghetto conditions and their effects, the impact of urban conditions on the new arrival, a comparison with the adaptation and treatment accorded earlier migrants, the validity of the melting pot concept, and a comparison of the life styles of various minority groups. Prerequisite: NYIT#BES2411.

Child Psychology (NYIT#BES2439)   3 credits

The study of human growth and development. This course is designed to give the student an understanding of children and who they change while passing through the major phases of growth. Emphasis is placed on physical, emotional, and personality development with an aim toward understanding the period of human growth on which adulthood is founded. Special topics include: identification of conditions in childhood leading to normal psychological development. Prerequisite: NYIT#BES2401.

Adolescent Psychology (NYIT#BES2441)   3 credits

An introduction to the study of that portion of human development called adolescence. Some of the topics treated: significance of puberty, biological and social sex roles, adolescent image, the emergence of new figures such as peers and idols, society at large as agents of socialization in place of parents and family, the extinction of old habits and practices and their replacement with new behavioral patterns. Theoretical consideration will be supplemented with observational experience. Prerequisite: NYIT#BES2401.

Theories of Personality (NYIT#BES2445)   3 credits

A survey of the major theoretical approaches to understanding the development, structure, & dynamics of personality. Prereq.: NYIT#BES2401.

Behavioral Science Marketing (NYIT#BES2451)   3 credits

An investigation of the behavioral sciences disciplines as they affect marketing decisions. Consideration of such fields as psychology, sociology, and anthropology as the basis for studying consumer motivation and behavior. Prerequisite: NYIT#BES2401.

Community Mental Health (NYIT#BES2454)   3 credits

An analysis of the current status of the community mental health movement which attempts to define and anticipate future trends. Topics include health and social environment, preventative health education, type and quality of community mental health services, organizational complexities, manpower, consumer attributes, consumer participation, and impact on other mental health organizations. Prerequisites: NYIT#BES2401, NYIT#BES2411.

Communication and Interviewing Techniques (NYIT#BES2460)   3 credits

The examination of communication from various standpoints, as illustrated by different types of interviews. Interviewing techniques employed for personnel selection are compared with those sued in interrogation and those used for the therapeutic purposes. Practice in interviewing. Prerequisites: NYIT#BES2401, NYIT#BES2411.

Abnormal Psychology (NYIT#BES2465)   3 credits

A study of mental health and abnormal behavior. The topics covered include: definitions of mental health and mental illness; problems of adjustment; the causes, diagnosis, treatment, and prevention of mental disorders. Case studies supplement and illustrate the theoretical parts of the course material. Prerequisite: NYIT#BES2401.

Environmental Psychology (NYIT#BES2467)   3 credits

A study of man's relationship to the physical environment. Topics include the effects of architecture on behavior, design in selective environments, social uses of space, urban and environmental stressors encouraging ecological behaviors. Prerequisite: NYIT#BES2401.

Introductory Research Methods (NYIT#BES2470)   4 credits

This course stresses the classical approach to experimental research on human behavior. Students conduct and report on experiments in the fields of psychophysics, psychomotor learning, memory and perceptions. These laboratory experiments permit the student to apply knowledge gained in former course about measurements, statistical inference, and the design of experiments. Prerequisites: NYIT#BES2401, NYIT#BES2421 and NYIT#BES2428.

Juvenile Delinquency (NYIT#BES2473)   3 credits

An inquiry into the causes of juvenile delinquency and the social and psychological factors involved in the predictive studies and theories concerning the development of delinquency. Topics also include formation of youth gangs, methods of coping with gang activity, the types of crime committed by children and youths, narcotics problems, neglected and retarded children, the youthful offender and wayward minor, the operation of the Children's Court, crime prevention programs. Prereq.: NYIT#BES2401, NYIT#BES2411, NYIT#BES2477.

Social Problems (NYIT#BES2475)   3 credits

A sociological analysis of social problems in American society. All social problems will be viewed from a structural perspective, i.e., the root cause of a social problem lies in the institutional arrangements of American society that give rise to social problems will be evaluated in terms of value-conflicts, power structures, and economic institutions. Major topics include: inequality, poverty, environmental destruction, ageism, educational institutions, social deviance, unemployment, problems of the city. Prerequisites: Completion of 12 BES credits including NYIT#BES2401 and NYIT#BES2411.

Criminology (NYIT#BES2477)   3 credits

An examination of crime and theories of crime causation. Topics include: the white collar criminal, the professional criminal, and the structure of organized crime. The criminal justice process is analyzed, including the role of the police, the criminal courts, the probation officer, correctional services, and the reentry of the offender into society. Prerequisites: NYIT#BES2401 and NYIT#BES2411.

Community Psychology (NYIT#BES2495)   3 credits

The broad range of activities of psychologists and councilors in community settings will be examined. An intensive study will be made of between twenty and twenty-five special areas of community involvement, including hospitals, rehabilitation services, halfway houses and outreach clinics, crisis intervention centers, and correctional institutions. Emphasis is on the prevention, recognition and remediation of problems, including field experience. The social, professional, and personal rationales for community psychology as a separate academic and professional entity will be considered. Prerequisites: NYIT#BES2401, NYIT#BES2411, NYIT#BES2454.

Rehabilitation Psychology (NYIT#BES2496) 3 credits

Review of contemporary theories, practices and research in rehabilitation of the emotionally, mentally and physically disabled. Selected topics will include various addictions, mental retardation, learning disabilities, emotional disorders, and physical incapacities. Prerequisites: NYIT#BES2401, NYIT#BES2445.

Introduction to Counseling (NYIT#BES2497) 3 credits

Theories and practical techniques of counseling, including advisement, guidance, and supportive psychotherapy, by both directive and non-directive methods. Counseling is considered both as a career in itself and as a component of one's job in such fields as teaching, business and personnel management, health occupations, social work, and the law.

Social Work II (NYIT#BES2498) 3 credits

This is the second social work course open to students who have completed BES 2494/ It is designed to meet the dual purpose of providing students with a framework for assessing and understanding the range of policy issues posed in the current organization, financing, and delivery of social services in the United States, and for evaluating proposals being made in the arenas of public policy for more comprehensive systems of social service. Emerging models of social service delivery systems will be reviewed. Prerequisites: NYIT#BES2401, NYIT#BES2411.

Introduction to Marketing (NYIT#BUS3400) 3 credits

Study of the process by which consumer needs and wants are analyzed and satisfied within the context of a modern marketing system. Investigation of current developments in the external environment affecting the marketing process. The role of marketing institutions in facilitating the flow of goods and services from producers to consumers is analyzed.

Sales Management (NYIT#BUS3401) 3 credits

Planning, supervising and evaluation of sales force efforts within the guidelines set by strategic marketing planning are the principal responsibilities of sales managers. This course examines both the theory and practices which are encompassed within the role of sales manager. Prerequisite: NYIT#BUS3400.

Management of Promotion (NYIT#BUS3405) 3 credits

A firm's promotional efforts focus on developing and managing marketing communications. This course studies the planning and implementation of demand stimulating promotion, i.e., advertising, personal selling, sales promotion and publicity/public relations.. Promotion is seen as a key element of the marketing mix which contributes to an organization's cohesive marketing strategy. Prerequisite: NYIT#BUS3400.

Marketing Research (NYIT#BUS3406)   3 credits

Research activity in the field of marketing, methods of data collection and analysis thereof, quantitative techniques in marketing, the role of the computer in marketing research, control and evaluation of the marketing function. Prerequisites: NYIT#BUS3400 (or Hotel and Restaurant Administration, not offered online).

Managerial Accounting (NYIT#BUS3501)   3 credits

Special emphasis is placed on the collection and interpretation of data for managerial decision-making purposes. A study is made of cost concepts used in planning and control, cost-profit-volume analysis, and budgeting. This course carries no credit for the public accounting major. Prerequisite NYIT#BUS3511.

Accounting I (NYIT#BUS3511)   3 credits

A study of accounting fundamentals. Topics include the accounting cycle, statement preparation, systems, assessed valuations, accounting concepts, and principles for the sole proprietorship.

Accounting II (NYIT#BUS3521)   3 credits

Continues the study of accounting fundamentals. Topics include partnership, corporations, liabilities, manufacturing, accounting, and statement analysis. Prerequisite: NYIT#BUS3511.

Business Law I (NYIT#BUS3529)   3 credits

An introductory course with emphasis on the law of contracts and agency. Designed to give a basic understanding of the legal aspects of contractual obligations and agency relationships.

Business Law II (NYIT#BUS3532)   3 credits

Law of property, bailments, secured transactions, bankruptcy, and related subjects. As analysis of the Uniform Commercial Code as it applies to the law of sales. Designed to give a basic understanding of legal problems in the marketing and transportation of goods. Prerequisite: NYIT#BUS3529.

Business Law III (NYIT#BUS3533)   3 credits

A study of the forms of business organization with emphasis on the law of partnership and corporations. An analysis of the Uniform Commercial Code with respect to commercial paper. When appropriate, problems from professional examinations will be introduced. Prerequisite: NYIT#BUS3532.

Corporate Finance (NYIT#BUS3630)   3 credits

Overview of the financial management function in modern business, emphasizing the time value of money and financial analysis. The financial and economic environment and capital markets and securities are covered. Prerequisites or corequisites: NYIT#EC2072 and NYIT#BUS3511, NYIT#MA3010.

Introduction to EDP in Business (NYIT#BUS3801)   3 credits

The role of computers in business organizations will be explored. There will be an emphasis on the use of such software packages as spreadsheets, database and word processing.

315

Collective Bargaining and Labor Relations (NYIT#BUS3902)   3 credits

This course is designed to meet the two objectives: to introduce the student to the background and relationships between economies, public policy, unionism, and business management and their impact upon management-labor relations; to provide a basic orientation to the framework, processes and strategies involved in collective bargaining and the resolution of labor grievances and arbitration in management-labor relations. Prerequisite: NYIT#BUS3917.

Organizational Behavior (NYIT#BUS3903)   3 credits

An introduction to the fundamental concepts of human behavior within organizations. Topics covered include: motivation, group dynamics, informal organizational design, leadership, performance measurement, organizational changes, conflict management and organizational behavior. Prerequisites: NYIT#BUS3906 or NYIT#BUS3900.

New Product Management (NYIT#BUS3904)   3 credits

Techniques and practices applied to conceiving, developing, launching and management new products. An in-depth evaluation of the life cycle concept will analyze various stages and how careful planning and managing can extend it. The product management concept and its effectiveness as a management tool will also be studied. Prerequisite: NYIT#BUS3400.

Small Business Management (NYIT#BUS3905)   3 credits

An examination of required skills, resources, and techniques which transform an idea into a viable business. Entrepreneurial decision making will be stressed and the role it plays in idea generation, conception, opportunity analysis, marshaling of resources, implementation of plans, management of ongoing operations, and providing for growth will be stressed. Prerequisites: NYIT#BUS3906, NYIT#BUS3400, NYIT#BUS3511.

Introduction to Business (NYIT#BUS3906)   3 credits

Broad overview of functions, institutions, principles and practices of business; provides basic foundation for the student who will specialize in some aspect of business in college and emphasize the dynamic nature of business and the role of change as evidenced by current events.

Introduction to International Business (NYIT#BUS3907)   3 credits

Techniques for analyzing and understanding the world of international business. Students will examine the challenges posed by the multinational firm and the dynamic nature of international business. Case studies and discussions will complement lectures. Prerequisites: NYIT#SS2010 or NYIT#SS2011, NYIT#BUS3900 and NYIT#BUS3400.

Computer Concepts (NYIT#COM5641)   3 credits

A course designed to provide an understanding of what the computer can do and how it does it for the non technically oriented student. The course covers the basic concepts of computer operation and programming, applications of computers, and the effects of computers on society.

Principles of Economics I (NYIT#EC2010)   3 credits

A study of basic economic concepts emphasizing analysis of the aggregate economy. The fundamental concepts of national income and its determination, economic fluctuations, monetary and fiscal policies, and economic growth, are covered.

Basic Economics (NYIT#EC2011)   3 credits

A basic introduction to economic analysis, with emphasis on the problems and issues of a modern economy. This course is not available to business, economics and political science majors.

Principles of Economics II (NYIT#EC2020)   3 credits

Examination of the processes of price determine, output, and resource allocation in perfect competition. Also covers labor economics, international trade and finance, and alternative economic systems. Prerequisite: NYIT#EC2010.

Money and Banking (NYIT#EC2072)   3 credits

The structure and function of the banking system and financial markets in the United States. The use of monetary policy in the regulation of the national economy. The role of the Federal Reserve System. Prerequisite: NYIT#EC2020.

International Economics and Finance (NYIT#EC2088)   3 credits

A study of international trade, investment, finance and economic cooperation. Topics will include theory and techniques of international trade, the US in international trade, tariffs and quotas, foreign aid programs, foreign exchange markets and hedging exposure to foreign exchange risk. Operations of multinational corporations, economic integration and cooperation, balance of payments and international adjustment mechanisms and international indebtedness. Prerequisite: NYIT#EC2072.

Introduction to Computer Conferencing (NYIT#EN1006)   3 credits

Students learn how a computer conferencing system is structured, how it works and how to use it. Particular attention is paid to user behavior in a computer conference and to the application of computer conferencing in a distance learning environment.

Basic Reading and Writing (NYIT#EN1E07)   3 credits

A course designed for students whose English placement test reveals the need for improved basic writing and reading skills. Students will read and write various kinds of essays, and practice prewriting, composing revising and editing. The course will improve the use of standard grammar and mechanics and develop comprehension strategies, vocabulary and study skills. Prerequisite: English placement test.

Basic Reading & Writing - International Students (NYIT#EN1008) 3 credits

A course for international students whose English placement test reveals need for improved basic writing and reading skills. Students read and write various essays and practice prewriting, composing, revising and editing. The course will improve use of standard grammar and mechanics and develop comprehension strategies, vocabulary and study skills. Coursework includes a computer lab component. Prerequisite: English placement test.

College Composition I (NYIT#EN1010)   3 credits

Instruction in and application of the principles and skills involved in effective expository writing, with most readings from nonfiction prose. Required of all freshmen. Coursework includes a computer lab component. Prerequisite: English placement test.

College Composition II (NYIT#EN1020)   3 credits

Further Development of the expository writing and reading skills taught in English 1010. Introduction to literature and library research.

Business Writing (NYIT#EN1042)   3 credits

An intermediate-level writing course for students in business. Instruction and practice in all phases of business communications, such as reports, memoranda and correspondence, as well as in-depth study of research methods. Required of all business and management majors. Coursework includes a computer lab component.

Technical Writing (NYIT#EN1043)   3 credits

An intermediate-level writing course for students in the physical and life sciences and technology. Emphasis on style in technical writing, modes of technical discourse (definition, description, analysis, interpretation), and strategies for effective business communication, including resume writing and technical reports. Methods and procedures of research are explored in depth. Recommended for all science and technology majors. Coursework includes a computer lab component.

Report Writing (NYIT#EN1044)   3 credits

An intermediate-level course for students of the behavioral and social sciences. Methods and procedures of research; emphasis on reports and advanced research papers and strategies for effective business communication including resume writing. Recommended for all majors in the behavioral sciences, political science, and economics. Coursework includes a computer lab component.

Advanced Scientific and Technical Writing (NYIT#EN1048)   3 credits

Continued training and practice in the techniques and forms of scientific and technical writing. Topics covered include: longer report forms, manuals, patent disclosures, preparation of forms, promotional materials, business and product plans, specification writing graphic techniques, information gathering, strategic planning, group problem solving, legal aspects of technical publishing, introduction to new technologies, including industrial use of film/videotape, audience analysis, rhetorical techniques, logical organization and clarity. Prerequisites: any Group B course.

Advanced Writing and Editing Techniques (NYIT#EN1049)   3 credits

An advanced workshop in business and technical writing techniques including technical aspects of editing and interpersonal skills employed by successful editors Participants practice revising writing for specific audiences; strengthen their techniques in revising for style, clarity, and conciseness; increase their command of grammar and mechanics; practice production editing and using style manuals; utilize word processors and computerized text editors; and develop important interpersonal editing skills through the use of role playing and peer evaluation. Participants also continue to be exposed to a variety of common forms of career-oriented business and technical writing. Prerequisites: Any Group B course.

The Art of Drama (NYIT#EN1053)   3 credits
An intermediate-level course in which the student explores dramatic literature in an effort to discover its ritual origins, historical role, and current significance. Prerequisite: NYIT#EN1020.

The Art of Fiction (NYIT#EN1054)   3 credits
An intermediate-level course in which selected works of fiction are examined in an effort to understand the approaches, strategies, and techniques of artists in this compelling medium. This course may be chosen to fulfill the Group A requirement. Prerequisite: NYIT#EN1020.

The Art of Prose: Scientific & Tech. Literature (NYIT#EN1056)   3 credits
An intermediate-level course in which the art of prose writing is explored in depth. This course focuses on style and rhetoric and covers the development of scientific and technical literature. This course may be chosen to fulfill the Group A requirement. Prerequisite: NYIT#EN1020.

Internship in Professional Writing (NYIT#EN1080)   3 credits
An advanced elective course which permits the student to gain supervised on-the-job experience as a technical communicator in a professional environment. Prerequisites: NYIT#EN1048, NYIT#EN1049, and/or permission of advisor.

Shakespeare (NYIT#EN1083)   3 credits
An advanced course in which selected texts and critiques from Shakespearean literature are examined intensively. Prerequisite: Any Group A course.

Literature Seminar (NYIT#EN1100)   3 credits
An advanced course which explores in depth each semester one major literary figure, one historical, period, one movement, one literary type, one work, or the writing of literature in the areas of fiction, nonfiction, poetry, or drama. The subject will vary from offering to offering. A student may repeat the seminar but not at any one given course content. Prerequisite: Any Group A course.

Capstone Seminar (NYIT#CAP1009)   3 credits
this is a senior seminar, the final course before awarding the Interdisciplinary Studies degree. Students write an autobiographical essay, give a series of reports, and carry our library research. Some of the time is devoted to preparing for careers and/or graduate school.

Humanities and the Biological Universe (NYIT#SCI4422)   3 credits
This course acquaints students with basic biological, health and environmental issues of the modern world. To achieve intended awareness, students will study basic anatomy, physiology, genetics and microbiology.

Special attention will be given to contemporary problems: AIDS, genetic engineering, cancer, heart disease, pollution. Students will use mathematical, computer and quantitative reasoning skills to present cohesive written summations of learning.

Environmental Sciences (NYIT#SCI9500)   3 credits

A multidisciplinary approach to the environmental and ecological sciences emphasizing principles, problems, and alternative approaches to solutions. The issues are treated in sufficient depth to permit quantitative reasoning and assessment, especially in such topics as the demographic trends of humanity in a resource-limited biosphere. Human physiological and behavioral requisites are interwoven with the fabric of culture and technology in modern society. In addition to lectures and seminars, students are required to become involved in a term activity, project, or paper which may integrate several disciplines.

Finite Mathematics (NYIT#MA3010)   3 credits

Review of elementary algebra and selected topics in statistics and probability. Sets, real numbers, graphing, linear and quadratic equations and inequalities, relations and functions, solving systems of linear equations, descriptive statistics, frequency distribution, graphical displays of data, measures of central tendency and dispersion, introduction to probability. Prerequisite: MA 3008 or MA 3013 or Math placement test.

Developmental Mathematics I/II (NYIT#MA3013)   3 credits

Designed for the accelerated student who has had some skills in algebra and is more motivated to finish at a faster pace. Topics covered include basic operations of algebraic fractions, exponents and radicals, functions and graphs, and equations. Prerequisite: Math placement test.

College Algebra and Trigonometry (NYIT#MA3014)   4 credits

A study on selected topics in mathematics for students of the humanities, especially in communication arts. Topics include: graphs, matrices, elements of linear programming, finite probabilities, introduction to statistics. Applications to real-life situations are emphasized. The place of these topics in the history of mathematics is outlined.

Introductory Concepts of Mathematics (NYIT#MA3015)   3 credits

A course on selected topics in mathematics for students of the humanities, especially in communication arts. Topics include: graphs, matrices, elements of linear programming, finite probabilities, introduction to statistics. Applications to real-life situations are emphasized. The place of these topics in the history of mathematics is outlined.

Introduction to Probability (NYIT#MA3017)   3 credits

Functions, curve equation relationship, set theory, random events, probability functions, mathematical expectation, conditional probability, special distributions (e.g. binomial, fnormal, and notion of a statistic). Prerequisite: NYIT#MA3014 or equivalent.

Quantitative Methods in Business (NYIT#MA3019)   3 credits

Applications of calculus to business and social science. Intuitive use of limits and continuity. Derivatives, extrema, concavity, and applications such as marginal analysis, business models, optimization of tax revenue, and minimization of storage cost. The exponential and logarithm functions. Antiderivatives and the definite integral. Areas of consumer's surplus. Some concepts of probability extended to discrete and continuous sample spaces. Prerequisites: NYIT#MA3101 or NYIT#MA3014.

Technical Mathematics I (NYIT#MA3310)   3 credits

Review of algebra: exponents, factoring, fractions. Linear equations, ratio, proportions. Applications to concrete problems. Coordinate systems and graphs of functions: straight line, slope. Systems of linear equations and their applications. Complex numbers. Quadratic equations. Introduction to trig. Applications to problems in engineering technology are emphasized throughout. Prerequisite: NYIT#MA3008 or NYIT#MA3013 or Math placement test.

Technical Mathematics II (NYIT#MA3320)   3 credits

Topics include trigonometric functions, identities and equations, the sine and cosine laws, graphs of the trigonometric functions; functions of a composite angle; DeMoivre's Theorem; logarithms; binomial theorem; and Cramer's rule. Prerequisite: NYIT#MA3310.

Humanity and the Physical Universe (NYIT#PHY4024)   3 credits

A survey course in the physical sciences for the non-technical student. The course will examine conceptually a broad range of topics including: motion; electromagnetism; optics; atomic physics; heat; energy and power generation; earth science; and modern concepts (relativity and quantum physics). The interactions between physical science and technology and their impact upon society and the quality of life will be considered.

Problems of Philosophy (NYIT#SS1510)   3 credits

An introduction to philosophy by way of selected problems from various areas of philosophy. Topics include: the nature of priori knowledge and of scientific explanation, the existence of God, whether or not there can be moral knowledge, and the problem of free will. The course objective is to acquaint students with these philosophical issues, and through detailed discussion, to teach them how to analyze ideas critically.

Logic and Scientific Method (NYIT#SS1515)   3 credits

An introduction to the valid forms of reasoning and the methods of inquiry practiced by the natural, social and behavioral sciences.

Philosophy and History of Religion (NYIT#SS1525)   3 credits

This course acquaints the student with major elements associated with the development of religion as examined by psychologists, anthropologists, sociologists, and historians, as well as selected theologians. Special attention is paid to the philosophical analysis of religious phenomena, clarifying issues such as the existence of God and gods, the nature of religious experience, the belief in the soul and other typically religious subjects.

Ethics and Social Philosophy (NYIT#SS1530)   3 credits

An examination of some of the most critical issues of moral and social philosophy. these include subjects such as the linguistic analysis of terms such as 'good', 'evil', 'duty', 'right', and others. The basis of different moral systems will be studied, and selections from ethical and social philosophers will be read.

Technology, Society and Values (NYIT#SS1535)   3 credits

Concerned with the impact of machines on man, of technological systems on social structures, and modes of production on values. Special attention is paid to the link between new technologies and the study of ethics.

American History I (NYIT#SS2500)   3 credits

The political, social, cultural, and economic factors pertaining to American history and civilization up to the year 1865. Two major areas of study are the colonial era through the American Revolution, and the 19th century.

American History II (NYIT#SS2510)   3 credits

A survey of American history from 1865 to the present. Particular attention is given to the various political movements and the four major wars. The American position as a world power and its role in international affairs. Effects of the growth of labor unions and corporations as integrated into merging historical patterns. Prerequisite: NYIT#SS2500.

Contemporary World (NYIT#SS2540)   3 credits

The transformation of Europe as a consequence of the first and Second World Wars; the polarity of the postwar world; the impotence of the superpowers; the impact of science and technology; the image of contemporary man in literature and visual arts; and the search for meaning in the twentieth century.

American Government and Politics (NYIT#SS2700)   3 credits

An introduction to the processes of the American form of government. The nature and structure of government, its characteristics and functions. The intimate relation of government to other interests.

Government and Metropolitan Problems (NYIT#SS2705)   3 credits

The first part comprises the political framework; state governmental structure, its functions, services, and financing; local, rural, and urban government, their structures, services and functions. The second half focuses on metropolitan problems and their interaction with metropolitan government; housing, schooling, transportation, sanitation, pollution, and taxation. Prerequisite: NYIT#SS2700.

Government and Business (NYIT#SS2708)   3 credits

A consideration of relationships between business enterprise and the societal and political milieu in which these enterprises operate. New concepts in business ethics and corporate responsibility. Government regulation of business activity. Prerequisite: NYIT#SS2700.

Comparative Government (NYIT#SS2710)   3 credits

An introduction to comparative political structures and institutions covering the major European governments as well as non-Western political systems. Prerequisite: NYIT#SS2700.

Basic Speech Communication (NYIT#SP1023)   3 credits

Study of the fundamentals of verbal communication including public communication, interpersonal communication, and small group interaction. Training in methods of obtaining and organizing materials and ideas for effective verbal communication.

Introduction to Telecommunication (NYIT#TN4701)   3 credits

An overview of the telecommunications field. Brief historical overview of major events in the technology, regulation and business applications. The roles of telecommunications management in the organization describes and introduces the terminology of voice and data transmission, media, switching and signaling, networks, terminals and codes, traffic engineering, etc.

Voice Communications (NYIT#TN4703)   3 credits

This course discusses telephones, PBX systems, key systems, and network design. Review of acoustics of voice generation. Bandwidth requirements for successful information carriage and interfacing. Digital and analog voice signal processing. Prerequisite: NYIT#TN4701.

Data Communications (NYIT#TN4704)   3 credits

Data concepts and terminology, transmission, networks, packet and other protocols, modulation techniques. Analog and digital data transmission.

Pennsylvania State University - 14 courses

Accredited by the Middle States Association of Colleges and Schools.

Department of Distance Education
207 Mitchell Building
University Park PA 16802-3601

Last year, more than 16,000 adult students chose Penn State Independent Learning as a way to begin their college education, return to college after many years, earn special certification, or find personal enrichment. At Independent Learning, we're proud of our past, but we're also firmly committed to your future. When you choose Penn State and Independent Learning, you're putting the resources of a world-class university to work for you. Getting a college education has never been easy, but we're prepared to work with you to ensure your success.

Independent Learning is a vital part of Continuing and Distance Education's innovative system of programs that uses both traditional and nontraditional methods of delivering education to a wide range of students around the globe.

Penn State's Independent Learning Program does not have an official online component, but a number of instructors have decided to accept email participation in their courses. It is expected that increasing numbers of these continuing and distance education courses will be available online, as more instructors select this option. Currently there are fourteen courses that offer this option. Contact the university's Independent Learning Program for additional information via email at: psude@cde.psu.edu.

Students choose to enroll in Independent Learning courses for a variety of reasons. Some enroll in one or two courses for personal or professional enrichment. Others enroll to pursue a degree or certificate. The semester-hour credits earned through Penn State's courses may be applied to baccalaureate and associate degree programs at most other colleges and universities in fulfillment of their requirements.

Tuition and Fees: Your costs to enroll in Independent Learning courses include charges for tuition and course materials. You will also need to add mailing and handling and processing charges. Tuition for college-credit courses is $98 per credit; for a 3-credit course, tuition is $294.

Jody Heckman
The Pennsylvania State University
Department of Distance Education
207 Mitchell Building
University Park PA 16802-3601

phone: 814-865-5403, 800-252-3592

email: psude@cde.psu.edu
URL: http://
    www.cde.psu.edu/de/

Pennsylvania State University Course Descriptions

Introductory Managerial Accounting (PASU#ACCT204)   3 credits

Actual and stand cost systems; managerial uses of cost data. Prerequisite ACCTG 200 Introductory financial Accounting.

Women and the American Experience (PASU#AMST104)   3 credits

Selected aspects of the role of women in US history and culture from colonial to modern times. Students will need a copy of the Bible, and will be asked to choose from a number of currently available videos found in video stores to vie for discussion and analysis. Students will read newspapers and magazines.

Legal Environment of Business (PASU#BLAW243)   3 credits

Social control through law: courts, basic policies underlying individual and contractual rights in everyday society.

The Profession of Dietetics (PASU#DSM100)   1 credit

Introduction to the profession and exploration of the roles and responsibilities of dietetic professionals.

Management of Food Service Operations (PASU#DSM260)   4 credits

Major Principles related to managing the purchasing, food and labor subsystems of a health care food service system. Prerequisite: DAM 250 Quantity Food Production Management.

Rhetoric and Composition (PASU#ENGL015)   3 credits

Instruction and practice in writing expository prose that shows sensitivity to audience and purpose. Prerequisite: Basic Writing Skills (ENGL004) or satisfactory performance on the English placement examination.

Introduction to Creative Writing (PASU#ENGL050)   3 credits

Practice and criticism in the reading, analysis, and composition of fiction, nonfiction and poetry writing. This course is now being revised/ developed. If you're interested in this course, call for availability.

Introduction to Article Writing (PASU#ENGL215)   3 credits

Written exercises in, and a study of, the principles of article writing; practice in the writing of specific articles. Prerequisite: Rhetoric and Composition (ENGL 015) or Honors Freshman Composition (ENGL 030). This course deals with writing the popular magazine article - generating ideas, drafting queries, researching, interviewing, organizing, preparing articles and submitting them for publication

Security Markets (PASU#FIN204)   3 credits

Analysis of the organization and operation of stock and bond markets; security speculation, brokerage houses; exchange relations with other institutions; security price behavior; exchange regulation.

Introduction to the Middle East (PASU#HIST181)   3 credits

Origins of Islamic civilization; expansion of Islam; the Ottoman Empire; the Middle East since 1918.

Survey of Management (PASU#MGMT100)   3 credits

Introduction to organizational factors relevant to management processes, including leadership, motivation, job design, technology, organizational design and environments, systems, change.

Organizational Behavior (PASU#MGMT321)   3 credits

Theories, concepts, applications appropriate to the study of the individual and small group organizations. Prerequisite Survey of Management (MGMT 100) or Basic Management Concepts (PASU#MGMT301), or three credits in psychology, sociology , or cultural anthropology.

Introduction to Management Information Sys. (PASU#MIS100)   3 credits

Business computer systems and impact on management decision making.

Critical Thinking and Argument (PASU#PHIL010)   3 credits

Principles of correct thinking; deductive and inductive inference; use and misuse of language in reasoning.

University of Phoenix - 60 courses

Accredited by the North Central Association of Colleges and Schools.

University of Phoenix - Online Campus
100 Spear Street, 2d Floor
San Francisco CA 94105

Online is one of several instructional formats in addition to standard classroom delivery offered by the University of Phoenix, an accredited private institution whose mission it is to meet the educational needs of working professionals. Through a customized computer conferencing system, Online has created an electronic classroom in which students who have access to a personal computer equipped with a modem are able to engage in dynamic interactive exchange with their instructor and classmates regardless of location or time of day. Online education permits working adults whose schedules or locations prevent them from attending a physical classroom to receive all the benefits of group-based learning.

The University of Phoenix has taken this new domain and built the most successful and widely recognized programs in business and management in the country. Combining the strengths of interactive, group-based learning with the flexibility previously restricted to individual study, these programs free you to participate in a classroom liberated from the constraints of time and place.

High academic standards, commitment to quality, and intensely focused programs have earned the University of Phoenix a reputation as a leader within both the academic as well as the business communities. Our unique blend of proven academic practices and innovative instructional delivery systems has helped build what is now the largest private business school in the country with more than 20 campuses and learning centers in six western states. While we are proud of our academic reputation, and the more than 60,000 adults who have come to us because of it, we take our greatest pride in our unyielding pursuit of excellence and in making each and every student feel as if he or she were our only student.

Upon registration, you and your fellow classmates (eight to thirteen other working adults) will be provided access to a special group mailbox. This group mailbox will serve as your electronic classroom. One of the first things you'll do there is get to know one another through an exchange of professional and personal information. It is also there where your faculty member will provide instruction, issue assignments, and stimulate and facilitate class discussions. In addition, you'll also receive a well-organized course guide in which you'll find a convenient outline of each week's learning activities.

Each of your class meetings and the accompanying class discussions will be spread out over a full seven days, giving you the weekends to get much of your reading and papers completed. As discussions build throughout the week, it is important to visit your classroom at least five days out of every week, but at times you choose and that best suit your individual circumstances. Before each week of class begins, your instructor will typically submit a lecture and review the assignments for the upcoming week. Then, throughout the week, he or she will be involved in the class discussions - providing expertise, guidance, feedback, and answers to questions.

At the conclusion of each week, you will be asked to provide a summary of the concepts covered. Based upon your summary and contributions to the class discussions, your instructor will let you know how you are doing and respond to any issues or concerns you might have. Whether undergraduate or graduate, business or management, the University of Phoenix degree you earn will be unlike any other. The reason is the project course built right into each program.

For more information: 800-742-4742 7am-6pm PST M-F

Cori Anne Capizzi, Public Affairs Administrator
University of Phoenix - Online Campus
100 Spear Street, 2d Floor
San Francisco CA 94105

University of Phoenix Course Descriptions:

Skills for Professional Transition (PHOE#GEN300) 3 credits

Designed to help working adults re-acclimate to the formal educational setting, and more specifically to introduce the skills that will enhance academic performance, especially within the context of an electronic classroom. Students will examine their own personal learning styles and refine the communications and small group process skills critical to success in the workplace.

Management and Leadership (PHOE#MGT402) 3 credits

This course focuses on the planning, organization, staffing, leading, and controlling functions of the manager. Students are exposed to effective employee motivation techniques and acquire tools useful in the solving of frequently encountered management problems.

Writing for Professionals (PHOE#COM205) 3 credits

Basic writing skills involved in fulfilling the communications responsibilities of the manager. Emphasis is on the importance of lucid writing in letters, memoranda, brief informal documents, and comprehensive business reports.

Mathematics for Management (PHOE#MTH201) 3 credits

This course is designed to build specific problem solving skills that rely on mathematical operations. Emphasis is placed upon concepts of basic algebra as they are commonly applied in day-to-day business environment.

Business Law (PHOE#BUS415) 3 credits

In this course, students examine the role of the manager in dealing with issues related to the law. Federal and state court systems, civil litigation, and consumer and antitrust law as relates to the conduct of business.

Business Communications (PHOE#COMM410) 3 credits

This course covers communication process models, issues in business correspondence, international business communication, editorial process, presentation techniques, and interviewing strategies.

Economics for Business (PHOE#ECO460/461) 6 credits

These courses are structured to equip students with the ability to analyze a wide array of economic indicators and to evaluate the implications of those indicators on their own business or discipline. Business cycles, money supply, taxation, productivity, supply and demand, governmental policies and controls, and international trade are all covered.

Financial Accounting (PHOE#ACC462/463) 6 credits

These courses cover accrual accounting concepts, analysis of financial statements, annual report analysis, inventory valuation analysis, financial controls, depreciation of operational assets, and accounting theory. Students learn how to integrate and make use of accounting information.

Managerial Finance (PHOE#FIN475/476) 6 credits

These courses cover working capital, leveraging, long-term financing, and financial forecasting. Students are provided an overview of the fundamentals of financial administration which make it possible to understand the financial consequences management decisions have on organizations.

Business Research Project (PHOE#488A/B/C) 8 credits

This course is divided into three parts. Together, they cover the uses of business research, research methods, report writing, instrument design, measurement criteria, interviewing techniques, and empirical analysis. Using the business-related skills acquired in the course, students are able to plan, conduct, and evaluate a study which they themselves have designed. Students are also able to more effectively analyze a broad spectrum of business problems.

Marketing (PHOE#MKT421) 3 credits

This course covers marketing strategies, opportunity analysis, new product development, pricing, and the product life cycle. An emphasis is placed on relationship of the marketing function to other managerial and organizational functions.

Statistics in Business (PHOE#QNT421/422) 6 credits

In these courses students learn how to apply the concepts of probability, sampling, and hypothesis testing to the solution of business problems. Covers statistical analysis, including correlation and regression.

Computers and Information Processing (PHOE#CIS419) 3 credits

This course focuses on the effective use of information systems in the management process. Students examine ways in which computers can improve the productivity and efficiency of an organization.

Organizational Behavior (PHOE#MGT432) 3 credits

In this course, students study the application of organizational theory to the managerial functions of planning, controlling, staffing, and directing. Various management systems, motivational techniques, organizational dynamic, and effective change strategies are examined.

Personnel Management (PHOE#MGT435) 3 credits

In this course, students examine some of the critical issues and responsibilities involved with managing people. Performance appraisal methods and strategies, staff training and development, wage and salary structure, and legal responsibilities are among the topics explored.

Finance and Accounting for Managers (PHOE#FIN424/425) 6 credits

These courses specifically address the needs of managers who are not directly involved in the financial or accounting area but must integrate and make use of accounting and financial information in their planning and control responsibilities. Students are provided an in-depth overview of financial and accounting principles which affect common managerial and organizational decision making processes.

Contemporary Issues in Management (PHOE#MGT405) 3 credits

This course examines a broad array of contemporary issues facing today's managers. Topics include ethics, prejudice, manager/employee communications, harassment, conflict of interests, and values. Students have the opportunity to analyze the ways in which these and other issues impact the management function within their own organizations.

Executive Management in a Global Economy (PHOE#MGT548)   2 credits

This course focuses on the social, cultural, and political dimensions of managing resources and business transactions in a global economy.

Legal Environment of Business (PHOE#BUS526)   3 credits

This course covers the American legal system as it relates to the regulation of business, organizational structure, commercial property, consumer law.

Manager Ethics & Professional Responsibility (PHOE#MGT592) 3 credits.

This course focuses on ethics issues confronted by individuals in carrying out their managerial and professional responsibilities. The application of moral concepts to ethical decision making is stressed.

Human Relations & Organizational Behavior (PHOE#MGT532)   3 credits

In this course, students analyze how individuals and groups function within the context of the organization, with emphasis on motivation and productivity, decision making, problem solving, and personal relations.

Financial Accounting (PHOE#ACC515)   3 credits

In this course, students are introduced to fundamental accounting concepts and processes. An emphasis is placed on methods of collecting and processing accounting information for external financial reporting purposes, and on the interpretation and use of this information. Special attention is given to emerging issues in accounting related to doing business internationally.

Managerial Accounting (PHOE#ACC514)   3 credits

This course examines the fundamental systems of managerial accounting based upon an overview of accounting principles and conventions currently observed in business and industry. Emphasis is placed on the preparation, analysis, and use of financial statements, budgeting, and planning.

Strategy Formulation and Implementation (PHOE#MGT549)   3 credits

This course examines a variety of ways in which business strategies are developed, implemented, and, when necessary, reformulated. Emphasis is placed on the need for responsiveness to changes that occur to an organization's internal and external environments.

Information Management (PHOE#CIS564)   3 credits

This course is designed to provide student with the necessary knowledge to understand and effectively use a broad spectrum of management information systems. the analysis and design of information systems are covered from the operational, tactical, and strategic perspectives with an emphasis on isolating especially effective tools and techniques. Actual systems are examined and used as models in exploring management roles and issues, and in case study analysis.

Statistics for Managerial Decision Making (PHOE#QNT522)   3 credits

In this course, students are introduced to the basic statistical tools managers need to possess in order to apply quantitative thinking skills to the decision process. Topics include descriptive statistics, probability, sampling, and introductory estimation and hypothesis testing.

Statistical Applications for Business (PHOE#QNT523)   3 credits

This course covers the application of statistical procedures used in quality control and business forecasting. Major topics include correlation and regression, analysis variance, chil-square analysis of categorical data, non-parametric procedures.

Applied Microeconomics (PHOE#ECO524)   3 credits

This course demonstrates ways in which economic theory can be applied to the analysis of market demand, production processes and costs, competitive conditions, pricing, and investment decisions. Relationships between economic concepts and areas of finance, accounting, marketing, strategy.

Macroeconomics for Decision Making (PHOE#ECO525)   3 credits

This course covers economic institutions and public policy processes through which market activities are coordinated and controlled at the national and international levels. Methods of using aggregate economic indicators for business decision making are studied.

Operations Management for Total Quality (PHOE#BUS540)   3 credits

Techniques for designing, analyzing, and managing operations processes in both manufacturing and service industries. Methods for developing operations systems that support a total quality management objective are examined.

Financial Analysis and Planning (PHOE#FIN539)   3 credits

This course examines ways in which to integrate risk analysis, capital budgeting, and financial forecasting into the business planning and decision making processes. International capital markets and the role of the finance function in building a total quality organization also discussed.

Advanced Marketing Management (PHOE#MKT541)   3 credits

This course analyzes the manager's role in overseeing the marketing function. Particular attention will be given to the creative resolution of problems having to do with product, pricing, promotion, and distribution.

Applied Management Science Project Seminar (PHOE#BUS583)   3 cr.

This course is designed to familiarize students with a variety of research skills and methodologies. The development of business plans and traditional business research papers are covered.

Applied Management Science Project (PHOE#BUS584)   2 credits

In this course, each student will work one-on-one with a faculty member to select an important business or organizational problem that will be attacked using the skills and knowledge learned throughout the program. The faculty member will serve as an advisor and resource as the student is guided through the preparation of either a business plan, process improvement plan, or research paper. Students will have a full four months in which to work on the project.

Introduction to Technology Systems (PHOE#MGT500)   3 credits

Roles management must play to integrate business and technology decision making to achieve both the strategic and operational objectives of the enterprise. The challenges to management are explored in the context or an environment of global competition driven technological change.

Information Technology and Decision Making (PHOE#MGT510)   3 cr.

This course investigates various elements of information theory, technologies, and the information systems tools as they apply to the decision making process. Students examine the risks and challenges associated with the introduction of information technologies.

Technology Forecasting & Strategic Planning (PHOE#MGT555)   3 credits

Describes and demonstrates the application of technology forecasting methods and techniques, their implementation within organizations, and their use in the development of a competitive strategic plan.

Strategic Mgt of Research Development (PHOE#MGT565)   3 credits

This course presents specific system concepts, methodologies and tools to strategically plan technology developments and how to integrate new technologies into existing or future products. The employment of R&D as a front end function is emphasized.

Intellectual Property Management (PHOE#MGT575)   2 credits

This course covers national and international patents, copyright law, trademarks and trade secrets. Focus is placed on the role of intellectual property in research and development, venture cost management, forecasting.

Managerial Finance (PHOE#FIN538)   3 credits

This course introduces students to the fundamental principles of finance, including common methods for obtaining operating and venture capital. The management of financial assets, the mathematics of finance, and basic techniques used in financial analysis are covered.

New Venture Cost Management (PHOE#MGT515)   3 credits

This course focuses on the unique dynamics, issues, and challenges of funding and analyzing costs that are associated with new products and technology projects. Emphasis is placed on the tools and skills required to evaluate the cost-benefit relationship prior to, and in the early stages of a product's or project's life cycle.

Project and Program Management Tools (PHOE#MGT525)   3 credits

This course presents specific system concepts, methodologies, and tools to effectively manage complex, interfunctional technology development projects and programs. Critical performance parameters for planning, cost control, scheduling, and productivity are examined and evaluated in the context of traditional and state-of-the-art tools and systems.

Innovative Processes (PHOE#MGT530)   2 credits

This course explores techniques used to stimulate and manage innovation in the work place. The role of the manager as a shepherd who nurtures ideas from concept to market are examined.

Human Factors in the Changing Organization (PHOE#MGT534)   3 cr.

This course provides the tools necessary to effectively employ Human Factor Analysis in the understanding and resolution of organizational change, technology and productivity. The issues, requirements, criteria, and impact involved when introducing a new or improved technology within a defined organizational context are explored.

Managing Change in Operations & Mfg. (PHOE#MGT542)   3 credits

Explores past, present, and future trends in manufacturing technology and focuses on the management skills necessary to relate and exploit different processes within various types of organizations and industries.

Technology Transfer & Global Strategy Mgt. (PHOE#MGT585)   3 credits

This course addresses a broad range of challenges and opportunities faced by organizations which conduct business globally. The curriculum focuses on the contribution that technology makes in managing a geographically diverse organization.

Applications of Technology Management (PHOE#MGT595)   3 credits

In this capstone course, students will review the broad range of subject matter covered in the program and focus it and the knowledge gained on the design of a project or plan which describes the launch of a new product or process selected by the student.

Applications of Technology Management Project (PHOE#MGT597)   2 cr.

In this course, each student will work one-on-one with a faculty member who will serve as an advisor and resource as the student is guided through the preparation and completion of the individual project defined in the previous course. Students have 4 months to work on their projects.

Fundamentals of Executive Management (PHOE#MGT512)   3 credits

This course focuses on the role of executive management in directing an organization and improving organizational performance. Students analyze the basic functions of management and their interrelationships.

Strategic Planning (PHOE#MGT535)   3 credits

Covers strategic planning and implementation, strategy analysis models, and contingency planning. Students study internal forces which shape strategy, develop long-term goals, and draw up operational plans.

Human Resource Management (PHOE#MGT 537)   3 credits

In this course, students examine employee recruitment strategies, staff training and development issues, benefits and compensation packages, and other responsibilities of the human resource department.

Managing Information (PHOE#MGT540)   3 credits

In this course, students explore different ways in which information is managed and how information needs and flow are evaluated. The course focuses on the manager as an end user and on the role a manager plays in evaluating the components and effectiveness of an information system.

Budgeting (PHOE#MGT546)   3 credits

In this course, students study the relationship of the budgeting process to the organization's strategic plan and objectives. Forecasting, evaluation and control, and cost/expense allocation are covered.

Decision Making (PHOE#MGT551)   3 credits

This course covers individual and group decision making processes, goal setting, and the relationship of decision making to personal and organizational values. Examines decision making models to job situations.

Advanced Budgeting (PHOE#MGT568)   3 credits

A continuation of Budgeting (PHOE#MGT546), this course addresses such issues as financial controls, data analysis, spreadsheet application, and the application of key financial ratios.

Applied Managerial Statistics (PHOE#QNT572)   3 credits

In this course, students learn how to apply the concepts of probability, sampling, and hypothesis testing to the solution of business problems.

Project Management (PHOE#MGT570)   3 credits

This course examines the key components necessary to effectively manage projects. Students study production and performance evaluation, quality control, and work flow analysis.

Applied Management Science Project (PHOE#BUS582A/B)   4 credits

This course is divided into two parts. Together, they cover the uses of business research, research methods, report writing, instrument design, measurement criteria, interviewing techniques, and empirical analysis. Using the business-related skills acquired in the course, students plan, conduct, and evaluate a study which they themselves have designed. The quantitative tools that are employed can also be used to analyze a broad spectrum of other business problems.

Marketing for Customer Satisfaction (PHOE#MGT577)   3 credits

Students examine the context in which the manager assumes a marketing role within the organization. Pricing policy, product life cycle, marketing research, and ethics are covered.

External Environment of Business (PHOE#MGT580)   3 credits

Through case study analysis, students examine the various ways in which governmental regulation, economy, technology, and competition affect the way in which business is conducted.

Rochester Institute of Technology - 72 courses   ROCH

Accredited by the Middle States Association of Colleges and Schools

College of Continuing Education
Rochester Institute of Technology
31 Lomb Memorial Drive
Rochester, NY 14623-5603

Since 1979, when the Rochester Institute of Technology (RIT) offered its first telecourse, the Institute has been a leader in offering interactive distance learning programs based on flexible and affordable technology. Today, over 3,000 students each year enroll in RIT's distance learning programs throughout New York, the United States and overseas.

RIT's distance learning courses have the same objectives, rigorous workload, tuition, and academic credit as RIT's on-campus courses. Students may register, order their required course materials, contact professors, and submit assignments by phone, fax, or email or mail - following the same procedures as for on-campus courses. For more information contact the Office of Distance Learning: 716-475-5089 or 1-800-CALL-RIT.

RIT DISTANCE LEARNING PROGRAMS INCLUDE:
* Master of Science in Telecommunications Software Technology
* Master of Science in Software Development and Management
* Master of Science in Health Sustems Administration
* Bachelor of Science in Applied Arts and Science with concentrations in: Telecommunications, Applied Computing, Management, Health Systems, Emergency Management and Environmental Management: Solid Waste Management & Technology
* Certificate in Health Systems Administration
* Certificate in Emergency Management
* Certificate in Environmental Management: Solid Waste Management
* Certificate in Voice Communications
* Certificate in Data Communications
* Certificate in Applied Computing and Communications
* Certificate in Telecommunications Network Management

Rochester Institute of Technology offers an Associate and Bachelor of Science Degree in Applied Arts and Science on line. In the multidisciplinary program students can select concentrations from Applied Computing, Health Systems, Management, Telecommunications, Emergency Management, and Solid Waste-Environmental Management. Credit from previous college courses successfully completed with a C or better can be transferred. The entire degree can be completed without coming to the RIT campus. RIT also offers three masters degrees in this format.

Certificates in Applied Computing, Health Systems, Data Communications, Voice Communications, Telecommunications Network Management, Emergency Management and Solid Waste-Environmental Management can also be earned and applied toward a degree.

To obtain more information through the automated response system:

1) Send e-mail to: RITDL@ritvax.isc.rit.edu

2) Enter subject as:

BSAAS	(BS in Applied Arts and Science)
MSTST	(MS in Telecommunications Software Technology)
MSSDM	(MS in Software Development and Management)
CERACC	(Cert. in Applied Computing & Communications)
CERHSA	(Cert. in Health Systems Administration)
CERDC	(Cert. in Data Communications)
CERVC	(Cert. in Voice Communications)
CERSWM	(Cert. in Solid Waste Management Technology)
CEREM	(Cert. in Emergency Management)

3) Type a message (if you have specific questions) or leave message blank.

4) Send message

5) Wait for the automatic reply.

For additional information call the Office of Distance Learning 1-800-CALL-RIT

Rochester Institute of Technology Course Descriptions:

Role of Accounting in the Organization (ROCH#0101-435)   4 credits

The course objective is to give students an understanding of how accounting is used to help achieve goals. Students will learn how to account and the reasons why we account as we do. Special emphasis will be placed on the resolution of controversial accounting issues within the context of the firm's goals. Positive accounting theory and agency theory will be discussed throughout.

Introduction to Work Organizations (ROCH#0102-405)   4 credits

This course will introduce students to the concept of work organizations and how they function. Students will learn of the different industries in which work organizations fall and how to become and help others become effective members of organization through motivation, leadership, interpersonal conflict management, an stress handling. Additionally, the student will learn about diverse workforce, social issues, and government regulation of work.

Management Concepts (ROCH#0102-406)   4 credits

This course introduces you to the four functions of management: planning, organizing, staffing and controlling. Topics such as organizational change, stress, productivity, and decision making are covered.

Theory & Application of Basic Finance (ROCH#0104-420)   4 credits

This course develops some of the basic principles of finance and shows some of the ways in which they can be applied to business decisions and problems. Concepts and applications include time value of money, ratio analysis, cash budgeting and pro forma forecasting, credit decisions, capital budgeting techniques, forms of borrowing, and capital structure decisions.

Marketing for Total Customer Satisfaction (ROCH#0105-415)   4 credits

This course will review the fundamentals of marketing: formulating marketing strategy (segmentation and positioning) and the marketing mix (price, product, promotion, and distribution decisions). The mechanisms of delivering total customer satisfaction throughout the marketing mix will be emphasized through applying quality management principles to the marketing function.

Tools for Total Quality Management (ROCH#0106-425)   4 credits

This course examines the concepts of quality and total quality. It addresses, as a theme, "What tools and techniques may be used, and in what manner, to 1) help understand and capture customer requirements accurately the first time; 2) transmit and translate the requirements faithfully to those who design products and operations; 3) control and continuously improve the production, delivery, and repair or recovery of goods and services; and 4) assure that customer requirements are satisfied the first time, every time?" Course perspectives include quality planning, control, and improvement. The basic tools for total quality are covered, including quality function deployment (QFD), check sheets, Pareto diagrams, flow charts, histograms, run charts, statistical control charts, and benchmarking. (Background in statistics recommended.)

Financial Accounting (ROCH#0201-201)   4 credits

Emphasis is placed on analyzing and recording business transactions, and understanding the results of these transactions. Preparation of basic financial statements required by any business are included.

Personal Financial Management (ROCH#0204-204)   4 credits

This course is to enables you to manage your personal finances more effectively. The course deals with personal budgeting, protection of personal assets, consumer credit, investments, and estate planning.

Survey of Health Care Systems (ROCH#0206-310)   4 credits

An overview of the development, structure, and current forces transforming the health care system. Topics will include the status of the national and regional populations, physician practice and payment, private and government health insurance, the impact of medical technology, manpower issues, hospital services and reimbursement systems, ambulatory care and alternative delivery systems, and mental health and long-term care. Prerequisite: previous experience or coursework in health care and permission of chair.

Health Systems Administration (ROCH#0206-320)   4 credits

A survey of administration in health care facilities focusing on the application of general management principles in the unique health care environment. Issues such as organizational structures, planning and performance monitoring, personnel management, finance and the respective roles of medical professional and administrator in managing the facility will be discussed. Prerequisite: course ROCH#0206-310 or previous experience or coursework in health care and permission of the chair.

Health Care Economics and Finance (ROCH#0206-351)   4 credits

This course will provide a knowledge of the efficiency, effectiveness, and equity of the new economics of health care, and a conceptual and practical knowledge of health care finance, including sources of funding, accounting and reporting, and the influence of third-party payers. No previous work in economics is assumed. Prerequisite: ROCH#0206-310 or ROCH#0206-320.

Legal Aspects of Health Care Admin. (ROCH#0206-421)   4 credits

An overview of statute and regulation as they apply to the health care field. Topics include an overview of the American legal system, licensure of institutions, licensure and discipline of practitioners, physician-patient relationship, reproductive issues, the right to die, organ donations, medical records, legal liability, malpractice, and labor law.

Health Care Quality Assurance (ROCH#0206-431)   4 credits

Introduction to quality assurance in health care. Course will explore past and current definitions and competing concepts of quality assurance; review existing quality assurance requirements and accrediting organizations, federal and state agencies, and third party payers; describe and explain quality assurance methods and tools and their application in various settings. Prereq.: ROCH#0206-310 or ROCH#0206-320.

Health Planning and Program Development (ROCH#0206-441)   4 credits

A review of the methodology of planning effectively for health care services. The use of data systems, forecasting, and identifying and analyzing problems is explored, along with the process of strategic planning, setting priorities, developing projects, and allocating resources. Students will prepare actual applications for new programs to regulatory agencies. Prerequisite: ROCH#0206-310 or ROCH#0206-320.

Communications (ROCH#0236-220)   4 credits

This course focuses on refining writing skills - emphasizing organization, support, and effective expression of ides in multi-paragraph papers. The major exercise is preparation of a position paper and an oral defense of the paper's thesis. Research methods and principles of effective argumentation are studied. Requires pre-test.

Communicating in Business (ROCH#0236-307)   4 credits

Focuses on the development of those communication skills essential to functioning effectively in the business world. Students learn the process of analyzing communication situations and responding to them appropriately. Topics include reports, memos, letters, oral presentations, and interpersonal skills. Prerequisite: coursework approved by the chair.

Technical Mathematics I (ROCH#0240-201)   4 credits

A two-quarter sequence introducing college algebra and trigonometry, covering basic algebraic concept and operations, algebraic and transcendental (trigonometric, logarithmic, and exponential) functions. Prerequisite: three years of high school math, or equivalent; requires pre-test.

Technical Mathematics II (ROCH#0240-202)   4 credits

Continuation of Technical Mathematics I (ROCH#0240-201).

Contemporary Science: Oceanus (ROCH#0246-224)   4 credits

An introduction to the fundamental principles of oceanography for nonscience majors, and the application of those concepts to areas of interest and concern in our contemporary technological society. The marine environment will be investigated in terms of basic scientific concepts, and topics to be discussed will include plate tectonics and earthquake prediction, the impact of ocean pollutants, climate fluctuations, cetacean intelligence and resources from the sea.

Contemporary Science: Mechanical Universe (ROCH#0246-289)   4 cr.

This course is an introduction to physics for nonscience majors that uses the video course, "The Mechanical Universe ... and Beyond," as the main method for presentation of material. The topics covered include: units and dimensional analysis, motion, force, energy, heat, waves, light, relativity, atoms and quantum mechanics.

Introduction to Computers & Programming (ROCH#0250-200)   4 credits

Basic concept and overview of computer science. The topics include historical development, algorithms, flowcharting and programming in BASIC. Exposure to hardware concepts, software concepts, binary and hex

340

numbers and logic. Application of the computer to various disciplines. Prerequisite: high school intermediate algebra.

Earth Science for the Emergency Manager (ROCH#0285-201)   4 credits

Introduction to applied meteorology and crystal dynamics. The meteorological topics include basic atmospheric parameters, air mass theory, weather maps, generation and effects of severe weather, atmospheric stability, and the simple Gaussian model of plume transport. The crystal dynamics segment includes a qualitative treatment of plate tectonics and faults with emphasis on earthquake generation, Richter scales, damage from earthquakes, and the state of the art of earthquake prediction.

Man-Made Hazards (ROCH#0285-202)   4 credits

Survey of the chemistry of hazardous materials, including toxics, causics, flammables, and reactives. Industrial storage and transportation practices; effects of exposure on humans; protective measures. Intro to the physics of radiation. Radioisotopes in common use; methods of storage and transportation. Effects of exposure on humans; protective actions. Design of commercial power reactors and safety features.

Emergency Management Laws & Regulations (ROCH#0285-301)   4 cr.

An introduction to the principal statues, regulations, and court cases governing emergency preparedness in New York State. The chief topics are NYD Executive Law (Article 2-B), Title III, of the Superfund Amendment and Reauthorization Act of 1986, NuReg-0654 governing radiological accident preparedness, federal and state disaster aid statutes, and the principles of NYS liability law as they apply to disaster clean-up. Prerequisites: ROCH#0285-202 or ROCH#0285-202.

Emergency Planning & Methodology (ROCH#0285-302)   4 credits

Quantitative methods of risk and hazard analysis; the scope of a comprehensive emergency plan; classes of protective actions; evacuations; turf problems associated with multi-agency plans; command structures; the post-incident recovery phase; the design of exercises; the role of new technologies in disaster response. Students will prepare hazard analyses and write sections of comprehensive plans for actual communities.

Emergency Operations (ROCH#0285-381)   4 credits

Classroom study of the roles of fire, police, emergency medical services, and volunteer agencies like the Red Cross at various types of major disasters; how to set up on-scene command posts and off-site operations centers; the Incident Command system; role of the media; how to critique incidents; Students will gain familiarity with on-scene command responsibilities through role plays on an incident simulator. Prerequisites: ROCH#0285-201, ROCH#0285-202 and ROCH#0285-301.

Principles of Environmental Management (ROCH#0286-201)   4 credits

Introduction to municipal solid waste systems. The topics include an overview of the relationship of municipal solid waste, environmental protection, protection of public health, and public service; solid waste generation and natural resources; and the unit operations of municipal solid waste collection, transfer, resource recovery, and disposal.

Recycling (ROCH#0286-301)   4 credits

A survey of recycling technology and its relationship to the general problem of municipal solid waste management. Explores both the mechanics and the economics of the problem. Topics include the separation and collection of recyclable materials, recycling as a manufacturing process, the development of markets, and public education issues. Prerequisite: ROCH#0286-201.

Waste Reduction (ROCH#0286-311)   4 credits

A study of the techniques and strategies being developed and used to reduce the generation of waste in both public and private sectors. Examines methods of reducing waste toxicity and quantity and of increasing the recyclability of waste materials.

Land Disposal and Treatment (ROCH#0286-401)   4 credits

A survey of the technological factors in siting, designing, and operating modern landfills and composting facilities. Topics to be discussed include the dynamic processes occurring in landfills and composting sites, site selection, facility design and operation, special operational needs, and the closure of landfills and end uses for the sites.

Energy Recovery (ROCH#0286-411)   4 credits

A survey of solid waste energy recovery and material conversion technologies. Course will examine MSW as a feedstock for the production of energy and material products. Topics include mechanical, thermal, chemical, and biological processes and conversions.

Special and Hazardous Wastes (ROCH#0286-475)   4 credits

A survey of the techniques and strategies used to manage hazardous wastes, non-hazardous industrial wastes, infectious wastes, and other problematic materials that enter municipal solid waste systems.

Technical Writing (ROCH#0502-444)   4 credits

This course develops in students those skills necessary for completing technical writing tasks, such as instructional memos; letters of inquiry; reports (trip, progress/status, accident, research, feasibility); problem analyses; specifications; flow charts; technical manuals. Students enrolling in Technical Writing should have command of clear and logical standard written English prose.

English Composition II (ROCH#0502-450)   4 credits

An introduction to the study of the mass media. The focus of the course is on the history, development and law and regulation of the mass media in the United States. Prerequisiste: English Composition.

Introduction to Literature (ROCH#0504-332)   4 credits

The students study some of the great literary works of our culture to enrich their lives and reinforce their analytical abilities. The students read representative poems, dramas, and narratives drawn from the Ancient, Medieval-Rennaissance, and Modern Periods.

Modern American History (ROCH#0507-301)   4 credits

This course examines the political, social, cultural, and economic development of the American people in the modern period. Studies the United States in its foreign relations.

Selected Problems in Black History (ROCH#0507-492)   4 credits

A seminar approach to the thought of key black leaders (Washington, Garvey, King) and the study of civil rights and black-power movements.

Black Civil Rights in the 20th Century (ROCH#0507-495)   4 credits

This course examines the social and legal history of civil rights in the US with particular attention to the demonstrations of the 1950s and the 1960s and the philosophy of the Rev. Dr. Martin Luther King Jr. Finally, it will compare his views with those of the recent Black Power Movement.

Modern Warfare & Arms Control Problems (ROCH#0508-486)   4 credits

In this course we will study the importance of science and technology in defense matters. We investigate how modern weapons, both nuclear and conventional, their delivery systems, and reconnaissance and surveillance methods have seriously affected the charter of armed conflict and of preventing wars. However, we shall also see how scientists, by providing their expertise, have been able to influence national security and attempts to control arms.

Philosophy of Science (ROCH#0509-443)   4 credits

An examination of the nature of the scientific enterprises; possible discussion topics include the presuppositions of science, its logic, its claims to reliability, and its relationships to society and to problems of human values. Prerequisite: at least one prior course in either philosophy or one of the natural sciences - physics, chemistry, biology.

Special Topics in Philosophy: Prof. Ethics (ROCH#0509-449)   4 credits

This course will be a critical examination of issues in Professional Ethics as it relates to the discipline of philosophy. Other topics covered under this course might be: metaphysics, epistemology, the philosophy of mind, and the philosophy of language.

Principles of Economics I (ROCH#0511-301)   4 credits

This is the first course in a two-quarter sequence designed to introduce the student to the basic principles of economics. This course will focus on basic economic concepts and macroeconomics. Topics of primary interest include economic methodology, the economizing probe, capitalist ideology, supply and demand, national income accounting, income determination, inflation, money, and the role of government in the economy. Other topics in basic economics will be selected by the instructor.

Principles of Economics II (ROCH#0511-302)   4 credits

This is the second course in a two-quarter sequence designed to introduce the student to the basic principles of economics. This course will focus on microeconomics. Topics of primary interest include market structure, supply and demand analysis involving elasticity, the theory of cost in the short and long run, perfect competition, monopoly, monopolistic competition oligopoly,

343

marginalist distribution theory, the labor market, and general equilibrium analysis. Other topics in microeconomics will be selected by the individual instructor.

American Politics (ROCH#0513-211)   4 credits

This course is a study of the American national political system, its theoretical foundations and institutions, and contemporary issues confronting it.

Government & Politics of Russia and the CIS (ROCH#0513-442)   4 cr.

This course provides an analysis of the politics and governmental systems in Russia and the former republics of the Soviet Union that now comprise the Commonwealth of Independent States (CIS). Emphasis will be on the dynamics of political, economic, and social change, as well as political leadership and contemporary issues. Prereq.: ROCH#0513-211.

Introduction to Psychology (ROCH#0514-210)   4 credits

This course is designed to introduce the student to the scope and methodology of psychology. Topics will include: aims and methods, sensation and perception, learning and memory, emotion and motivation, normal and abnormal personality, and social psychology.

Abnormal Psychology (ROCH#0514-447)   4 credits

This course examines the major categories of mental disorder not only from descriptive point of view, but also in terms of the major theoretical explanations of the causes of disorder. The major treatment modalities also are covered. Prerequisite: Intro. to Psychology (ROCH#0514-210).

Foundations of Sociology (ROCH#0515-210)   4 credits

This course introduces students to the way sociologists interpret social reality, the major elements of the field and the most important research findings. Included are such topics as cultural differences and ethnocentrism, socialization, social statuses and roles, group dynamics, social institutions, stratification, collective behavior.

Sociology of Health (ROCH#0515-446)   4 credits

This course is a survey of the sociological aspects of health and illness. some areas of study will be the definition, causes (etiology) and cure of disease in various societies and social groups. Also, a discussion of the epidemiology of disease, access to, and delivery of health care in contemporary US society, problems of patient care, and the study of mental illness and death and/or dying. Prerequisite: ROCH#0515-210.

Senior Seminar (ROCH#0520-501)   4 credits

Course enables students to sharpen and demonstrate their ability to define a research task or problem, gather and evaluate scholarly evidence in a paper or project. While the content and focus of the seminar will change from year to year, it will always direct student attention toward a broad issue or aspect of contemporary culture and equip them to understand that subject more fully, investigate one facet of it in depth, and provide an advanced experience of problem solving and value clarification.

Organizational Communications (ROCH#0535-415)   4 credits

This course examines both interpersonal and small-group communication in organizational settings. Topics include information flow and networks, organizational theory, managerial decision making, interviewing, organizational development, and conflict resolution.

Human Communications (ROCH#0535-480)   4 credits

This course is an overview of the field of communication, including the contexts of interpersonal, group, mass, and public communication.

Persuasion (ROCH#0535-481)   4 credits

An in-depth study of the theories, practices, effects and ethics of persuasion. Persuasion is defined as human communication designed to influence one's beliefs, values, attitudes, and actions.

Mass Communication (ROCH#0535-482)   4 credits

An introduction to the study of the mass media. The focus of the course is on the history, development, and law and regulation of mass media in US.

Introduction to Programming (ROCH#0602-208)   4 credits

A first course in programming using C++ in writing modular, well-documented programs. Topics include an overview of problem solving methods, C++ control structures and their uses, procedures and functions with parameters, elementary data types, arrays, records, and modular programming. The course is organized around weekly programming assignments that stress features of structured programming and C++.

Programming Design & Validation (ROCH#0602-210)   4 credits

A second course in programming and data structures, where students use C++ to implement moderately large programs. Topics include sorting, searching, arrays of records, text files, files of records, multidimensional arrays, recursion, pointers, classic data structures and their implementations (stacks, queues, linked lists, trees), and the application of these concepts to solve problems of intermediate complexity. The role of testing in the validation and acceptance of a program will be stressed. Programming projects required. Prerequisite: ROCH#0602-208.

Computer Concepts and Software Systems (ROCH#0602-410)   4 credits

An introduction to the overall organization of digital computers and operating systems of non-majors. Topics include basic machine organization, an overview of machine and assembly language, properties of common I/O devices, synchronization and scheduling of processes, physical and virtual memory management techniques, resource allocation and protection, and user interface issues. Prereq.: ROCH#0602-208.

Data Communications & Computer Networks (ROCH#0602-411)   4 cr.

An introduction to data communications hardware and software, and use of these components in computer networks. Topics include communica-tion system components, communications software, packet switching, network control, common carrier issues, long-haul vs. local area networks, and performance consideration. Prerequisite: ROCH#0602-208.

Data Communications Technology (ROCH#0602-477)   4 credits
(Course description not available.)

Applied Database Management (ROCH#0602-483)   4 credits
An introduction to issues in data management in organizations, and the role of database management systems in addressing these issues. Topics include the uses and needs for data in organizations, review of simple data structures, the influence of computer architecture and I/O devices on the management of data, basic file organizations supporting data management (sequential, direct access, indexed sequential), logical data models and their physical implementation, database administration, and DBMS selection. Prerequisite: ROCH#0602-208 or permission of instructor.

Telecommunications Fundamentals (ROCH#0609-271)   4 credits
A survey of and introduction to the structure and regulation of the telecommunications industry is provided. the basics of data communications, telephony, switching systems, ISDN, multiplexing, and networks are introduced. Data communication components, codes and techniques are identified. Methods for selecting, implementing, and managing a computer network or telephone system are reviewed.

Data Communications (ROCH#0609-343)   4 credits
(Course description not available.)

Voice Communications: Principles & Tech. (ROCH#0609-474)   4 credits
Provides an understanding of basic telephony concepts and associated voice-based applications. Various telephone architectures are studied. Topic highlights include audiotext, ISDN (Integrated Service Digital Networks), and voice mail. Practical assignments emphasize 'real-world' applications. Prerequisites: ROCH#0609-271, ROCH#0602-200 or ROCH#0602-208.

Switching Technologies (ROCH#0609-475)   4 credits
To familiarize the student with the various switching methods and equipment used in the telephone network. Voice and data switching methods such as matrix, circuit, message packet, burst, and LAN are studied and compared. The function of the switch in the network and network routing methods are examined. Prerequisites: ROCH#0609-474, ROCH#1016-309.

Data Communication Technology (ROCH#0609-477)   4 credits
Provides a practical overview of data communications environment, historical evolution, technology and applications. Topics highlights include networking concepts, cellular/mobile communications, FDDI (fiber distributed data interface), digital-fiber networks and applications.

Telecommunications Policy and Issues (ROCH#0609-480)   4 credits
This course provides an introductory overview of domestic and global information/telecommunications policy, standards, and regulation. Topic highlights include the European Unification, the automatic number identification (ANI)/call ID (CID) debate, privacy in the information age, transborder flow of information and security, and Personal Communications Network (PCN) standards. Prerequisite: ROCH#0609-271.

Network Management (ROCH#0609-572)   4 credits

Provides an intensive practical experience in network management. The technical and management issues associated with the administration of complex, highly integrated networks are examined using various hardware and software tools. Case studies and lab-based assignments emphasize 'real-world' experience. Prerequisites: ROCH#0609-474, ROCH#0609-477.

Elementary Statistics (ROCH#1016-309)   4 credits

An introduction to elementary techniques of statistical description and inference. Topics include descriptive statistics, probability, estimation of parameters, hypothesis testing, and simple linear regression. The statistical package MINITAB will be used.

Fundamentals of Radiation (ROCH#1017-250)   4 credits

In this course we will study the various aspects, applications, and hazards of ionizing radiation. X-rays, alphas, betas, and gamma rays will be discussed. Nuclear medicine, diagnostic and therapeutic aspects of radiology, nuclear reactors, radioactive waste, and other contemporary issues involving ionizing radiation will be presented.

Monitoring & Measuring for Solid Waste Mgt. (ROCH#0286-361)   4 cr.

This course provides an in-depth view of environmental monitoring and measurement, giving the student the knowledge to plan, execute, and interpret a sampling project. The course will cover techniques for sampling air, soil, surface water and groundwater with an empahsis on landfill construction and monitoring. Student will learn to plan sampling events, determine the number and type of samples needed, collect quality assurance/quality control samples, determine correct sampling techniques, and document sampling.

Geology for Solid Waste Management (ROCH#0286-371)   4 credits

An introduction to Environmental Geology including a survey of basic geology and topics applicable to environmental management. Basic geology topics include earth materials, earth's internal processes and earth's external processes. Environmental geology topics include erosion and slope stability, soil properties, glacial geology of Monroe county, and geologic aspects of landfill siting.

Hydrology for Solid Waste Management (ROCH#0286-381)   4 credits

An introduction to hydrology covering surface water, groundwater and water chemistry. Students learn theoretical background, as well as practical application of the science to environmental management. Topics include the hydrologic cycle, surface water, vadose zone, groundwater glow, groundwater monitoring, normal and polluted water chemistry, landfill hydrology, and hydrology of Monroe County.

Rogers State College - 33 courses

Accredited by the North Central Association of Colleges and Schools

Electronic University Network
1977 Colestin Rd.
Hornbrook CA 96044

800-225-3276

Rogers State College is a public, two-year school, and is part of the Oklahoma State System of Higher Education. Rogers State offers courses for credit, taught by regular faculty, through the Electronic University Network.

It's easy to get started at Rogers State College online. If you're over 21, you may take up to 9 credits (generally 3 courses) before you apply for admission to the college. Just look through the Course List, the Course Descriptions, and the Course Fees. Then call us at 1-800-22LEARN (1-800-225-3276). One of our Admissions Counselors will get you started. Later, if you decide you want to become a fully admitted Rogers State student, you can apply for admission.

Note that you may earn a Rogers State College degree by taking as few as 12 credits (4 courses) from the college. The rest of your credits may be transferred from other colleges, or you may earn credit through recognized examination programs such as CLEP, TECEP, ACT PEP or DANTES.

Students go to campus with a personal computer and modem and a local phone call. The campus is accessible 24 hours a day from home, office, hotel room, military base . . . wherever the student may be. Faculty members are ready to help, by electronic mail and conferencing, whenever and wherever students need help. And that help is personal, responsive to each student's needs, not prepackaged or impersonal. Rogers State College and the Electronic University Network bring the Electronic Campus to students all over the U.S. and around the world.

You can choose one of three degrees that Rogers State College offers online: Associate of Science in Computer Science, Associate of Arts in Business Management, and Associate of Arts in Liberal Arts. All these degree programs prepare you to transfer to a four-year institution where you'll complete a B.S. or B.A. degree. Each degree requires that you take 60-62 credits -- but only 12 of these credits need be from Rogers State College online. The rest can be courses you've taken from other regionally accredited colleges, or college-level exams you've passed. You need not take any courses on campus at Rogers State. All your work may be done online.

<u>Fees and costs:</u> Online courses may cost you more than going to a local college, especially a low-cost community college--though even this is questionable, if you consider commuting costs, babysitters, and lost earnings. You'll find that our courses cost the same or less than other distance-learning courses -- and ours, we believe, offer all the elements you need to succeed:

-- One-on-one tutorials
-- Discussions and seminars online
-- Videotape lectures
-- Course teleguide with AOL documentation
-- Text and study guide
-- The Electronic University Campus Online

COSTS: For the 1994 fall semester, the all-inclusive fee for each 3-credit course is $545. This includes college tuition; videotape instruction; one-on-one tutoring with your instructor; class discussions and seminars; the course teleguide; final exam and transcript; and academic and technical support. Textbooks and shipping are extra. Courses without a video component are $50 less.

All new Electronic University Network students pay a one-time administrative fee of $75. This fee is only paid once as long as you are enrolled in at least one course each year.

Rogers State College
Will Rogers & College Hill
Claremore OK 74017-2099

Rogers State College Course Descriptions

Accounting I: Financial Accounting (ROGE#ACCT2103)   3 credits

Everyone who manages in business - whether a mom and pop store or a huge multinational corporation - needs to understand and speak the language of accounting. This course introduces you to the language and concepts of accounting. The course takes you through basic accounting theory, classified financial statement preparation, accounting systems design, and corporate stocks and bonds, as well as other subjects. When you've finished the course, you'll understand the theory of accounting, be able to read and understand financial statements and stories in the financial press, and be ready to go on to more advanced accounting courses.

Accounting II: Managerial Accounting (ROGE#ACCT2203)   3 credits

Managerial accounting is what you, the manager, will use to run the daily operations of a business and make decisions about its future. Managerial accounting uses past data and future predictions as information for decision-making about such practical matters as pricing the items to be sold, purchasing and maintaining inventories, and ensuring profitability. The course covers cash flow statements, financial statement analysis, manufacturing accounting, budgeting, breakeven analysis, profit analysis, and competitive pricing theory. when you're finished, you should be able to analyze and think better about personal and business finances, read and understand the business press better, and better understand your other business classes and apply accounting principles to them.

Economics I: Macroeconomics (ROGE#ECON2113)   3 credits

Does economics affect your life? Of course it does, and if you'd like to know how, this course will let you find out. Understanding economics will enable you to address issues ranging from national and international politics to your professional and personal life. Economics I is a theory-oriented course that introduces basic economic principles and develops them through the study of important social issues: inflation, unemployment, consumer expectations, surpluses, shortages, and international trade. This course gets you ready for Economics II and for courses in international business, money and banking, financial institutions, and stocks and bonds.

Economics II: Microeconomics (ROGE#ECON2114)   3 credits

A theory-oriented approach to the study of economics. Elementary principles of price theory and national income theory are developed systematically with emphasis on their use in analyzing economic issues and for recommending appropriate economic policy. Prerequisite: Math proficiency at the level of College Algebra.

Horse and Ranch Management (ROGE#HSMG2303)   3 credits

A study of horse and ranch management, designed to allow students the opportunity to study special topics.

Contemporary Marketing (ROGE#BMA2143)   3 credits

Introduction to basic marketing concepts with emphasis on practical application and relationship to contemporary living. Includes evaluation of environmental factors which influence marketing decisions and how a marketing manager interacts with diverse areas of business. Covers fundamental principles of product strategy, promotion, pricing and distribution and the interrelationships between them.

Principles of Management (ROGE#BMA2013)   3 credits

Introduction to practical management with an emphasis on the role of the manager/supervisor within the organization. Includes communication, leadership, motivation, organizational structure, the effects of organizational change, and decision-making as applied to management systems, organizations, interpersonal relationships, and production. Suggested for all students who may supervise on their jobs, regardless of major.

Introduction to Business (ROGE#BMA1203)   3 credits

This course is for everyone who wants to expand their understanding of business. It provides a comprehensive view of the contemporary business environment from the internal functions of a business to the challenges of business on an international scale. After completing this course you should have a better understanding of several areas of business and have a foundation to build on in related business courses. One area is heavily emphasized -- the global marketplace. Challenges and opportunities are not only to be found within the borders of the United States. Success will depend on how well the individual can develop a broader, more global perspective on business. Today, the world of business is indeed the entire world.

Introduction to Computer Programming (ROGE#CS1213)   3 credits

If you're getting ready to work in computing or related fields, or want to participate more knowledgeably in our increasingly computerized world, this is the course for you! The instructor is Julie Luscomb, an RSC faculty member and an experienced distance-learning instructor. The course includes a review of the DOS operating environment and leads into actually writing programs in the C computer programming language. There is an equipment requirement. You need a computer that can support the C compiler (provided with the textbook) -- either an MS-DOS computer, or a Macintosh with PC emulation or with Soft PC* installed.

Microcomputer Applications (ROGE#CS2113)   3 credits

This course is for *everybody* -- those who want to continue in computer science, those working toward a business degree, and those who just want to know more about computers and applications programs. The course introduces Windows and gives you hands-on experience with word processing, spreadsheets, and database management on IBM personal computers. There is no prerequisite. Software used in the course includes Windows plus Word for Windows 6.0, Excel 5.0 and Access 2.0. If you don't currently have the software, you will be able to purchase The Microsoft Office Professional at a substantially discounted student price. Note: If you do not have Windows you must have it installed before you can install the course software. Requirements: PC with 386 or faster microprocessor; MS-DOS version 3.1 or higher; 4 MB RAM Memory (8 recommended); 30 MB of hard disk space (for minimum installation) to 85-100 MB (for full installation); VGA or higher graphics card; mouse; high density disk drive). For PowerPoint graphics program, 256-color video adapter recommended.

C Programming (ROGE#CS2223)   3 credits

This course is a must for serious computer professionals and anyone who wants a degree in computer science. You will learn to write, debug, and run programs in C -- the increasingly popular UNIX-related, intermediate-level software development language. The course covers operators, variables, loops, functions, pointers, input-output, data types, structures, and file operations. The instructor is Julie Luscomb, an experienced distance-learning instructors in the Advanced Technologies Division at Rogers State College. The prerequisite for this course is Introduction to Computer Programming or a programming language or the instructor's permission (to get permission, you must be able to convince the instructor that you have absorbed the equivalent knowledge on the job or through your own study). You need a computer that can support the C compiler (provided with the text) -- either an MS-DOS computer, or a Macintosh with PC emulation or with Soft PC* installed.

C++ Computer Programming (ROGE#CS2323)   3 credits

C++ is an object-oriented extension of the C computer language. Object-oriented approaches to creation of software are covered in this course using C++ for illustration. You need a computer that can support the C++ compiler (Borland's Turbo C++ for DOS, available at an educational discount) -- either an MS-DOS computer, or a Macintosh with PC emulation or with Soft PC* installed.

Operating Systems (ROGE#CS2153)   3 credits

What's the most popular operating system in the world? If you thought MS-DOS, you'd be wrong. It's UNIX, and that's the system that's covered in great detail in this course. You'll study the components, functions, and relationships of computer operating systems and their interactions with user programs. You'll become familiar with popular operating systems other than UNIX. The instructor is Cliff Layton, director of the Advanced Technologies Division at Rogers State College, an experienced distance-learning instructor, and the co-coordinator of the RSC online program. The prerequisite is a course in a programming language (C or another language). Your computer must support the required software: Coherent Operating System, v4.2 (386 computer with 4 MB RAM and 20 MB hard space.

Software Systems Analysis & Design (ROGE#CS2133)   3 credits

To be a successful computer science, professional, you need to know more than programming languages. You need to know how to analyze and organize the work. This is the course that teaches you those critical skills. In this course, engineering and computer science methods are applied to the production of software, according to problem specifications, and time and budget constraints. Methodologies for project definition, analysis, design, coding, testing and maintenance, are interrelated with management, costing, and communication considerations. To take this course, you need the following equipment: an MS-DOS Computer (286 or faster); a VGA or EGA graphics monitor; and a mouse. You also need Object Craft Software. EUN arranges for you to get the software at an educational discount. The software is available through EUN at an educational discount.

English Composition I (ROGE#ENGL1113)   3 credits

Practical writing experience emphasizing basic sentence structure, vocabulary, spelling and other mechanics. The focus is on student-written essays and improving self-expression.

English Composition II (ROGE#ENGL1213)   3 credits

This course will benefit you as a student, a professional, and a person. You're already a writer. Now you can become a better writer. Learn to better express the self you are - in writing. Learn about the relationship that you already have with literature. Take a leap into the pool of the writer's experience - yours, and others'! The main goals of Composition II are to help you write better in any area of your life, and to help you learn to prepare a college research paper. The first goal is useful no matter who you are or what you do for a living. The second is essential for success in a college program.

Creative Writing (ROGE#ENGL2023)   3 credits

This course covers devices and techniques necessary to write and publish, particularly fiction. It includes an introduction to publishing markets and proper manuscript submission. This course challenges students to regain their eloquence with the written word and with each other. It encourages you to rediscover your unique voice and to take pride in your own words and experiences. The course focuses on the practical aspects of writing, introducing students to revision and editing techniques. For those interested in publishing, the course outlines standard submission techniques and strategies. One of the special features of the course is that each lesson contains mini-interviews with some of the country's leading writers. The major objectives of the course are: to encourage you to communicate clearly with others, to think and live creatively, to broaden your vision of the world around you and to encourage you to be your own biographer -- to discover yourself and others through words. Prerequisite: English Comp I and/or English Comp II or permission of instructor.

Medical Terminology (ROGE#NURS1103)   3 credits

The course presents a physiological systems approach to the principles of medical word building. Providing medical vocabulary for anatomy, physiology, systems, diagnostic testing and pharmacology, the course is appropriate for health science students such as nursing, dental hygiene, paramedic, and physical therapy assistant.

Art History II (1400-1850) (ROGE#ART2723)   3 credits

The study in chronological sequence of major art styles and movements from 1400 to 1850 AD.

Humanities I (ROGE#HUM2113)   3 credits

Humanities is the study of culture ... a study which encompasses all of the arts as well as philosophy and religion. Although this course is taught chronologically, history will be a frame and not the focus. We will note the WHY of human achievements in the context of WHAT, WHEN, and WHERE.

Humanities II (ROGE#HUM2223)   3 credits

This is a course about people and their creativity . . . about achievements and values . . . about how you can learn about yourself and the world you live in by studying worlds and people no longer in existence. Learn what you have in common with Tutankhamen, Mozart, and me! The focus of this course - which has a strong and engaging video series as its core - is seven of the major art forms: film, drama, music, literature, painting, sculpture, and architecture. The textbook focuses briefly on dance and photography.

General Environmental Biology (ROGE#BIOL1134)   4 credits

A general survey of environmental science. Includes an introduction to basic ecological principles with an emphasis on major modes of environmental pollution.

Basic Mathematics (ROGE#MATH0013)   3 credits

Pre-college math; preparation for college level courses. Includes operations with real numbers, percentages, volumes, areas, perimeters of simple geometric figures, metric system, English system, scientific notation, basic rules of exponents, and solving algebraic equations. This course is for students who need a refresher course in basic mathematics.

Elementary Algebra (ROGE#MATH0113)   3 credits

Includes signed numbers, exponents, and algebraic expressions through quadratic equations.

Intermediate Algebra (ROGE#MATH0213)   3 credits

This course covers the real numbers system, exponents and polynomials, factoring polynomials, rational expressions, linear equations, absolute value, linear inequalities, linear functions and their graphs, rational exponents and radicals. Prerequisite: MATH0113 or a firm understanding of elementary algebra.

College Algebra (ROGE#MATH1513)   3 credits

Includes special products, factoring, fractions, exponents, radicals, functions, inequalities, polynomials, systems of equations, matrices, determinants, and progressions.

Values and Ethics (ROGE#PHILO1113)   3 credits

The study of ethics and values from a comparative and structural basis includes origin and base formulation and applications to social issues and ethical problems in contemporary living. What would the philosophers of the past have to say about abortion, nuclear weapons, health care reform, genetic engineering? The style of this course emphasizes interactive discussion among participants -- a course which will engage both your mind and your emotions.

Astronomy (ROGE#PHYS2003)   3 credits

Course includes history of astronomy, techniques and tools of the astronomer, and structure of the universe. A knowledge of basic algebra is helpful but not required.

354

Chemistry (ROGE#CHEM1115)   5 credits

Study of basic concepts involved in chemical combination, valences, gas laws, liquids, solids, and solutions. For students who have not had high school chemistry.

American Federal Government (ROGE#POLSC1113)   3 credits

Course topics cover the development of the national government with emphasis on state origins, constitutionalism and basic structures and theories of the federal government.

American History I (to 1865) (ROGE#HIST2483)   3 credits

The great drama of the discovery of America and the founding of our nation as a series of tiny, struggling colonies marks the beginning of this course. The course explores how European settlers, seeking religious freedom and economic opportunity, shaped our nation out of the wilderness, developed a culture, and set a revolution in motion. It takes us through the shaping of our political system, the burgeoning of the industrial revolution, through the years before the Civil War and the war itself.

American History II (from 1865) (ROGE#HIST2493)   3 credits

The drama of the development of American society continues as the country grows into a world power. Topics include: Reconstruction, closing of the frontier, industrialism, overseas expansion, progressivism, the Twenties, depression and the New Deal, world leadership.

History of Aviation (ROGE#AVIA2233)   3 credits

Did you know that the Wright Brothers were not the first to fly? (But they did make a unique contribution to aviation history!) Did you know that a lot of exciting aviation history happened in Europe? This course examines aviation history, from those who dreamed of flight to those who made it happen. It covers the evolution of flight from kites to gliders, from balloons to aircraft, from uncontrolled flight to controlled, powered flight. You'll have a chance to explore events or topics or periods of aviation history that are especially interesting to you.

Salve Regina University - 12 courses

Accreditation by the New England Association of Schools and Colleges.

Electronic University Network
1977 Colestin Rd.
Hornbrook CA 96044
800-225-3276

Salve Regina University was first chartered in the state of Rhode Island in 1934. It was established as an independent university in the Catholic tradition of education, which acknowledged the critical importance of higher education for women and for men.

The master's degree, first offered in 1974, now includes 15 concentrations. In 1990 the University initiated a humanities program leading to the doctoral degree. Thus, in combination with undergraduate programs in the arts, sciences, management, business, information systems, nursing, education, and social work, the curriculum presently provides opportunities for over 50 areas of concentration leading to an associate, bachelor's, master's, or Ph.D. degree.

The University presently serves 2,200 men and women in 38 states and 10 foreign countries, and has more than 10,000 alumni/ae. The University is located in Newport, Rhode island. The University is a member of numerous organizations concerned with the advancement of higher education. A partial list includes: Association of American Colleges; American Council on Education; College Entrance Examination Board; Council for the Advancement and Support of Education; National Catholic Educational Association; Council for the Advancement of Small Colleges.

Salve Regina University of Newport, RI, has announced it will offer the Master of Arts in International Relations to distance learners via computer and modem. Courses will begin in the Fall of 1994.

With the dawn of the 21st century, dynamic changes have occurred, and others are taking place that will impact on virtually every person in the world community of nations. The prospects for peace over war, for economic well-being over poverty, and for fulfillment of certain political, social, and cultural aspirations influence the relations of states and continue to challenge the emerging new world order. It is in this context that the International Relations program focuses on the world not only as it is, but also as it should be, in light of the enduring central values of the world's great civilizations.

The courses, designed for graduates seeking a broader and deeper understanding of the contemporary world, will help prepare them for their role in the increasingly interdependent world of the 21st century. The chief focus of the program is a search for new avenues to global harmony and justice. Courses in the program, however, are designed to meet the individual needs of students and help them prepare for or enhance their careers in government, international organizations, business, finance, teaching, research or further study.

To receive more information as it becomes available, please send email to our Admissions Office (EUNGrad@aol.com). Include your name, address, phone number, and the name of your employer.

Tuition is $300.00 per credit hour or $900.00 per 3 credit course. All courses are 3 credits and full payment is required at the time of registration for each course. Additional fees also apply.

The telephone number is 800-637-0002. Students may call the 800 number 24 hours a day to leave a message. The FAX number is 401-849-0702. Students may also contact the Director by electronic mail using MISTOL@Salve3.Salve.EDU or Mistol.aol.com.

Sister Leona Misto, Ed.D., Director
Graduate Extension Study
Salve Regina University
100 Ochre Point Ave.
Newport RI 02840

Salve Regina University Course Descriptions

Research Seminar (SALV#HUM500)   3 credits

In this course, students explore various research techniques and apply that knowledge not only in critically analyzing existing research but also in designing and implementing their own research project. Concepts addressed in the course include preparation of a literature review, qualitative and quantitative approaches, triangulation methods, research designs and their inherent threats to internal and external validity, sampling techniques, data collection methods, and ethical considerations. Note: for degree students, this course must be taken in the first year of the program.

Ethical Perspectives on Global Issues (SALV#HUM501)   3 credits

Students examine and compare the ethical standards and approaches of Western and non-Western moralists in the resolution of major moral issues. Readings include such topics as nuclear proliferation, the search for peace, ecological issues, world hunger, and genetic engineering.

Foundations of International Relations (SALV#INR502)   3 credits

Students explore the salient issues involving conflict or cooperation in contemporary international politics. The major topics include nation-state systems; struggle for power among nations; continuities and changes in current international relations; the role of diplomacy, ideology, economics, military force, war, nuclear weapons, international law and organizations; the quest for community; and the relationship of moral and religious values to some of the problems of international relations.

International Law (SALV#INR504)   3 credits

Students examine the role international law plays in today's dynamic world. Topics include the ever-evolving concepts of legal order, jurisdiction, territoriality, nationality, extradition, and sovereignty over land, sea, and air space, as well as the broadening impact of human rights, statehood, diplomacy, treaties, and international economic regulations. Students examine, too, the ongoing quest to regulate the use of force, including UN peacekeeping operations.

Russia and Eastern European Politics (SALV#INR518)   3 credits

Establish a conceptual framework for understanding the international relations of the Eastern European states since 1945. Special attention is devoted to recent changes in the Russian government's approach toward foreign policy. The global impact of these developments is considered.

Africa's Global Perspectives (SALV#INR524)   3 credits

Students analyze the fundamental factors in influencing the relations of contemporary African states within the continent and with the outside world. Such factors as African social, economic, political, and cultural developments are considered, as well as reaction to African developments by other states.

China, Japan, and the Pacific Rim (SALV#INR528)   3 credits

Students examine the major political, economic, military, and cultural factors influencing the current relations of China and the Asian states.

Special emphasis is on the broader Asian and global trends, including Japan and the developing impact of the Pacific Rim states.

Foreign Policy Concerns: Central Asia & India (SALV#INR535)   3 credits

Central Asia, long divided between Russia and China, partially returned to an international system. Five ex-Soviet republics - Turkmenistan, Tadzhikistan, Kyrgystan, Uzbekistan, Kazakhstan - as well as Out Mongolia must rapidly develop their weak economies, revive fragile cultures, and devise astute foreign policies if they are to survive. This course considers their history, politics, and relationships with neighboring states, stressing their impact upon the Indian Sub-continent.

North America in the New World (SALV#INR550)   3 credits

Topics studied include the postwar "revolution" in North American foreign policy and the effects of rapid change and economic ecological crisis on that policy.

Contemporary Problems in Latin America (SALV#INR561)   3 credits

Students focus on the major political, social, and economic problems facing Central and South America today. They examine the political culture and processes, political interest groups, and the solutions proposed by constitutional, military, and leftist regimes to the problem of political instability. Other issues discussed are economic underdevelopment and dependency, including demographic problems, urbanization, and agrarian reform.

Contemporary International Issues (SALV#INR568)   3 credits

Problems in international relations are analyzed in a seminar on a selected case-study basis. Topics include global concerns ranging from nuclear proliferation through international terrorism to world overpopulation, hunger, degradation of the global environment, and a new international economic order.

The Middle East (SALV#INR586)   3 credits

Students examine these interrelated subject areas in an effort to better understand how they influence and shape events in the Middle East: the Peoples of the Middle East, Islam, the Arab-Israeli Problem, Oil, Iran's Revolution, the Iran-Iraq War, the Iraq-Kuwait War, and Gulf Security.

Thomas Edison State College - 9 courses

Distance and Independent Adult Learning (DIAL) Program
Accredited by the Middle States Association of Colleges and Schools

Electronic University Network
1977 Colestin Rd.
Hornbrook CA 96044

800-225-3276

Thomas Edison State College offers courses through its On-Line Computer Classroom to students around the world. Current offerings include eight courses, ranging from 3 to 9 credits, in subjects such as Introduction to Marketing, Computers and Society, Marriage and the Family, and other topics (see below).

Take courses online using Thomas Edison State College's Computer Assisted Lifelong Learning (CALL) Network. Earn college credit using a computer and modem to "call" into class, eliminating worries about bad weather or scheduling conflicts. Participate in course discussions required) with faculty mentors and fellow students at a time which is convenient for you. *You set your own schedule.*

Use the privacy of email to send assignments to faculty mentors and to receive corrected assignments back. Interact with other students, form study groups and undertake collaborative learning projects. Join students in the *electronic student union* for informal discussions. All this and more is available through Thomas Edison's On-Line Computer Classroom.

New courses are coming online periodically, and information about these is available online by dialing (609)292-7200 or by calling DIAL at (609)292-6317 for information by mail. Course descriptions are available on-line by dialing (609) 292-7200 (Data-8, Parity-none, Stop-1, Emulation-full, VT-100) or by calling for information by mail.

Courses offered for three- and six-credits have a 16-week semester, while nine-credit courses have a 24-week semester. You attend class weekly by computer, discuss questions through a computer conference and submit written assignments on email for evaluation by faculty.

Proctored exams are administered at conveniently located sites. Even course materials are delivered directly to your home. Textbooks, study guides, and either video and/or audio tapes, or computer disks, could be part of your courseware depending on the structure. Course material fees are separate from tuition fees. Contact Specialty Books for information and prices: (800)466-1365

Registration in Guided Study courses is open to all adult learners. All of the courses listed are applicable toward both associate and baccalaureate degrees at Thomas Edison State College. However, by registering for a course, you are not enrolling in the College. You can contact the Thomas Edison Office of Admissions Services at (609) 984-1150 for information about enrolling in the College. It is not necessary to be enrolled in Thomas Edison in order to register for Guided Study courses.

Course fees:

New Jersey residents pay $51 per credit hour.
Out-of-state students pay $76 per credit hour.
All students pay a $12 registration fee.
Students who are not enrolled in a Thomas Edison degree program pay a $35 technology fee. Students who register during late registration are charged a $50 late fee.

Mr. William J. Seaton, Director
Distance and Independent Adult Learning (DIAL)
Thomas Edison State College
101 W. State St.
Trenton NJ 08608-1176
(609) 292-6317

Thomas Edison State College Course Descriptions

Computers and Society (THOM#COS161)   6 credits

This course aims to develop a working vocabulary associated with computers, explain at a general level how a computer works and use problem-solving approaches that lend themselves to computer solutions. Different types of languages are described, with attention to the capabilities and limitations of BASIC/Q BASIC and Logo. The student is expected to use the four simple software packages provided with the course (such as word processing, database management, a graphics program and an electronic spreadsheet package). the course is designed to equip the student with the knowledge and the skills to be an informed consumer of computing services. Course uses IBM-PC software tutorials and commercial tutorials.

Global Environmental Change (THOM#ENS311)   6 credits

Course description unavailable.

American Cinema (THOM#FIL110)   3 credits

Course description unavailable.

Marriage & the Family (THOM#SOC210)   3 credits

This course provides students with an understanding of various approaches to studying the family and the varieties of US family forms. It explores family life - mate selection, parenting and the major processes of family interaction.

Principles of Management (THOM#MAN301)   3 credits

For those who have decided upon a career in business, government or educational management, this introductory course in the concepts of management will provide a valuable introduction to a successful career. The course is designed for the managerial candidate who is newly graduated, or who has worked but not had formal training in business management. It is intended to provide essential skills in planning and organizing, staffing and directing, controlling, decision-making,, motivation, communication and the application of management principles to the business organization.

Managing in Organization (THOM#MAN351)   9 credits

This course will introduce you to the field of management in complex organizations, addressing the subject from three related viewpoints: the systems view, an approach to understanding and managing organizations, stressing the interdependence of people and functions, and focusing on the organization as a whole; the behavioral viewpoint, emphasizing the interactions of individuals and groups, and how their behavior affects organizational performance; and the management practice approach, addressing the actual functions and activities of managers in organizations.

Introduction to Marketing (THOM#MAR301)   3 credits

The overall aim of this course is to provide an introduction to marketing as it relates to contemporary living and society's changing needs. Learning will focus on how a marketing manager interacts with diverse areas of business, as well as basic marketing principles, including product promotion, pricing, distribution and their inter-relationships..

Social Psychology (THOM#PSY370)   6 credits

This course surveys the field of social psychology and explores major topics, including communication, friendship, prejudice, conformity, leadership, aggression and altruism. The course aims to teach students to evaluate interpersonal communication and media presentations of current issues.

The Religious Quest (THOM#REL405)   9 credits

This course is designed as in intensive one-semester course in world religions. Emphasis is on specific forms of religious expression and practice, rather than the more abstract or theological aspects. Religions covered by the course are those of the majority of humankind and living traditions in today's world (Hinduism, Buddhism, religions of China and Japan, Judaism, Christianity, Islam, and several African religions.

University of Washington - 75 courses

Accredited by the Western Association of Schools and Colleges

> University of Washington Extension
> 5001 25th Ave. NE
> Seattle WA 98195

Each registrant receives a course guide containing the course outline, a list of required texts and materials, study instructions, supplementary information and specific lesson assignments. Sometimes additional media such as video or audio tapes or laboratory kits are offered to further expand the scope of study. These materials provide a basic focus and discipline for your study, as well as a means of establishing and maintaining communication with your instructor.

Assignments are completed at your convenience and mailed to the UW Distance Learning office for routing to your instructor for evaluation. Two weeks are usually required for the return of an assignment through regular mail. You may contact your instructor to request a personal conference. Most UW Distance Learning courses are designed by the faculty who teach the same courses on the University of Washington campus. The instructors are familiar with students' questions and needs and have developed the appropriate methods to help students achieve the course objectives in a distance learning format.

Two calendar months is the minimum time required for completing a UW Distance Learning course. Completion of a course in this amount of time cannot be guaranteed. *Be cautious in estimating the time you need to complete a course, especially if you haven't taken a UW Distance Learning course before*. You are allowed 6, 9 or 12 months, depending on the course, from the date of enrollment to complete a UW Distance Learning course. If all assignments and examinations have not been completed at the end of your enrollment period, your enrollment on extensions for an additional six months. For information on extensions, contact the administration.

The University of Washington's Distance Learning courses are open to any high school graduate or any person 18 years or older who chooses distance learning for such reasons as remote location, full-time career, physical disabilities or educational preference. High school students may enroll in courses upon recommendation of a high school counselor.

In addition to academic considerations, prospective UW Distance Learning students should consider their personal strengths and preferences. The qualities of independence, self-direction and discipline characterize the successful UW Distance Learning student.

The University of Washington Distance Learning program includes courses for which high school students may receive high school credit and/or college credit. High school students should consult with their high school advisers to determine if a distance learning course will further the student's educational goals. Taking college-level courses by UW Distance Learning offers beginning-level foreign language, natural science, social science, English and mathematics courses which can be used to meet these requirements.

Your account provides access to library catalogs of the UW and other major universities, Grolier's Encyclopedia, Webster's Dictionary, the Oxford English Dictionary, Usenet, the UW campus calendar and other resources. The latest version of this catalog is also available on UWIN (UW Information), the University's computer network for students, faculty and staff.

To select the email option, request a free Uniform Access account, which is available to students who have a Macintosh or IBM-PC (or compatible) computer, a modem (preferably 2400 baud or higher), communications software and a phone line. If you do not have communications software, the UW Distance Learning will sell you a copy of Kermit, a UW-supported program, for $1. If you have any questions about the email option, call Corliss Harmer at (206) 543-2350 or (800) 543-2320.

Email address: instudy@u.washington.edu

Proctors: Students who reside outside of Washington state, as well as Washington residents, may take an examination under the supervision of a suitable proctor. The student is responsible for locating a proctor and sending a *Proctor Verification* form to UW Distance Leaning.

Tuition is $66 per quarter credit for all students, including residents of other states and countries.

UW Distance Learning, GH-23
University of Washington Extension
5001 25th Ave. NE
Seattle WA 98195

(206)543-2350
(800) 543-2320

University of Washington Course Descriptions

Introduction to Technical Writing (WASH#ENGR-C231)   3 credits

Principles of organizing, developing and writing technical information. Report forms and rhetorical patterns common to scientific and technical disciplines. Technical writing conventions such as headings, illustrations, style and tone. Numerous writing assignments required. Required for all engineering majors. Prerequisite: one 5-credit composition course.

Science Education: Elementary School (WASH#EDC&I-C470)   3 credits

Students perform in-home experiments with assistance from instructor via email. Designed for classroom teachers with reference to the teaching and learning of science from kindergarten through grade six. Emphasis is placed on objectives, methods and materials as related to the concepts of processes of science. Prerequisite: teaching experience.

Basic Educational Statistics (WASH#EDPSY-C490)   3 credits

Measures of central tendency and variability, point and interval estimation, linear correlation, hypothesis testing.

Nutrition for Today (WASH#FDSC-C300)   3 credits

Basic applied nutrition and food science. Identification and physiological roles of nutrients, nutritional requirements, problems with over- and under-nutrition and nutritional food-related diseases. Food additives, processing, safety and their effects on overall nutrition.

Reading Literature (WASH#ENGL-C200)   5 credits

Techniques and practice in reading and enjoying literature. Examines some of the best works in English and American literature and considers such features of literary meaning as imagery, characterization, narration and patterning in sound and sense. Emphasis on literature as a source of pleasure and knowledge about human experience.

Reading Fiction (WASH#ENGL-C242)   5 credits

Critical interpretation and meaning in fiction. Different examples of fiction representing a variety of types from medieval to the modern periods.

Shakespeare (WASH#ENGL-C225)   5 credits

Survey of Shakespeare's career as dramatist. Study of representative comedies, tragedies, romances and history plays.

Intermediate Expository Writing (WASH#ENGL-C281)   5 credits

(NOTE: This course may be previewed electronically.) Writing papers communicating information and opinion to develop accurate, competent and effective expression. Recommended: sophomore standing. Interested students can view the study guide through the World Wide Web at http://weber.u.washington.edu/~instudy/.

Beginning Short Story Writing (WASH#ENGL-C281)   5 credits

Introduction to the theory and practice of writing the short story. Recommended: sophomore standing. Purchase of blank cassette tape for instructor comments in required. Minimum enrollment period is 3 mo.

Shakespeare to 1603 (WASH#ENGL-C323)   5 credits
Shakespeare's career as dramatist before 1603 (including *Hamlet*). Study of history plays, comedies and tragedies.

Shakespeare After 1603 (WASH#ENGL-C324)   5 credits
Shakespeare's career as dramatist after 1603 (including *Hamlet*). Study of comedies tragedies and romances.

English Literature: Late Renaissance (WASH#ENGL-C325)   5 credits
A period of skepticism for some, faith for others, but intellectual upheaval generally. Poems by John Donne; poems and plays by Ben Johnson and other late rivals to Shakespeare; prose by Sir Francis Bacon and others.

Milton (WASH#ENGL-C333)   5 credits
Milton's early poems and the prose; *Paradise Lost, Paradise Regained* and *Samson Agonistes*, with attention to the religious, intellectual and literary contexts.

The Modern Novel (WASH#ENGL-C340)   5 credits
The novel on both sides of the Atlantic in the first half of the 20th century. Includes Joyce, Waugh, Lawrence, Steinbeck, and Hemingway.

Fantasy (WASH#ENGL-C349)   5 credits
Nonnatralistic literature, selected folktales, fairy tales, fables, nonsense, ghost stories, horror stories, science fiction and/or utopian literature - the supernatural and surreal, the grotesque, the fantastical.

American Literature: The Early Nation (WASH#ENGL-C352)   5 credits
Conflicting visions of the national destiny and the individual identity in the early years of America's nationhood. Works by Emerson, Thoreau, Hawthorne, Melville, and such other writers as Poe, Cooper, Irving, Whitman, Dickinson and Douglass.

American Lit.: Early Modern Period (WASH#ENGL-C354)   5 credits
Literary responses to the disillusionment after World War I, experiments in form and in new ideas of new period. Works by such writers as Anderson, Toomer, Cather, O'Neill, Frost, Pound, Eliot, Cummings, Hemingway, Fitzgerald, Faulkner, Stein, Hart Crane, Stevens and Porter.

American Literature: Contemporary (WASH#ENGL-C355)   5 credits
Works by such writers as Ellison, Williams, O'Connor, Lowell, Barth, Rich and Hawkes.

Advanced Expository Writing (WASH#ENGL-C381)   5 credits
Concentration on the development of prose style for experienced writers. Recommended: sophomore standing.

Short Story Writing (WASH#ENGL-C384)   5 credits
Exploring and developing continuity in the elements of fiction writing. Methods of extending and sustaining plot, setting, character, point of view and tone. Permission of instructor is required. Purchase of blank cassette tape for instructor comments is required. Minimum enrollment period is three months.

367

Elementary German (WASH#GERMAN-C326)   5 credits
For persons who have had no previous instruction in German. Acquisition of a large vocabulary; grammar; practice in reading and writing.

Elementary Italian (WASH#ITAL-C101)   5 credits
Basic study of Italian grammar and idiomatic usage of the language. All assignments and examinations are written, with tape recordings used.

Introduction to Linguistic Thought (WASH#LING-C200)   5 credits
Introduction to the scientific study; language and writing; phonological and grammatical analysis; language change; related disciplines.

Language Development (WASH#LING-C457)   4 credits
First-language acquisition and use by children. Emphasis on theoretical issues and research techniques.

History of Jazz (WASH#MUSIC-C331)   3 credits
Survey of major periods and styles of jazz, New Orleans jazz to the avant-garde and popular jazz today. Studies main characteristics of each style.

Introduction to World Religions: Eastern (WASH#ENGL-C202)   5 credits
Introductory course in the history of religions, concentrating on religions that have developed in South Asia and East Asia. Primary attention to Hinduism and Buddhism. Other important Asian religions are discussed in relation, with emphasis on basic conceptual and symbolic structures.

First Year Russian (WASH#RUSS-C101)   5 credits
Introduction to Russian. Emphasis on oral communication with limited vocabulary. Basic grammatical features and some reading. Student must purchase a blank cassette tape for oral exercises.

Elementary Spanish (WASH#SPAN-C101)   5 credits
Recommended for those who wish to work primarily toward a reading knowledge of the languages. Instructional video tape supports learning.

Astronomy (WASH#ASTR-C101)   5 credits
Introduction to the universe, with emphasis on conceptual, as contrasted with mathematical, comprehension. Modern theories, observations and ideas concerning nature and evolution of galaxies, quasars, stars, black holes, planets and solar systems.

The Planets (WASH#ASTR-C150)   5 credits
For liberal arts and beginning science students. Survey of the planets of the solar system, with emphasis on recent space exploration of the planets and on the comparative evolution of the Earth and other planets.

Weather (WASH#ATM-C101)   5 credits
The earth's atmosphere, with emphasis on weather observations and forecasting. Daily weather discussions. Highs, lows, fronts, clouds, storms, jet streams, air pollution and other features of the atmosphere, weather phenomena.

General Chemistry (WASH#CHEM-C140)   4 credits

For science, engineering and other majors who plan to take a year or more of chemistry courses. Atomic nature of matter, nuclear chemistry, periodic table, quantum concepts, chemical bonding, gas laws.

Algebra with Applications (WASH#MATH-C111)   5 credits

Use of graphs and algebraic functions as found in business and economics. Algebraic and graphical manipulations to solve problems. Exponential and logarithmic functions; various applications to growth of money.

Applications of Calculus to Business (WASH#MATH-C112)   5 credits

Rates of change, tangent, derivative, accumulation, area, integral in specific contexts, particularly economics. Techniques of differentiation and integration. Application to problem solving. Optimization.

Introduction to Environmental Studies (WASH#ENV-C101)   5 credits

Natural history and human modifications of the natural world. Evolutionary biology, geography, toxicology, energy, economics, law, public policy.

Precalculus (WASH#MATH-C120)   5 credits

Polynomial, rational, exponential and trigonometric functions.

Elementary Linear Algebra (WASH#MATH-C205)   3 credits

Systems of equations, vector spaces, matrices, linear transformations, vectors.

Introduction to Differential Equations (WASH#MATH-C307)   3 credits

Taylor series, first and second order ordinary differential equations.

Intermediate Algebra (WASH#MATH-C101)   0 credits

Similar to the third term of high school algebra. Prerequisite: one year of high school algebra.

Survey of Oceanography (WASH#OCEAN-C101)   5 credits

Origin and extent of the oceans; nature of the sea bottom; causes and effects of currents and tides; animal and plant life in the sea.

Psychology as a Social Science (WASH#PSYCH-C101)   5 credits

Behavior from a social-science viewpoint. Emphasizes personality, individual differences, attitudes, and social behavior and influence. Includes related aspects of cognition, behavior disorders, states of awareness, motivation and emotion, learning, development and research methods.

Personality & Individual Differences (WASH#PSYCH-C205)   4 credits

Basic concepts, methods and background for more intensive study in the field of personality.

Abnormal Psychology (WASH#PSYCH-C305)   5 credits

An overview of major categories of psychopathology, including description and classification, theoretical models and recent research on etiology and treatment. Prerequisites: 10 credits in psychology.

Introduction to Drugs and Behavior (WASH#PSYCH-C322)   3 credits

Basic concepts of drug action emphasizing the behavioral consequences of the intake of a variety of drugs.

Survey of Cognitive Psychology (WASH#PSYCH-C355)   5 credits

Current theory and research in perception, attention, memory and learning, attitudes, thinking and decision making and language. For the student who wishes a survey in any of the above content areas. Prerequisite: eight credits in psychology, including an introductory course.

Personality Development of the Child (WASH#PSYCH-C415)   5 credits

Socialization theory and research, infant attachment and social relationships, development of aggressive and altruistic behaviors, sex-role development, moral development, parent and adult influences. Applied issues in social development and policy.

Basic Statistics (WASH#STAT-C220)   5 credits

Objectives and pitfalls of statistical studies. Structure of data sets, histograms, means and standard deviations. Correlation and regression. Probability theory, the binomial and normal distributions. Interpretations of statistical estimates, confidence intervals and significance tests.

Basic Statistics with Applications (WASH#STAT-C301)   5 credits

Objectives and pitfalls of statistical studies Structure of data sets, histograms, means and standard deviations. Correlation and regression. Probability, binomial and normal distributions. Interpretation of estimates, confidence intervals and significance tests. Application to problems in the student's major field.

Elements of Statistical Methods (WASH#STAT-C311)   5 credits

Elementary concepts of probability and sampling, the binomial and normal distributions. Basic concepts of hypothesis testing, estimation and confidence intervals, t-tests and chi-square tests. Linear regression theory and the analysis of variance.

Legal Aspects of Communications (WASH#CMU-C320)   5 credits

Regulations governing publication and broadcast in the mass media. The course focuses on the limits of free speech, whom the law protects and the goals of mass media law.

History Communication and Journalism (WASH#CMU-C201)   5 credits

History and development of communication from prehistoric times; social and technical inventions; political and economic contexts.

The Phenomena of Communicating (WASH#CMU-C202)   5 credits

Types of communicating behaviors in progressively more complex situations, from individual cognition through interpersonal interactions to mass communicating.

Introduction to Microeconomics (WASH#ECON-C200)   5 credits

Introduction to analysis of markets; consumer demand, production, exchange, the price system, resource allocation, government intervention.

Introduction to Macroeconomics (WASH#ECON-C201)   5 credits
Analysis of the aggregate economy: national income, inflation, business fluctuations, unemployment, monetary system, federal budget, international trade and finance.

Intermediate Microeconomics (WASH#ECON-C300)   5 credits
Choice decisions of individuals and firms: consequences of these decisions in product and factor markets. Consumption production and cost, exchange.

Geography of Cities (WASH#GEOG-C277)   5 credits
Study of (1) systems of cities - their location, distribution, functions and competition, and (2) their internal structure - the location of activities within urban areas. Particular emphasis on current urban problems - sprawl, housing, segregation, economic growth and metropolitan transportation.

Biological Aspects of Aging (WASH#UCONJ-C440)   3 credits
Introductory course on aspects of the biology of human aging and of functional changes associated with normal aging and with those illnesses that may be present in the elderly. Focus on the relationship between changes in physical function, environment and quality of life. Includes theoretical perspective on aging as well as the aging process in specific physiological systems. Designed for upper-level undergraduate students with an interest in aging. Prerequisite: introductory course in biology or permission of instructor.

A History of the US Since 1940 (WASH#HSTAA-C135)   5 credits
Through study of documents, personal testimony and other source materials, through written reports on historical problems, and through discussions, lectures, films and audiovisual presentations, students are encouraged to examine evidence and to think 'historically' about persons, events and movements within the memory of their own generation and that immediately preceding theirs.

History of Modern Japan (WASH#HSTAA-C432)   5 credits
Political, social, economic and cultural development of Japan from the late Tokugawa period to the present with special emphasis on the cultural impact of the West.

Philosophical Issues in the Law (WASH#PHIL-C114)   5 credits
Analysis and critical assessment of various philosophical issues in law and legal reasoning. Material drawn from actual law cases, as well as writings by contemporary philosophers of law and lawyers. Topics include criminal responsibility, civil disobedience, abortion, reverse discrimination and enforcement of morals. No special legal or philosophical training required.

Practical Reasoning (WASH#PHIL-C115)   5 credits
Introduction to logic emphasizing concepts and methods used for practical analysis of arguments in everyday contexts. Meaning, syllogism, logical diagrams, inductive and statistical inference, informal fallacies, argument structure, perhaps some beginning symbolic logic. a wide variety of examples, including logical puzzles are considered.

Introduction to Logic (WASH#PHIL-C120)   5 credits

Elementary symbolic logic. The development, application and theoretical properties of an artificial symbolic language designed to provide a clear representation of the logical structure of deductive arguments.

Introduction to Politics (WASH#POLS-C101)   5 credits

Introduction to thinking about the political problems that affect our lives and shape the world around us. Recommended for nonmajors, for students who are thinking about political science majors who haven't decided on an area of specialization.

Introduction to American Politics (WASH#POLS-C202)   5 credits

Introduction to people, institutions and politics in the American Political system. Provides various ways of thinking about how significant problems, crises and conflicts of American society are resolved politically.

The Politics of Mass Communi. in US (WASH#POLS-C305)   5 credits

Role of mass audiences in politics from the standpoint of the communi-cation strategies used to shape their political involvement. Topics include: social structure and political participation, political propaganda and persuasion, political uses of public opinion, and mass media and politics.

Intro to Personality & Differences (WASH#PSYCH-C205)   4 credits

Basic concepts, methods and background for more intensive study in the field of personality. Prerequisite: Psych 101 or 102, or equivalent.

Fundamentals of Psych. Research (WASH#PSYCH-C209)   4 credits

Psychological research methodology and techniques. Topics include the logic of hypothesis testing, experimental design, research strategies and techniques, fundamentals of scientific writing and ethical issues in psychological research. Prerequisite: Psych 101 or 102, or equivalent.

Elementary Psychological Statistics (WASH#PSYCH-C213)   6 credits

Applied statistics in psychology. Describing data, probability theory, stating and testing hypotheses in psychology. Covers the more commonly used inference tests. Required for majors registered in psychology bachelor of arts program. Prerequisites: Psych 209 and one and one-half years of high school algebra, or permission of instructor.

Developmental Psychology (WASH#PSYCH-C306)   5 credits

Analysis of psychological development of the child in relation to biological, physical and sociological antecedent conditions from infancy to adolescence. Prerequisite: Psych 101 or 102, or equivalent.

Social Psychology (WASH#PSYCH-C345)   5 credits

The effects of the social environment upon the formation of individual attitudes, values and beliefs, and upon individual attitudes, values and beliefs, and upon individual and group behavior. Discussion of major theoretical approaches and presentation of field and experimental research findings. Prerequisite: Psych 101 or 102, or equivalent.

Survey of Sociology (WASH#SOC-C110)   5 credits

Human interaction, social institutions, social stratification, socialization, deviance, social control, social and cultural change. Course content may change depending upon instructor.

Introduction to the Sociology of Deviance (WASH#SOC-C271)   5 credits

Examination of deviance, deviant behavior and social control. Deviance as a social process; types of deviant behavior (e.g., suicide, mental illness, drug use, crime, 'sexual deviance', delinquency); theories of deviance and deviant behavior; nature and social organization of societal reactions ad social and legal policy issues.

Socialization (WASH#SOC-C347)   5 credits

How social systems control the behavior of their constituents through the socialization process, sanctions, power, allocation of status and rewards.

Criminology (WASH#SOC-C371)   5 credits

Survey of legal definitions, types of criminal behavior, trends and patterns, recidivism, offender characteristics, environmental influences, diagnostics, prediction, theories of crime and delinquency prevention, social policy.

Developing a C Application (WASH#CPROG-C900)   4 CEUs

Students work one-on-one with the instructor to develop a C or C++ application which demonstrates their knowledge and skills. Participants taking this noncredit Distance Learning course prepare a proposal for an application project and develop a schedule for the project. They develop general source code, debug, improve and enhance the program, and prepare appropriate documentation to design a significant application in C or C++ in the areas of graphics, database or statistics. Participants who want to communicate with their instructors via email or need access to a C compiler receive a free six-month Uniform Access account when they register for the course. *This course is not offered for academic credit.* Prerequisite: a sequence of four C programming courses or six months of on-the-job C programming experience.

Webster University - 3 courses

Accredited by the North Central Accrediting Agency

> Webster University
> 470 East Lockwood Ave.
> St. Louis MO 63119

Webster University offers three courses by way of the Internet. The courses are regular university courses, 3 credits each. The usual tuition applies, but the application fee will be waived for non-degree seeking students.

phone: (314) 968-7170   email: bumbaugh@webster2.websteruniv.edu

Webster University Course Descriptions:

Introduction to Critical Thinking (WEBS#PHIL 1010)   3 credits

This course will be taught entirely via the Internet. Regular class meetings will be held in a social virtual reality space known as a MOO. Students will interact further with each other and with the instructor by some combination of electronic mail and additional meetings at the MOO. The standard format will be for the entire class to meet in the social virtual reality space for lecture and discussion during the scheduled period. Students will have assigned reading and writing to do in the intervening weeks. Students require full, interactive Internet access -- having just email won't do.

Contemporary Moral Problems (WEBS#PHIL 2032)   3 credits

This course will be taught exclusively on the net and all materials used will be taken from the net. Students will need access and must have use of email, news groups, ftp and World Wide Web. We will study six contemporary moral problems. Some of the student writings will be posted on various appropriate newsgroups and students will be responsible to respond to replies from both members of the class and non-members. At times we will arrange group discussions on a MOO (more details later) and these group sessions will be mandatory. However, most of the course will be run on time guidelines that will allow the student to maximize his or her own time choices.

Haitian History (WEBS#HST 2045)   3 credits

This course will be taught exclusively on the and all materials used will be taken from the with the exception of one book, which students must read and report on . Different students will read different books, depending on what is available at local libraries. Students will need access and must have use of email, news groups, ftp and World Wide Web. The guiding theme or thesis of the course is that in order to understand contemporary Haiti one must understand her in her development. Consequently, the course will be a constant dialectic between contemporary Haiti and her history.

University of Wisconsin - Madison - 12 courses   WISM

Accredited by the North Central Association of Colleges and Schools

Department of Engineering Professional Development
College of Engineering
University of Wisconsin-Madison
432 North Lake Street
Madison, Wisconsin 53706

MISSION STATEMENT

The Department of Engineering Professional Develoment is an internationally recognized, self-sustaining academic department of the University of Wisconsin-Madison. Our mission is to improve the practice of engineering and related professions for the benefit of society by:

* providing objective continuing education and credit instruction to practicing professionals and students
* conducting and disseminating research and
* enhancing the public's understanding of science and technology.

EPD Independent Study Courses

This is a listing of courses in engineering, disaster management, and computer science developed and administered by the University of Wisconsin-Madison, Department of Engineering Professional Development (EPD). Taking courses through EPD's Independent Study Program allows you to study when and where you choose, work at your own pace and receive one-on-one help from your instructor through the mail - or through the Internet. You may begin your course anytime and take up to one year to complete it.

Anyone may access these lessons for free. If you would like to register for continuing education credit, please contact Judy Faber by e-mail to faber@engr.wisc.edu.

For registration information please contact:
faber@engr.wisc.edu

Department of Engineering Professional Development
432 North Lake Street
Madison, Wisconsin 53706

Phone: 800-462-0876
Fax: 608-263-3160

University of Wisconsin-Madison Course Descriptions

These courses can be taken free of charge:

Most of the courses detailed below (except for the LISP programming ones) are available for free. You may use this material freely for educational purposes, giving credit to the authors and UW-Madison/ Extension. If you would like to register for credit, please write Judy Faber, Department of Engineering Professional Development, Correspondence Course Office, University of Wisconsin-Madison, 432 North Lake Street, Madison, WI 53706. Or by e-mail to faber@engr.wisc.edu, fax at 608/263-3160, toll-free phone at 800/462-0876 or direct phone at 608/262-1735.

Solid Waste Landfills (WISM#A180)   2 CEUs

Dealing with the vast quantities of waste our industrial society produces has become a major challenge for business and government. Improper disposal practices cause environmental degradation, need for costly corrective actions, and public opposition to the locating of new facilities. All solid waste professionals, those working in the solid waste industry, lawyers who have clients in the solid waste industry, citizens and public officials involved in developing solid waste policies, and other interested individuals will benefit from this course. This course presents the issues important for the design, planning, operation, closure and long term care of landfills. The lessons will describe the basic principles involved in developing and operating a state-of-the-art landfill.

Introduction to Solid Waste Landfills
Landfilling Principles
Landfill Gas Movement, Control and Uses
Leachate Control and Treatment
Evaluating a Potential Sanitary Landfill Site
Sanitary Landfill Design Procedure
Landfill Site Plan Preparation
Sanitary Landfill Operation
Disposal of Hazardous and Special Wastes
Landfill Closure and Long-term Care
Extended Reading List - Optional Sources

Solid Waste Recycling (WISM#A182)   2 CEUs

The objective of the course is to describe the available opportunities for recycling and the steps necessary to develop a successful recycling program. Subjects covered include:
- Recycling opportunities and approaches
- Alternative technologies for recycling materials
- Marketing recycled materials
- Planning a community recycling program
- Organizing a voluntary recycling program
- Implementing a mandatory recycling program
- Developing a recycling center
- Operating a commercial recycling service

<u>Solid Waste Composting (WISM#A184)</u>   <u>2 CEUs</u>

The objective of the course is to describe the available opportunities for composting and the steps necessary to develop a successful composting program. Subjects covered include:
- Recycling opportunities and approaches
- Alternative technologies for recycling materials
- Marketing recycled materials
- Planning a community recycling program
- Organizing a voluntary recycling program
- Implementing a mandatory recycling program
- Developing a recycling center

<u>Collecting & Transport Recyclables & Solid Waste (WISM#A186)</u>   <u>2 CEUs</u>

Learn principles and methods for developing an effective and efficient system for collecting recyclables and solid wastes. This course presents ways to meet the increasing pressure on haulers and municipalities to handle more materials in more ways, all without increasing costs. This self-study course consists of ten lessons with self-graded assignments and two university- graded exams. Only the two exams are mailed in. Satisfactory grades are required on the exams to earn the course CEU and Certificate of Completion. The course table of contents is listed below. The objective of the course is to describe the principles and methods of developing an effective and efficient system for collecting recyclables and solid wastes. Subjects to be covered include:

Defining Collection Needs and Developing an Integrated
Collection Strategy
Planning a High-Performance Collection System
Alternative Methods for Collection of Residential
Recyclables
Collection of Recyclables from Multi-Family Housing and Businesses
Collection of Yard Materials and Special Wastes
Collection Equipment Selection and Maintenance
Contracting for Collection Services
Financing Options for Collection Systems
Transfer Stations and Long-Haul Transport Systems
Safety, Health and Training for Collection Workers

<u>Aim and Scope of Disaster Management (WISM#AA02)</u>   <u>2 CEUs</u>

At the University of Wisconsin-Madison, the Disaster Management Center (UW-DMC) offers a program of continuing professional education in natural disaster and refugee emergency management.There is a curriculum for those involved worldwide in emergency preparedness, disaster relief and disaster mitigation. Educational materials have been prepared as self-study modules. While courses focus on third world disasters and emergencies, many under-lying principles can apply anywhere.

This self-study course will meet the needs of people involved in disaster management for both sudden-onset natural disasters (i.e., earthquakes, floods, hurricanes) and slow-onset disasters (i.e., famine, drought). This course is designed for government personnel, representatives of private voluntary agencies, and other individuals interested in disaster management. Course objectives:

<u>Lesson 1</u>: Develop an understanding of why and how the modern disaster manager is involved with pre-disaster and post-disaster activities. Understand the four work objectives of the disaster manager. Know the key personnel or specialists related to disaster management and associate them with the types of disasters and phases in which they are useful. Understand the six elements of disaster management.

<u>Lesson 2</u>: Develop an awareness of the chronological phases of natural disaster response and refugee relief operations. Understand how the phases of each are parallel and how they differ. Understand the key concepts of a) disaster management related to development, and b) the relationship of different disaster management activities to the appropriate disaster phase. Understand the relationship of disaster phases to each other and the linkage of activities from one phase to the next. Identify the major disaster types. Understand the "relief system" and the "disaster victim."

<u>Lesson 3</u>: Identify the organizations that are involved in natural disaster assistance. Differentiate between disaster assistance for refugee operations and for natural disasters. Understand traditional patterns of foreign assistance. Be able to relate victims to assistance models.

<u>Lesson 4</u>: Describe the four sets of tools available to disaster managers Describe the three planning strategies useful in mitigation. Identify the regulatory controls used in hazard management. Describe public awareness and economic incentive possibilities. Understand the tools of post-disaster management.

<u>Lesson 5</u>: Describe the eight principal disaster management technologies with which a disaster manager should be familiar. Identify other supplemental skills that could be useful.

Principles of Disaser Management (WISM#AA04)   2 CEUs

Disaster management as an identifiable profession is relatively new. The tasks of a disaster manager, however, have been around for a long time. They have typically been thought of as disaster relief assistance, or of specific ad hoc activities during and after a disaster emergency. Many people have been disaster managers without thinking of themselves in that term. There has been a growing awareness in recent years that all of these activities, in fact, comprise the process of disaster management. By understanding this as an identifiable role, we can describe a coherent and cohesive direction for people who are involved in the field of disasters. This, of course, includes the spectrum of activities from administration to project implementation; from disaster prevention to disaster mitigation to disaster preparedness to disaster response.

Disaster management is not necessarily a full-time activity. Indeed, for most people in the field, their concerns for disaster issues form only a part of their total responsibilities. Similarly, this course is not designed for only full-time professional disaster managers. Rather it is intended to be useful even for individuals who expect to be active only during some aspect of disaster related operations. One of the ideal objectives of this course and of the Disaster Management Center (DMC) is for disaster managers eventually to work themselves out of their job. The ultimate success of disaster management would be the elimination of the underlying causes of disasters which would contribute to disaster prevention. Obviously, total prevention will not be feasible, but minimizing the people's vulnerability to disaster and responding to emergencies in positive ways will make an enormous impact on the current deadly state of disaster events.

This self-study course will meet the needs of people involved in disaster management for both sudden-onset natural disasters (i.e., earthquakes, floods, hurricanes) and slow-onset disasters (i.e., famine, drought). This course is designed for government personnel, representatives of private voluntary agencies, and individuals interested in disaster management.

Natural Hazards: Causes and Effects Introduction (WISM#BB02) 3 CEUs

This course is an introduction to the topic of natural hazards, their causes and their consequences. The subject is so vast that this course cannot begin to provide a definitive treatment of all aspects of these hazards. Instead, it seeks to present an overview of the general subject. The course begins with a definition of each major natural hazard that disaster managers may encounter in developing countries. Historical examples are presented to give perspective to the potential scope of these natural events and their actual effects within a community or country. The geographical distribution of the hazard type, indicating the possibility of its occurrence in all parts of the world, is shown. The natural pre-conditions that must exist for the phenomenon to occur are described. The actual event is described in its physical/natural manifestation, with a detailed account of what happens and why, before, during and after the event. The impact on the natural and human- produced environment-the reason it becomes a "disaster" rather than simply a natural phenomenon-is reviewed. Each lesson then discusses what disaster managers in particular and the public in general can do to prepare for disasters, to reduce their effects, or to respond to them in case they occur.

There are extensive libraries covering all the aspects that are touched on in this course, and it is not possible to give a definitive treatment to each topic within the context of an introductory text. Consequently, the editors of this course have sought to identify and utilize the most current and authoritative information and resources on the issues addressed here. In some cases, this has meant not using the most scholarly or in-depth resource, but rather the most useful to a professional disaster manager who is probably a lay person in terms of the earth sciences. Disaster management as an identifiable profession is relatively new. The tasks of a disaster manager, however, have been around for a long time. They have typically been thought of as disaster relief assistance, or as specific ad hoc activities during and after a disaster emergency. Many people have been disaster managers without thinking of themselves in that term.

There has been a growing awareness in recent years that all of these activities, in fact, comprise the process of disaster management. By understanding this as an identifiable role, we can describe a coherent and cohesive direction for people who are involved in the field of disasters. This, of course, includes the spectrum of activities from administration to project implementation: disaster prevention, disaster mitigation, disaster preparedness, and disaster response. Disaster management is not necessarily a full-time activity. Indeed, for most people in the field, concerns for disaster issues form only a part of their total responsibilities. Similarly, this course is not designed for only full-time professional disaster managers. Rather it is intended to be useful even for individuals who expect to be active only during some aspect of disaster-related operations.

Disaster Preparedness (WISM#BB04)   2.5 CEUs

Disaster management as an identifiable profession is relatively new. The tasks of a disaster manager, however, have been around for a long time. They have typically been thought of as disaster relief assistance, or as specific ad hoc activities during and after a disaster emergency. Many people have been disaster managers without thinking of themselves in that term. There has been a growing awareness in recent years that all of these activities, in fact, comprise the process of disaster management. By understanding this as an identifiable role, we can describe a coherent and cohesive direction for people who are involved in the field of disasters. This, of course, includes the spectrum of activities from administration to project implementation: disaster prevention, disaster mitigation, disaster preparedness, and disaster response.

Disaster management is not necessarily a full-time activity. Indeed, for most people in the field, concerns for disaster issues form only a part of their total responsibilities. Similarly, this course is not designed for only full-time professional disaster managers. Rather it is intended to be useful even for individuals who expect to be active only during some aspect of disaster-related operations.

Damage and Needs Assessment (WISM#BB06)   3 CEUs

Disaster management as an identifiable profession is relatively new. The tasks of a disaster manager, however, have been around for a long time. They have typically been thought of as disaster relief assistance, or as specific ad hoc activities during and after a disaster managers without thinking of themselves in that term.

There has been a growing awareness in recent years that all of these activities, in fact, comprise the process of disaster management. By understanding this as an identifiable role, we can describe a coherent and cohesive direction for people who are involved in the field of disasters. This, of course, includes the spectrum of activities from administration to project implementation: disaster prevention, disaster mitigation, disaster preparedness, and disaster response.

Disaster management is not necessarily a full-time activity. Indeed, for most people in the field, concerns for disaster issues form only a part of their total responsibilities. Similarly, this course is not designed for only full-time professional disaster managers. Rather it is intended to be useful even for individuals who expect to be active only during some aspect of disaster-related operations.

One of the ideal objectives of this course and of the Disaster Management Center (DMC) is that disaster managers eventually work themselves out of their jobs. The ultimate success of disaster management would be the elimination of the underlying causes of disasters; this would contribute to minimizing the people's vulnerability to disaster. Positive responses to emergencies will make an enormous impact on the current deadly state of disaster events.

To move towards those idealize objectives will require more form disaster managers than an understanding of the aim and scope of their jobs. It will also require development of several skills and technologies. The Disaster Management Center views this course as one component of a training program that will contribute towards those skills and techniques.

Disaster Response (WISM#BB08)   3 CEUs

This course introduces disaster managers at various operational levels to decisions and actions required at the disaster site by local, regional, national and international agencies involved in disaster relief and reconstruction. The text is primarily oriented to disasters occurring in the Third World and is aimed at government officials who are responsible for any aspect of disaster preparedness or response. Another primary audience is the middle management of voluntary agencies. Sections have been included which explain the roles of these non-governmental organizations and international organizations. In this way, all those involved in disaster response should benefit from an awareness of the needs and requirements of other agencies.

This textbook is essentially an anthology from recent disaster literature, drawing on the knowledge of a large number of people and institutions currently working in the disaster field. It reflects not only the growing experience on the part of professional disaster managers but also the awareness of the need to document these experiences and lessons learned. This volume, Disaster Response, is a companion to the texts Disaster Preparedness, Disaster Assessment, and Aim and Scope of Disaster Management. These are self-study courses offered by the Disaster Management Center. They have a similar format to this course and complement the information of this text.

NOTE: The courses detailed below are not available for free, as are the ones described above.

Introduction to AutoLISP Programming (WISM#A430)   4 CEUs

The CADalyst/University of Wisconsin--Madison Introduction to AutoLISP Programming is an eight-lesson correspondence course. The series of lessons shows you how to customize AutoCAD, turning the general purpose design package into an even more powerful tool for your particular needs. Designed for experienced users of AutoCAD, the course does not require prior knowledge of programming. You only need to know a little about creating menu macro commands and to have used a text editor, such as the DOS EDLIN. At the end of the course, you will be able to write intelligent programs that will make AutoCAD conform to your own unique requirements.

1. Lesson One - An introduction to AutoLISP
   o What is AutoLISP?
   o AutoLISP data types and atoms
   o Executing AutoLISP
   o Execution by typing in an AutoLISP expression
   o Execution from an ASCII file
   o AutoLISP execution from menu macros
   o Global and local variables
   o Homework questions
2. Lesson Two - AutoLISP program evaluation and control
   o Special characters for programming
   o AutoLISP Function Formats and Arguments
   o Assignment and use of variables
   o AutoLISP evaluation - Evaluation and quote
   o Nesting of functions and parenthesis control
   o Error checking for parentheses and variable values
   o Example programs
   o Homework questions
3. Lesson Three - Manipulating lists with AutoLISP
   o Program structure
   o Manipulating lists - list, car, cdr examples and combinations
   o nth item of a list
   o Constructing lists - cons, append, and member functions
   o Do's and don'ts for appending expressions
   o Examples of working with lists
   o Homework programming assignments
4. Lesson Four - AutoLISP functions for math and geometry
   o Math functions
   o Converting angles in degrees to radians
   o Geometry with AutoLISP
   o Drawing geometric shapes
   o Some 'GET...' functions
   o Polar and Cartesian coordinates
   o Using internally defined functions
   o Programming examples
   o Homework programming assignments

5. Lesson Five - User interaction in AutoLISP
    o User interaction with the GET... function
    o Initial conditions for GET... functions
    o Printing functions
    o Prompting for user input
    o Programming examples
    o Homework programming assignments
6. Lesson Six - Input/output and file handling with AutoLISP
    o Printing functions - using print functions for 'clean' endings
    o Testing and debugging techniques
    o Programming techniques for reducing the number of variables
    o Error handling
    o A modular approach to programming
    o Example programs
    o Homework programming assignments
7. Lesson Seven - Logic and branching out with AutoLISP
    o Relational functions - equality, ">", "<", 'not' functions
    o Logical functions - and, or, not, null functions
    o Branching functions - 'if' functions, use of 'progn' functions, branching with 'cond'
    o Example programs
    o Homework programming assignments
8. Lesson Eight - Intelligent programming with AutoLISP
    o Looping functions - while and foreach
    o An intelligent cross-hatching program
    o Menus for AutoLISP program development
    o Homework programming assignments

Advanced AutoLISP Programming (WISM#A432)   5.0 CEUs

The CADalyst/University of Wisconsin--Madison Advanced AutoLISP Programming is an eight-lesson correspondence course. The series of lessons shows you how to customize AutoCAD, turning the general purpose design package into an even more powerful tool for your particular needs. Designed for experienced users of AutoCAD, the course requires that you know AutoLISP programming through looping and branching functions. If you do not have this level of expertise with AutoLISP, you should enroll in the Introduction to AutoLISP Programming course instead. At the end of the advanced course, you will be able to delve into AutoCAD objects, and more for a variety of applications.

Lesson One - AutoLISP Programming Techniques
    o Program Structure
    o The AutoLISP error handler
    o Techniques for 'test' arguments in looping and branching
    o Program development
    o Prototype programs
Lesson Two - System Variables and Interfacing with AutoCAD
    o Some useful system variables for AutoLISP
    o AutoCAD tables and the Drawing Exchange Format (DXF)
    o DXF group codes and AutoLISP association lists

o Table association lists
o Example programs
o Homework questions
Lesson Three - Entity Selection for AutoLISP
o Entity selection functions
o Using filter lists
o Manipulating selection lists
o Homework programming assignments
Lesson Four - AutoLISP Data Base Manipulations
o Entity functions
o Association and substitution
o Programming examples
o Homework programming assignments
Lesson Five - AutoCAD Complex Entities
o Blocks and inserts
o Making blocks
o Listing the data structure for blocks and inserts
o Programming examples
o Homework programming assignments
Lesson Six - AutoLISP Anonymous Blocks
o The structure of anonymous blocks
o Creating anonymous blocks
o Extended entity data - an introduction
o Example programs
o Homework programming assignments
Lesson Seven - Extended Entity Data
o Extended entity DXF group codes
o Applications and registration for XDATA
o Creating and appending XDATA
o Example programs
o Homework programming assignments
Lesson Eight - More Programming Techniques
o Programming for surface modeling
o Fast processing of point lists
o Menus for AutoLISP program development
o Homework programming assignments

University of Wisconsin - Stout - 6 courses

Accredited by the North Central Association of Colleges and Secondary Schools and the National Council for Accreditation of Teacher Education.

Electronic University Network
1977 Colestin Rd.
Hornbrook CA 96044
800-225-3276

UW-Stout provides statewide, national and international service through its educational programs. With an enrollment of about 7,200, the university offers undergraduate, graduate, and postgraduate degrees in a variety of majors, most of them specialized subjects related to the fields of industry, commerce, education, and human services. Recently, an undergraduate degree in manufacturing engineering, and a graduate degree in training and development were approved.

UW-Stout is the second oldest graduate institution in the University of Wisconsin System. More than 7,000 students have graduated from UW-Stout's 13 master's degree programs and two educational specialist programs since the institution began offering graduate programming in 1935. For more information about UW-Stout's graduate college, write to: Graduate College, 417 Bowman Hall, UW-Stout, Menomonie WI 54751; or call: (715-232-2211); or send email to: tknous@uwstout.edu.

UW-STOUT'S MISSION: UW-Stout, as a special mission institution, serves a unique role in the University of Wisconsin System. UW-Stout is characterized by a distinctive array of programs leading to professional careers focused on the needs of society. These programs are presented through an approach to learning which involves combining theory, practice, and experimentation. Extending this special mission into the future requires that instruction, research and public service programs be adapted and modified as the needs of society change.

The University of Wisconsin Stout, in partnership with the Electronic University Network and America Online, is linking professors and students. Anyone anywhere in the country with access to a modem-equipped computer may register for these online courses. Online students meet with their instructors, socialize with other students, and obtain instructional resources using the electronic conferencing facilities of the Electronic University Networks online campus.

COURSE FEES include the following: college tuition; one-on-one tutoring with your instructor; class discussions and seminars; the course teleguide; final exam and transcript; and academic and technical support. Textbooks and shipping are extra and cost about $50 per course.

Child Development I (4 credits)
Residents of:
Wisconsin, $386.39
Minnesota, $439.39
All other states, $1184.39

Technical Writing (3 credits)
Residents of:
Wisconsin, undergrad $289.98
    grad $473.20
Minnesota, undergrad $329.73
    grad $470.20
Other states, undergrad, $888.48
    grad $1429.45

Nutrition for Healthy Living (2 cr.)
Residents of:
Wisconsin, $193.57
Minnesota, $220.07
All other states, $592.57

Foundations in Rehab. (3 cr.)
Residents of:
Wisconsin, $473.20
Minnesota, $470.20
*All other states, $1429.45

*Out of state tuition waiver may be available

Director of Admissions
University of Wisconsin-Stout
PO Box 790
Menomonie, Wisconsin 54751-0790

Call 1-800-225-3276 between 8:30 am and 5:30 pm Pacific time, M-F.
Email: EUNCouncil@aol.com   or   conted@uwstout.edu

Course Descriptions:

Child Development (WISS#212-124(50))   4 credits

The study of growth and development in the young child ages prenatal through late childhood are explored in this foundational course. Emphasis is placed on basic principles of development, fundamental sequences, and the context in which development occurs. Advanced placement high school students interested in a career in Early Childhood Education, Human Development and Family Studies, or Family and Consumer Educational Services are encouraged to register for this course.

Foundations in Rehabilitation (WISS#459-701(50))   3 credits

The foundations of vocational rehabilitation as practiced in the United States will be explored in this course. The course will include discussions of the philosophical foundations of rehabilitation, including historical development and current organization; professional roles, responsibilities, and practices; and future trends. This course would be appropriate for professionals working in the human service field, allied helping professions, and anyone interested in exploring the rehabilitation field.

Individual Research I (WISS#479-480(50))   1 credit

Preliminaries of active research through the development of a research proposal which includes the problem statement, review of the literature and the design of the research project is covered in this class designed to be immediately followed by 479-481(50), Individual Research II. These tandem courses may well serve professionals interested in gathering information related to diverse fields, such as personnel, quality control, sales, etc.

Individual Research II (WISS#479-481(50))   1 credit

Research in a personal area of interest within the behavioral sciences. Requirements include the completion of a research report which meets American Psychological Association guidelines. Individual Research I, 479-480(50) is prerequisite to this course.

Nutrition for Healthy Living (WISS#229-202(50))   2 credits

Food selection and eating patterns, standards, applied nutrition knowledge and interrelationships, nutrition information source analysis, weight management, and the nutrition-exercise-fitness connection will be explored in this course. The course is appropriate for nursing assistants, direct care staff in group homes and nursing homes, foodservice workers, and daycare providers as well as early childhood educators and individuals interested in their personal health.

Technical Writing (WISS#326-515(50))   3 credits

Technical writing is the practical writing that people do as part of their job. This course will focus on designing technical documents for on-the-job professionals. Students will learn to develop a sophisticated sense of audience, to define their communication purpose, to organize technical information effectively, and to present information in a professional format. Course activities will mirror actual on-the-job writing situations where people frequently collaborate on projects and edit and review colleagues' writing. This course satisfies tech prep requirements for secondary teachers.

Lists

Lists

Internet Study Resources for Students:

There are eight lists in this section. These are sources of information for you to use in study and research. Bear in mind that things are changing so fast on the Internet that any source you check may have moved to another address or gone out of business all together! For updates check subsequent editions of **The Internet University - College Courses by Computer**; or be sure and check out this book's website. Just point your browser to this URL:

http://www.caso.com/

These eight lists are provided to get you on your way. Lists are best presented online, since updates can be made regularly, a fact that is impossible with paper-based lists, but these have been designed to be useful to you, the online student. A summary of the lists:

List 1 - Internet Providers by Area Code: will give you some providers in your area to gather price and service from. Identify some in your area and apply the questionnaire on pages 38-40. Bear in mind that this market is very volatile, and that providers come and go with remarkable speed.

List 2 - Mailing Lists for the Student: Review the section on mailing lists (pages 31 and 65) and subscribe to one or two as an experiment. Some are very useful and some are loaded with 'noise'. Review the 'history of mailing lists' on page 66.

List 3 - Usenet Newsgroups for the Student: Usenet Newsgroups are something like globally-based bulletin boards, and there are literally thousands of interest groups which run an ongoing conversation via this medium. List 3 contains the names of hundreds of newsgroups. You can gather from the name what the subject matter of the list is.

List 4 - Telnet Sites for the Student: Colleges and libraries generally allow free remote logon to their computer systems. This list includes many of these addresses with passwords. Remember that we are allowed to visit these sites without charge as a courtesy, and don't try to 'wander' into prohibited sites.

List 5 - FTP Sites for the Student: These are servers in the Internet world that allow you to log on 'anonymously' and download files to your own computer. These will include academic or scientific papers, programs, or graphics, etc.

List 6 - Educational Websites: A random assortment of URLs. If you visit the companion website for The Internet University you will find this list in a 'live' format, and be able to visit them with the click of the mouse. Or, you can enter the chosen URL into your browser and away you go.

List 7 - College and University Websites: A list of 'official' websites for some of the world's colleges and universities. This list is certainly destined multiply in size over the next months and years.

List 8 - Yanoff's Internet Services List: An excerpt of one of the most comprehensive collection of Internet resources available on the Internet. This one is maintained by Scott Yanoff, an Internet hero and legend; it provides Gopher and WWW addresses for a wide variety of sites.

Please consider this request from your publisher. Any list is only as comprehensive as the data-collection process that preceeded it. If you know of any online resource that you think would improve any of these lists, please forward the information to us. To aid in this process we have designated a 'mailbox' on our server for this information. Simply forward any suggestions, additions or corrections that may occur to you via email to:

tellus@caso.com

To demonstrate our appreciation for your help, every month we draw a name from among all contributors and send that lucky person a free copy of the latest edition of our book The Internet University.

List 1 - Internet Providers by Area Code

Area Code 202

Connection	(201) 435-4414	info@cnct.com
Dorsai Embassy	(718) 392-3667	info@dorsai.org
Echo Communications	(212) 255-3839	info@echonyc.com
Global Enterprise Services	(800) 358-4437	info@jvnc.net
INTAC Access Corporation	(201) 944-1417	info@intac.com
Interactive Networks, Inc.	(800) 561-1878	info@interactive.net
Mordor International	(201) 433-7343	info@ritz.mordor.com
National Internet Source, Inc.	(201) 825-4600	info@maple.nis.net
Neighborhood Internet Connect.	(201) 934-1445	info@nic.com
New York Net	(718) 776-6811	info@new-york.net
Planet Access Networks	(201) 691-4704	info@planet.net
Zone One Network Exchange	(718) 549-8078	info@zone.net

Area Code 202

Capitol Area Internet Service	(703) 448-4470	info@cais.com
Charm Net	(410) 558-3900	info@charm.net
Clark Internet Services Inc.	(410) 730-9764	info@clark.net
Digital Express Group	(800) 969-9090	info@digex.net
Global Enterprise Services	(800) 358-4437	info@jvnc.net
Merit Network, Inc.	(313) 764-9430	info@merit.edu
Meta Network	(703) 243-6622	info@tmn.com
NCM, Inc.	(703) 749-9150	info@tpe.ncm.com
NovaNet, Inc.	(703) 524-4800	info@novanet.com
US Net, Inc.	(301) 572-5926	info@us.net

Area Code 203

Connix	(203) 349-7059	info@connix.com
Dorsai Embassy	(718) 392-3667	info@dorsai.org
Global Enterprise Services	(800) 358-4437	info@jvnc.net
NetAxis	(203) 969-0618	info@netaxis.com
New York Net	(718) 776-6811	info@new-york.net
PCNet	(800) 664-4638	info@pcnet.com

Area Code 204

MBnet	(204) 474-8230	info@mbnet.mb.ca

Area Code 205

InterQuest Online Services	(205) 464-8280	info@iquest.com
Nuance Network Services	(205) 533-4296	info@nuance.com
Planet Access Networks	(201) 691-4704	info@planet.net
Traveller Information Services	(800) 840-8638	info@traveller.com

Area Code 206

Cyberlink Communications	(206) 281-5397	info@cyberspace.com
Eskimo North	(206) 367-7457	info@eskimo.com
Halcyon	(206) 426 9298	info@halcyon.com
NETCOM Online	(800) 501-8649	info@netcom.com
Network Access Services	(206) 733-9279	info@nas.com
NorthWest CommLink	(206) 336-0103	info@nwcl.net

Provider	*Phone*	*Email*
Northwest Nexus Inc.	(206) 455-3505	info@nwnexus.wa.com
NorthWestNet	(206) 562-3000	info@nwnet.net
Olympus	(206) 385-0464	info@pt.olympus.net
Pacific Rim Network, Inc.	(206) 650-0442	info@pacificrim.com
Pacifier Computers	(206) 693-2116	info@pacifier.com
SeaNet	(206) 343-7828	info@seanet.com
Skagit On-Line Services	(206) 755-0190	info@sos.net
Townsend Communcations, Inc.	(206) 385-0464	info@olympus.net
WLN Internet Services	(800) 342-5956	info@wln.com
World dot Net	(206) 576 7147	info@world.net

Area Code 207
maine.net, Inc.	(207) 780-6381	info@maine.net

Area Code 208
WLN Internet Services	(800) 342-5956	info@wln.com

Area Code 209
California West Coast Online!	(707) 586-3060	info@calon.com
Sacramento Network Access, Inc.	(916) 565-4500	info@sna.com

Area Code 210
Freeside Communications	(800) 968-8750	info@fc.net

Area Code 212
Blythe Systems	(212) 348-2875	info@blythe.org
Dorsai Embassy	(718) 392-3667	info@dorsai.org
Echo Communications	(212) 255-3839	info@echonyc.com
Escape	(212) 888-8780	info@escape.com
Global Enterprise Services	(800) 358-4437	info@jvnc.net
Ingress Communications	(212) 679-8592	info@ingress.com
Interport Communications	(212) 989-1128	info@interport.net
Maestro Technologies, Inc.	(212) 240-9600	info@maestro.com
Mordor International	(201) 433-7343	info@ritz.mordor.com
Network 23, Inc.	(212) 786-4810	info@net23.com
New York Net	(718) 776-6811	info@new-york.net
PANIX Public Access Unix	(212) 741-4400	info@panix.com
Phantom Access Technologies	(212) 989-2418	info@phantom.com
Pipeline Network	(212) 267-3636	info@pipeline.com
Zone One Network Exchange	(718) 549-8078	info@zone.net

Area Code 213
DHM Information Management	(310) 214-3349	info@dhm.com
DigiLink Network Services	(310) 542-7421	info@digilink.net
Earthlink Network	(213) 644-9500	info@earthlink.net
KAIWAN Corporation	(714) 638-2139	info@kaiwan.com
Primenet	(800) 463-8386	info@primenet.com
ViaNet Communications	(415) 903-2242	info@via.net

Area Code 214
Dallas Vietnamese Network	(214) 248-8701	info@sdf.lonestar.org

Provider	Phone	Email
DFW Internet Services, Inc.	(817) 332-5116	info@dfw.net
Metronet, Inc.	(214) 705-2900	info@metronet.com
NETCOM Online	(800) 501-8649	info@netcom.com

Area Code 215

FishNet	(610) 337-9994	info@pond.com
Global Enterprise Services	(800) 358-4437	info@jvnc.net
PREPnet	(412) 268-7870	info@prep.net
VoiceNet/DCS	(215) 674-9290	info@voicenet.com
You Tools Corporation	(610) 954-5910	info@youtools.com

Area Code 216

APK Network Services	(216) 481-9445	info@wariat.org
Exchange Network Services, Inc.	(216) 261-4593	info@en.com
OARnet	(800) 627-8101	info@oar.net

Area Code 217

FGInet, Inc.	(217) 544-2775	info@mail.fgi.net

Area Code 218

Minnesota Regional Network	(612) 342-2570	info@mr.net
Red River Net	(701) 232-2227	info@rrnet.com

Area Code 300

Community News Service	(719) 592-1240	info@cscns.com

Area Code 301

Capitol Area Internet Service	(703) 448-4470	info@cais.com
Charm Net	(410) 558-3900	info@charm.net
Clark Internet Services Inc.	(410) 730-9764	info@clark.net
Digital Express Group	(800) 969-9090	info@digex.net
FredNet	(301) 698-2386	info@fred.net
Gotham Communications	(301) 924-5998	info@gotham.com
Merit Network, Inc.	(313) 764-9430	info@merit.edu
Meta Network	(703) 243-6622	info@tmn.com
NCM, Inc.	(703) 749-9150	info@tpe.ncm.com
NovaNet, Inc.	(703) 524-4800	info@novanet.com
SURAnet	(301) 982-4600	info@sura.net
US Net, Inc.	(301) 572-5926	info@us.net

Area Code 302

SSNet, Inc.	(302) 378-1386	info@ssnet.com
Systems Solutions	(800) 331-1386	info@marlin.ssnet.com

Area Code 303

Colorado Internet Coop Assoc.	(303) 443-3786	info@coop.net
Colorado SuperNet	(303) 296-8202	info@csn.org
Denver Area Super Hwy.	(800) 624-8597	info@dash.com
Internet Express	(800) 592-1240	info@usa.net
NETCOM Online	(800) 501-8649	info@netcom.com
New Mexico Technet, Inc.	(505) 345-6555	info@technet.nm.org
Nyx, the Spirit of the Night	(303) 871-3308	info@nyx.cs.du.edu

Provider	Phone	Email
Rocky Mountain Internet	(800) 900-7644	info@rmii.com
Westnet	(914) 967-7816	info@westnet.net

Area Code 304

WVNET	(304) 293-5192	info@wvnvms.wvnet.edu

Area Code 305

Acquired Knowledge Sys.	(305) 525-2574	info@aksi.net
CyberGate	(305) 428-4283	info@gate.net
Florida Online	(407) 635-8888	info@digital.net
IDS World Network	(800) 437-1680	info@ids.net
SatelNET Communications	(305) 434-8738	info@satelnet.org

Area Code 306

SASK#net	(306) 966-4860	info@admin.usask.ca

Area Code 309

netILLINOIS	(708) 866-1825	info@illinois.net

Area Code 310

DHM Information Management	(310) 214-3349	info@dhm.com
DigiLink Network Services	(310) 542-7421	info@digilink.net
Earthlink Network	(213) 644-9500	info@earthlink.net
ISI Network Associates	(310) 822 1511	info@isi.edu
KAIWAN Corporation	(714) 638-2139	info@kaiwan.com
Lightside, Inc.	(818) 858-9261	info@lightside.com
NETCOM Online	(800) 501-8649	info@netcom.com
ViaNet Communications	(415) 903-2242	info@via.net

Area Code 312

American Info Systems	(708) 413-8400	info@ais.net
MCSNet	(312) 248-8649	info@mcs.net
Net Information Systems	(708) 983-6064	info@xnet.com
NETCOM Online	(800) 501-8649	info@netcom.com
Ripco Communcations, Inc.	(312) 665-0065	info@ripco.com
Tezcatlipoca, Inc.	(312) 850-0181	info@tezcat.com
WorldWide Access	(708) 367-1870	info@wwa.com

Area Code 313

Merit Network, Inc.	(313) 764-9430	info@merit.edu
Innovative Concepts	(313) 998-0090	info@ic.net
Innovative Data Services	(810) 478-3554	info@id.net
MSen Connection Services	(313) 998-4562	info@msen.com

Area Code 314

ThoughtPort Inc.	(314) 474-6870	info@thoughtport.com
MOREnet	(314) 882-2000	info@more.net
STARnet	(314) 935 7390	info@wugate.wustl.edu

Area Code 315

NYSERNet	(315) 453-2912	info@nysernet.org

Provider	*Phone*	*Email*

Area Code 316
Tyrell Corp.   (800) 897-3551   info@tyrell.com

Area Code 317
IQuest Network Services   (800) 844-8649   info@iquest.net
Network Link, Inc.   (619) 278-5943   info@tnl1.tnwl.com

Area Code 319
Planet Access Networks   (201) 691-4704   info@planet.net

Area Code 401
Anomaly   (401) 273-4669   info@anomaly.sbs.risc.net
Global Enterprise Services   (800) 358-4437   info@jvnc.net
IDS World Network   (800) 437-1680   info@ids.net

Area Code 402
Internet Nebraska Corp.   (402) 434-8680   info@inetnebr.com
MIDnet   (402) 472-7600   info@westie.mid.net
Synergy Communications   (402) 346-4638   info@synergy.net

Area Code 403
PUCnet Computer Connections   (403) 448-1901   info@pucnet.com
UUNET Canada, Inc.   (416) 368-6621   info@uunet.ca

Area Code 404
Intergate, Inc.   (404) 429-9599   info@intergate.net
Internet Atlanta   (404) 410-9000   info@atlanta.net
Internet Services of Atlanta   (404) 454-4638   info@is.net
Lyceum   (404) 377-7575   info@lyceum.com
MindSpring Enterprises, Inc.   (404) 888-0725   info@mindspring.com
NETCOM Online   (800) 501-8649   info@netcom.com
Ping   (800) 746-4835   info@ping.com

Area Code 405
GSS Internet   (918) 835-3655   info@galstar.com

Area Code 406
WLN Internet Services   (800) 342-5956   info@wln.com

Area Code 407
CyberGate   (305) 428-4283   info@gate.net
InternetU   (407) 952-8487   info@iu.net
Florida Online   (407) 635-8888   info@digital.net
IDS World Network   (800) 437-1680   info@ids.net

Area Code 408
a2i communications   (408) 293-8078   info@rahul.net
Aimnet Information Svs.   (408) 257-0900   info@aimnet.com
Best Internet Communications   (415) 964-2378   info@best.com
California West Coast Online!   (707) 586-3060   info@calon.com
CCnet Communications   (510) 988-0680   info@ccnet.com
Darex Associates   (415) 903-4720   info@darex.com

Provider	*Phone*	*Email*
Duck Pond	(408) 249-9630	info@kfu.com
ElectriCiti Incorporated	(619) 338-9000	info@electriciti.com
Internet Connection	(408) 461-4638	info@ico.net
InterNex Information Services	(415) 473-3060	info@internex.net
NETCOM Online	(800) 501-8649	info@netcom.com
Portal Information Network	(800) 433-6444	info@portal.com
Portal System	(408) 973-9111	info@cup.portal.com
Scruz-Net	(800) 319-5555	info@scruz.net
South Valley Internet	(408) 683-4533	info@garlic.com
ViaNet Communications	(415) 903-2242	info@via.net
zNET	(408) 477-9638	info@znet.com

Area Code 409

Info-Highway International, Inc.	(800) 256-1370	info@infohwy.com
Internet Connect Services	(512) 572-9987	info@icsi.net

Area Code 410

Capitol Area Internet Service	(703) 448-4470	info@cais.com
Charm Net	(410) 558-3900	info@charm.net
Clark Internet Services Inc.	(410) 730-9764	info@clark.net
Digital Express Group	(800) 969-9090	info@digex.net

Area Code 412

PREPnet	(412) 268-7870	info@prep.net
PSCNET	(412) 268-4960	info@psc.net
Telerama Public Access Internet	(412) 481-3505	info@telerama.lm.com

Area Code 414

BINCnet	(608) 233-5222	info@binc.net
Exec-PC	(800) 393-2721	info@earth.execpc.com
Internet Connect, Inc.	(414) 476-4266	info@inc.net
MIX Communications	(414) 228-0739	info@mixcom.com

Area Code 415

a2i communications	(408) 293-8078	info@rahul.net
Aimnet Information Svs.	(408) 257-0900	info@aimnet.com
Best Internet Communications	(415) 964-2378	info@best.com
California West Coast Online!	(707) 586-3060	info@calon.com
CCnet Communications	(510) 988-0680	info@ccnet.com
Darex Associates	(415) 903-4720	info@darex.com
ElectriCiti Incorporated	(619) 338-9000	info@electriciti.com
Institute for Global Comm.	(415) 442-0220	info@igc.apg.org
Internet Service Provider	(415) 941-2641	info@aplatform.com
InterNex Information Services	(415) 473-3060	info@internex.net
LineX Communcations	(415) 455-1650	info@linex.com
Little Garden	(415) 487-1902	info@tlg.org
NETCOM Online	(800) 501-8649	info@netcom.com
North Bay Network	(415) 472-1600	info@nbn.com
Portal System	(408) 973-9111	info@cup.portal.com
QuakeNet	(415) 655-6607	info@quake.net
Scruz-Net	(800) 319-5555	info@scruz.net

Provider	_Phone_	_Email_
Sirius Connections	(415) 284-4700	info@sirius.com
ViaNet Communications	(415) 903-2242	info@via.net
WELL	(415) 332-4335	info@well.com

Area Code 416

HookUp Communication	(519) 747-4110	info@hookup.net
ONet	(905) 525 9140	info@onet.on.ca
UUNET Canada, Inc.	(416) 368-6621	info@uunet.ca
UUnorth	(416) 225-8649	info@uunorth.north.net

Area Code 419

OARnet	(800) 627-8101	info@oar.net

Area Code 501

Sibylline, Inc.	(501) 521-4660	info@sibylline.com

Area Code 502

IgLou Internet Services	(800) 436-4456	info@iglou.com

Area Code 503

Hevanet Communications	(503) 228-3520	info@hevanet.com
Internetworks	(503) 233-4774	info@i.net
NETCOM Online	(800) 501-8649	info@netcom.com
RainDrop Laboratories	(503) 293-1772	info@agora.rain.com
RAINet	(503) 297-8820	info@rain.com
Teleport	(503) 223-0076	info@teleport.com
WLN Internet Services	(800) 342-5956	info@wln.com

Area Code 504

NeoSoft Internet Services	(713) 684-5969	info@neosoft.com
Tyrell Corp.	(800) 897-3551	info@tyrell.com

Area Code 505

Internet Express	(800) 592-1240	info@usa.net
New Mexico Technet, Inc.	(505) 345-6555	info@technet.nm.org

Area Code 507

Millennium Online	(507) 282-8943	info@mill.com

Area Code 508

Anomaly	(401) 273-4669	info@anomaly.sbs.risc.net
CapeINTERNET	(508) 790-1501	info@capecod.net
CCSNet	(508) 477-6181	info@ccsnet.com
Channel 1	(617) 864-0100	info@channel1.com
Destek Group, The	(508) 363-2413	info@destek.net
DMConnection	(508) 568-1618	info@dmc.com
intuitive information, inc.	(508) 342-1100	info@iii.net
NEARnet	(617) 873-8730	info@nearnet
North Shore Access	(617) 593-3110	info@shore.net
NovaLink	(800) 274-2814	info@novalink.com
Schunix	(508) 853-0258	info@schunix.com
The Internet Access Company	(617) 276-7200	info@tiac.com

Provider	*Phone*	*Email*
UltraNet Communications, Inc.	(800) 763-8111	info@ultranet.com

Area Code 509

Internet On-Ramp, Inc.	(509) 927-7267	info@on-ramp.ior.com
WLN Internet Services	(800) 342-5956	info@wln.com

Area Code 510

Access InfoSystems	(707) 422-1034	info@community.net
Aimnet Information Svs.	(408) 257-0900	info@aimnet.com
Beckemeyer Development	(510) 530-9637	info@bdt.com
Best Internet Communications	(415) 964-2378	info@best.com
California West Coast Online!	(707) 586-3060	info@calon.com
CCnet Communications	(510) 988-0680	info@ccnet.com
Community ConneXion	(510) 841-2014	info@c2.org
ElectriCiti Incorporated	(619) 338-9000	info@electriciti.com
Global Enterprise Services	(800) 358-4437	info@jvnc.net
Info. Access Technologies	(510) 704-0160	info@holonet.net
InterNex Information Services	(415) 473-3060	info@internex.net
NETCOM Online	(800) 501-8649	info@netcom.com
Sacramento Network Access, Inc.	(916) 565-4500	info@sna.com
Zocalo Engineering	(510) 540-8000	info@zocalo.net

Area Code 512

Eden Matrix	(512) 478-9900	info@eden.com
Freeside Communications	(800) 968-8750	info@fc.net
Illuminati Online	(512) 462-0999	info@io.com
Internet Connect Services	(512) 572-9987	info@icsi.net
MoonTower, Inc.	(512) 837-8670	info@moontower.com
Onramp Access, Inc.	(512) 322-9200	info@onr.com
RealTime Communications	(512) 451-0046	info@realtime.net
THEnet	(512) 471-2444	info@nic.the.net
Zilker Internet Park	(512) 206-3850	info@zilker.net

Area Code 513

EriNet Online Communications	(513) 436-1700	info@erinet.com
Freelance Systems Programming	(513) 254-7246	info@dayton.fsp.com
IgLou Internet Services	(800) 436-4456	info@iglou.com
Internet Access Online	(513) 887-8877	info@iac.com
OARnet	(800) 627-8101	info@oar.net

Area Code 514

Comm. Accessibles Montreal	(514) 931-0749	info@cam.org
RISQ	(514) 340-5700	info@crim.ca
UUNET Canada, Inc.	(416) 368-6621	info@uunet.ca

Area Code 516

Cosmic Communications	(516) 342-7597	info@cosmic.com
Creative Data Consultants	(718) 229-0489	info@silly.com
Echo Communications	(212) 255-3839	info@echonyc.com
Global Enterprise Services	(800) 358-4437	info@jvnc.net
LI Net, Inc.	(516) 476-1168	info@li.net

Provider	*Phone*	*Email*
Long Island Information	(516) 248-5381	info@liii.com
Network Internet Services	(516) 543-0234	info@netusa.net
New York Net	(718) 776-6811	info@new-york.net
Phantom Access Technologies	(212) 989-2418	info@phantom.com
Savvy Internet Access	(516) 626-2090	info@savvy.com
Zone One Network Exchange	(718) 549-8078	info@zone.net

Area Code 517
Concentric Research	(517) 895-0500	info@cris.com
Innovative Concepts	(313) 998-0090	info@ic.net
Merit Network, Inc.	(313) 764-9430	info@merit.edu

Area Code 518
Wizvax Communications	(518) 271-6005	info@wizvax.com

Area Code 519
HookUp Communication	(519) 747-4110	info@hookup.net
UUNET Canada, Inc.	(416) 368-6621	info@uunet.ca
UUnorth	(416) 225-8649	info@uunorth.north.net

Area Code 602
Data Basix	(602) 721-1988	info@data.basix.com
Evergreen Communications	(602) 230-9330	info@enet.net
Internet Direct, Inc.	(602) 274-0100	info@indirect.com
Internet Express	(800) 592-1240	info@usa.net
Network 99, Inc.	(800) 638-9947	info@cluster.mcs.net
New Mexico Technet, Inc.	(505) 345-6555	info@technet.nm.org
Primenet	(800) 463-8386	info@primenet.com

Area Code 603
Destek Group, The	(508) 363-2413	info@destek.net
MV Communications, Inc.	(603) 429-2223	info@mv.com
NEARnet	(617) 873-8730	info@nearnet
NETIS Public Access Internet	(603) 437-1811	info@scoot.netis.com

Area Code 604
UUNET Canada, Inc.	(416) 368-6621	info@uunet.ca

Area Code 606
IgLou Internet Services	(800) 436-4456	info@iglou.com

Area Code 608
BINCnet	(608) 233-5222	info@binc.net
FullFeed Communications	(608) 246-4239	info@fullfeed.com
WiscNet	(608) 262-8874	info@cs.wisc.edu

Area Code 609
New Jersey Computer Connection	(609) 896-2799	info@pluto.njcc.com
Global Enterprise Services	(800) 358-4437	info@jvnc.net
New York Net	(718) 776-6811	info@new-york.net

Area Code 610
FishNet	(610) 337-9994	info@pond.com

401

Provider	*Phone*	*Email*
SSNet, Inc.	(302) 378-1386	info@ssnet.com
You Tools Corporation	(610) 954-5910	info@youtools.com

Area Code 612

Cloudnet	(612) 240-8243	info@cloudnet.com
InterNetwork Services	(612) 391-7300	info@inet-serv.com
Minnesota MicroNet	(612) 681-8018	info@mm.com
Skypoint Communications, Inc.	(612) 475-2959	info@skypoint.com
StarNet Communications, Inc.	(612) 941-9177	info@winternet.com

Area Code 613

UUnorth	(416) 225-8649	info@uunorth.north.net
fONOROLA	(613) 235-3666	info@fonorola.net
UUNET Canada, Inc.	(416) 368-6621	info@uunet.ca

Area Code 614

OARnet	(800) 627-8101	info@oar.net
InfiNet (Infinite Systems)	(614) 268-9941	info@infinet.com

Area Code 615

Edge Network	(615) 726-8700	info@edge.net

Area Code 616

Merit Network, Inc.	(313) 764-9430	info@merit.edu
Dorsai Embassy	(718) 392-3667	info@dorsai.org
Innovative Concepts	(313) 998-0090	info@ic.net

Area Code 617

CENTnet	(617) 354-5800	info@ora.com
Channel 1	(617) 864-0100	info@channel1.com
DELPHI Internet Services	(800) 695-4005	info@delphi.com
NEARnet	(617) 873-8730	info@nearnet
NETCOM Online	(800) 501-8649	info@netcom.com
North Shore Access	(617) 593-3110	info@shore.net
NovaLink	(800) 274-2814	info@novalink.com
Pioneer Global	(617) 375-0200	info@pn.com
The Internet Access Company	(617) 276-7200	info@tiac.com
Wilder Systems, Inc.	(617) 933-8810	info@id.wing.net
World	(617) 739-0202	info@world.std.com
Xensei Corporation	(617) 773-4785	info@xensei.com

Area Code 619

CTS Network Services	(619) 637-3637	info@cts.com
Cyberspace Station	(619) 634-1376	info@cyber.net
Data Transfer Group	(619) 220-8601	info@access.thegroup.net
ElectriCiti Incorporated	(619) 338-9000	info@electriciti.com
ESNET Communications	(619) 278-4641	info@cg57.esnet.com
NETCOM Online	(800) 501-8649	info@netcom.com
Network Link, Inc.	(619) 278-5943	info@tnl1.tnwl.com
SDSCnet	(619) 534 8328	info@sdsc.net

Provider	*Phone*	*Email*

Area Code 702

Great Basin Internet Services	(702) 829-2244	info@greatbasin.com
info@wizard.com	(702) 871-4461	info@wizard.com
Network 99, Inc.	(800) 638-9947	info@cluster.mcs.net
NevadaNet	(702) 784-6861	info@nevada.edu
Sacramento Network Access, Inc.	(916) 565-4500	info@sna.com
Sierra-Net	(702) 832-6911	info@sierra.net

Area Code 703

Capitol Area Internet Service	(703) 448-4470	info@cais.com
Charm Net	(410) 558-3900	info@charm.net
Clark Internet Services Inc.	(410) 730-9764	info@clark.net
Meta Network	(703) 243-6622	info@tmn.com
NovaNet, Inc.	(703) 524-4800	info@novanet.com
NCM, Inc.	(703) 749-9150	info@tpe.ncm.com
US Net, Inc.	(301) 572-5926	info@us.net
PSINet	(800) 827-7482	info@psi.com
SprintLink	(703) 904-2156	info@sprintlink.net
NETCOM Online	(800) 501-8649	info@netcom.com
Digital Express Group	(800) 969-9090	info@digex.net
Merit Network, Inc.	(313) 764-9430	info@merit.edu
UUNET Communication Services	(703) 204-8000	info@uunet.uu.net

Area Code 704

CONCERT Network	(919) 248-1999	info@concert.net
Vnet Internet Access, Inc.	(800) 377-3282	info@vnet.net

Area Code 706

MindSpring Enterprises, Inc.	(404) 888-0725	info@mindspring.com
Internet Atlanta	(404) 410-9000	info@atlanta.net

Area Code 707

Access InfoSystems	(707) 422-1034	info@community.net
California West Coast Online!	(707) 586-3060	info@calon.com
Northcoast Internet	(707) 443-8696	info@northcoast.com
Pacific Internet	(707) 468-1005	info@pacific.net

Area Code 708

American Info Systems	(708) 413-8400	info@ais.net
Global Enterprise Services	(800) 358-4437	info@jvnc.net
MCSNet	(312) 248-8649	info@mcs.net
Net Information Systems	(708) 983-6064	info@xnet.com
netILLINOIS	(708) 866-1825	info@illinois.net
Ripco Communications, Inc.	(312) 665-0065	info@ripco.com
Tezcatlipoca, Inc.	(312) 850-0181	info@tezcat.com
WorldWide Access	(708) 367-1870	info@wwa.com

Area Code 709

NLnet	(709) 737-8329	info@kean.ucs.mun.ca

Provider	_Phone_	_Email_
Area Code 713		
Black Box	(713) 480-2684	info@blkbox.com
Info-Highway International, Inc.	(800) 256-1370	info@infohwy.com
Internet Connect Services	(512) 572-9987	info@icsi.net
NeoSoft Internet Services	(713) 684-5969	info@neosoft.com
SESQUINET	(713) 527-4988	info@sesqui.net
South Coast Computing Services	(800) 221-6478	info@sccsi.com
Area Code 714		
DHM Information Management	(310) 214-3349	info@dhm.com
DigiLink Network Services	(310) 542-7421	info@digilink.net
Digital Express Group	(800) 969-9090	info@digex.net
KAIWAN Corporation	(714) 638-2139	info@kaiwan.com
Lightside, Inc.	(818) 858-9261	info@lightside.com
NETCOM Online	(800) 501-8649	info@netcom.com
Network Intensive	(800) 273-5600	info@ni.net
Area Code 715		
BINCnet	(608) 233-5222	info@binc.net
Area Code 717		
PREPnet	(412) 268-7870	info@prep.net
SuperNet Internet Services	(800) 466-5338	info@success.net
You Tools Corporation	(610) 954-5910	info@youtools.com
Area Code 718		
Blythe Systems	(212) 348-2875	info@blythe.org
Creative Data Consultants	(718) 229-0489	info@silly.com
Dorsai Embassy	(718) 392-3667	info@dorsai.org
Escape	(212) 888-8780	info@escape.com
Ingress Communications	(212) 679-8592	info@ingress.com
Interport Communications	(212) 989-1128	info@interport.net
Maestro Technologies, Inc.	(212) 240-9600	info@maestro.com
Mordor International	(201) 433-7343	info@ritz.mordor.com
NETCOM Online	(800) 501-8649	info@netcom.com
New York Net	(718) 776-6811	info@new-york.net
PANIX Public Access Unix	(212) 741-4400	info@panix.com
Phantom Access Technologies	(212) 989-2418	info@phantom.com
Pipeline Network	(212) 267-3636	info@pipeline.com
Zone One Network Exchange	(718) 549-8078	info@zone.net
Area Code 719		
Colorado SuperNet	(303) 296-8202	info@csn.org
Community News Service	(719) 592-1240	info@cscns.com
Internet Express	(800) 592-1240	info@usa.net
Old Colorado City Commun.	(719) 528-5849	info@oldcolo.com
Rocky Mountain Internet	(800) 900-7644	info@rmii.com
Area Code 801		
XMission	(801) 539-0852	info@xmission.com

Provider	*Phone*	*Email*

Area Code 802
Destek Group, The   (508) 363-2413   info@destek.net

Area Code 803
A World of Difference   (803) 769-4488   info@awod.com
Global Vision, Inc.   (803) 241-0901   info@globalvision.net
SIMS, Inc.   (803) 762-4956   info@sims.net
South Carolina SuperNet, Inc.   (803) 748-1207   info@scsn.net

Area Code 804
Widomaker Communications   (804) 253-7621   info@widomaker.com
Wyvern Technologies, Inc.   (804) 627-7837   info@wyvern.com
VERnet   (804) 924-0616   info@ver.net

Area Code 805
Datawave Network Services   (805) 730-7775   info@datawave.net

Area Code 808
Hawaii OnLine   (808) 246-1880   info@aloha.net
PACCOM   (808) 956-3499   info@hawaii.edu

Area Code 809
Global Enterprise Services   (800) 358-4437   info@jvnc.net

Area Code 810
Innovative Concepts   (313) 998-0090   info@ic.net
Innovative Data Services   (810) 478-3554   info@id.net
Merit Network, Inc.   (313) 764-9430   info@merit.edu
MSen Connection Services   (313) 998-4562   info@msen.com
Rabbit Network   (800) 456-0094   info@rabbit.net

Area Code 812
IgLou Internet Services   (800) 436-4456   info@iglou.com
Point Network   (812) 246-8032   info@thepoint.com

Area Code 813
CENTURION Technology   (813) 572-5556   info@cent.com
Florida Online   (407) 635-8888   info@digital.net
PacketWorks, Inc.   (813) 446-8826   info@packet.net

Area Code 814
PREPnet   (412) 268-7870   info@prep.net

Area Code 815
American Info Systems   (708) 413-8400   info@ais.net
MCSNet   (312) 248-8649   info@mcs.net
Net Information Systems   (708) 983-6064   info@xnet.com
WorldWide Access   (708) 367-1870   info@wwa.com

Area Code 816
Tyrell Corp.   (800) 897-3551   info@tyrell.com
SkyNET Corp.   (816) 483-0002   info@sky.net

Provider	*Phone*	*Email*
Area Code 817		
DFW Internet Services, Inc.	(817) 332-5116	info@dfw.net
Metronet, Inc.	(214) 705-2900	info@metronet.com
ACM Network Services	(817) 776-6876	info@acm.org
Area Code 818		
DHM Information Management	(310) 214-3349	info@dhm.com
DigiLink Network Services	(310) 542-7421	info@digilink.net
Earthlink Network	(213) 644-9500	info@earthlink.net
Lightside, Inc.	(818) 858-9261	info@lightside.com
NETCOM Online	(800) 501-8649	info@netcom.com
Primenet	(800) 463-8386	info@primenet.com
ViaNet Communications	(415) 903-2242	info@via.net
Area Code 902		
NSTN	(902) 468 6786	info@hawki.nstn.ns.ca
PEINet	(902) 566 0552	info@peinet.pe.ca
Area Code 904		
Florida Online	(407) 635-8888	info@digital.net
SymNet	(904) 385-1061	info@symnet.net
Jax Gateway to the World	(904) 730-7692	info@jax gttw.com
Area Code 905		
UUNET Canada, Inc.	(416) 368-6621	info@uunet.ca
ONet	(905) 525 9140	info@onet.on.ca
Area Code 906		
Merit Network, Inc.	(313) 764-9430	info@merit.edu
Innovative Concepts	(313) 998-0090	info@ic.net
Area Code 907		
University Of Alaska Southeast	(907) 465-6453	info@alaska.edu
Internet Alaska	(907) 562-4638	info@alaska.net
Area Code 908		
Digital Express Group	(800) 969-9090	info@digex.net
Global Enterprise Services	(800) 358-4437	info@jvnc.net
New York Net	(718) 776-6811	info@new-york.net
Planet Access Networks	(201) 691-4704	info@planet.net
SkyNET Corp.	(816) 483-0002	info@sky.net
Tyrell Corp.	(800) 897-3551	info@tyrell.com
Zone One Network Exchange	(718) 549-8078	info@zone.net
Area Code 909		
Lightside, Inc.	(818) 858-9261	info@lightside.com
Area Code 910		
CONCERT Network	(919) 248-1999	info@concert.net
Area Code 912		
Internet Atlanta	(404) 410-9000	info@atlanta.net

Provider	*Phone*	*Email*

Area Code 914

Cloud 9 Internet	(914) 682-0626	info@cloud9.net
Dorsai Embassy	(718) 392-3667	info@dorsai.org
IDS World Network	(800) 437-1680	info@ids.net
MHVNet	(800) 998-7131	info@mhv.net
New York Net	(718) 776-6811	info@new-york.net
Phantom Access Technologies	(212) 989-2418	info@phantom.com
TZ-Link	(914) 353-5443	info@j51.com
Zone One Network Exchange	(718) 549-8078	info@zone.net

Area Code 915

New Mexico Technet, Inc.	(505) 345-6555	info@technet.nm.org

Area Code 916

California West Coast Online!	(707) 586-3060	info@calon.com
NETCOM Online	(800) 501-8649	info@netcom.com
Sacramento Network Access, Inc.	(916) 565-4500	info@sna.com
Sierra-Net	(702) 832-6911	info@sierra.net

Area Code 917

Network 23, Inc.	(212) 786-4810	info@net23.com
New York Net	(718) 776-6811	info@new-york.net
Zone One Network Exchange	(718) 549-8078	info@zone.net

Area Code 918

GSS Internet	(918) 835-3655	info@galstar.com

Area Code 919

CONCERT Network	(919) 248-1999	info@concert.net
Vnet Internet Access, Inc.	(800) 377-3282	info@vnet.net
Interpath	(800) 849-6305	info@interpath.net

List 2 - Mailing Lists for the Student

The usual way to subscribe to a mailing list is to send email to the server program by using the email address. Remember that you can recognize an email address by the presence of the ampersand (the '@' character) located somewhere in the middle. Also remember that even though these lists are free in that they do not charge money for subscriptions, time and energy will be needed to handle what may be a trickle or may be a flood of postings. Keep the instructions (generally the first or second transmission, often obtainable by sending the message 'help' or 'info') to find out how to 'unsubscribe' when you are ready to 'unsubscribe' from the list.

A.Word.A.Day - *A new English word with definition is posted every day*
```
Subscribe to:     wsmith@wordsmith.org
Enter subject:    subscribe <your full name>
```

ACTION - *Activism Online: forum for profess. & volunteer online activists*
```
Subscribe to:     listserv@eff.org
Enter message:    ADD action
```

AFRICA-N - *News and information from Africa from a variety of sources*
```
Subscribe to:     LISTSERV@utoronto.bitnet
Enter message:    SUBSCRIBE AFRICA-N <your full name>
```

AGMODELS-L - *A forum for discussion of agricultural simulation models*
```
Subscribe to:     listserv@unl.edu
Enter message:    SUB AGMODELS-L <your full name>
```

ai-nat - *Artificial intelligence as applied to natural world problems*
```
Subscribe to:     Majordomo@adfa.oz.au
Enter message:    Please send information
```

AE - *Alternative energy and renewable energy discussion list*
```
Subscribe to:     listserv@sjsuvm1.sjsu.edu
Enter message:    subscribe ae <your full name>
```

AMgtAcc-L - *Management accounting discussion*
```
Request info:     AMgtAcc-L-owner@scu.edu.au
Enter message:    Please send information
```
(Note: archives at URL: http://anet.scu.edu.au/anet.lists)

Apple-Internet-(lists) - *Lists for Apple computer users on the Internet*
```
Request info:     listproc@abs.apple.com
Enter message:    info apple-internet-announce
```

ATeach-L - *Discussion of teaching and learning in accounting*
```
Request info:     ATeach-L-owner@scu.edu.au
Enter message:    Please send information
```
(Note: archives at URL: http://anet.scu.edu.au/anet.lists)

Biodiv-L - *Discussion of the establishment of a biodiversity network*
  Subscribe to: `listserv@bdt.ftpt.ansp.br`
  Enter message: `subscribe biodiv-l <your full name, org.>`

Biomch-L - *Discussion of biomechanics and human or animal movement*
  Subscribe to: `listserv@nic.surfnet.nl`
  Enter message: `subscribe biomch-l <your full name>`

Biosph-L - *Interdisciplinary discussion of Earth's ecology and biosphere*
  Subscribe to: `listserv@ubvm.cc.buffalo.edu`
  Enter message: `subscribe biosph-l <your full name>`

BIZ-WIRE - *Discussion of issues re: creation and operation of businesses*
  Subscribe to: `listserv@ais.net`
  Enter message: `subscribe biz-wire <your full name>`

bpr-l - *Discussing the newly-emerging field of Business Process Redesign*
  Subscribe to: `listserv@is.twi.tudelft.nl`
  Enter message: `SUB BPR-L <your full name>`

CBR-MED - *Discussion of CBR (Case-Based Reasoning) in Medicine*
  Subscribe to: `listproc@cs.uchicago.edu`
  Enter message: `subscribe CBR-MED <your full name>`

CEI - *Competitive Enterprise Institute, supports free trade and limited gov't*
  Request info :   `volokh@netcom.com`
  Enter message: `please send information`

CFCP-Members - *Confederation of Future Computer Professionals*
  Request info: `mlindsey@nyx.cs.du.edu`
  Enter message: `please send information`

chem-eng - *Chemical engineering newsletter*
  Request info: `trayms@cc.curtin.edu.au`
  Enter message: `please send information`

civil-liberty-index - *Distribution of civil liberties article indexes*
  Subscribe to: `listserv@eff.org`
  Enter message: `subscribe <your full name>`

classical-request - *Discussion of classical music from all periods*
  Subscribe to: `classical-request@webcom.com`
  Enter message: `subscribe classical-request <your full name>`

CMPLAW-L - *Discussion of the Internet, computers and the law*
  Subscribe to: `listserv@nervm.nerdc.ufl.edu`
  Enter message: `subscribe cmplaw-l <your full name>`

comp-academic-freedom-talk - *Computers and academic freedom*
  Subscribe to: `listserv@eff.org`
  Enter message: `subscribe comp-academic-freedom-talk <your name>`

CompuNotes - *Free weekly publication on computer news and reviews*
Subscribe to: subscribe@supportu.com
Enter message: subscribe compunotes <your name>

CussNet-List - *Computer Users in the Social Sciences discussion list*
Request info: cussnet-list-request@stat.com
Enter message: Please send information

cybermind - *Computer Users in the Social Sciences discussion list*
Subscribe to: majordomo@jefferson.village.virginia.edu
Enter message: subscribe cybermind <your full name>
(Note URL: http://www.uio.no/~mwatz/cybermind/)

Dinosaur - *Amateur discussion of dinosaurs*
Subscribe to: listproc@lepomis.psych.upenn.edu
Enter message: subscribe dinosaur <your full name>

Document Search and Retrieval - *Electronic retrieval technique forum*
Subscribe to: search-request@imsworld.com
Enter message: subscribe search <your full name>

Earth and Sky - *Weekly publication on earth science and astronomy*
Subscribe to: majordomo@lists.utexas.edu
Enter message: subscribe earthandsky <your email address>

econ-soc-devt - *Discussion of international economic and social development*
Subscribe to: mailbase@mailbase.ac.uk
Enter message: subscribe econ-soc-devt <your full name>

Economic-growth - *Discussion list related to issues of economic growth*
Subscribe to: majordomo@ufsia.ac.be
Enter message: info economic-growth <your full name>

effector-online - *Electronic Frontier Foundation's bi-weekly newsletter*
Subscribe to: listserv@eff.org
Enter message: subscribe effector-online

Forest Management DSS - *Discussion of forest management systems*
Subscribe to: listserv@pnfi.forestry.ca
Enter message: subscribe fmdss-l <your full name>

forestgen - *Discussion of forest genetics and tree breeding*
Subscribe to: majordomo@metla.fi
Enter message: subscribe forestgen <your full name>

Forestry - *General discussions on forestry*
Subscribe to: mailserver@nic.funet.fi
Enter message: subscribe forestry <your full name>

Fungus - *Dedicated to hobby and commercial mushroom cultivation*
 Subscribe to: fungus-request@teleport.com
 Enter message: subscribe fungus <your email address>

fuzzy-mail - *Discussion of fuzzy logic and fuzzy sets*
 Subscribe to: listserver@vexpert.dbai.tuwien.ac.at
 Enter message: subscribe fuzzy-mail <your full name>

Genesis - *Project Genesis: furthering Jewish education on the Internet*
 Subscribe to: listproc@shamash.nysernet.org
 Enter message: subscribe genesis <your full name>

gwm - *Groundwater monitoring list*
 Subscribe to: majordomo@gwrp.cciw.ca
 Enter message: subscribe gwm-l <your full name>

handicap - *Discussion of issues related to physically/mentally impaired*
 Request info: wtm@bunker.shel.isc-br.com
 Enter message: Please send information
 (Note: postings are also found in Usenet Newsgroup "misc.handicap")

HELP-NET - *Instruction and guidance for beginning Internet user*
 Subscribe to: help-net@vm.temple.edu
 Enter message: subscribe help-net <your full name>

HEPROC-L - *Discussion of major issues of higher education*
 Subscribe to: listserv@american.edu
 Enter message: subscribe heproc-l <your full name>

home-ed - *Discussion of home schooling and home-based education*
 Request info: home-ed-request@think.com
 Enter message: Please send information

home-ed-politics - *Discussing political issues of home-based education*
 Subscribe to: listproc@mainstream.com
 Enter message: help

Homeopathy - *Exchange of info relative to the practice of homeopathy*
 Request info: homeopathy-request@dungeon.com
 Enter message: Please send information

hs-computing - *Addresses advanced pre-college computing and training*
 Subscribe to: majordomo@delos.com
 Enter message: subscribe hs-computing

ht lit - *Discussion of hypertext fiction, theory and literary studies*
 Subscribe to: subscribe@journal.biology.carleton.ca
 Enter message: subscribe ht_lit
 Note: http://chat.carleton.ca/~kmennie/ht_lit.html>

Humanist Initiatives - *Postings by humanist organizations*
Subscribe to: `listproc@phantom.com`
Enter message: `subscribe hs-computing`

HYDROLOGY - *Discussion of the science of water in the environment*
Subscribe to: `listserv@eng.monash.edu.au`
Enter message: `subscribe hydrology <your full name>`

I-TV - *Discussion two-way interactive television and educational uses*
Subscribe to: `majordomo@zilker.net`
Enter message: `info i-tv`   (line one)
                 `end`   (line two)

IAMS - *Internet Amateur Math Society: math puzzles and problems*
Request info: `majordomo@zilker.net`
Enter message: `Please send information`

immune - *Support group for people with immune-system breakdowns*
Request info: `immune-request@weber.ucsd.edu`
Enter message: `Please send information`
(Note: archives are available via ftp: `wever.ucsd.edu/pub/immune`)

INDEX-L - *Discussion of good indexing practice and techniques*
Subscribe to: `listserv@bingvmb.bitnet`
Enter message: `subscribe indel-l <your full name>`

info-gnu - *Reports of the GNU Project of the Free Software Fdn. (free-Unix)*
Subscribe to: `info-gnu-request@prep.ai.mit.edu`
Enter message: `subscribe indel-l <your full name>`

Infoterra - *Support group for people with immune-system breakdowns*
Subscribe to: `listproc@pan.cedar.univie.ac.at`
Enter message: `subscribe infoterra`

interest-groups - *Support group for human immune-system breakdowns*
Subscribe to: `listproc@pan.cedar.univie.ac.at`
Enter message: `subscribe infoterra`

isig - *Internet technical info for beginners and intermediate users*
Subscribe to: `majordomo@netf.org`
Enter message: `subscribe`

JAM - *Oceanography and earth science trivia and miscellanea*
Request info: `oldnic@soton.ac.uk`
Enter message: `Please send information`

jewish - *Discussion of Jewish topics with an emphasis on Jewish law*
Subscribe to: `listserv@israel.nysernet.org`
Enter message: `subscribe mail-jewish <your full name>`

Jewishnt - *Discussion of the Global Jewish Information Network*
    Subscribe to: `listserv@bguvm.bgu.ac.il`
    Enter message: `sub jewishnt <your full name>`

JOB-LIST - *Posting available entry-level positions for college graduates*
    Subscribe to: `listserv@sun.cc.westga.edu`
    Enter message: `subscribe job-list <your full name>`

JOBPLACE - *For job search trainers, career counselors and specialists*
    Subscribe to: `listserv@ukcc.uky.edu`
    Enter message: `subscribe jobplace <your full name>`

KIDSPHERE - *International network for use of children and their teachers*
    Request info: `kidsphere-request@vms.cis.pitt.edu`
    Enter message: `Please send information`

List-Managers - *Discussions for managers of Internet mailing lists*
    Subscribe to: `majordomo@greatcircle.com`
    Enter message: `subscribe list-managers`

lit-med - *Discussion of Literature And Medicine humanities database, &c.*
    Request info: `lit-med-request@popmail.med.nyu.edu`
    Enter message: `Please send information`

MAR-FACIL - *For managers & technical staff at marine research facilities*
    Subscribe to: `mailserv@ac.dal.ca`
    Enter message: `subscribe mar-facil`

Media Access - *Making electronic media accessible to disabled persons*
    Subscribe to: `listmanager@hookup.net`
    Enter message: `subscribe access`

met-study - *Discussion of issues related to meteorology*
    Subscribe to: `listproc@bibo.met.fu-berlin.de`
    Enter message: `subscribe met-sub <your full name>`

Migra-List - *On international migration*
    Request info: `migra-list-request@lists.utah.edu`
    Enter message: `Please send information`

moonlight-l - *Discussion for people moonlighting at home with a computer*
    Subscribe to: `listserv.netcom.com`
    Enter message: `subscribe moonlight-l`

Music-Research - *On applications of computers & music*
    Request info: `music-research-request@cattell.upenn.psych.edu`
    Enter message: `Please send information`

NA-net - *Discussions of numerical analysis*
    Subscribe to: `na.join@na-net.ornl.gov`
    Enter message: `<your first name>`   (line 1)

```
            <your last name>        (line 2)
            <your email address>    (line 3)
```

NASAINFO - *Postings by NASA about space missions; no discussion*
Subscribe to: `listserv@amsat.org`
Enter message: `subscribe nasainfo <your full name>`

NativeLit-L - *Discussion of Native American literature*
Subscribe to: `listserv@cornell.edu`
Enter message: `subscribe nativelit-1 <your full name>`

NativeNet - *Discussion of indigenous peoples and threats to their cultures*
Subscribe to: `gst@gnosys.svle.ma.us`
Enter message: `subscribe nativelit-1 <your full name>`

net-guide - *Monthly updates to EFF's Guide to the Internet*
Subscribe to: `listserv@eff.org`
Enter message: `subscribe net-guide <your full name>`

net-lawyers - *Discussion of how to use the Internet in study and practice*
Subscribe to: `net-lawyers-request@webcom.com`
Enter message: `subscribe`

newlists - *Announcements of new Internet mailing lists that are starting*
Subscribe to: `listserv@vml.nodak.edu`
Enter message: `subscribe newlists <your full name>`

OB-GYN-L - *Discussion of gynocology and obstetrics*
Subscribe to: `listserv@bcm.tmc.edu`
Enter message: `subscribe ob-gyn-1 <your full name>`

our-kids - *Care, diagnosis and therapy for developmental delays*
Subscribe to: `majordomo@tbag.osc.edu`
Enter message: `subscribe our-kids`

PAGEMAKER - *Discussing desktop publishing emphasizing Pagemaker*
Subscribe to: `listserv@indycms.iupui.edu`
Enter message: `subscribe pagemaker <your full name>`

plays - *Discussion of theatre and plays*
Subscribe to: `majordomo@world.std.com`
Enter message: `subscribe plays`
(Note: postings are in Usenet newsgroup "rec.arts.theatre.plays")

project-management - *Discussion of project management techniques*
Subscribe to: `mailbas@mailbase.ac.uk`
Enter message: `join project-management <your full name>`

ProMED - *Management of emerging infectious disease worldwide*
Subscribe to: `promed-request@usa.healthnet.org`
Enter message: `subscribe promed`

PSYCHE-D - *Exploration of consciousness and its relationship to the brain*
    Subscribe to: `listserv@iris.rfmh.org`
    Enter message: `subscribe psyche-d <your full name>`

PSYCHE-L - *A refereed electronic journal on consciousness and the brain*
    Subscribe to: `listserv@iris.rfmh.org`
    Enter message: `subscribe psyche-l <your full name>`

Quotations - *Inspirational quotations posted daily*
    Subscribe to: `majordomo@trg2.saic.com`
    Enter message: subscribe serial-quotes-digest
    Note info at ftp: `//trg2.saic.com/pub/quotes/serial-quotations.info`

RC_WORLD - *Discussing respiratory care and general health care issues*
    Subscribe to: `listserv@indycms.iupui.edu`
    Enter message: `subscribe rc_world <your full name>`

remote-work - *Forum for telecommuters or those working at remote sites*
    Subscribe to: `remote-work-request@unify.com`
    Enter message: `subscribe remote-work`

RESIDENTS - *Mutual support group for medical residents of all specialties*
    Subscribe to: `listserv@beach.utmb.edu`
    Enter message: `subscribe residents <your full name>`

reviewers - *Book reviewer discussion forum*
    Request info: `reviewers-request@armory.com`
    Enter message: `Please send information`

rockhounds - *Discussion for gem and mineral collectors*
    Request info: `rockhounds-request@infodyne.com`
    Enter message: `Please send information`

rocks-and-fossils - *Discussion for rock and fossil collectors*
    Subscribe to: `majordomo@world.std.com`
    Enter message: `subscribe rocks-and-fossils`

ROOTS-L - *Genealogy discussion list*
    Subscribe to: `listserv@vml.nodak.edu`
    Enter message: `subscribe roots-l <your full name>`
    (Note: postings also are in Usenet newsgroup "`soc.roots`")

RSI Network Newsletter - *Repetitive Strain Injury support group, info*
    Subscribe to: `majordomo@world.std.com`
    Enter message: `subscribe rsi`

RTVJ-L - *Radio and television journalism discussion group*
    Subscribe to: `listproc@listserv.umt.edu`
    Enter message: `subscribe rtvj-l <your full name>`

sched-l - *Discussing scheduling techniques and manufacturing processes*
Subscribe to:	`listserver@vexpert.dbai.tuwien.ac.at`
Enter message:	`subscribe sched-l <your full name>`

Software Entrepreneuers - *Entrepreneurial software publishing*
Request info:	`softpub-request@toolz.atl.ga.us`
Enter message:	`Please send information`

SOILS-L - *Discussion of soil sciences*
Subscribe to:	`listserv@unl.edu`
Enter message:	`subscribe soils-l <your full name>`

specieslist - *Information regarding the World Species List (WSL)*
Request info:	`rstafursky@envirolink.org`
Enter message:	`Please send information`

SSIN - *Student Solar Info Network: solar and renewable energy*
Request info:	`m.e.thornton@bham.ac.uk`
Enter message:	`Please send information`

stagecraft - *Discussion of theatrical stage work & management*
Request info:	`stagecraft-request@zinc.com`
Enter message:	`Please send information`

Student Media - *Discusses issues faced by college media*
Subscribe to:	`listserv@uabdpo.uab.edu`
Enter message:	`sub stumedia <your full name>`

Technology Review - *MIT's magazine of technology & policy: 8 per year*
Subscribe to:	`listserv@uabdpo.uab.edu`
Enter message:	`sub stumedia <your full name>`

Telecom-Tech - *Discussion of technical aspects of telecommunications*
Request info:	`TeleTech-Request@zygot.ati.com`
Enter message:	`Please send information`

TESL-L - *Discusses teaching English abroad*
Subscribe to:	`listserv@cunyvm.cuny.edu`
Enter message:	`sub tesl-l <your full name>`

Testing-Research - *MIT's magazine of technology & policy: 8 per year*
Request info:	`Testing-Research-Request@cs.uiuc.edu`
Enter message:	`Please send information`

theatre-misc - *Discussion of theater and theatrical arts*
Subscribe to:	`majordomo@world.std.com`
Enter message:	`subscribe theatre-misc`

(Note: postings are in Usenet Newsgroup "`rec.arts.theatre.misc`")

ToxList - *Studies effects of toxins on man and environment*
Subscribe to:	`listserv@cornell.edu`

Enter message: subscribe toxlist <your full name>

usenet-oracle - *An active, cooperative effort for creative humor*
Subscribe to: oracle@cs.indiana.edu
Enter message: help

Visions - *Discusses Christian prophecies and spiritual visions*
Subscribe to: listserv@ubvm.cc.buffalo.edu
Enter message: subscribe visions <your full name>

VISTA-L - *Volunteers in Service to America: monthly bulletin*
Subscribe to: listserv@american.edu
Enter message: subscribe vista-l <your full name>

VOCALIST - *Classical singing discussion list*
Subscribe to: majordomo@phoenix.oulu.fi
Enter message: subscribe vocalist

VOCNET - *Discussion of issues of vocational education*
Subscribe to: listserv@cmsa.berkeley.edu
Enter message: subscribe vocnet <your full name>

WSTN - *Wall Street News financial newsletter and forecasts*
Request info: listserv@cmsa.berkeley.edu
Enter message: Please send information

The Wellness List - *Discussion of health, nutrition, wellness, fitness*
Subscribe to: majordomo@wellnessmart.com
Enter message: subscribe wellnesslist

Wildnet - *Discussion of issues of vocational education*
Request info: wildnet-request@tribune.usask.ca
Enter message: Please send information

Wind Energy Weekly - *Discusses wind energy development worldwide*
Request info: tgray@igc.apc.org
Enter message: Please send information

WLREHAB - *Wildlife rehabilitation discussions*
Subscribe to: LISTSERV@VM1.NODAK.EDU
Enter message: subscribe wlrehab <your full name>

WMN-HLTH - *Center for Women's Health Research newsline*
Subscribe to: listproc@u.washington.edu
Enter message: subscribe wme-hlth <your full name>

YSN - *Employment issues for scientists at the start of their careers*
Request info for: ysnadm@crow-t-robot.stanford.edu
Enter message: Please send information

List 3 - Usenet Newsgroups for the Student

Alt Newsgroups (481 groups)

alt..jobs
alt.3d
alt.3d.studio
alt.abortion.inequity
alt.abuse.recovery
alt.abuse.transcendence
alt.activism
alt.activism.death-penalty
alt.adoption
alt.agriculture.misc
alt.aldus.freehand
alt.aldus.pagemaker
alt.alien.visitors
alt.america.online
alt.anagrams
alt.angst
alt.angst.xibo.sex
alt.animals.dolphins
alt.animals.felines
alt.animals.foxes
alt.animals.lampreys
alt.animation.warner-bros
alt.anonymous
alt.anonymous.messages
alt.answers
alt.aol-sucks
alt.appalachian
alt.aquaria
alt.archery
alt.architecture
alt.architecture.alternative
alt.architecture.int-design
alt.artcom
alt.arts.nomad
alt.arts.storytelling
alt.ascii-art
alt.ascii-art.animation
alt.astrology
alt.atheism
alt.atheism.moderated
alt.atheism.satire
alt.bbs

alt.bbs.ads
alt.bbs.doors
alt.bbs.first-class
alt.bbs.internet
alt.bbs.lists
alt.bbs.majorbbs
alt.bbs.pcboard
alt.bbs.pcbuucp
alt.bbs.searchlight
alt.bbs.unixbbs
alt.best.of.internet
alt.binaries.clip-art
alt.binaries.misc
alt.binaries.multimedia
alt.binaries.pictures
alt.binaries.pictures.animals
alt.binaries.pictures.anime
alt.binaries.pictures.arts.bodyart
alt.binaries.pictures.ascii
alt.binaries.pictures.astro
alt.binaries.pictures.cartoons
alt.binaries.pictures.children
alt.binaries.pictures.fine-art.digitized
alt.binaries.pictures.fine-art.graphics
alt.binaries.pictures.fractals
alt.binaries.pictures.furniture
alt.binaries.pictures.misc
alt.binaries.pictures.utilities
alt.binaries.pictures.vehicles
alt.bio.hackers
alt.birthright
alt.bonsai
alt.books.anne-rice
alt.books.deryni
alt.books.isaac-asimov
alt.books.m-lackey
alt.books.reviews
alt.books.stephen-king
alt.books.technical
alt.books.tom-clancy
alt.business.import-export

alt.business.misc
alt.business.multi-level
alt.cable-tv.re-regulate
alt.cad
alt.cad.autocad
alt.california
alt.callahans
alt.cascade
alt.cd-rom
alt.cd-rom.reviews
alt.celebrities
alt.censorship
alt.cereal
alt.cesium
alt.chess.bdg
alt.chess.ics
alt.child-support
alt.chinchilla
alt.chinese.computing
alt.chinese.text
alt.christnet
alt.christnet.bible
alt.christnet.christianlife
alt.christnet.comp.dcom.telecom
alt.christnet.dinosaur.barney
alt.christnet.ethics
alt.christnet.evangelical
alt.christnet.hypocrisy
alt.christnet.philosophy
alt.christnet.theology
alt.clearing.technology
alt.co-evolution
alt.co-ops
alt.cobol
alt.coffee
alt.collecting.autographs
alt.college.college-bowl
alt.college.food
alt.college.fraternities
alt.college.sororities
alt.college.tunnels
alt.college.us
alt.colorguard
alt.comedy.british
alt.comedy.firesgn-thtre
alt.comedy.standup

alt.comedy.vaudeville
alt.comics.alternative
alt.comics.batman
alt.comics.buffalo-roam
alt.comics.elfquest
alt.comics.lnh
alt.comics.superman
alt.comp.acad-freedom.news
alt.comp.acad-freedom.talk
alt.comp.compression
alt.comp.databases.xbase.clipper
alt.comp.fsp
alt.comp.hardware.homebuilt
alt.comp.periphs.mainboard.asus
alt.comp.shareware
alt.comp.virus
alt.computer.consultants
alt.conference-ctr
alt.config
alt.consciousness
alt.conspiracy.jfk
alt.consumers.free-stuff
alt.control-theory
alt.crackers
alt.culture.alaska
alt.culture.argentina
alt.culture.austrian
alt.culture.electric-midget
alt.culture.internet
alt.culture.theory
alt.culture.usenet
alt.current-events.bosnia
alt.current-events.net-abuse
alt.current-events.russia
alt.current-events.ukraine
alt.current-events.usa
alt.cyb-sys
alt.cyberpunk
alt.cyberspace
alt.dads-rights
alt.dcom.catv
alt.dcom.telecom
alt.dear.whitehouse
alt.desert-storm
alt.desert-storm.facts
alt.dev.null

419

alt.discordia
alt.discrimination
alt.divination
alt.dreams
alt.dreams.lucid
alt.drugs
alt.drugs.usenet
alt.drumcorps
alt.education.disabled
alt.education.distance
alt.education.research
alt.energy.renewable
alt.etext
alt.exotic-music
alt.fashion
alt.fax
alt.feminism
alt.feminism.individualism
alt.fishing
alt.flame
alt.flame.spelling
alt.folklore.college
alt.folklore.computers
alt.folklore.ghost-stories
alt.folklore.herbs
alt.folklore.military
alt.folklore.science
alt.folklore.suburban
alt.folklore.urban
alt.food
alt.fractals
alt.fractals.pictures
alt.fraternity.sorority
alt.freaks
alt.freemasonry
alt.freenet
alt.galactic-guide
alt.gambling
alt.gathering.rainbow
alt.geek
alt.genealogy
alt.good.morning
alt.good.news
alt.gopher
alt.gothic
alt.grad-student.tenured

alt.graffiti
alt.great-lakes
alt.guitar
alt.guitar.bass
alt.guitar.tablature
alt.hackers
alt.hackers.malicious
alt.hangover
alt.health.ayurveda
alt.hemp
alt.heraldry.sca
alt.hindu
alt.history.living
alt.history.what-if
alt.home.repair
alt.horror
alt.housing.nontrad
alt.human-brain
alt.humor.best-of-usenet
alt.humor.puns
alt.hypertext
alt.hypnosis
alt.illuminati
alt.image.medical
alt.india.progressive
alt.individualism
alt.industrial
alt.infertility
alt.internet.access.wanted
alt.internet.media-coverage
alt.internet.services
alt.internet.talk-radio
alt.internet.talk.bizarre
alt.irc
alt.japanese.text
alt.journalism
alt.journalism.criticism
alt.journalism.gonzo
alt.kalbo
alt.ketchup
alt.kids-talk
alt.lang.asm
alt.lang.awk
alt.lang.basic
alt.lang.teco
alt.law-enforcement

alt.lefthanders
alt.lemmings
alt.life.internet
alt.locksmithing
alt.lycra
alt.magic
alt.magick
alt.manga
alt.med.cfs
alt.med.fibromyalgia
alt.meditation
alt.meditation.transcendental
alt.memetics
alt.mens-rights
alt.messianic
alt.military.cadet
alt.mindcontrol
alt.misanthropy
alt.missing-kids
alt.models
alt.motherjones
alt.motorcycles.harley
alt.msdos.programmer
alt.mud
alt.music.alternative
alt.mythology
alt.native
alt.newbie
alt.news-media
alt.news.macedonia
alt.news.microsoft
alt.non.sequitur
alt.obituaries
alt.online-service
alt.online-service.america-online
alt.online-service.compuserve
alt.online-service.delphi
alt.online-service.freenet
alt.online-service.prodigy
alt.org.toastmasters
alt.os.linux
alt.os.multics
alt.paranet.abduct
alt.paranet.paranormal
alt.paranet.psi
alt.paranet.science

alt.paranet.skeptic
alt.paranet.ufo
alt.paranormal
alt.parents-teens
alt.pcnews
alt.peace-corps
alt.periphs.pcmcia
alt.personals
alt.philosophy.jarf
alt.philosophy.objectivism
alt.philosophy.zen
alt.planning.urban
alt.politics.british
alt.politics.bush
alt.politics.clinton
alt.politics.correct
alt.politics.datahighway
alt.politics.democrats.d
alt.politics.ec
alt.politics.economics
alt.politics.elections
alt.politics.equality
alt.politics.europe.misc
alt.politics.greens
alt.politics.homosexuality
alt.politics.india.progressive
alt.politics.libertarian
alt.politics.media
alt.politics.org.batf
alt.politics.org.cia
alt.politics.org.misc
alt.politics.org.nsa
alt.politics.org.un
alt.politics.perot
alt.politics.radical-left
alt.politics.reform
alt.politics.usa.constitution
alt.politics.usa.misc
alt.politics.usa.republican
alt.polyamory
alt.postmodern
alt.president.clinton
alt.prisons
alt.privacy
alt.privacy.anon-server
alt.privacy.clipper

alt.prophecies.nostradamus
alt.prose
alt.psychoactives
alt.psychology.help
alt.psychology.personality
alt.pub.coffeehouse.amethyst
alt.pulp
alt.quotations
alt.radio.digital
alt.radio.networks.cbc
alt.radio.networks.npr
alt.radio.pirate
alt.radio.scanner
alt.rap
alt.rap-gdead
alt.rave
alt.rec.camping
alt.recovery
alt.recovery.catholicism
alt.recovery.codependency
alt.religion.all-worlds
alt.religion.christian
alt.religion.computers
alt.religion.islam
alt.religion.mormon
alt.religion.scientology
alt.restaurants
alt.revisionism
alt.revolution.counter
alt.rissa
alt.rock-n-roll
alt.romance
alt.rush-limbaugh
alt.satanism
alt.save.the.earth
alt.sci.astro.aips
alt.sci.physics.acoustics
alt.sci.physics.new-theories
alt.sci.physics.plutonium
alt.sci.planetary
alt.sci.sociology
alt.scooter
alt.security
alt.self-improve
alt.sewing
alt.sex

alt.sexual.abuse.recovery
alt.shenanigans
alt.showbiz.gossip
alt.skate
alt.skate-board
alt.skinheads
alt.skunks
alt.slack
alt.smokers
alt.snail-mail
alt.snowmobiles
alt.soc.ethics
alt.society.anarchy
alt.society.civil-liberties
alt.society.conservatism
alt.society.cu-digest
alt.society.futures
alt.society.generation-x
alt.society.neutopia
alt.society.resistance
alt.society.revolution
alt.soft-sys.corel.draw
alt.soft-sys.tooltalk
alt.soulmates
alt.sources
alt.sources.index
alt.sources.mac
alt.sources.patches
alt.sources.wanted
alt.stagecraft
alt.suburbs
alt.suicide.holiday
alt.support
alt.surfing
alt.surrealism
alt.sustainable.agriculture
alt.tarot
alt.tasteless
alt.tasteless.jokes
alt.technology.misc
alt.technology.obsolete
alt.tennis
alt.test
alt.toys.hi-tech
alt.transgendered
alt.travel.road-trip

alt.true-crime
alt.ufo.reports
alt.unix.wizards
alt.usage.english
alt.usenet.offline-reader
alt.visa.us
alt.wais
alt.war
alt.war.civil.usa
alt.war.vietnam
alt.wedding
alt.whistleblowing
alt.winsock
alt.wired
alt.wolves
alt.women.attitudes
alt.zen
alt.zines

Bionet Newsgroups (42)

bionet.agroforestry
bionet.announce
bionet.biology.computational
bionet.biology.n2-fixation
bionet.biology.tropical
bionet.cellbiol
bionet.drosophila
bionet.general
bionet.genome.arabidopsis
bionet.genome.chromosomes
bionet.immunology
bionet.info-theory
bionet.jobs
bionet.journals.contents
bionet.metabolic-reg
bionet.molbio.bio-matrix
bionet.molbio.embldatabank
bionet.molbio.evolution
bionet.molbio.genbank
bionet.molbio.genbank.updates
bionet.molbio.gene-linkage
bionet.molbio.genome-program
bionet.molbio.hiv
bionet.molbio.proteins
bionet.molbio.rapd
bionet.molbio.yeast

bionet.mycology
bionet.neuroscience
bionet.photosynthesis
bionet.plants
bionet.population-bio
bionet.sci-resources
bionet.software
bionet.software.acedb
bionet.software.gcg
bionet.users.addresses
bionet.virology
bionet.women-in-bio
bionet.xtallography

Bit Newsgroups (42)

bit.admin
bit.general
bit.listserv.aix-l
bit.listserv.autism
bit.listserv.autocat
bit.listserv.banyan-l
bit.listserv.c+health
bit.listserv.catholic
bit.listserv.cinema-l
bit.listserv.coco
bit.listserv.deaf-l
bit.listserv.dectei-l
bit.listserv.disarm-l
bit.listserv.film-l
bit.listserv.games-l
bit.listserv.gaynet
bit.listserv.geograph
bit.listserv.govdoc-l
bit.listserv.hellas
bit.listserv.help-net
bit.listserv.history
bit.listserv.hungary
bit.listserv.i-amiga
bit.listserv.ibm-main
bit.listserv.ibmtcp-l
bit.listserv.lawsch-l
bit.listserv.libref-l
bit.listserv.literary
bit.listserv.mideur-l
bit.listserv.museum-l
bit.listserv.muslims

bit.listserv.novell
bit.listserv.os2-l
bit.listserv.pacs-l
bit.listserv.pagemakr
bit.listserv.politics
bit.listserv.scuba-l
bit.listserv.seasia-l
bit.listserv.simula
bit.listserv.slovak-l
bit.listserv.techwr-l
bit.listserv.travel-l

Comp Newsgroups (72)

comp.admin.policy
comp.ai
comp.answers
comp.apps.spreadsheets
comp.archives
comp.bbs.majorbbs
comp.bbs.misc
comp.benchmarks
comp.cad.synthesis
comp.client-server
comp.cog-eng
comp.compilers
comp.compression
comp.constraints
comp.databases
comp.doc
comp.doc.techreports
comp.dsp
comp.editors
comp.edu
comp.edu.composition
comp.edu.languages.natural
comp.emacs
comp.emulators.misc
comp.fonts
comp.graphics
comp.groupware
comp.home.automation
comp.home.misc
comp.human-factors
comp.infosystems
comp.internet.net-happenings
comp.jobs

comp.lang.misc
comp.laser-printers
comp.mail.misc
comp.misc
comp.multimedia
comp.music
comp.newprod
comp.object
comp.org.acm
comp.org.eff.news
comp.org.eff.talk
comp.org.fidonet
comp.parallel
comp.patents
comp.periphs
comp.programming
comp.publish.prepress
comp.realtime
comp.risks
comp.robotics
comp.security.misc
comp.simulation
comp.society
comp.sources.misc
comp.specification
comp.speech
comp.std.misc
comp.sw.components
comp.sys.ibm.pc
comp.sys.laptops
comp.sys.mac
comp.sys.mentor
comp.sys.misc
comp.sys.novell
comp.text
comp.theory
comp.unix.misc
comp.virus
comp.windows.misc

Info Newsgroups (5)

info.big-internet
info.firearms
info.firearms.politics
info.grass.programmer
info.grass.user

K12 Newsgroups (17)

k12.chat.elementary
k12.chat.junior
k12.chat.senior
k12.chat.teacher
k12.ed.art
k12.ed.business
k12.ed.comp.literacy
k12.ed.health-pe
k12.ed.life-skills
k12.ed.math
k12.ed.music
k12.ed.science
k12.ed.soc-studies
k12.ed.special
k12.lang.art
k12.library
k12.sys.projects

Misc Newsgroups (50)

misc.activism.militia
misc.activism.progressive
misc.answers
misc.books.technical
misc.business.consulting
misc.consumers
misc.creativity
misc.education.adult
misc.education.home-
school.christian
misc.education.home-school.misc
misc.education.language.english
misc.education.medical
misc.education.multimedia
misc.education.science
misc.educational.medical
misc.emerg-services
misc.entrepreneurs
misc.entrepreneurs.moderated
misc.fitness
misc.forsale
misc.handicap
misc.headlines
misc.health.aids
misc.health.alternative
misc.health.arthritis

misc.health.diabetes
misc.immigration.misc
misc.industry.utilities.electric
misc.int-property
misc.invest
misc.jobs.misc
misc.kids
misc.kids.computer
misc.kids.consumers
misc.kids.health
misc.kids.info
misc.kids.pregnancy
misc.kids.vacation
misc.legal
misc.misc
misc.news.bosnia
misc.rural
misc.survivalism
misc.taxes
misc.transport.air-industry
misc.transport.rail.americas
misc.transport.rail.misc
misc.transport.urban-transit
misc.wanted
misc.writing

Rec Newsgroups (69)

rec.animals.wildlife
rec.answers
rec.antiques
rec.aquaria
rec.arts.animation
rec.arts.ascii
rec.arts.books
rec.arts.comics
rec.arts.dance
rec.arts.fine
rec.arts.marching.misc
rec.arts.misc
rec.arts.movies
rec.arts.mystery
rec.arts.poems
rec.arts.prose
rec.arts.sf.misc
rec.arts.theatre
rec.arts.tv

rec.audio
rec.autos
rec.aviation
rec.backcountry
rec.bicycles.misc
rec.birds
rec.boats
rec.climbing
rec.collecting
rec.crafts.misc
rec.equestrian
rec.folk-dancing
rec.food.recipes
rec.gambling
rec.games.misc
rec.gardens
rec.guns
rec.heraldry
rec.humor
rec.humor.oracle
rec.hunting
rec.juggling
rec.kites
rec.mag
rec.martial-arts
rec.misc
rec.motorcycles
rec.music.info
rec.org.mensa
rec.pets
rec.photo
rec.ponds
rec.puzzles
rec.pyrotechnics
rec.radio.amateur.misc
rec.railroad
rec.running
rec.scouting
rec.scuba
rec.skate
rec.skiing
rec.skydiving
rec.sport.misc
rec.toys.misc
rec.travel
rec.video

rec.windsurfing
rec.woodworking

Sci Newsgroups (84)

sci.aeronautics
sci.agriculture
sci.answers
sci.anthropology
sci.aquaria
sci.archaeology
sci.astro
sci.bio
sci.bio.conservation
sci.bio.ecology
sci.bio.entomology.lepidoptera
sci.bio.ethology
sci.bio.evolution
sci.bio.fisheries
sci.bio.herp
sci.bio.microbiology
sci.bio.paleontology
sci.bio.technology
sci.chaos
sci.chem
sci.chem.electrochem
sci.chem.labware
sci.chem.organomet
sci.classics
sci.cognitive
sci.comp-aided
sci.cryonics
sci.crypt
sci.crypt.research
sci.data.formats
sci.econ
sci.econ.research
sci.edu
sci.electronics
sci.electronics.cad
sci.electronics.repair
sci.energy
sci.energy.hydrogen
sci.engr
sci.environment
sci.fractals
sci.geo.earthquakes

sci.geo.eos
sci.geo.fluids
sci.geo.geology
sci.geo.hydrology
sci.geo.meteorology
sci.geo.oceanography
sci.geo.petroleum
sci.geo.satellite-nav
sci.image.processing
sci.lang
sci.logic
sci.materials
sci.math
sci.med
sci.military
sci.misc
sci.nanotech
sci.nonlinear
sci.op-research
sci.optics
sci.philosophy.meta
sci.philosophy.tech
sci.physics
sci.polymers
sci.psychology
sci.research
sci.research.careers
sci.research.postdoc
sci.skeptic
sci.space
sci.space.news
sci.space.policy
sci.space.science
sci.space.shuttle
sci.space.tech
sci.stat.consult
sci.stat.edu
sci.stat.math
sci.systems
sci.techniques.microscopy
sci.virtual-worlds

Soc Newsgroups (26)

soc.answers
soc.bi
soc.college

soc.college.grad
soc.college.gradinfo
soc.couples
soc.couples.intercultural
soc.couples.wedding
soc.culture.misc
soc.feminism
soc.genealogy.computing
soc.genealogy.misc
soc.history
soc.history.moderated
soc.libraries.talk
soc.misc
soc.net-people
soc.org.nonprofit
soc.penpals
soc.politics
soc.rights.human
soc.roots
soc.singles
soc.veterans
soc.women

Talk Newsgroups (23)

talk.abortion
talk.answers
talk.environment
talk.origins
talk.philosophy.humanism
talk.philosophy.misc
talk.politics.animals
talk.politics.china
talk.politics.crypto
talk.politics.drugs
talk.politics.guns
talk.politics.libertarian
talk.politics.medicine
talk.politics.mideast
talk.politics.misc
talk.politics.theory
talk.politics.tibet
talk.rape
talk.religion.buddhism
talk.religion.misc
talk.religion.newage
talk.rumors

List 4 - Telnet Sites for the Student

Advanced Technology Info Net - *world-wide agricultural news*
URL: `telnet://caticsuf.csufresno.edu`
Login: `super` or `public`
(To exit: type "0" (zero) at the main menu)

Air Force Institute of Technology - *Wright-Patterson AFB OH*
URL: `telnet://sabre.afit.af.mil`
Login: 1. Type username `AFITPAC`
            2. Type password `LIBRARY`
(To exit: 1. type `CTRL-Z`
            2. Type `QUIT`)

Albert Einstein College of Medicine - *Bronx NY*
URL: `telnet://lis.aecom.yu.edu`
Login: Hit `<RETURN>` twice

Baylor University - *Waco TX*
URL: `telnet://library.baylor.edu`
Login: At the Username prompt, enter `BAYLIS`
(To exit: type `PF1` until you are logged out of the system)

Boston Library Consortium - *Boston MA*
URL: `telnet://blc.lrc.northeastern.edu`
Login: 1. Select `BLC`
            2. Select 5 for VT100
(To exit: type `//EXIT`)

Boston University - *Boston MA*
URL: `telnet://library.bu.edu`
Login: `library`
(To exit: select D on main menu)

Bowman Gray School of Medicine - *Wake Forest, Winston-Salem NC*
URL: `telnet://152.11.242.245`
Login: type `opac`
(To exit: select D on the main menu)

Brandeis University - *Waltham MA*
URL: `telnet://library.brandeis.edu`
Login: Type username: `louis`
(To exit: type `quit`)

Catholic U of America Law Library - *Washington DC*
URL: `telnet://colombo.law.cua.edu`
Login: type `library`

(To exit: type Q on main menu)

College of the Holy Cross - *Worcester MA*
   URL: `telnet://hcacad.holycross.edu`
   Login: At the Username prompt, enter LIBRARY

Columbia U - *Manhattan NY*
   URL: `telnet://cli.cul.columbia.edu`
   Login: 1. When connected, hit RETURN
             2. Enter terminal type: vt100
   (To exit: type STOP)

Environmental Protection Agency - *Libraries, US & global info*
   URL: `telnet://epaibm.rtpnc.epa.gov`
   Login: follow instructions
   (To exit: 1. to escape type: <control>]
             2. to quit type: q

Federal Information Exchange (FEDIX) - *links to higher education*
   URL: `telnet://fedix.fie.com`
   Login: FEDIX
   (To exit: type the zero key)

Fenway Libraries Online - *Boston MA*
   URL: `telnet://flo.org`
   Login: Type username: GUEST
   (To exit: type ex, then 0 (zero) on main menu)

Food & Drug Administation (US) - *actions, testimony, news releases*
   URL: `telnet://fdabbs.fda.gov`
   Login: 1. At login prompt type: bbs (lower case)
             2. Follow instructions
   (To exit: type QUIT at any BBS COMMAND prompt)

Gallagher Law Library - *University of Washington*
   URL: `telnet://uwin.u.washington.edu`
   Login: 1. Select I on main menu
             2. Select LIB
             3. Select UWLIB
             4. Select GCAT
   (To exit: type Q)

Harvard University - *Boston MA*
   URL: `telnet://hollis.harvard.edu`
   Login: 1. Press RETURN when Mitek Server screen appears
             2. Type hollis Office for Info. Tech. screen
   (To exit: type <ESCAPE> xx)

Hytelnet - *assists access to libraries, CWISs, BBSs, &c. by Telnet*
URL: `telnet://access.usask.ca`
Login: Type as password hytelnet

International Centre for Distance Learning - *Open University (UK)*
URL: `telnet://acsvax.open.ac.uk`
Login: Type as username: icdl

InterNIC - *Directory and Database Services Telnet Interface*
URL: `telnet://ds.internic.net`
Login: Type as password guest

IPAC Extragalactic Database - *extragalactic objects literature*
URL: `telnet://ned.ipac.caltech.edu`
Login: type ned; no password needed

Jewish Theological Seminary of America - *New York NY*
URL: `telnet://jtsa.edu`
Login: 1. Type username ALEPH
         2. Select 3 for VT102 emulation
(To exit: type the <escape> key)

Kent State University - *Kent OH*
URL: `telnet://catalyst.kent.edu`
Login: 1. At ENTER TERMINAL TYPE, enter VT100
         2. At SELECT APPLICATION, type D
         3. At CICS, type LUKS

Lawrence Livermore National Laboratory - *Berkeley CA*
URL: `telnet://library.llnl.gov`
Login: Type username: PATRON
(To exit: type Q on main menu)

Library of Congress Information System (LOCIS)
URL: `telnet://locis.loc.gov`
(To exit: type 12 at the main menu)

Los Alamos National Laboratory - *Los Alamos NM*
URL: `telnet://admiral.lanl.gov`
Login: library
(To exit: select 2 on main menu)

Loyola Marymount University - *Los Angeles CA*
URL: `telnet://linus.lmu.edu`
Login: library

Martin Luther King Bibliography - *contains 2,700+ on King, civil rights*
URL: `telnet://forsythetn.stanford.edu`

Login: 1. At Account? prompt, type: Socrates
2. At Type of terminal? prompt, type: VT100
3. At YOUR RESPONSE prompt, type: select mlk
(To exit: type END)

Metro Boston Library Network - *Boston MA*
URL: telnet://mbln.bpl.org
Login: Type Username LIBRARY
(To exit: select EXIT on main menu)

Miami University - *Oxford OH*
URL: telnet://watson.lib.muohio.edu
Login: type library
(To exit: type H on the main menu)

Morehouse School of Medicine - *Atlanta GA*
URL: telnet://library.msm.edu
Login: Type username NEXPUBCAT
(To exit: 1. Return to the main menu
2. press <RETURN> to get Welcome screen
3. type EXIT)

National Center for Atmospheric Research - *Boulder CO*
URL: telnet://library.ucar.edu
Login: Select VT100 as your terminal type
(To exit: type END on the main menu)

National Institutes of Health
URL: telnet://nih-library.nih.gov
Login: When connected, type <ESCAPE>
(To exit: type D on main menu)

New York Institute of Technology - *Online Campus*
URL: telnet://acl.nyit.edu

New York Univ.; *Ehrman Medical, Waldmann Dental, & Law Libraries*
URL: telnet://mclib0.med.nyu.edu
Login: Type library
(To exit: type D)

OCEANIC (Oceanic Network Info Center) - *projects database, U. Delaware*
URL: telnet://delocn.udel.edu
Login: 1. At Username prompt: type INFO
2. Enter first/last name
(To exit: at SELECTION type $)

Pennsylvania State University - *University Park PA*
URL: telnet://lias.psu.edu

Login: Type `TERMINAL VT100` at the >>> prompt
(To exit: type `QUIT`)

Princeton Manuscripts Catalog - *Princeton NJ*

URL: `telnet://pucc.princeton.edu`
Login: 1. Type `FOLIO`
   2. When the list of choices appear, choose 3
(To exit: type `LOGOFF`)

Princeton University - *Princeton NJ*

URL: `telnet://catalog.princeton.edu`
(To exit: Type `LOGOFF` or `END`)

Rensselaer Polytech Institute - *Troy NY*

URL: `telnet://infotrac.rpi.edu`
Login: 1. At the Welcome screen, type `LIB`
   2. An the Library Information screen, type `CAT`
(To exit: Type `STOP`)

Rutgers University CWIS - *wide range of information services*

URL: `telnet://info.rutgers.edu`
(To exit: type `quit`)

Science & Tech. Info System (STIS) - *National Science Found. publications*

URL: `telnet://stis.nsf.gov`
Login: type `public` (there is no password required)
(To exit: 1. type `<ESC>` key to return to main menu
   2. choose logoff command)

Seattle Public Library - *Seattle WA*

URL: `telnet://spl.lib.wa.us`
Login: `library` (lowercase only)
(To exit: select "Logoff" from the main menu)

Smithsonian Astrophysical Observatory - *Cambridge MA*

URL: `telnet://asc.harvard.edu`
Login: Type `ascinfo`

Space Shuttle Earth Observations Project - *Houston TX*

URL: `telnet://sseop.jsc.nasa.gov`
Login: 1. Type username `photos`
   2. Type password `photos`

Stanford University - *Palo Alto CA*

URL: `telnet://forsythetn.stanford.edu`
Login: 1. At the Account? prompt, type `socrates`
   2. At the OK to proceed? prompt, type `YES`
(To exit: type `END`)

State Library of Pennsylvania

URL: `telnet://192.102.245.100`
Login: When connected, type <RETURN>
(To exit: type the <escape> key)

SUNY College of Environmental Science & Forestry - *Syracuse NY*

URL: `telnet://acsnet.syr.edu`
Login: 1. At the > prompt, type SUMMIT
2. At the Enter Terminal Type prompt, type VT100
3. At the Enter Summit prompt, type SUMMIT
(To exit: 1. Type LOGOFF
2. Type UNDIAL)

SWAIS Politics Databases - *speeches, briefings, papers, & documents*

URL: `telnet://sunsite.unc.edu`
Login: 1. type politics
2. screen will scroll until user sees "term=(unknown)"
3. press <enter> at this point
(To exit: type q)

Texas A&M - *College Station TX*

URL: `telnet://venus.tamu.edu`
Login: 1. Type username VTAM
2. At Texas A&M Statewide screen, type NOTIS
3. At the CICS screen, type <RETURN>
(To exit: type CTRL-Z)

Tufts University - *Boston MA*

URL: `telnet://library.tufts.edu`
Login: Type username TULIPS
(To exit: 1. Type CTRL-Z
2. Type QUIT)

Uniformed Services U of the Health Sciences - *Bethesda MD*

URL: `telnet://131.158.2.160`
Login: 1. Type catalog
2. Select v for VT100
(To exit: type D on the main menu)

U of Delaware - *Oceanographic Institute, Newark DE*

URL: `telnet://delocn.udel.edu`
Login: Type username INFO
(To exit: type EXIT)

U of MD CWIS - *archives, incl. computers, economic data, and government*

URL: `telnet://info.umd.edu`
Login: 1. type info

2. type terminal type (default is VT100)

(To exit: type Q for Quit)

U of Medicine and Dentistry of New Jersey - *Newark NJ*

URL: `telnet://library.umdnj.edu`

Login: 1. Type username LIBRARY

         2. At the Selection prompt, type OC (in uppercase)

(To exit: 1. Type CTRL-Z

         2. At the Selection prompt, enter QU)

U of Miami - *Miami FL, Integrated Bibliographic Information System*

URL: `telnet://stacks.library.miami.edu`

Login: 1. Type `library`

         2. Select v for VT100

(To exit: type QUIT)

U of New Mexico - *General library*

URL: `telnet://129.24.8.195`

Login: Type start to display LIBROS welcome screen

U of North Caronlina - *Coastal Library Consortium*

URL: `telnet://uncclc.coast.uncwil.edu`

Login: 1. Type `library`

         2. OPAC = INNOPAC <OP009>

(To exit: select Q on main menu)

U of Oregon - *Eugene OR*

URL: `telnet://janus.uoregon.edu`

Login: 1. Press <RETURN> several times

         2. At the login: prompt, type janus

         3. When asked for terminal type, enter v

(To exit: type x)

U of Texas Health Science Center - *San Antonio, TX*

URL: `telnet://athena.uthscsa.edu`

Login: Type username LIS

(To exit: 1. Type EXIT

         2. Press <RETURN>

         3. Type QUIT)

U of Virginia - *Charlottesville VA*

URL: `telnet://ublan.acc.virginia.edu`

Login: 1. Press <RETURN> until >> prompt appears

         2. Type C VIRGO at the >> prompt

         3. Enter VT100 at the terminal type prompt

(To exit: 1. Use the stop command or % to back out of menus

         2. When at the >> prompt, use the <escape> key)

U of Virginia Law Library - *Charlottesville VA*
    URL: `telnet://innopac.law.virginia.edu`
    Login: `library`
    (To exit: select D on main menu)

U.S. National Library of Medicine - *Bethesda MD*
    URL: `telnet://locator.nlm.nih.gov`
    Login: `locator` (lower case)
    (To exit: 1. return to the main menu by pressing <F2>
              2. select <Exit> or press X)

Vanderbilt University - *Nashville TN, Jean & Alexander Heard Library*
    URL: `telnet://ctrvax.vanderbilt.edu`
    Login: 1. Type username ACORN
              2. Press <RETURN> when "SysAvl Appl" appears
    (To exit: type CTRL-Z)

Washington and Lee Law Library - *many services & resources*
    URL: `telnet://liberty.uc.wlu.edu`
    Login: `lawlib` (in lower case letters)
    (To exit: type x)

Washington College of Law - *Washington DC*
    URL: `telnet://leagle.wcl.american.edu`
    Login: Type `library`
    (To exit: select D on main menu)

Weather Underground - *Complete U.S. Weather Service info*
    URL: `telnet://madlab.sprl.umich.edu`   3000
    (To exit: choose option <X>)

Wellesley College - *Wellesley MA*
    URL: `telnet://library.wellesley.edu`
    Login: Type `library`
    (To exit: type Q)

Yale University - *New Haven CT*
    URL: `telnet://umpg.ycc.yale.edu`   6520
    Login: 1. press <RETURN>
              2. terminal type: `vt100`
    (To exit: type STOP)

List 5 - FTP Sites for the Student

Archive of Electronic Magazines - *collection of various 'e-zines'*
URL: ftp://etext.archive.umich.edu pub/Zines/

Artwork - *OTIS project to collect online art*
URL: ftp://sunsite.unc.edu/pub/multimedia/pictures/OTIS/

ASCII Art FAQ - *by Jorn Barger*
URL: ftp://ftp.mcs.com/mcsnet.users/jorn/asciifaq.txt

AUPs - *Network acceptable use policies*
URL: ftp://nic.merit.edu/acceptable.use.policies/

BBS Internet List - *by F. Zamfield*
URL: ftp://sunsite.unc.edu/pub/docs/about-the-net/libsoft/internet_bbs.txt

Beginner's Guide to the Internet - *by P. Suarez*
URL: ftp://oak.oakland.edu/SimTel/msdos/info/bgi20.zip

Bibliographic Databases - *by Billy Barron and Marie-Christine Mahe*
URL: ftp://ftp.utdallas.edu/pub/staff/billy/libguide/

Byte - *Byte Magazine archives*
URL: ftp://oak.oakland.edu/pub/misc/byte/

Campus-Wide Info Systems - *by Judy Hallman, a paper*
URL: ftp://sunsite.unc.edu/pub/docs/about-the-net/cwis/hallman.txt

Community Nets - *by Arthur R. McGee, an information resource*
URL: ftp://ftp.netcom.com/pub/am/amcgee/community/

Comp Sci - *Computer Science Bibliographies available on the Internet*
URL: ftp://ftp.cs.umanitoba.ca/pub/bibliographies/index.html

Computer Jargon - *A complete list of hacker terminology & slang*
URL: ftp://aeneas.mit.edu/pub/gnu/jargon-README

Computer Mediated Communications - *by John December, a list*
URL: ftp://ftp.rpi.edu/pub/communications/internet-cmc.bib

Current Cites - *A journal citing articles on networks & computers*
URL: ftp://ftp.lib.berkeley.edu/pub/Current.Cites/

Democracy, Technology, and the Arts - *by Richard A. Lanham*
URL: ftp://press-gopher.uchicago.edu/pub/Excerpts/lanham.txt

Dir. of Electronic Journals & Newsletters - *by Michael Strangelove*
URL: ftp://ftp.cni.org/pub/net-guides/strangelove/

Dir. of Internet User Guides - *assembled by Library of Congress*
  URL: `ftp://ftp.loc.gov/pub/iug/`

Dir. of Scholarly Electronic Conferences - *by Diane K. Kovacs*
  URL: `ftp://ksuvxa.kent.edu/library/acadlist.readme`

Dr. E's Compendium - *J. Ellsworth, resources for adult education*
  URL: `ftp://ftp.std.com/pub/je/dre-list.txt`

Educator's Email - *An Educator's Guide to E-Mail Lists*
  URL: `ftp://nic.umass.edu/pub/ednet/educatrs.lst`

Educator's USENET - *guide to Usenet newsgroups*
  URL: `ftp://nic.umass.edu/pub/ednet/edusenet.gde`

Effector Online - *Electronic Frontier Foundation Newsletter*
  URL: `ftp://ftp.eff.org/pub/EFF/newsletters/Index`

EJournal Archive - *implications of electronic networks and texts*
  URL: `ftp://ftp.hanover.edu/pub/ejournal`

Electric Mystics Guide - *by M. Strangelove, directory of religious studies*
  URL: `ftp://panda1.uottawa.ca/pub/religion/`

Electronic Frontier Foundation - *cyberspace-related papers*
  URL: `ftp://ftp.eff.org/pub/Publications/CuD/Papers/`

Email 101 - *by John Goodwin, how to use email, etc.*
  URL: `ftp://mrcnext.cso.uiuc.edu/etext/etext93/email025.txt`

Email Services - *by David DeSimone, a list*
  URL: `ftp://sunsite.unc.edu/pub/docs/about-the-net/`
        `libsoft/email_services.txt`

FAX by Internet FAQ - *by Kevin Savetz*
  URL: `ftp://rtfm.mit.edu/pub/usenet/news.answers/`
        `internet-services/fax-faq`

Federal Information Resources - *documents from U.S. government*
  URL: `ftp://nic.merit.edu/omb/INDEX.omb`

Free Databases - *catalogs databases available without payment*
  URL: `ftp://idiom.berkeley.ca.us/pub/free-databases`

Gender Issues in Computer Networking - *by Leslie Regan Shade*
  URL: `ftp://alfred.carleton.ca/pub/freenet/93conference/papers/`

GILS - *Government Information Locator Service*
  URL: `ftp://ftp.cni.org/pub/gils/`

GNET Archive - *bringing the Internet to poor parts of the world*
  URL: `ftp://dhvx20.csudh.edu/global_net/`

Gold in Networks! - *by J. Martin, 'nuggets' in the network*
URL: `ftp://nic.merit.edu/documents/fyi/fyi_10.txt`

HelpNet Archives - *reference base for new users to the Internet*
URL: `ftp://ftp.temple.edu/pub/info/help-net`

High Weirdness by Email - *a list by (author unknown)*
URL: `ftp://slopoke.mlb.semi.harris.com/pub/weirdness/`

Human-Computer Interaction - *bibliography repository*
URL: `ftp://archive.cis.ohio-state.edu pub/hcibib/`

Infobot - *hotlist database*
URL: `ftp://ftp.netcom.com/pub/ksedgwic/hotlist/hotlist.html`

Information Delicatessen - *by Peter Kaminski, collection of Internet info*
URL: `ftp://ftp.netcom.com/pub/info-deli/bookmark.html`

Institute for Academic Tech. Bibliography - *by Carolyn Kotlas*
URL: `ftp://gandalf.iat.unc.edu/user/home/anonftp/`
`guides/irg-14.txt`

Institute for Academic Technology - *archive site*
URL: `ftp://gandalf.iat.unc.edu/user/home/anonftp/guides/`

Institute on Academic Info Resources - *by staff at Kenyon College*
URL: `ftp://ftp.kenyon.edu/pub/pub/e-pubs/workbook/`

Interest Groups List - *listing of special interest group mailing lists*
URL: `ftp://sri.com/netinfo/interest-groups.txt`

Internet Access Guide - *by Ellen Hoffman*
URL: `ftp://nic.merit.edu/introducing.the.internet/access.guide`

Internet Access - *by James Milles, covering individual Internet access*
URL: `ftp://sluaxa.slu.edu/pub/millesjg/internet.access`

Internet and Education - *by Noel Estabrook*
URL: `ftp://ftp.msu.edu/pub/education/`

Internet Books - *by Kevin Savetz, a comprehensive list*
URL: `ftp://rtfm.mit.edu/pub/usenet/news.answers/`
`internet-services/book-list`

Internet FAQs - *Lists of frequently asked questions*
URL: `ftp://rtfm.mit.edu/pub/usenet/news.answers/`
`internet-services/faq`

Internet Glossary - *terminology of the Internet defined*
URL: `ftp://nic.merit.edu/documents/fyi/fyi_18.txt`

Internet History - *by E. H. Hardy, master's thesis*
  URL:
  `ftp://umcc.umich.edu/pub/users/seraphim/doc/nethist8.txt`

Internet Hunt - *an Internet learning game*
  URL: `ftp://ftp.cni.org/pub/net-guides/i-hunt/`

Internet Mall - *Commercial services available on the Internet (monthly)*
  URL: `ftp://netcom.com/pub/Guides/`

Internet Navigating - *by Richard J. Smith, a workshop list*
  URL: `ftp://ubvm.cc.buffalo.edu/navigate/`

Internet News - *by C. Sam Sternberg, news, press services, and publications*
  URL: `ftp://ftp.shell.portal.com/pub/jshunter/news.html`

Internet Press - *Guide to electronic journals about the Internet*
  URL: `ftp://rtfm.mit.edu/pub/usenet/news.answers/`
        `internet-services/internet-press`

Internet Resource Directory for Educators
  URL: `ftp://tcet.unt.edu/pub/telecomputing-info/IRD`

Internet Society - *charts of traffic, connectivity, hosts, etc.*
  URL: `ftp://ftp.isoc.org/isoc/charts/`

Internet Talk Radio - *by Carl Malamud*
  URL: `ftp://sunsite.unc.edu/pub/talk-radio/ITRintro.readme`

Internet Tools - *by John December, summary Internet tools & CMC*
  URL: `ftp://ftp.rpi.edu/pub/communications/`
        `internet-tools.readme`

Internet Training - *by Bill Wheeler, handouts*
  URL: `ftp://s850.mwc.edu/nettrain/`

Internet Wiretap - *electronic books and information*
  URL: `ftp://wiretap.spies.com/About/`

Internet Writer Resources - *by L. Detweiler, a list*
  URL: `ftp://rtfm.mit.edu/pub/usenet/news.answers/`
        `writing/resources`

InterText - *an electronically distributed magazine of fiction*
  URL: `ftp://network.ucsd.edu/intertext/`

JAUC - *The Journal Of American Underground Computing*
  URL: `ftp://etext.archive.umich.edu pub/Zines/JAUC/`

Journalism Directory - *by J. Makulowich, Internet resources*
URL: `ftp://ftp.clark.net/pub/journalism/`

Libraries on the Internet - *internet material for librarians*
URL: `ftp://nic.funet.fi/pub/doc/library/`

Library Catalogs & Databases - *by Art St. George and Ron Larsen*
URL: `ftp://nic.cerf.net/internet/resources/library_catalog/`

Library Catalogs - *by Dana Noonan, online library catalogs*
URL: `ftp://sunsite.unc.edu/pub/docs/about-the-net/`
`libsoft/guide2.txt`

Library Resources on the Internet - *edited by Laine Farley*
URL: `ftp://dla.ucop.edu/pub/internet/libcat-guide`

Library Services for CMC - *a paper by the OCLC Research Group*
URL: `ftp://ftp.rsch.oclc.org/pub/`
`internet_resources_project/report/`

LIBRES - *Library and Information Science Electronic Journal*
URL: `ftp://cc.curtin.edu.au/LIB-RESEARCH/`

Media List - *by Adam Gaffin, e-mail addresses of media outlets*
URL: `ftp://ftp.std.com/customers/periodicals/`
`Middlesex-News/medialist`

Meta Magazine - *news and editorials on and by the net community*
URL: `ftp://ftp.netcom.com/pub/mlinksva/meta.html`

MOO Papers - *Pavel Curtis' collection of MU* papers*
URL: `ftp://ftp.parc.xerox.com/pub/MOO/papers/`

National Academy of Sciences - *archives*
URL: `ftp://ftp.nas.edu`

National Science Foundation - *resource guide to Internet resources*
URL: `ftp://ds.internic.net/resource-guide/overview`

Navigating the Internet - *by Richard J. Smith, a workshop via email*
URL: `ftp://ftp.sura.net/pub/nic/training/`

Net Etiquette Guide - *by Arlene H. Rinaldi, user behavior, propriety*
URL: `ftp://ftp.lib.berkeley.edu/pub/net.training/FAU/`

Network Knowledge for the Neophyte - *by M. Raishstuff, navigation*
URL: `ftp://hydra.uwo.ca/pub/libsoft/`
`network_knowledge_for_the_neophyte.txt`

New User's Questions - *by Malkin and Marine, FAQs*
URL: `ftp://nic.merit.edu/documents/fyi/fyi_04.txt`

REACH - *Research & Ed. Applications of Computers in Humanities*
  URL: `ftp://ucsbuxa.ucsb.ed/hcf/`

Retrieval Success Stories - *by Karen Schneider, Internet for reference*
  URL: `ftp://mailbase.ac.uk/pub/lists/unite/files/`
        `internet-stories.txt`

Rovers' Anonymous FTP Sites - *by Perry Rovers, list*
  URL: `ftp://rtfm.mit.edu/pub/usenet/news.answers/ftp-list/`

Scholarly Communication by Network - *by Brian Kahin*
  URL: `ftp://ftp.cni.org/CNI/projects/Harvard.scp/kahin.txt`

Scholarly Communication Libraries - *by Mellon Foundation*
  URL: `ftp://ftp.cni.org/ARL/mellon/`

Social Organization of Computer Underground - *Gordon R. Meyer*
  URL: `ftp://ftp.eff.org/pub/Publications/CuD/Papers/meyer/`

Society of Professional Journalists - *archives*
  URL: `ftp://ftp.netcom.com/pub/spj/html/spj.html`

Student Aid Sources - *grants, scholarships and funding*
  URL: `ftp://riceinfo.rice.edu/`

Sunsite Communication - *by David Barberi, archive*
  URL: `ftp://sunsite.unc.edu/pub/academic/communications/`

Surfing the Internet - *by Jean Armour Polly, a narrative of services*
  URL: `ftp://nysernet.org/pub/resources/`
        `guides/surfing.2.0.3.txt`

Texas Internet Consulting - *Internet demographics, study*
  URL: `ftp://ftp.tic.com/survey/`

The BigFun List - *by Jeremy Smith, telnet, ftp, and other sites*
  URL: `ftp://owl.nstn.ns.ca/pub/netinfo/bigfun.txt`

The Online World - *by Odd De Presno Guide, shareware book*
  URL: `ftp://ftp.eunet.no/pub/text/`

US Government Information - *by Blake Gumprecht*
  URL: `ftp://ftp.nwnet.net/user-docs/government/`
        `gumprecht-guide.txt`

USENET FAQs - *collection of files from Usenet newsgroups*
  URL: `ftp://rtfm.mit.edu/pub/usenet/`

USENET Maps - *Maps of Usenet news feeds/backbones*
  URL: `ftp://gatekeeper.dec.com/pub/maps/`

USENET University - *online learning, teaching or tutoring*
URL: `ftp://nic.funet.fi/pub/doc/uu/FAQ`

User Network Interface To Everything - *Internet tools & systems list*
URL: `ftp://mailbase.ac.uk/pub/lists/unite/files/`
        `systems-list.txt`

WAIS Sources - *grouped into relevant categories*
URL: `ftp://kirk.bond.edu.au/pub/Bond_Uni/doc/wais/readme`

Where to Start for New Internet Users - *by James Milles*
URL: `ftp://sluaxa.slu.edu/pub/millesjg/newusers.faq`

List 6 - Educational Websites

Adult Education, Votech ed, Corrections ed site
http://WWW.coled.umn.edu/votech/default.html

American Education Research Association
http://info.asu.edu/aff/aera/home.html

American universities
http://www.clas.ufl.edu/CLAS/american-universities.html

Argonne National Laboratory, Dept. of Ed.
http://www.newton.dep.anl.gov

AskERIC
http://gopher.ericse.ohio-state.edu/
http://www.indiana.edu
http://eryx.syr.edu/Main.html
http://ericir.syr.edu/
http://eryx.syr.edu/Main.html
http://eryx.syr.edu/COWSHome.html

Association for Support of Graduate Students
http://www.wpm.com/asgs/

Athena University (Formerly Virtual Online University)
http://core.symnet.net/~VOU/
http://symnet.net/~VOU

Audio and Video on Demand
http://mcindy.cs.colorado.edu/home/homenii/demand.html

Business Guide for Internet; S. Sternberg
http://www.phoenix.ca/Phoenix/whats-new.html

Career Resource Center
http://www.seanet.com/Vendors/careers

Centre for Research into the Ed. of Adults; Univ. of Nottingham, UK
http://acorn.educ.NOTTINGHAM.AC.UK/AdultEd/Welcome.html

Changing the Face of the Earth
http://www.peg.apc.org/~shelter/ctfote

Classroom Connect; More than 800 links to educational information
http://www.wentworth.com/classroom/

Commonwealth of Learning
http://www.col.org

Computer News Daily
http://nytsyn.com/cgi-bin/times/lead/go

Computer-based education links
http://www.uct.ac.za/projects/cbe

443

Computer-Mediated Communication, by John December
http://www.rpi.edu/~decemj/cmc/mag/current/toc.html

Connecting With Nature: Ecopsychology
http://www.pacificrim.net/~nature/

Cyber High School
http://www.webcom.com/~cyberhi

Desktop Video Conferencing Products
http://www2.ncsu.edu/eos/service/ece/project/
succeed_info/dtvc_survey/products.html

Directory of Literacy and Adult Ed. Resources, by Tom Eland
http://www.cybernetics.net/users/sagrelto/elandh/home.htm

Distance Education Links
http://joe.uwex.edu/stremiki/edresources
http://dolphin.csudh.edu/~dlearn/
http://lemming.uvm.edu/
http://mcindy.cs.colorado.edu/home/homenii/distance.html
http://ollc.mta.ca
http://www.crl.com/~gorgon/distance.html
http://www.yahoo.com/yahoo/education/on_line_teaching_and_learning/

Distance Education webpage by Thomas R. Ramage
http://www.dacc.cc.il.us/~ramage

Distance Learning Directory
http://www.ed.uiuc.edu/collis/

Distance Learning site
http://www.con-ed.howard.edu/WebPages/dll/DIST-LRN/dll.htm

Dr. E's Eclectic Compendium of Resources for Adult/Distance Education
http://www.oak-ridge.com/ierdrep1.html

Edith Cowan University Virtual Campus Australia (ECU)
http://www.cowan.edu.au/ecuwis/docs/virtcamp/virt.html

Educational Technology Journal: "FROM NOW ON"
http://www.pacificrim.net/~mckenzie

EDUTEL
http://www.mailbase.ac.uk

EdWeb (educational computing and networking on-line,by the CPB)
http://k12.cnidr.org:90/resource.cntnts.html
http://edweb.cnidr.org

Electronic Prehistoric Shark Museum
http://turnpike.net/emporium/C/celestial/epsm.html

Environmental Protection Agency (US)
http://www.epa.gov/Rules.html

ERIC Clearinghouse for Science, Math and Environmental Education
http://gopher.ericse.ohio-state.edu/

European Assn of Distance Teaching Universities/Open U, Netherlands
http://www.ouh.nl

FEDIX/MOLIS (Federal Education Information Database
http://web.fie.com

Foreign to US currency conversions
http://gnn.com/cgi-bin/gnn/currency?United_States

FredNet
http://www.fred.net/nhhs/nhhs.html
http://www.fred.net/nhhs/html/cassutto.html

From Now On - A Monthly Commentary on Ed Technology Issues
http://www.pacificrim.net/~mckenzie/

Global Campus
http://www.calpoly.edu:80/~delta/

Globewide Network Academy
http://uu-gna.mit.edu:8001/uu-gna/index.html

GNN Education Center - Houghton Mifflin
http://gnn.com/edu/

HandsNet
http://www.handsnet.org/handsnet

Henry W. Grady Coll. of Journalism and Mass Communication, U of GA
http://www.grady.uga.edu/ProtoPapers/Reports/Reports.html

Humanities External Degree Program (MA in Humanities)
http://dolphin.csudh.edu/~huxindex.html

Institute for Advanced Metaphysical Studies
http://www:tagsys.com/Ads/MetaPhysical/

Intelligent Tutoring Media Journal
http://www.dcs.ex.ac.uk/~masoud/yazdani/editor/itm.html

Interactive Age
http://techweb.cmp.com/ia

Interactive Age Daily
http://techweb.cmp.com/ia

Interactive frog dissection
http://paul.spu.edu/~mmorrell/fun.html

International Centre for Distance Learning (ICDL)
http://acs-info.open.ac.uk/info/other/ICDL/ICDL-Facts.html

International News
http://www.auburn.edu/~vestmon/news.html

International universities
http://www.mit.edu:8001/people/cdemello/geog.html

Internet Chess Club
http://www.hydra.com/icc/

Internet Job Locator
http://mtc.globesat.com/jobs

Internet Resources (by Heriot-Watt University Library)
http://www.hw.ac.uk/libWWW/irn/irn.html

Introductory Mechanics using Interactive Physics app; U of Ill at Chicago
http://halliwell.phy.uic.edu/IP/instructions/*IP.html

Italian universities and research centers
http://dibe.unige.it/hp_dli/hpdli_hp.html

Living Your Dream - The Option Institute
http://www.human.com/mkt/option, gopher human.com

Macintosh Educators Page for K-12 Educators
http://www.netinw.net/showcase/macintosh/

Map of the Internet
http://ucmp1.berkeley.edu/subway.html
http://www.ziff.com:8010/~pccomp/webmap/
http://www.kumc.edu/Internet/InternetClass/internet_class.html

Media-Link
http://www.dds.nl/~kidon/media.html

MediaInfo Interactive: online newspaper services, 165 Web sites, etc.
http://www.mediainfo.com/edpub

Michigan Information Technology Distance Learning Directory
http://www.mitn.msu.edu/distance.htm

Mind Extension University (MEU)
http://www.meu.edu/

Mindmedia; personality tests and self-improvment site
http://www.mindmedia.coms

Montana State University - *Graphical Data Analysis*
http://www.math.montana.edu/~umsfjban/STAT438/Stat438.html

Montana State University - *use of web in teaching*
http://www.math.montana.edu/~umsfjban/Seminar.html

NASA news site
http://spacelink.msfc.nasa.gov

NASA shuttle launch timetable
   http://www.ksc.nasa.gov/shuttle/missions/missions.html

National-Louis University - *Dept. of Adult & Continuing Education*
   http://nlu.nl.edu/ace/ACEHome.html

Netscape's "push" demonstration site
   http://www.razorfish.com/

NetWatch web magazine
   http://www.pulver.com/netwatch

New York Times 'TimesFax'
   http://nytimesfax.com

Oak Ridge National Laboratory Review
   http://www.ornl.gov/ORNLReview/rev26-2/text/home.html

Open University (UK)
   http://www.open.ac.uk/

Peterson's Guides
   http://www.petersons.com

Public Libraries with Internet access
   http://sjcpl.lib.in.us/homepage/PublicLibraries/

Réseau scolaire canadien (RSC)(SchoolNet en francais)
   http://schoolnet.carleton.ca/french/schlnetf.html

SchoolNet (English)
   http://schoolnet2.carleton.ca

Science for children
   http://scitech.lm.com/index.html

Smithsonian - *exhibit: "DRYLANDS - Bright Edges of the World"*
   http://drylands.nasm.edu:1995

Social Science Information Technology
   http://www.gamma.rug.nl

Speech/communication disorders (from Gus Communications Inc.
   http://www.direct.ca/gus/index.html

Star Schools: high school, middle school, and staff development courses
   http://www.scsn.net/~serc/

Student Services Scholarship Search
   http://www.studentservices.com/search/

Study Educational Technology Institute - course 'Online Learning'
   http://130.89.41.97/Marco/online/campus.html

TeleEducation New Brunswick
http://ollc.mta.ca

Teleport
http://www.teleport.com/~illum

The Educational Technology Journal
http://www.pacificrim.net/~mckenzie

The Higher Education Database
http://www.access.digex.net/~reimann/heproc

The Internet Mall (1,900 online stores)
http://www.mecklerweb.com/imall

The Internet Society
http://www.isoc.org/

The Open Learning Agency
http://oilpatch.schdist60.bc.ca/ola.html

Training & Management Development
http://www.garlic.com/rfwilson/trdev.html

Training courses listed by topic
http://www.tregistry.com/ttr

Travel and tourist information
http://www.city.net/
http://wings.buffalo.edu/world/
http://www.neosoft.com/citylink/

Tutorials: Courses on html's, primers, do-it-yourself web pages
http://emmetal.cs.wisc.edu:1994/bob.html
http://www.webcom.com/~greeting/diy/diy.html
http://www2.pcy.mci.net/whats-new/editors/index.html
http://www.ets.bris.ac.uk/ets/resource/tutorial/tutorial.html

Tutorial: Modem Workshop (a shareware book-on-disk) for IBM PC
http://turnpike,net/emporium/C/celestial/celest.html

Tutorials on C, C++, VC++, Motif, etc.
http://www.iftech.com

U of No Carolina Offc for Info Tech
http://sunsite.unc.edu/pjones/

U.S. Budget Simulator (by UC Berkeley)
http://garnet.berkeley.edu:3333/budget/budget.html

U.S. Department of Education
http://www.ed.gov.

University of Cape Town, South Africa's Computer-Based Education (CBE)
http://www.uct.ac.za/projects/cbe/

University of Georgia Center for Continuing Education
http://www.gactr.uga.edu/

US Postal Service Zip code generator
http://www.usps.gov/ZIP4Form.html

USENET search service, by keyword
http://www.dejanews.com/

Video Conferencing
http://fiddle.ee.vt.edu/succeed/videoconf.html
http://mcindy.cs.colorado.edu/home/homenii/videoconf.html

Video Webalog
http://figment.fastman.com/vweb/html/vidmain.html

Web Developer's Virtual Library
http://WWW.Stars.com/

Web Map in clickable HTML format
http://www.ziff.com:8010/~pccomp/webmap/

Web tools (written in Tcl/Tk)
http://hplyot.obspm.fr/~dl/wwwtools.html

WebAholics Site
http://www.ohiou.edu/~rbarrett/webaholics/ver2/

WebChat Broadcasting System
http://www.irsociety.com/wbs.html

World Lecture Hall
http://wwwhost.cc.utexas.edu/world/instruction/index.html
http://www.utexas.edu/world/lecture/

Writers Alliance (Internet training workshops), by John Makulowich
http://www.clark.net/pub/journalism/brochure.html

WWW NewsLink (campus papers)
http://www.newslink.org/newslink/

WWW Virtual Library: *biology depts, institutes, acad. programs, prof. orgs*
http://golgi.harvard.edu/afagen/depts/deptus.html

WWW Virtual Library
http://www.library.nwu.edu/.nul/libresources.html

Zines on the Internet
http://www.ora.com:8080/johnl/e-zine-list/

List 7 - College and University Websites:

Given the extreme rush to the Web, many universities and colleges have established websites. These range in complexity from extensive to 'under construction'. A list is provided for your exploration - bear in mind that this is a volatile environment and that sites come and go, and undergo dramatic changes, often overnight.

Abilene Christian University
http://cteserver.acu.edu/

Agnes Scott College
http://www.scottlan.edu/

Albert Einstein College of Medicine
http://www.aecom.yu.edu/

Albertson College of Idaho
http://www.acofi.edu/

Albion College
http://www.albion.edu/

Alderson-Broaddus College
http://www.mountain.net/ab/

Alfred University
http://screech.alfred.edu/

Allentown College
http://www.allencol.edu/

Amherst College
http://www.amherst.edu/start.html

Antioch University
http://college.antioc.edu/

Appalachian State University
http://www.acs.appstate.edu/

Arizona State University
http://info.asu.edu/

Assumption College
http://www.assumption.edu:80/

Auburn University
http://mallard.duc.auburn.edu/

Augsburg College
http://www.augsburg.edu/

Augustana College
http://www.augustana.edu/

Austin College
http://www.austinc.edu/

Azusa Pacific University
http://apu.edu/

Baker University
http://www.bakeru.edu/

Ball State University
http://virgo.bsu.edu:8080/

Bard College
http://www.bard.edu/

Bates College
http://abacus.bates.edu/

Baylor College of Medicine
http://www.bcm.tmc.edu/

Baylor University
http://www.baylor.edu/

Belmont University
http://acklen.belmont.edu/

Beloit College
http://stu.beloit.edu/

Berea College
http://www.berea.edu/

Bethany College
http://info.bethany.wvnet.edu/

Bethel College, Newton KS
http://www.bethelks.edu/

Binghamton University
http://www.binghamton.edu/

Biola University
http://www.biola.edu/

Bloomsburg University
http://www.bloomu.edu/

Boise State University
http://www.idbsu.edu/

Boston College
http://infoeagle.bc.edu/

Boston University
http://web.bu.edu/

Bowdoin College
http://www.bowdoin.edu/

Bowling Green State University
http://www.bgsu.edu/

Bradley University
http://www.bradley.edu/

Brandeis University
http://www.brandeis.edu/

Bridgewater College
http://www.bridgewater.edu/

Brigham Young University
http://www.byu.edu/

Brigham Young Univ. - Hawaii
http://www.byuh.edu/

Brown University
http://www.brown.edu/

Bucknell University
http://www.bucknell.edu/

Buena Vista Coll. - Storm Lake IA
http://othmar.bvc.edu/

Butler University
http://www.butler.edu/

California Lutheran University
http://robles.callutheran.edu/

Cal State Poly U. - S. Luis Obispo
http://www.calpoly.edu/

Cal State University - Chico
http://www.csuchico.edu/

Cal State Univ. - Dominguez Hills
http://dolphin.csudh.edu/
~huxindex.html

Cal State University - Fullerton
http://www.fullerton.edu/

Cal State University - Hayward
http://www.mcs.csuhayward.edu/

Cal State University - Long Beach
http://www.csulb.edu/

Cal State University - Los Angeles
http://www.calstatela.edu/

Cal State University - Northridge
http://www.csun.edu/

Cal State University - Sacramento
http://ww.csus.edu/

Cal State Univ. - San Bernadino
http://www.csusb.edu/

Cal State University - San Marcos
http://coyote.csusm.edu/

Cal State University - Stanislaus
http://lead.csustan.edu/

California Institute of Technology
http://www.caltech.edu/

California Institute of the Arts
http://www.calarts.edu/

Calvin College
http://www.calvin.edu/

Carleton College
http://www.carleton.edu/

Carnegie Mellon University
http://www.cmu.edu/

Carroll College
http://carroll1.cc.edu/

Case Western Reserve University
http://www.cwru.edu/

451

Cedarville College
http://www.cedarville.edu/DPMA/

Centenary College of Louisiana
http://alpha.centenary.edu/

Central Michigan U - Computers
http://www.cps.cmich.edu/

Central Missouri State University
http://cmsuvmb.cmsu.edu/

Central Washington University
http://www.cwu.edu/

Centre College, Danville KY
http://www.centre.edu/

Cerritos College
http://www.cerritos.edu

Chapman University
http://www.chapman.edu

Chicago-Kent College of Law
http://www.kentlaw.edu

Christopher Newport University
http://www.pcs.cnu.edu/

City University of New York
http://www.cuny.edu/

City U, Seattle WA
http://www.cityu.edu/inroads/

Clark University
http://www.clarku.edu/

Clarke College
http://www.clarke.edu/

Clemson University
http://www.clemson.edu/home.html

Cleveland State University
http://www.csuohio.edu/

Coe College
http://www.coe.edu/

Colby College
http://www.colby.edu/

Colgate University
http://cs.colgate.edu/

College of Aeronautics
http://www.mordor.com/coa/coa.html

College of Charleston
http://www.cs.cofc.edu/

College of Eastern Utah
http://www.ceu.edu/

College of St. Benedict
http://www.csbsju.edu/

College of the Holy Cross
http://www.holycross.edu/

College of William and Mary
http://www.wm.edu/

Colorado Christian University
http://www.ccu.edu/

Colorado College
http://www.cc.coloradoedu/

Colorado School of Mines
http://gn.mines.colorado.edu:80/

Colorado State University
http://www.colostate.edu/

Columbia College
http://www.colum.edu/

Columbia University
http://www.columbia.edu/

Concordia College
http://www.cord.edu/

Connecticut College
http://camel.conncoll.edu/

Cornell College, Iowa
http://www.cornell-iowa.edu/

Cornell University
http://www.cornell.edu/

Creighton University
http://bluejay.creighton.edu/

Dakota State University
http://www.dsu.edu/

Dana College
http://www.dana.edu/

Dartmouth College
http://www.dartmouth.edu/

Denison University
http://louie.cc.denison.edu/

DePaul Universty
http://www.depaul.edu/

Diablo Valley College
http://www.dvc.edu/

Dixie College
http://sci.dixie.edu/

Drake University
http://www.drake.edu/default.html

Drew U, Academic Tech.
http://tarzan.drew.edu/athome.html

Drexel University
http://www.drexel.edu/

Duke University
http://www.duke.edu/

Duquesne University
http://www.duq.edu/

Earlham College
http://http.earlham.edu/

East Carolina University
http://ecuvax.cis.ecu.edu/

East Central U, Ada OK
http://student.ecok.edu/

East Stroudsburg State University
http://www.esu.edu/

East Tennessee State University
http://etsu.east-tenn-st.edu

East Texas State University
http://www.etsu.edu

Eastern Illinois University
http://www.eiu.edu/

Eastern Michigan University
http://www.emich.edu/

Eastern New Mexico State Univ.
http://www.enmu.edu/

Eastern Washington University
http://www.ewu.edu/

Edinboro Univ. of Pennsylvania
http://www.edinboro.edu/

Elizabeth City State University
http://www.ecsu.edu/

Embry-Riddle Aeronautical Univ.
http://macwww.db.erau.edu/

Emmanuel College
http://www.emmanuel.edu/

Emporia State University
http://www.emporia.edu/Index.html

Fayetteville State University
http://www.fsufay.edu/

Ferris State University
http://about.ferris.edu/

Fisk University
http://www.fisk.edu/

Florida Atlantic University
http://www.fau.edu/

Florida Institute of Technology
http://www.fit.edu/

Florida International University
http://nomadd.fiu.edu/

Florida State University
http://www.fsu.edu/

Fort Hays State University
http://fhsuvm.fhsu.edu/

Franklin and Marshall College
http://www.fandm.edu/

Fredonia State University
http://www.fredonia.edu/

Fullerton College
http://www.fullerton.edu/

Furman University
http://www.furman.edu/

Gallaudet University
http://www.gallaudet.edu/

George Mason University
http://www.gmu.edu/

George Washington University
http://gwis.circ.gwu.edu/

Georgetown University
http://www.georgetown.edu/

Georgia Institute of Technology
http://www.gatech.edu/

Georgia State University
http:://www.gsu.edu/

Gettysburg College
http://www.gettysburg.edu/

Gonzaga University
http:://www.gonzaga.edu/

Goshen College
http:://www.goshen.edu/

Goucher College
http:://www.goucher.edu/

Grace College
http:://www.grace.edu/

Graceland College
http://www.graceland.edu/

Gustavus Adolphus College
http://www.gac.edu/

Hahnemann University
http://www.hahnemann.edu/

Hamilton College
http://www.hamilton.edu/

Hamline University
http://www.hamline.edu/

Hampden-Sydney College
http://lion.hsc.edu/

Hampshire College
http://www.hampshire.edu/

Hanover College
http://www.hanover.edu/

Harding University
http://www.harding.edu/

Hartwick College
http://www.hartwick.edu/

Harvard University
http://www.harvard.edu/

Harvey Mudd College
http://www.hmc.edu/

Haverford College
http://www.haverford.edu/

Heidelberg College
http://www.heidelberg.edu/

Hendrix College
http://192.131.98.11/

Hiram College
http://www.hiram.edu/

Hobart & William Smith Colleges
http://hws3.hws.edu:9000/

Hofstra University
http://www.hofstra.edu/

Hope College
http://www.hope.edu/

Howard University
http://www.howard.edu/

Humboldt State University
http://rocky.humboldt.edu/

Huntington College
http://www.huntcol.edu/

Idaho State University
http://www.isu.edu/

Illinois Institute of Technology
http://www.iit.edu/

Illinois State University
http://www.ilstu.edu/

Incarnate Word College
http://www.iwctx.edu/

Indiana Institute Technologyy
http://www.indtech.edu/

Indiana State University
http://www.indstate.edu/

Indiana University
http://www.indiana.edu/

Indiana Univ. of Pennsylvania
http://www.lib.iup.edu/

Iowa State University
http://www.iastate.edu/

Ithaca College
http://www.ithaca.edu/

Jacksonsonville State University
http://jsucc.jsu.edu/home.html

James Madison University
http://www.jmu.edu/

Johnson C. Smith University
http://www.jcsu.edu/index.html

Kalamazoo College
http://www.kzoo.edu/

Kansas State University
http://www.ksu.edu/

Keene State College
http://kilburn.keene.edu/

Kent State University
http://www.kent.edu/

Kenyon College
http://www.kenyon.edu/

Kutztown University of PA
http://www.kutztown.edu/

La Sierra University
http://www.lasierra.edu/

La Sierra University
http://www.lasierra.edu/

Lafayette College
http://www.lafayette.edu/

Lake Forest College
http://www.lfc.edu/

Lamar University
http://www.lamar.edu/

Langston University
http://www.lunet.edu/

Lasalle University
http://www.lasalle.edu/

Lawrence University
http://www.lawrence.edu/

Lehigh Univervsity
http://www.lehigh.edu/

Lewis & Clark College
http://www.lclark.edu/

Lock Haven University
http://www.lhup.edu/

Louisiana State University
http://unix1.sncc.lsu.edu/

Louisiana Tech University
http://aurora.latech.edu/

Loyola College
http://www.loyola.edu/

Loyola Marymount University
http://www.lmu.edu/

Loyola U, Chicago
http://www.luc.edu/

Lycoming College
http://www.lycoming.edu/

455

Macalester College
http://www.macalstr.edu/

Manhattan College
http://www.cc.mancol.edu/

Mankato State University
http://www.mankato.msus.edu/

Mansfield University
http://157.62.12.80/

Marist College
http://www.marist.edu/

Marshall University
http://www.marshall.edu/

Mary Washington College
http://www.mwc.edu/

Mass. Institute of Technology
http://web.mit.edu/

Mass. Maritime Academy
http://www.mma.mass.edu/

McNeese State University
http://www.mcneese.edu/

Medical College of Georgia
http://www.mcg.edu/

Medical College of Ohio
http://www.mco.edu/

Medical College of Wisconsin
http://www.mcw.edu/

Medical Univ. of SC, Oncology
http://www.radonc.musc.edu/

Meharry Medical College
http://ccmac.mmc.edu/

Mercer University
http://www.mercer.peachnet.edu/

Mercyhurst College
http://utopia.mercy.edu/

Metro State College of Denver
http://www.mscd.edu/

Metropolitan State University
http://www.metro.msus.edu/

Miami University of Ohio
http://www.muohio.edu/

Michigan State University
http://www.msu.edu/

Michigan Technological Univ.
http://www.mtu.edu/

Middle Tennessee State Univ.
http://www.mtsu.edu/

Middlebury College
http://www.middlebury.edu/

Midwestern State University
http://www.mwsu.edu/

Millersville University
http://marauder.millersv.edu/

Millsaps College
http://www.millsaps.edu/

Milwaukee School of Engineering
http://www.msoe.edu/

Mississippi College
http://www.mc.edu/

Mississippi State University
http://www.msstate.edu/

Missouri Western State College
http://www.mwsc.edu/

Monmouth College
http://www.monmouth.edu/

Montana State U-Bozeman
http://www.montana.edu/

Montana State U-Northern Havre
http://cis.nmclites.edu/

Montclair State University
http://www.montclair.edu/

Monterey Institute of Int'l Studies
http://www.miis.edu/

Moravian College
http://www.moravian.edu/

Mount Holyoke College
http://www.mtholyoke.edu/

Mount Union College
http://www.mu.edu/default.html

Muskingum College
http://www.muskingum.edu/

National Technological University
http://www.ntu.edu/

National University
http://nunic.nu.edu/

NC Agricultural & Technical Univ.
http://www.ncat.edu/

New Jersey Institute of Tech.
http://www.njit.edu/

N. Mexico Inst. of Mining & Tech.
http://www.nmt.edu/

New Mexico State University
http://www.nmsu.edu/

New York University
http://www.nyu.edu/

Nicholls State University
http://server.nich.edu/

North Carolina State University
http://www.ncsu.edu/

North Dakota University System
http://www.nodak.edu/

Northeast Louisiana University
http://www.nlu.edu

Northeast Missouri State Univ.
http://www.nemostate.edu/

Northeastern University
http://www.northeastern.edu

Northern Arizona University
http://www.nau.edu

Northern Illinois U, Bio Sciences
http://www.niu.edu

Northern Michigan University
http://www-ais.acs.nmu.edu

Northwest Nazarene College
http://www.nnc.edu/

Northwestern Michigan College
http://leo.nmc.edu/

Northwestern State U, Louisiana
http://server.nsula.edu/

Northwestern University
http://www.acns.nwu.edu/

Nova Southeastern University
http://alpha.acast.nova.edu/

Oakland University
http://www.acs.oakland.edu/

Oberlin College
http://www.oberlin.edu/

Occidental College
http://www.oxy.edu/

Ohio Northern University
http://www.onu.edu/

Ohio University
http://www.ohiou.edu/

Ohio Wesleyan University
http://192.68.223.4:8000/

Oklahoma City University
http://frodo.okcu.edu/

Oklahoma State University
http://www.okstate.edu/index.html

Old Dominion University
http://www.odu.edu/

Olivet Nazarene University
http://www.olivet.edu/

OR Graduate Ins. of Sci. & Tech.
http://www.ogi.edu/welcome.html

Oregon Health Sciences Univ.
http://www.ohsu.edu/

Oregon State University
http://www.orst.edu/

Pace University
http://pacevm.dac.pace.edu/

Pacific Lutheran University
http://www.plu.edu/

Pennsylvania State University
http://www.psu.edu/

Pepperdine University
http://www.pepperdine.edu/

Pittsburg State University
http://www.pittstate.edu/

Plymouth State College, NH
http://www.plymouth.edu/

Polytechnic University of NY
http://www.poly.edu/

Pomona College
http://www.pomona.claremont.edu/

Portland State University
http://www.pdx.edu/

Prairie View A&M University
http://www.pvamu.edu/

Princeton University
http://www.princeton.edu/

Purdue University
http://www.purdue.edu/

Purdue U, Indianapolis
http://indyunix.iupui.edu/

Quincy University
http://www.quincy.edu/

Radford University
http://www.runet.edu/

Randolph-Macon College
http://www.rmc.edu/

Randolph-Macon Woman's College
http://www.rmwc.edu/

Reed College
http://www.reed.edu/

Regent University
http://www.regent.edu/

Rensselaer Polytechnic Institute
http://www.rpi.edu/

Rhodes College
http://www.rhodes.edu/

Rice University
http://www.rice.edu/

Richard Stockton University
http://odin.stockton.edu/

Roanoke College
http://www.roanoke.edu/

Rochester Institute of Technology
http://www.rit.edu/

Rose-Hulman Institute of Technol.
http://www.rose-hulman.edu/

Rowan College of New Jersey
http://www.rowan.edu/

Rutgers University
http://www.rutgers.edu/

Rutgers U-Camden
http://camden-www.rutgers.edu/

Saint Joseph College
http://www.sjc.edu/

Saint Joseph's College
http//www.saintjoe.edu/

Saint Joseph's University
http://www.sju.edu/

Salve Regina U, Cliffwalk Library
http://198.49.179.4/cliffwalk.html

Sam Houston State University
http://oliver.shsu.edu/

Samford University
http://server1.samford.edu/

San Diego State University
http://www.sdsu.edu/

San Francisco State University
http://sfsuvax1.sfsu.edu/

San Jose State University
http://amalthea.sjsu.edu/

Sangamon State University
http://www.sangamon.edu/

Santa Clara University
http://www.scu.edu/

School of the Visual Arts
http://www.sva.edu/

SD School of Mines & Tech
http://www.sdsmt.edu/

Seattle Pacific University
http://www.spu.edu/

Seattle University
http://www.seattleu.edu/

Seton Hall University
http://www.shu.edu/

Shippensburg U of Pennsylvania
http://www.ship.edu/

Simon's Rock College
http://www.simons-rock.edu/

Simpson College
http://www.simpson.edu/

Skidmore College
http://www.skidmore.edu/

Slippery Rock University
http://www.sru.edu/

Smith Chapel Bible College
http://144.174.145.13/

SMU, Cox School of Business
http://www.cox.smu.edu/

Sonoma State University
http://www.sonoma.edu/

South Dakota State University
http://www.sdstate.edu/

Southeast Missouri State Univ.
http://www.semo.edu/

Southern College of Technology
http://www.sct.edu/

Southern Connecticut State Univ.
http://scwww.ctstateu.edu/

Southern Illinois University
http://www.siu.edu/

Southern Ill. U, Edwardsville
http://www.siue.edu/

Southern U, Baton Rouge
http://www.subr.edu/

Southwest Missouri State Univ.
http://sy.smsu.edu/

Southwest Texas State University
http://www.swt.edu/

Southwestern Adventist College
http://www.swac.edu/

Southwestern College
http://swc.cc.ca.us/

St. John's U, Collegeville MN
http://www.csbsju.edu/

St. John's U, Jamaica NY
http://sjuvm.stjohns.edu/

St. Louis U, School of Law
http://lawlib.slu.edu/

St. Mary's College of Minnesota
http://www.mnsmc.edu/

St. Michael's College
http://waldo.smcvt.edu/

St. Olaf College
http://www.stolaf.edu/

Stanford University
http://www.stanford.edu/

SUNY at Albany, ComSci
http://www.cs.albany.edu/

SUNY at Buffalo
http://wings.buffalo.edu/

SUNY at Oswego
http://www.oswego.edu/

SUNY at Stony Brook
http://www.sunysb.edu/

SUNY College at Brockport
http://www.acs.brockport.edu/

SUNY College at Cortland
http://www.cortland.edu/

SUNY College at Geneseo
http://mosaic.cc.geneseo.edu/

SUNY College at Oneonta
http://137.141.153.38/

SUNY College at Potsdam
http://www.potsdam.edu/

State U of NYIT at Utica/Rome
http://fang.csci.sunyit.edu/

Stephen F. Austin State Univ.
http://www.sfasu.edu/

Stetson University
http://thoth.stetson.edu/

Stevens Institute of Technology
http://www.stevens-tech.edu/

Swarthmore College (Computing)
http://www.cc.warthmore.edu/

Syracuse University
http://cwis.syr.edu/

Temple University
http://astro.ocis.temple.edu/

Tennessee Technological Univ.
http://www.tntech.edu/

Tenton State College
http://www.trenton.edu/

Texas A&M University
http://www.tamu.edu/

Texas A&M U, Corpus Christi
http://www.tamucc.edu/

Texas A&M U, Kingsville
http://mullet.taiu.edu/

Texas Christian University
http://www.tcu.edu/

Texas Tech University
http://www.ttu.edu/

Texas Woman's University
http://192.135.186.50/twu/1.html

The American University
http://www.american.edu/

The Catholic Univ. of America
http://www.cua.edu/

The Citadel, Math Dept.
http://macs01.mathcs.citadel.edu/

The Johns Hopkins University
http://www.jhu.edu/

The Naval Postgraduate School
http://www.nps.navy.mil/

The Ohio State University
http://www.acs.ohio-state.edu/

The Rockefeller University
http://www.rockefeller.edu/

The Sage Colleges
http://www.sage.edu/

Thomas College
http://www.thomas.edu/

Thomas Jefferson University
http://www.tju.edu/

Towson State University
http://www.towson.edu/

Trinity College
http://www.trincoll.edu/

Trinity University
http://www.trinity.edu/

Tufts University
http://www.tufts.edu/

Tulane University
http://www.tulane.edu/

University of Akron
http://www.uakron.edu/

University of Alabama
http://www.sa.ua.edu/

Univ. of Alabama, Bimingham
http://www.uab.edu/

Univ. of Alabama, Huntsville
http://info.uah.edu/

University of Alaska System
http://www.alaska.edu/

University of Alaska, Anchorage
http://orion.alaska.edu/www/

University of Alaska, Fairbanks
http://zorba.uafadm.alaska.edu/

University of Arizona
http://www.arizona.edu/

Univ. of Arkansas, Fayetteville
http://comp.uark.edu/uoa.html

Univ. of Arkansas, Little Rock
http://www.ualr.edu/

Univ. of Arkansas, Monticello
http://cotton.uamont.edu/

University of Baltimore
http://www.ubalt.edu/

Univ. of Cal, SFrancisco Library
http://www.library.ucsf.edu/

Univ. of California, Berkeley
http://www.berkeley.edu/

University of California, Davis
http://www.ucdavis.edu/

University of California, Irvine
http://peg.cwis.uci.edu/

Univ. of California, Los Angeles
http://www.ucla.edu/

Univ. of Cal., Office of President
http://www.ucop.edu/

Univ. of California, Riverside
http://www.ucr.edu/

Univ. of California, San Diego
http://www.ucsd.edu/

Univ. of California, Santa Barbara
http://www.ucsb.edu/

Univ. of California, Santa Cruz
http://www.ucsc.edu/

University of Central Arkansas
http://aix1.uca.edu/

University of Central Florida
http://www.ucf.edu/

University of Chicago
http://www.uchicago.edu/

University of Cincinnati
http://www.uc.edu/

University of Colorado
http://www.colorado.edu/

U. of Colorado, Colorado Springs
http://www.uccs.edu/

University of Colorado, Denver
http://www.cudenver.edu/

University of Connecticut
http://www.uconn.edu/

University of Dallas
http://www.udallas.edu/

University of Dayton
http://www.udayton.edu/

University of Delaware
http://www.udel.edu/

University of Denver
http://www.du.edu/

University of Evansville
http://www.evansville.edu/

University of Florida
http://www.ufl.edu/

University of Georgia
http://www.uga.edu/

University of Hartford
http://www.hartford.edu/

University of Hawaii
http://www.hawaii.edu/uhinfo.html

University of Houston
http://www.uh.edu/

Univ. of Ill. at Urbana-Champaign
http://www.uiuc.edu/

University of Illinois, Chicago
http://www.uic.edu/

University of Iowa
http://www.uiowa.edu/

Univ. of Kansas Medical Center
http://www.kumc.edu/

University of Kentucky
http://www.uky.edu/

University of Louisville
http://www.louisville.edu/

University of Maine
http://kramer.ume.maine.edu/

University of Maine System
http://www.maine.edu/

University of Maryland System
http://www.umd.edu/

Univ. of Maryland, Baltimore Co.
http://www.umbc.edu/

Univ. of Maryland, College Park
http://inform.umd.edu/

University of Mass. at Dartmouth
http://www.umassd.edu/

University of Mass. at Amherst
http://www.umass.edu/

University of Mass. at Boston
http://www.umb.edu/

University of Mass. at Lowell
http://www.uml.edu/

University of Mass. System
http://www.umassp.edu/

Univ. of Med. & Dentistry of NJ
http://njmsa.umdnj.edu/umdnj.html

University of Memphis
http://www.memphis.edu

University of Miami
http://www.miami.edu/

University of Michigan-Ann Arbor
http://www.umich.edu/

University of Michigan-Dearborn
http://www.umd.umich.edu/

University of Minnesota
http://www.umn.edu/

University of Mississippi
http://www.olemiss.edu/

University of Missouri-Columbia
http://www.missouri.edu/

Univ. of Missouri-Kansas City
http://www.umkc.edu/

University of Missouri-Rolla
http://www.umr.edu/

University of Missouri-St. Louis
http://www.umsl.edu/

University of Montana
http://www.umt.edu/

University of Nebraska, Lincoln
http://www.unl.edu/index.html

University of Nebraska, Omaha
http://www.unomaha.edu/

University of Nevada Las Vegas
http://www.nscee.edu/

University of Nevada Reno
http://www.scs.unr.edu/

University of Nevada System
http://www.nevada.edu/

University of New Haven
http://www.newhaven.edu/

University of New Mexico
http://www.unm.edu/

University of New Orleans
http://www.uno.edu/

University of NH, Durham
http://samizdat.unh.edu:70/1/unh

U. of No. Carolina - Wilmington
http://www.uncwil.edu/

U. of No. Carolina - Chapel Hill
http://www.unc.edu/

U. of No. Carolina - Greensboro
http://www2.uncg.edu/

U. of North Carolina - Asheville
http://ww.unca.edu/

U. of North Carolina - Charlotte
http://unccvm.uncc.edu/

University of North Dakota
http://www.und.nodak.edu/

University of North Florida
http://www.unf.edu/

University of North Texas
http://www.unt.edu/

University of Northern Iowa
http://www.uni.edu/

University of Notre Dame
http://www.nd.edu/NDHomePage/

University of Oklahoma
http://www.uoknor.edu/

University of Oregon
http://www.uoregon.edu/

University of Pennsylvania
http://www.upenn.edu:80/

University of Phoenix
http://www.uophx.edu/

University of Pittsburgh
http://www.pitt.edu/

University of Portland
http://www.up.edu/

University of Puget Sound
http://www.ups.edu/

University of Rhode Island
http://www.uri.edu/

University of Richmond
http://www.urich.edu/

University of Rochester
http://www.rochester.edu/

University of San Diego
http://www.acusd.edu/

University of San Francisco
http://www.usfca.edu/

University of Scranton
http://www.cds.uofs.edu/

University of South Carolina
http://www.csd.scarolina.edu/

University of South Dakota
http://www.usd.edu/

University of South Florida
http://www.usf.edu/

University of Southern California
http://cwis.usc.edu/

University of Southern Indiana
http://wsodeman.usi.edu/

University of Southern Maine
http://csir1.usmacs.maine.edu/

Univ. of Southern Mississippi
http://www.usm.edu/

Univ. of Southwestern Louisiana
http://www.usl.edu/

University of St. Thomas
http://www.stthomas.edu/

Univ. of Tenn., Genome Project
http://mickey.utmem.edu/

Univ. of Tennessee, Chattanooga
http://www.utc.edu/

Univ. of Tennessee, Knoxville
http://www.utk.edu/

University of Tennessee, Martin
http://www.utm.edu/

Univ. of Texas at Arlington, EE
http://www-ee.uta.eu/

University of Texas at Austin
http://www.utexas.edu/

Univ. of Texas at Brownsville
http://www.utb.edu/

University of Texas at Dallas
http://www.utdallas.edu/

University of Texas at El Paso
http://cs.utep.edu/utep/utep.html

University of Texas at Houston
http://www.uth.tmc.edu/

Univ. of Texas Medical Branch
http://www.utmb.edu/

Univ. of Texas SW Medical Center
http://www.swmed.edu/

University of Texas-Pan American
http://www.panam.edu

University of the Pacific
http://www.uop.edu/

University of the South
http://www.sewanee.edu/

University of the Virgin Islands
http://www.uvi.edu/

University of Toledo
http://www.utoledo.edu/

University of Tulsa
http://www.utulsa.edu/

University of Utah
http://www.utah.edu/

University of Vermont
http://www.uvm.edu/

University of Virginia
http://www.virginia.edu/

University of Washington
http://www.washington.edu/

Univ. of Wisconsin, Eau Claire
http://www.uwec.edu/

University of Wisconsin, Madison
http://www.wiscinfo.wisc.edu/

Univ. of Wisconsin, Milwaukee
http://www.uwm.edu/

University of Wisconsin, Oshkosh
http://www.uwosh.edu/

University of Wisconsin, Parkside
http://www.uwp.edu/

Univ. of Wisconsin, Platteville
http://www.uwplatt.edu/

Univ. of Wisconsin, River Falls
http://www.uwrf.edu/

Univ. of Wisconsin, Stevens Point
http://www.uwsp.edu/

Univ. of Wisconsin, Whitewater
http://www.uww.edu/

University of Wyoming
http://www.uwyo.edu/

Uiversity of Indianapolis
http://www.uindy.edu/

Uniformed Svs. U. of Health Sci.
http://net.usuhs.mil/

Union College
http://www.union.edu/

United States Air Force Academy
http://www.usafa.af.mil/

United States Naval Academy
http://www.nadn.navy.mil/

Utah State University
http://www.usu.edu/

Valparaiso University
http://www.valpo.edu/

Vassar College
http://vasweb.vassar.edu/

Vermont Technical College
http://www.vtc.vsc.edu/

Villanova University
http://infonet.vill.edu/

Virginia Commonwealth Univ.
http://www.vcu.edu/

Virginia Tech
http://www.vt.edu/

Wake Forest University
http://www.wfu.edu/www-data/

Walla Walla College
http://www.wwc.edu/

Warren Wilson College
http://www.warren-wilson.edu/

Washburn University
http://www.wuacc.edu/

Washington & Lee University
http://liberty.uc.wlu.edu/

Washington College
http://www.washcoll.edu/

Washington State University
http://www.wsu.edu/home.html

Washington Univ. in St. Louis
http://www.wustl.edu/

Wayne State U, Dept. of Physics
http://www.physics.wayne.edu/

Wellesley College
http://www.wellesley.edu/

West Virginia University
http://www.wvu.edu/

Western Carolina University
http://www.wcu.edu/

Western Kentucky University
http://www.wku.edu/

Western Michigan University
http://www.wmich.edu/

Western Washington University
http://www.wwu.edu/

Westminster College
http://keystone.westminster.edu/

Wheaton College, Illinois
http://www.wheaton.edu/

Wheaton College, Massachusetts
http://www.wheatonma.edu/

Wichita State University
http://www.twsu.edu/

Willamette University
http://www.willamette.edu/

Williams College
http://www.williams.edu/

Winona State University
http://gopher.winona.msus.edu/

Worcester Polytechnic Institute
http://www.wpi.edu/

List 8 - Yanoff's Internet Services List

This is a partial listing one of the most comprehensive collection of Internet resources available, and is maintained by Scott Yanoff, an Internet hero and legend. This list provides Gopher and WWW addresses for a wide variety of sites. For directions on downloading this list, email to yanoff@alpha2.csd.uwm.edu, or look for it in the newsgroup `alt.internet.services`.

AGRICULTURE
  Ag. Genome WWW
  Agricultural Index
  Agriculture Gophers
  Agriculture Lists
  University Networks
  Family Farm Issues
  Food & Nutrition
  Global Pest MIS
  Master Gardener
  National Agric. Library
  Soil Conservation
  Sustainable Agric.
  Veterinary Archives
  World Food Outlook

AVIATION
  Avion Newspaper
  Aviation Gophers
  Aviation Weather

BIOLOGY
  Biology Gophers
  Biological Services
  Frog Dissection
  Genetics Banks
  Genomic Databases
  Molecular Modeling
  Museum of Nat. Hist.

BOTANY
  Botanical Gardens
  Botany Databases

BUSINESS
  Business Resources
  Canadian Business
  Career Centers
  Currency Exchange
  Economics Gophers
  Enterprise Develop.
  Entrepreneurs WWW
  European Commission
  Financial Web Servers

Internet Biz Center
IRS
Mutual Funds
Patent Searching
Personal Finance
Small Business Admin.
Stock Market Reports
Stock Market Simulator

CHEMISTRY
  American Chemical Soc.
  Periodic Table

COMPUTERS
  Amiga User
  IBM-Compatibles
  Macintosh
  Shareware Search
  Software Exchange
  Unix Reference Desk
  Windows Archives

CONSUMER INFO.
  AT&T 800 Number Dir.
  Classified Ads
  Commercial WWW Sites
  Consumer News/Info.
  Criminal Justice
  Dance Resources
  Dictionary Servers
  Internet Mall

EDUCATION
  Celebrity Lectures
  Dewey School of Ed.
  Distance Ed. Dbase
  Educational Sources
  Fax via Internet
  Finger via Telnet
  IBM Kiosk for Ed.
  Instuct. Development
  International Ed. BBS
  K-12 Resources
  KidLink Gopher

Learning Link
MathMagic
MicroMUSE
Minority Assistance
Nanaimo SchoolsNET
Nat'l Education BBS
Plugged In
Teaching & Learning
Teaching Science
Univ. Extension

FTP
  Archie Mail Servers
  FTP via EMail
  FTP Sites/Archives
  FTP via Telnet

GAMES
  Backgammon Servers
  Bolo Tracker
  Chat Clients
  Chat Services
  Chess Servers
  Chinese Chess
  Comics on the Web
  Crossword Server
  Diplomacy
  Fingers for Fun
  Game Server
  Games Domain
  GO Server
  Multi-Trek
  Othello/Reversi

GEOSCIENCE
  Wegener Institute
  Ask-A-Geologist
  Earthquake Info.
  Geography Resources
  Geographic Server
  Geological Gopher
  Global Land Info.

466

GOPHER
Gopher Sites
Gopher Greats
GopherMail

GOVERNMENT
Air Pollution BBS
American Politics
C-SPAN Gopher
Census Information
Clinton Watch
Congress
FDA BBS
Federal GPO BBS
FedWorld Gateway
Gov't documents
Ham Radio Callbooks
History Databases
Hobbies Index
Internet Guides/Docs
InterNIC
IP Address Resolver
Library of Congress
Project Vote Smart
Telecommunications
Univ. & library catalogs
White House Summary

LAW
Gopher & WWW Servers
Law Library
Law Resources List
LawNet
Legal Directory
Supreme Court Rulings
WWW Law Servers

LITERATURE/LANGUAGES
Catalogue of texts
Dartmouth Library
French Literature
Human-Languages Page
Leeds Db of Verse
Online Book Initiative
Poetry Archives
Project Gutenberg

MATH
E-Math
Mathematical Software
Math Answers, K-12
Math Assoc. of America
Math Topics

NetLib
StatLib Server

MEDICAL/HEALTH
AIDS Information
Cancer Information
AIDS & Epilepsy
Child Health Policy
Disability & Rehab.
Drug Index (GenRx)
Educational Tech Net
GriefNet
Health Information
Health Services DB
HungerWeb
Medical Gophers
Medical Resources
Nursing Gophers
Pharmacy Resources
Radiology

MISCELLANEOUS TOPICS
Almanac of Events
Archeology
Art
Astronomy
Internet tutorials
Language Translation
Library Services
List of Lists
Military
Missing Children
Museums
Nationwide libraries
Personal Ads
Philosophy Gopher
Princeton Review
Psychology
Queer Resource Dir.
Recipe Archives
TheUsenet Oracle
Women's Studies
World-Wide Web

MOVIES & TV
Movie Databases
Movie Trailers
Movie Reviews
Nielsen TV Ratings
Satellite TV Info.
Theatre
TV & Movie FTP Site

TV Guide
TV News Archive

MUSIC
CD Databases/Clubs
Guitar Chords/TAB
Lyric/Music Server
Music & Brain D-base
Music Library
Music Newsletter
Music on the Web
Music Reviews
Sid's Music Server
Sound Databases
Used Music Server

NEWS
China News Digest
Business & econ. news
Electronic Journals
Global Network Navig.
International News
News Mail Filter
Newspapers On-line
Russia/America News
Time, Inc.

PARANORMAL
AwareNET
SPIRIT-WWW

PHYSICS
Nuclear Data Center
Particle Information
Physics

RELIGION
Atheism Web
Baha'i Faith
Chabad Lubavitch
Christian Resources
Jewish, Israel info.
NY-Israel Gopher
Religion on the Web

SPACE
Advanced Space Studies
Europe Space Agency
Extragalactics
Hubble Telescope
NASA Headline News
NASDA (Japan)
Research Data Analyis
Satellite Gopher/WWW

467

The INTERNET UNIVERSITY

SETI
Shuttle Payloads
Space Enviro. Effects
SpaceNews

SPORTS
Baseball Archives
Biking
Fishing
Football
Hockey
Olympics
Paddling Sports

Running
Sailing
Scores/Standings
Skydiving
Soccer
Sports on the Web
Tennis

TRAVEL
Roadside America
Subway Navigator
Train Schedules
Travel Information

WEATHER
Avalanche Forecast
Emergency Info.
Flood Information
NOAA
Oceanography
Solar Report
Tropical Storm Forecast
Weather Services

Glossary

Glossary

Welcome to the Internet University's **Glossary**.

While we were compiling this book we realized that this section will most likely be used by the beginners among us, and so we thought that we should take a little extra time and shape a list that would help in your the introduction to the Internet. As anybody who has gone online even once can attest, the whole of the Internet can appear a formidable phenomenon for the beginner.

Your Place In History: The concepts that the Internet engenders are new, and there is so much more than use of email, which is what most people think of when you say 'Internet'. In the years after WWI our ancestors were introduced to phone lines and automobiles for the first time, and this had an impact because several new factors and concepts were introduced. Society (in the actual experience of individuals) had to adapt and develop new responses to these tools.

With the Internet this process has been greatly accelerated. Electronic education, online library access, telecommuting, electronic commerce - all of these features of the Internet will have their own special effects, and these will take time to play their way out in our social fabric. So, sit back, relax, and realize: withing a few months other people will be looking at <u>you</u> as being somewhat of an authority on the Internet. They will be bringing their most vexing questions to you, or asking for suggestions for hot new information sources. Just learn a few of these terms, get connected, and away you go.

Obviously, nobody can know everything about online education. If you know of a resource or connection not covered in this book please let us know so we can update our next edition. Simply email your suggestions to:

tellus@caso.com

Thank you. May you be the lucky winner of our monthly drawing from those entries for a free copy of this book.

---

accreditation - a process that establishes public recognition that an educational institution meets certain basic academic criteria

algorithm - a step-by-step procedure which yields a predictable set of results from a computer program.

alias - a parallel computer file which 'points' to an actual file; this are used to ease (automate) access to the original, or to protect the underlying file system of the server which houses it.

anonymous logins - access is provided by numerous ftp servers throughout the world which are participating in the 'great information giveaway' of the Internet; the means of this file transfer is through 'anonymous' logon in which your login name is "anonymous" and your email address serves as your password.

AOL - America Online, an online service.

Archie - A search utility for finding files located on ftp servers; requires the exact filename of the desired document. This program catalogs files on well over one thousand file servers worldwide and users *query* it for file locations.

ASCII - Reference standard for numeric equivalents of all characters, numerals, punctuation, etc; includes 128 codes, each represented by a 7-digit binary number. Using the ASCII standard, an 'a' on my computer is an 'a' on yours.

asynchronous - literally 'a-synchronous', or 'not at the same time'; refers to the means of transmission of the vast majority of CMC (computer mediated communications) where you can communicate with me even though we are not online at the same moment - I'll pick up your messages later.

backbone - the actual trunks of communications lines connecting multiple networks; normally connecting routers only, which is what your Internet service provider connects your SLIP/PPP equipped computer with.

bandwidth - quantity of data that can be transmitted through a connection within a given time, usually measured in baud or bits-per-second. A greater bandwidth enables transfer of a given document in a shorter time.

BBS - Bulletin Board Service - a system that allows people to leave messages for each other, upload and download files, and broadcast announcements, all done 'asynchronously'.

BITnet - A precursor of the Internet, this is a major academic wide-area-network which links academic institutions. Email is the only tool available on BITnet and Internet users can email to these addresses.

boot up - start up your computer, or perhaps a particular application or program

bps - bits per second, roughly characters per second for plain text; a 28.8 Kbps modem can transmit or receive up to 28,800 bits per second.

browser - an application, usually graphically-based, which enables the user to access online sites (URLs) with the click of the mouse. See Mosaic, Netscape.

bulletin board - see BBS

cache - literally storage; a scheme where graphics and other pieces of data are stored on your hard disk - that way the computer can simply refer to them without putting you through the wait of downloading them again and again.

campus-wide information system (CWIS) - a wide area network housed on a college or university campus for the use of students and faculty, and to a lesser degree visitors through anonymous ftp, Telnet, or other linkages. Strong on academic data and applications, and a frequent vehicle for accessing campus libraries.

CEUs - continuing education units; The International Association for Continuing Education and Training maintains standards for CEUs, credits that professional persons often must atain as part of their continued certification requirements. One CEU is generally   469   469 defined as the equivalent of ten 'contact' hours of participation in an organized continuing education experience under qualified instruction.

CLEP - College Level Examination Program, which establishes proficiency in any of a list of subjects (page 78), verifying 'life experience' in the form of college credit equivalency.

CMC - computer-mediated communications; the new field of computers and networks, and the study of why the sum of these systems is more than the mere total of their parts. Computer-mediated communications of the education variety is the subject of this book.

compression - a computer data storage technique that makes files functionally smaller by removing all redundent information. A typical file may be 'squeezed' to half it's size, which saves transmission time and reduces storage requirements. Compression utilities have become highly automated and generally require little if any user intervention, but if you are going to be transferring large numbers of large files it would pay to learn more about this feature.

connect charges - two types of payment are often required of the person seeking access to the Internet: 1) paying the phone company for the connection to your service provider, and 2) paying the service provider for the connection to the Internet. If you are so fortunate to live within a local toll-free call of your provider's POP you will be spared the first of these. If you are so fortunate to work for an institution with Internet access you may well be relieved of all fees related to Internet use. If you are paying more than $1 or $2 per hour for connect charges you have our sympathies. Shop around for the best deal, and remember that in this volatile market pricing strategies are changing, usually downward.

cyberspace - that place that occurs in the collective mindset of all participants in Internet and online connection; a new piece of jargon invented to discuss the new world of global networking.

dedicated connection - typically a phone line that is for use of the computer alone. For an additional $20 per month it may be worth another line installed by the phone company (to use as a dedicated line) so that your Internet use does not interfere with household voice phone traffic.

domain - an indicator of a particular level of heirarchy in an Internet server's full nodename; to send suggestions to Cape Software for additions, corrections or deletions to The Internet University we ask you to email:

`tellus@caso.com.`

In this case the extended nodename is 'caso.com' which means our choice was 'caso' as short for Cape Software, followed by 'com', indicating that we are a commercial enterprise. We can therefore say that we are in the 'com' domain.

downloading - bringing a file from a remote server 'down' to your computer; the opposite of 'uploading'.

e-conference - electronic conference, generally an academic experience where 'speakers' post 'speeches' which are asynchronously 'attended' by subscribers. For futher information, read John Gresham's Guest Article on page 137.

e-journal - electronic journal, the functional equivalent of a scientific or literary journal which in this case is distributed to subscribers electronically. Subscriptions to e-journals is generally free and receipt is automatic through the medium of email.

email - electronic mail; comprised of messages which are electronically transmitted over the Internet by you to another individual (one-to-one) or to a mailing list (one-to-many).

EUN (Electronic University Network) - the 'grandfather' of online distance education, currently operating through America Online (AOL); see page 54.

encryption - distorting a message so that nobody can read it unless they have the code for restoring it to a readable form.

Ethernet - the most common of networking schemes used to tie LANs of personal computers together, usually in a shop, business or school. If you have the only computer on the site (such as at home) or if your computer is not wired to another computer, you likely have had nothing to do with Ethernet.

Eudora - a popular email management application, published by Qualcomm.

FAQ - frequently asked questions; files on virtually any topic of Internet use where answers to these questions are archived. This system developed out of self-defence by Internet users who were besieged by the same question one hundred times. Don't be a rank beginner - consult the FAQ before asking the nearest Intenet guru; save the hard questions for them. For more on FAQs, see page 68 and the ftp sites cited on pages 438 and 440.

Fetch - an ftp client program used to download files. Fetch asks the name of the host you wish to connect to and then displays the file struture of the site for your browsing.

flaming - social sanctions are applied through the informal community of the Internet by the medium of email. If you transgress someone else's idea of proper behavior or speech, they may register their objection by sending you an email message. If it is insulting, or if you get a series of 'bombs' (sometimes 'clogging' your mailbox), you have been flamed.

FTP - File Transfer Protocol - the most common method used to move files between two Internet sites (see download, upload, anonymous logon).

Gopher - a popular utility which presents online menus of files available via the Internet. This is a client/server utility, and while very useful it is being generally supplanted by the Web owing to the latter's enhanced ease-of-use. However, expect Gopher to remain an active part of the Internet's search toolkit for years to come.

GUI - graphical user interface, which refers to little pictures on the screen, like the trash can, windows, pull-down menus, etc. rather than a blinking line into which are typed arcane commands (command-line interface). Windows and Macintosh operating systems are both GUI-based; MS-DOS is not.

HTML - hypertext markup language - used for programming the pages that you will see at various websites that you visit on the World-Wide Web. Consider The Internet University's website at:

`http://www.caso.com`

These pages were created using html.

HTTP - hypertext transfer protocol - the step-by-step means whereby a click on your computer's screen is translated into instructions for your computer to retrieve a particular linked document.

hypertext - a word or image in an online document which is dynamically 'linked' to another document or location within the same document. This is usually identified by 'bold/blue' formatting or some other visual indicator. Adding the word 'hyper' to the word 'text' infers that this is not just ordinary text, and indeed, these links of hypertext make the dynamic environment of the Web possible. Hypertext is often used to create indexes and other structures for organizing the text, graphics, video, sound, and other files that can be transferred via the Web.

IBM-compatible - any of the many computers based on the Intel chip and typically operating MS-DOS or Windows operating systems.

Internet - The worldwide conection of literally millions of computers - PCs, minis and mainframes - which use the communications protocol TCP/IP. (You must have a pretty good idea of what the Intenet is or you wouldn't have gotten this far in the book.)

InterNIC - the Internet Network Information Center; the people that assign domain names and keep track of the various internet addresses. To apply for Cape Software's domain name (caso.com, as in the email address 'tellus@caso.com'), we had to apply to InterNIC. They verified that nobody else had claimed that domain name, and it was assigned to us.

Internet University - the title of this book; also a metaphoric invention of the publisher used to convey the concept of worldwide availability of college courses for adults who are interested in continuing their education, conducted via the Internet.

IP address - a 'dotted quad' number (e.g.; 214.126.210.2) which gives each servier on the Internet a unique address. These are translated by special servers to node names which are easier for people to remember (e.g.; caso.com)

IP routers - computer servers on the Internet which have the function of changing the node names in the IP address definition to the correct numeric IP address.

ISDN - acronym for 'Integrated Services Digital Network', which is touted as the 'future of the Internet', or at least as an interim step on the way to total integration of the 'electronic superhighway' into our social infrastructure. This technology allows for data transmission over existing phone lines at rates 3-4 times that of the fastest modem today.

LAN - Local Area Network - a collection of computers wired together so users can exchange files, share applications; usually located in one discrete area, floor or building. Users obtain access by 'logging on' to the 'network'.

listserv - a program which takes care of the details of operating a mailing list; there are others, but this is the most popular. If the email address starts with 'listserv' (i.e.; `listserv@ubvm.cc.buffalo.edu`) the simple email message 'help' or 'info' will usually automatically return a file describing the 'rules of engagement' for the mailing list.

login - when referring to a name, it is the shorthand version of your name that you have arranged with your network; when referring to a process it is the sequence of events that give you access to a network.

lurking - following the proceedings in a newsgroup or mailing list without contributing inputs; this is a polite way to begin involvement despite the unseemly flavor of the term. It is generally regarded as good Internet manners for the beginner to observe proceedings for awhile before posting responses to the ongoing discussions.

Lycos - a powerful search utilities; assists in locating resources on the Web by use of 'key words' that are entered describing the desired topic.

mail server - an Internet program which enables the operation of a mailing list; *listserv* is the most common, others are *majordomo* and *mailserv*.

mailing list - a system hosted by somebody (usually an institution) interested in the subject matter of the list, wherein submissions are sent to all subscribers either automatically upon posting (unmoderated) or after being 'screened' for appropriatness (moderated).

Mediated Classwork - generally a class where the professor moderates a class mailing list. For a description of this technique in action read Mary McComb's Guest Article on page 170.

message threads - in a Usenet newsgroup, it will often occur that you will want to respond directly to somebody else's posting. He or somebody else may then wish to respond to your response. This process can be continued, each entry pertainent to the ongoing discussion. This sequence of inter-related postings is referred to as a 'thread'.

modem - a device that allows your computer to communicate by telephone with another computer or network. Often confused with the phrase from the southern USA dialect of English meaning 'more of them'.

moderated lists - mailing lists which have all submissions for posting reviewed by the hosting institution; if deemed appropriate for the focus of the list the submission will then be distributed to the all subscribers.

Mosaic - the first popular browser, still appreciated today for its speed of access and caching capabilities.

Multimedia - whether online or by CD-ROM, this refers to a combination of outputs of various formats - audio, video, data - this gives the viewer a full experience, and offers the author a wide range of communicative expression.

Netscape - the most popular browser, published by one of the companies most responsible for the dramatic developments of the World-Wide Web.

Network - a combination of computers linked in such a way that the transfer of information in the form of files is possible.

newsgroup - discussion group on Usenet, you can generally gather the subject of the group by the name, such as `alt.animals.dolphins`.

newsreader - a program similar to a browser which enables the user to follow one or more Usenet newsgroups. As well as tracking those newsgroups you are interested in, the **newsreader** will notice which postings you have read so that you won't have to search through them again on subsequent sessions.

online - the state of having your computer connected to a remote computer by wiring of some sort, enabling transfer of data between the machines.

password - similar to a PIN (personal identification number) at an automatic teller machine - a **password** is known only to you and to the computer that you are trying to access. This is the system employed to allow only authorized use of accounts.

point and click - otherwise known as 'point-and-shoot', this is the innovation of computer interface design that gave the general public access to use of computers. With the mouse the user positions the cursor over a sensitized section of the screen marked, usually with a 'graphic', with a link to another screen or function.

POP - point-of-presence, a phone location that your internet service provider establishes in order to give you a local phone number to call to avoid phone company toll charges. When querying a prospective provider, ask them if they have a P-O-P in your dialing area.

PPP - this is an acronym for Point-to-Point Protocol, the most common resource which enables your modem-based computer to make a TCP/IP connection, enabling Web and other connections. If your Internet provider does not offer SLIP or PPP (preferrably the latter), find another Internet provider.

reboot - re-start the computer, usually when the computer 'crashes' or 'hangs'.

shell account - a UNIX command-line interface which provides basic (non-browser) access to the Internet. This is the format that you will have to learn if your Internet service provider does not offer SLIP/PPP access.

SLIP - this is an acronym for Serial Line Internet Protocol, a companion to the newer (and faster) protocol: PPP. If your Internet provider offers SLIP or PPP connections you can use that route to access the Web. If they don't, find another Internet provider.

SLIP/PPP - these terms are often used interchangeably though they are in fact different protocols. The latter is becoming the prodominant system due to its faster transfer of data.

synchronous - literally 'at the same time'; talking face-to-face is synchronous communications, leaving a message on an answering machine is not. Think: 'in synch'.

TCP/IP - acronym for Transmission Control Protocol/Internet Protocol - the basic building block of Internet traffic; information is broken down into discrete 'chunks'. With the development of this protocol a broad variety of computers can communicated despite their various operating systems.

Telnet - remote login; an application of the Internet which enables your computer to act as a terminal of a distant network. See pages 36 and 43.

threads - in a Usenet newsgroup, it will often occur that you will want to respond directly to somebody else's posting. He or somebody else may then wish to respond to your response. This process can be continued, each entry pertainent to the ongoing discussion. This sequence of inter-related postings is referred to as a 'thread'.

UNIX - one of the original programming languages, UNIX is the language of the Internet. Thankfully with today's browsers it is not necessary to learn it.

uploading - sending a file from your computer 'up' to a remote server; the opposite of 'downloading'.

URL - Universal Resource Locator; an Internet address. To visit The Internet University's website, type it's URL into your browser's 'go to' function. The URL for The Internet University is: `http://www.caso.com/`.

Usenet - picture a global bulletin board system; refer to pgs. 34 and 68.

userid - 'user identification code' or 'user-i-d'; your screen name, which your network will correlate with your password, which only you know, to verify authorized access.

Veronica - a search utility which is comprised of a database of the contents of thousands of gopher servers - sort of a gopher of gophers.

virtual - as in 'almost real', where the experience of a simulated event is so close to the experience of the real event that the participant has the feeling of 'being there'.

WAIS - Wide Area Information Servers; software that enables indexing of large amounts of information - this index is then searchable across the Internet according to content-oriented queries.

Website - a location on the World-Wide Web that is accessed by 'pointing' your browser to the site's URL. A site may have one page or screen, or many. Consider The Internet University's website (URL: http://www.caso.com). This site has literally hundreds of pages of material covering online distance education, all available through the index on the 'home' page.

Workarounds - techniques for using a program or network that are not what the original program or system administrator had in mind when they developed it, and which generall extend the resource's function. An example of an email workaround would be obtaining a web page by following the suggestions in Bob Rankin's Guest Article (pg. 153).

WWW - World-Wide Web; where the 'action' is on the Internet these days, the Web gives graphical 'point-and-click' ease of navigation to anyone with a PPP connection and a browser such as Netscape or Mosaic.

'zines - electronic magazines, which bring the power of publishing to anyone with a computer on the Internet and something to say.

Index

Index

D

E

F

Order Form

- [ ] *Please send* _____ *copies of*:

The Internet University - College Courses by Computer

✎ Name:_____

Address:_____

City:_____State_____ZIP_____

✉ *Postal orders*: **Cape Software Press**
P. O. Box 800-B
Harwich MA 02645

☎ *Call our order line*: 508-432-2435   *Order by fax*: 508-432-1499
Order via Email: books@caso.com

Price per book: **$26.95** (quantity pricing available)

Shipping:
Add $3.50 per copy.

Sales tax:
Add $1.15 per copy shipped to Massachusetts addresses.

Payment:
- [ ] Check   [ ] Money Order

- [ ] VISA   [ ] MasterCard   [ ] AMEX   [ ] Discover

Name on card:_____ Exp.date_____

Card number:_____

Call and order now !

Order Form

☐ *Please send* _____ *copies of*:

The Internet University - College Courses by Computer

✎ Name:_____

Address:_____

City:_____State_____ZIP_____

✉ *Postal orders*: **Cape Software Press**
P. O. Box 800-B
Harwich MA 02645

☎ *Call our order line*: 508-432-2435   *Order by fax*: 508-432-1499
Order via Email: books@caso.com

Price per book: **$26.95** (quantity pricing available)

Shipping:
    Add $3.50 per copy.

Sales tax:
    Add $1.15 per copy shipped to Massachusetts addresses.

Payment:
    ☐ Check   ☐ Money Order

    ☐ VISA   ☐ MasterCard   ☐ AMEX   ☐ Discover

    Name on card:_____ Exp.date_____

    Card number:_____

Call and order now !